FORGOTTEN HERO

BY: JOSEPH LINDLEY

**Second Edition
(2019)**

Published by BookLocker.com, Inc., St. Petersburg, Florida, U.S.A.

Printed on acid-free paper.

BookLocker.com, Inc.
2019

Second Edition

Cover photos: U.S. Army photos taken by SSG Earl Vanalstine
101st Airborne Division, Vietnam, 1967-1968.

TABLE OF CONTENTS

To The Reader

It's important to note that research used for this book includes primary sources such as U.S. Army after-action reports, U.S. Army daily staff journals, and personal affidavits from, and interviews with, the men with whom Calvin fought. The research also includes Calvin's medical and military records secured through the National Archives, the National Personnel Center, and Calvin's own personal files. These include his medical and psychological summaries, U.S. Army 201 File (his military personnel file), DD-214, individual U.S. Army orders, etc. Other sources include Calvin's personal affidavits and numerous interviews, the *Screaming Eagle* newspaper, and the Department of Veterans Affairs records. Any inconsistencies or disagreements between records or other sources are noted. The *story* was written from Calvin's perspective.

2019 Note from the author

Since I first published *Forgotten Hero* in early 2015, I have received a great deal of additional information from the men with whom Calvin served and fought, especially the men of Phantom Force. Since this work has become the definitive narrative of the March 1968 Battle of Bau Co Bong, I have incorporated that information in this Second Edition in hopes that the courage and bravery exhibited by all the men that day, is never *forgotten*.

Joseph Lindley,
2019

God and the soldier, all men adore
In time of danger, and not before.
When the danger has passed, and all things righted,
God is forgotten, and the soldier slighted.

John F. Kennedy's version of Francis Quarles poem

PROLOGUE

It was March 23, 2013, a bright, sunny afternoon. I was sitting at my kitchen counter deep in thought. My research, maps, and reference books were haphazardly scattered all over the kitchen, much to my wife's dismay. I was working feverishly to finish a book I was writing about Henry Washington Brown, a local Civil War soldier who fought with the 21st Massachusetts Infantry. Summer, with all the associated yard work, was rapidly approaching and I was hoping to finish the two-year project before the outside work began. Deeply engrossed in my work, I was startled by the sound of a car horn blowing in my driveway. In the 26 years I lived at my house in Thompson, Connecticut, there was only one person who would sit in the driveway tooting the horn like that – my old softball buddy – Calvin Heath.

Calvin and I played a great deal of softball together when we were younger, and he was probably the only person I have ever known who enjoyed playing the game more than I. About 15 years prior, sore joints and father time had forced us both to leave the game we loved. We always agreed it was one of the best times of our lives.

For a time, Calvin lived down the road from me and occasionally, he would stop at my house to shoot the breeze. Over the years, we developed a strong friendship and I always enjoyed his visits and, more importantly, his happy-go-lucky outlook on life. We had both served in the military and we often talked about life in the Army. I knew he was a Vietnam combat veteran serving with the famed 101st Airborne Division, and I greatly respected his service during the Vietnam War. I heard he received a raw deal after being severely wounded in Vietnam, but I knew few of the details. I did know that during the late 1980s and through the 1990s several of his combat buddies were helping him secure his VA benefits, but again, I knew little about who they were or what they were trying to accomplish.

After I quit playing softball in 1994, I didn't see much of Calvin except for his random drive-by horn blasts and waves he would give me on his way home. On July 12, 1999, he unexpectedly showed up in my driveway announcing himself with his characteristic tooting of the horn. Knowing immediately who it was, I went out to greet him. Stepping out of his pickup, he excitedly yelled, "Joe! I finally got it!"

"Got what Cal?"

"My medals! My Silver Star!"

Calvin, beaming with pride, handed me his Purple Heart and Silver Star neatly placed in their blue protective hinged boxes, and the citations that accompanied both medals. Before I started reading the citation, it struck me that despite my nearly 12 years of military service, I never saw a Silver Star medal, never mind hold one, and I quickly realized that this was something very special. After reading the citations, unexpected tears quickly developed, and I suddenly realized just how little I knew about Calvin's time in Vietnam. I gave Cal a big hug and congratulated him. We talked for another hour or so and as he drove away, I could not help but think… *Why the hell did it take so long?*

I saw Calvin on and off over the next few years. I heard that he had moved to Texas, and as time went on, his visits were less frequent. On the afternoon of March 23, 2013, after hearing that all-too-familiar tooting from the driveway, I jumped to my feet and rushed outside to find my old friend once again sitting there, like he had so many times before.

"Hey Cal! How the hell are you?" As soon as the words came out of my mouth, I knew something was seriously wrong.

He looked away and after a few seconds said, "Not good Joe, I'm dying."

Stunned, I said, "What?"

"I have brain cancer. The VA doctors think it might be from Agent Orange… I don't really know. I'm getting treated at the VA Center, but it doesn't look good."

"What's the prognosis?" I asked.

"Maybe a year, maybe less…"

Tears began swelling in his eyes, and then in mine as the message sank in.

"Why don't you come in for a coffee?" I asked.

Calvin sat down at the cluttered countertop, I made coffee, and with neither of us knowing where to start we talked a few minutes about the good ole' days and how we would both give anything to be playing just one more game.

Soon, we began talking about his Silver Star, how he earned it, and all the problems he had with the Army and the Veterans Administration after Vietnam. For the first time in our long friendship he opened up and shared the details about how he earned two of the most prestigious combat medals awarded by the U.S. Military – and the price, both physically and psychologically, he paid for those medals. I immediately thought, *this is an amazing story that needs to be captured!* I turned to him and said, "Cal, I'm just finishing up a book," showing him the mess that lay around the kitchen, "… your story needs to be told and I would be honored to write it."

He looked at me and once again tears began to flow. "What? You'd do that for me?"

"Cal, I'd be honored."

For a moment, I could see his pain disappear and his tears slowly develop into that contagious and familiar smile I so fondly remembered. Calvin would have a legacy and I would have a mission – record the details of my friend's time in Vietnam and the mistreatments he endured after the war by a broken military support system.

Over the next several months, Calvin visited me several times per week, sometimes with his younger brother Frank, bringing me personal files, pictures, and official reports. As the pieces of his life fell into place, I was rapidly gaining a better understanding of the battles and demons he fought during and after the war.

During one of his visits in April 2013, Calvin asked me if I would be interested in helping him raise the funds necessary to attend his unit's reunion being held in Oklahoma. We had talked about the reunions a number of times and he often mentioned that he would like to "See the guys just one more time." I agreed to do whatever I could but did not realize at that time just how important these reunions were to Calvin. That would take me another few months.

On May 23, 2013, I once again found myself sitting alone at my kitchen counter, this time staring at a large three foot by five foot poster board that the Thompson, Connecticut Historical Society created to announce my new book about Henry Washington Brown. The problem was… the book wasn't finished. I was struggling with the epilogue. Maybe with thoughts of Calvin now becoming a priority, I was losing interest in my current project. I knew that was unfair to Henry who also saw too much of war's cruelty. Frustrated, I was ready to call it quits when Calvin arrived. As I made coffee for the two of us, we talked about Henry. Calvin looked through the work I had scattered all over the kitchen and he became interested in the battles that Henry fought and the horrible experiences he had faced. I could see Calvin quickly developing a strange kinship to Henry. After a few minutes of examining the display board, he provided the ending I so desperately sought. That evening I wrote:

> *A year and a half after this project began, I struggled for weeks on how to end it. It turns out that the last few paragraphs were my most difficult to compose. I tried numerous times to summarize what I learned about Henry, his time during the war, the suffering he both witnessed and endured, and the tragic way in which he died. I naively envisioned crafting something clever and profound that would bring the story so perfectly together, but after weeks of struggling with the problem, I had nothing. Discouraged, I set my work aside.*
>
> *On May 23, 2013, I was visited by a good friend, Calvin Heath. Calvin served with the 101st Airborne during the Vietnam War and was awarded the Silver Star, the country's third highest award. In March of 1968, while on a reconnaissance mission, Calvin and his platoon were cut off and surrounded by North Vietnamese soldiers. Risking his life, Calvin, then severely wounded, opted to stay in harm's way with other wounded men providing them cover, and eventually guidance for a rescue force. His Silver Star*

citation reads, "For gallantry in action against a hostile and superior force..."[1] But that is another story...

During his visit, I showed Calvin a large poster board outlining Henry's life and the sacrifices he made. The board was created as a backdrop for a display the Thompson Historical Society was developing for Henry's letters. As Calvin examined the board, it became immediately apparent that in spite of being separated by more than 100 years, he knew a lot about Henry. He had seen what Henry had seen, felt what Henry had felt, and battled the same demons that Henry had battled. Calvin looked long and hard at the board, and for a second, I could tell he completely understood. After all those weeks of searching for an appropriate way to end this piece, my friend, who also faced the ugliness of war, provided the words I so desperately sought – he simply turned to me and said, "It's good to remember."

Throughout the balance of May, and through June 2013, Calvin stopped by the house numerous times, and we continued to work on recording the details of his life and listing the resources needed to write his story. During this period, I noticed Calvin had good days and bad days, but he always seemed to be at his best when we discussed the project. On June 27, 2013, he was especially upbeat. He told me that during an appointment the previous day, the oncologist informed him that he had responded exceptionally well to his surgery, radiation treatments, and chemotherapy. He stated that the "The doctors think they got it in remission, and I might have a few more years." Calvin's VA medical records dated June 26, 2013, indicate that he had indeed spoken with Dr. Nancy J. Freeman, Chief of Hematology and Oncology, Providence VA Medical Center. Dr. Freeman wrote that she and Calvin discussed his current condition and that Calvin had decided to try another round of chemotherapy due to the apparent success of the previous two cycles.

---

[1] Calvin Heath Silver Star award and citation, June 11, 1999.

A few days after Calvin's June 27th visit, I was scheduled to visit my parents in South Carolina for a week for my Dad's 80th surprise birthday. Initially, I was uncomfortable about missing time with Calvin, not knowing how much he had left, and considered cancelling my trip, or at least cutting it short. With Calvin's new optimistic update, I stuck to my original plans and stayed in South Carolina for a week. I understood Calvin's ultimate prognosis did not change, but I was glad he had a little longer to enjoy life and to help me tell his story.

I left Connecticut for South Carolina on July 6, 2013, bringing with me a large file of paperwork that Calvin had given me to review while I was away. Two days later, I showed my parents the material. My dad, a U.S. Air Force Korean War Era veteran, read the reports with more attention than I had ever seen him give such matters. As he read the stack of notes and reports, tears began to swell. This caught me off guard as I had only witnessed my father cry twice in my life, once when he buried his father and once when he buried his mother. Dad became incredibly upset with the way in which the U.S. Army and the U.S. Government treated a Silver Star recipient. After reviewing the entire file, he sat back and stared at the stacks of papers that covered his kitchen table with great disappointment. He shook his head, and said, "Why don't you call the book *Forgotten Hero*? The title was now set, and I could not wait to get home to tell Calvin. I was certain he would approve.

The following evening, July 9, 2013, I received an unexpected phone call from Jason Authier. Jason and I had worked together in the Thompson, Connecticut Little League for a number of years and my first assumption after seeing his name on caller I.D. was that the Little League was looking for some sort of help. "Joe, this is Jason. I thought I would give you a call to let you know that Calvin passed away." Stunned, it took me a few seconds to remember that Jason was also the son of Rob Authier, one of Calvin's best friends, and growing up, Jason was close enough to Calvin to call him "Uncle Calvin."

I was devastated. I asked a few questions, obtained what details I could, thanked Jason and hung up. I walked around my parents' spare bedroom for a while in a daze, trying to collect my thoughts. That night, I laid awake, unable to sleep, my mind swimming. I somehow felt that I should have stayed home, I should have done something… that I should be doing something now, but of course there was nothing I could do. Calvin was gone.

Through the balance of July, and into August and September my research intensified. I requested records from the National Archives, I contacted a number of men from Delta Company, 3/187th, 101st Airborne, Calvin's old unit, and I spoke with a number of Calvin's family, friends, and acquaintances.

On October 3, 2013, I received a phone call from Dave Dillard, one of Calvin's battle mates. Dave invited me to meet with him and two other former Rakkasans with whom Calvin had fought the day he earned his Silver Star.[2] The men were in Connecticut to attend a memorial service in Hartford, Connecticut, in honor of Calvin. Other battle mates joining Dave the following day to honor Calvin included Ray Palmer, Distinguished Service Cross recipient, Jeffrey Wishik, and Medal of Honor recipient, Paul "Bud" Bucha. I gladly accepted Dave's invitation. He gave me the address and we agreed on a time.

On the morning of October 9, 2013, I loaded all my research and Calvin's files in my car and headed south. As I drove along Route 95, I thought about the men I was about to meet and suddenly felt strangely uncomfortable. Even with more than a decade of service under my belt, I did not know how I should handle myself among these distinguished warriors.

I arrived at Bill Heaney's residence, a well-kept, two-story house located only a few blocks from Long Island Sound, shortly after noon. I was immediately met by a large pleasant man who introduced himself as Dave Dillard. Dave then introduced me to Bill Heaney and Mike Rawson; all three men served with Calvin in Vietnam during 1967-68. A few minutes later we were joined by freelance journalist Adam Piore. Adam had been working on producing a piece for public radio about the men of Delta Company and their time before, during, and after Vietnam. I hope he has great success with his project.

---

[2] Note: The unit to which Calvin belonged was the 187th Infantry (ABN), 101st Airborne Division – nicknamed the Rakkasans. The name's origin is explained later in this book.

I explained to the men my many conversations with Calvin and my promise to him to tell his story. I spoke of the work Calvin and I accomplished to date – and all the work that I felt remained. I handed them the records, documents, and pictures Calvin had provided. They reviewed the material with great interest and after a few minutes they began discussing their experiences in Vietnam and their experiences after the war. After a few minutes, I began to understand why I was initially so uncomfortable. After serving in the military myself, I was used to being around combat veterans, many of whom had told me their stories, most times over a beer at the Enlisted Man's Club, the VFW, or the American Legion, but this was the first time I sat *among* them as they shared their first-hand accounts of their experiences *together*. This was not a circle of men in which I belonged, and I could not help but think of the famous line from Shakespeare's Henry V, "We few, we happy few, we band of brothers. For he today that sheds his blood with me shall be my brother…" I was sitting among men who shed their blood together and truly *were* a band of brothers. What I quickly decided to do was to sit back and simply listen.

EARLY LIFE

Calvin William Heath, "Willy," was born on January 24, 1949 in Putnam, Connecticut. He was the sixth child of Wayland and Eva Brown Heath. The Heaths had a large family that eventually grew to 15 children, three of whom were from a previous marriage.

Wayland, was born on May 3, 1913, in Orleans, Vermont. The 1930 census records show 16-year-old Wayland living with his parents Albert and Ivah, and five brothers, Willard (age 14), Albert (age nine), Chester (age six), Rayburn (age four), and Raymond (age one). Wayland was listed as not attending school at that time and it's safe to assume he was working.[3] Ten years later, the 1940 census shows Wayland, then a 27-year-old single man, working and living in East Woodstock, Connecticut on the farm of 60-year-old Calvin Easterbrook, possibly Calvin's namesake.[4]

Calvin's mother, Eva Viola Brown, was a Nipmuc Indian born on January 10, 1923 in Woodstock, Connecticut. The 1940 census shows Eva as a 17-year-old maid working for 62-year-old widow, Ida Nelson of South Woodstock, Connecticut. It is most likely that Wayland and Eva met while Wayland was working at Easterbrook's farm. They were married soon after the census was taken.

Wayland and Eva had 12 children, Glen (1940), Bert (1943), Patricia (1944), Chester "Chet" (1946), Evelyn (1947?), Calvin (1949-2013), Melzer "Mel" (1950), Corrine (1952), Wayland Jr. "Spooky" (1953-1996), Roy (1954-1954), Linda (1953-2000), and Frank (1955).[5] Wayland also had three additional children from a previous marriage, Arnold who passed away as a youngster from pneumonia, Joyce (1933), and Lorraine (1934).[6]

---

[3] 1930 U.S. Census.
[4] Ibid.
[5] From a variety of sources to include the Heath family and the U.S. Census.
[6] Joyce Lefevre interview with author, March 30, 2014.

Above: Picture of Calvin Heath or his brother Chet circa 1951. Older sister Joyce Lefevre suggests it may have been taken at the Easterbrook Farm, Pomfret, CT. Whether the picture is Calvin or Chet, the photo provides a glimpse at the Heaths' life as children. Melzer and Curt Heath photo.

Throughout most of the family's early years, Calvin's father, a farm hand, had difficulty holding a good-paying job and the financial responsibilities of clothing, feeding, and caring for such a large family became overwhelming. As a result, in 1954, five of the children, Glen, Bert, Patricia, Chet, and Calvin, were removed from the family home and placed under Connecticut State foster care. They were not the first Heath children to be removed from the family. Calvin later said, "I was taken from my parents and put at a foster home on a farm... there was just too many of us in the family and my father

2

couldn't keep up with supporting all the kids."[7] After removing the children, the State of Connecticut had some difficulty finding suitable homes for the five children. Bert, Calvin's older brother, later noted that, "We were Native American and we didn't quite fit in."[8]

The children were first sent to the Windham County Home in Vernon, Connecticut, a State-run foster home, and shortly thereafter to the Putnam Town Farm, owned by Dr. and Anna Antell. Dr. Antell passed away and Anna, soon thereafter, married John Ciccone who owned a farm on Thurber Road, Putnam, Connecticut. The five children were then placed at the Ciccone Farm; Glen arriving in December of 1953, Chet and Bert around February 1954, Patricia in July and Calvin in August.[9] Fortunately for the Heath children, the Ciccones accepted all five children and the siblings, for a time, remained together.[10]

According to Bert, growing up on the farm was easier for Calvin, the youngest of the five, than it was for the older children. "We were there for one thing and one thing only, and that was to work. The [Ciccones] took good care of us. We were never hungry. We had clean clothes and the care was excellent… but we worked hard."[11]

Bert did have several fond memories of his time on the farm, especially when it came to Calvin. During an interview on October 24, 2013, he smiled and recalled that, "On the farm, Willy was Willy. He was always a happy-go-lucky kid that didn't have a care in the world." Bert continued, "One day Willy comes to me and says he wanted a fishing pole so he could fish in the small pond that we had on the farm. He would catch pout, bass and other fish down at the lake and bring them home and put them in our pond. I made this fishing pole from a long stick and a piece of string and it worked. He'd fish all day in that pond and just keep throwing the fish back in." Bert thought for a moment and added, "I think Willy had a good life

---

[7] Adam Piore interview with Calvin Heath, 2009.
[8] Bert Heath interview with author, October 24, 2013.
[9] Bert Heath interview with author, October 3, 2014.
[10] Bert Heath interview with author, October 24, 2013.
[11] Ibid.

when he was a kid..."[12] When I asked Calvin about his time on the farm, he simply said, "It was something we had to do. I never thought it was a big deal."[13]

My wife Sue and I built our home in Thompson, Connecticut in 1988. It is situated only a few hundred yards from the old Ciccone farmhouse where the five Heath children lived; maybe that's why Calvin liked visiting. The fields I now mow were some of the very same fields on which Calvin and his siblings worked and played as children. When Bert visited me in October of 2013, he looked out my back window and was transported back in time nearly 60 years. He chuckled as he recalled another story. "[Calvin] would collect manure worms, and he would take those worms and go down to the road with a sign, and of course you had all the traffic going by on their way to [Quaddick Lake]. He did pretty good selling those worms."[14] The story resulted in more smiles for the 70-year-old truck driver.

Many people in town did not know about the Heath children being removed from their house as young children. An old friend and former school mate of Calvin's, Tammy Hall, stated, "That's heartbreaking about the kids being removed from their home... not something most people knew about, I'm guessing. Cal was always smiling and cheerful as a child from my recollection, and even as I knew him later as an adult, he would greet me like a long-lost friend."[15]

Calvin attended elementary school at the Israel Putnam School, Putnam, Connecticut. School was not an easy affair for Calvin. As an American Indian, he struggled in the highly intolerant and narrow-minded society of the 1950's. John Cutler, a former classmate, remembers Calvin being singled out by a teacher at the beginning of their first grade year and being spanked in front of the whole class. "I think she was trying to make an example out of him."[16] John did not recall Calvin ever committing any real offense.

---

[12] Bert Heath interview with author, October 24, 2013.

[13] Calvin Heath interview with author, April 26, 2013.

[14] Bert Heath interview with author, October 24, 2013.

[15] Tammy Hall Email to author, October 29, 2013.

[16] Author interview with John Cutler October 2013.

During sixth grade, Calvin remembered a specific event that bothered him for the rest of his life. "When I went to school, I can remember I sat in the corner all day because I was Native American, Nipmuc Indian, and I said I was Indian. The [teacher] would say, 'There are no Indians left... you're lying!'"[17] Instead of helping Calvin embrace his heritage, she punished him because of it, something that would cost her her job today.

Throughout his childhood, Calvin was often belittled due to his socioeconomic status. When my own family moved to Putnam, Connecticut in 1964, I can remember people in town talking poorly about the large struggling families throughout town, and I now see how genuinely mean-spirited such talk was. My mother always suggested that, "Those with little who spoke about those with less, did so in order to feel better about themselves." In many cases, I think she was right.

After struggling through Israel Putnam Elementary School, Calvin attended the Putnam Middle School located on School Street, Putnam, Connecticut. The former three-story brick high school building was converted to a middle school when the Town of Putnam built a new high school in 1950 due to a rapid rise in student population. For Calvin, the greatest part of this new school was that it had an athletic program complete with an indoor basketball court and a large beautiful baseball field. According to Romeo Blackmar, a well-recognized and long-time baseball and basketball figure in Northeast Connecticut, Calvin and Romeo's older brother Bob, "...were mound rivals during their middle school days," Bob played for cross-town rival St. Mary School and Calvin for the public school. Romeo noted how great an athlete Calvin was as a youngster.[18]

During the fall of his seventh and eighth grade years, Calvin also played football for the St. Mary's football team. The St. Mary's Crusaders was a community-based effort that was "...opened to all youngsters," and founded in 1961 by local legend, Gerry St. Jean.[19] Crusaders' Football was a junior-high program that played against

[17] Adam Piore interview with Calvin Heath, 2009.
[18] Romeo Blackmar Email, October 28, 2013.
[19] St. Mary's Football Brochure, 1968, p. 23.

5

other organizations and school teams throughout Southern New England, sometimes travelling as far away as Camden, New Jersey for games. Coach St. Jean was impressed with Calvin's talent as a football player and in one of the team's programs stated that he was an "End with promise."[20] Calvin fondly remembered his days on the gridiron and stated:

I played wide receiver. I could play anywhere I wanted, but they wanted me to play running back. I didn't want to go out for passes, I just wanted the ball. The longest gain I had was 52 yards. And on defense, I played defensive end and defensive tackle. I was one of the bigger guys. I was like 185 pounds.[21]

While his weight might have been a slight overstatement, those who played with Calvin during those years remember him being larger than most players and one of the best on the field.

Left: Calvin Heath c.1961 while playing for the St. Mary's Crusaders. Legendary coach, Gerry St. Jean, said Calvin was back with promise. Many who knew Calvin as a youngster talk about his exceptional athletic skills. St. Mary's Football brochure.

One humorous story from this time period that deserves special note is brother Melzer and Cousin Curt's "skunk" story. With so many mouths to feed, the Heaths always had difficulty finding money to buy their children clothes. As a result, the family took advantage of rummage sales held throughout town by various volunteer groups.

---

[20] St. Mary's Football Brochure, 1968, p. 10.
[21] Adam Piore interview with Calvin Heath, 2009.

While visiting his mother and father one day, 13-year-old Calvin and his cousin Tyke, Curt's brother, were sent to a charity rummage sale that was being held at the Belding Hemingway Forman's Club building, located near Ballou Village, Putnam, Connecticut, close to where Calvin's family lived. The two boys took a well-worn shortcut by the Quinebaug River and unexpectedly crossed paths with a skunk. The odious animal did what came naturally. Neither boy realized they were sprayed, and both smelled awful. They entered the rummage sale without a care in the world and quickly had the place to themselves thinking nothing of the ladies scrambling for the doors. They tried on and selected several fashionable articles and when it came time to pay, the ladies gave the two boys everything they touched for a few pennies. The boys were then quickly escorted to the door. As Curt later said, laughing, "They smelled absolutely terrible! When they went into the rummage sale, all the ladies in the hall left!" Oblivious to their newly acquired "scent," the two boys returned home with their new clothes feeling pretty good about themselves and the generous women who assisted them. "When they arrived home, they were immediately taken out back by our moms and given a tomato juice bath!" finished Curt laughing.[22]

In September of 1964, at the age of 15, Calvin entered Putnam High School as a freshman. His time in high school did not last long. In January 1965, when Calvin turned 16, he was repatriated to his parents and was the last of the Heath children to leave the Ciccone farm.[23] Shortly thereafter, Calvin quit high school in order to help support his struggling family. Calvin stated, "My father was hurt. I needed to help the family by bringing in some money, so I quit school and went to work."[24] This was very unfortunate for Calvin for several reasons. First, his Armed Forces Qualification Test, taken a year and a half later, would show, that despite struggling through school, Calvin was quite intelligent. Second, had Calvin stayed in high school, his athletic abilities would have undoubtedly opened other opportunities that few in his family had ever had.

---

[22] Curt and Melzer Heath interview with author, January 31, 2014.
[23] Bert Heath interview with author, October 24, 2013.
[24] Calvin Heath interview with author, May 2014.

Calvin's first job was loading dye machines at the Hale's Manufacturing Company located on Pomfret Street, Putnam, Connecticut. Hale's was a well-established company that dated back to 1807. The company remained a major part of the Putnam landscape and economy for nearly 180 years and maintained a good reputation for treating its employees well.

The dye house, in which Calvin worked, was a brutally hot and dangerous environment due to the chemicals used, the constant heat, and the dangerous equipment used in the textile dying process. Temperatures in the dye house always exceeded 100°F and the work was usually assigned only to the hardiest of souls. Calvin was one of these hardy souls. Things seemed to be going well for Calvin at Hale's, but several months after he was hired, he was called to the front office. The company's personnel department realized they had a 16-year old working in an area where the minimum age was 18, leaving them little choice. It is uncertain if Calvin provided the wrong age when he was hired or if his age was an oversight by the company. Either way Calvin was looking for a new job.

A short time after leaving Hale's Manufacturing Company, in the summer of 1965, Calvin secured a job with the City of Putnam's Highway Department. For a little more than a year, he worked as a general laborer and enjoyed the work so much that he decided it would be in construction, specifically operating heavy equipment, where he would like to make a living

Several discussions with older brothers Bert, a former 101st Airborne Trooper, Chet, who was stationed in Korea as a personal driver for the deputy-post commander, Glen, who served as an Army engineer in Europe, and local Army recruiters, soon convinced Calvin that the best way to obtain this goal was to join the U.S. Army.[25] Given he was only 17 at the time, enlistment into the Army required his parents' permission. His father immediately consented, but because of the war raging in Southeast Asia, his concerned mother would not agree. Eight months later, in May 1967, after Calvin had

---

[25] Calvin Heath records, U.S. Army Enlistment Record, Fort Jackson, SC.

turned 18 years old, he enlisted. This time his mother had no choice but to accept her son's decision.[26]

---

[26] Calvin Heath interview with author, April 26, 2013.

VIETNAM

After World War II, the American-backed French government looked to reestablish and maintain control over its former colony, French Indochina, which included Laos, Cambodia, and Vietnam. German victories in France, the Japanese occupation of Indochina, and a rising local insurgency all conspired against the French maintaining control. By the end of WWII, French rule over their colonies was hanging by a thread. Over the next ten years, the situation in this part of the world continued to deteriorate. On April 7, 1954, during a press conference, concerned U.S. President Dwight D. Eisenhower stated:

Finally, you have broader considerations that might follow what you would call the "falling domino" principle. You have a row of dominoes set up, you knock over the first one, and what will happen to the last one is the certainty that it will go over very quickly. So, you could have a beginning of a disintegration that would have the most profound influences.[27]

One month later, on May 7, 1954, in spite of the growing support from America and its allies, the Communist-backed Viet Minh, under the leadership of General Vo Nguyen Giap, defeated a large French force at Dien Bien Phu, ending French control of the area. Soon after, Cambodia, Laos, and Vietnam were granted their independence and the struggle for political control in each country began.[28]

In 1954, Vietnam was partitioned according to the 1954 Geneva Accords, with the Communist government seeded in the North, and the anti-Communist regime led by Ngo Dình Diem in the South. Diem's corrupt regime, which favored the country's Catholics and

---

[27] Eisenhower, *The President's News Conference of April 7, 1954.*
[28] Jeffries, p. 388.

10

neglected the country's large Buddhist population, was eventually deposed and unrest ruled the land.

During his inaugural speech in 1961, President John F. Kennedy, agreeing with Eisenhower's "falling domino" theory, stated that America would "Pay any price, bear any burden, meet any hardship, support any friend, [and] oppose any foe, in order to assure the survival and success of liberty."[29] In June 1961, immediately following his now famous Vienna meeting with Khrushchev, he told James Reston of The New York Times that, "Now we have a problem making our power credible and Vietnam looks like the place." Kennedy would go on to use Vietnam as his line in the sand.[30] Throughout 1963, he increased the 900 American advisors that Eisenhower had sent to Vietnam to 16,000.[31] U.S. military advisors were now imbedded at all levels of the South Vietnam military.

When Lyndon Johnson became the U.S. President after the assassination of John F. Kennedy in November of 1963, the situation in Vietnam continued to escalate. A 1963 South Vietnam regime change and alleged attacks on the USS Maddox and the USS Turner Joy in August 1964, prompted Congress to approve the Gulf of Tonkin Resolution allowing President Johnson presidential power to conduct war without a declaration.[32] In the spring of 1965, U.S. Marines landed at Da Nang to protect the U.S. air base located there. One month later, President Johnson authorized the use of combat forces for offensive operations. This was the start of a rapid buildup that, by the end of 1967, resulted in more than 485,000 American troops in Vietnam.

In America, opposition to the war increased, and soon, organized and unorganized anti-war protests were popping up across the country, especially at colleges and universities like Berkeley, Cornell, Kansas, and Michigan. High profile figures like Dr. Martin Luther King, Muhammad Ali, and Eugene McCarthy all renounced the war. In 1967, a group called the Vietnam Veterans against the War was

---

[29] The Avalon Project found at the Yale Law School, *Inaugural Address of John F. Kennedy.*
[30] Mann, a *Grand Delusion.*
[31] Swarthmore College Peace Collection, "Vietnam War".
[32] Moise, p. 76.

formed and conducted protests in a variety of places starting with New York City's "Fifth Avenue Peace Parade." Dr. Martin Luther King, in 1968 said, "If America's soul becomes totally poisoned, part of the autopsy must read 'Vietnam.'"[33] More and more Americans felt the war was unwinnable and by the time Calvin joined the U.S. Army, the country was literally split in two over the issue.[34]

What should be noted is that Calvin, a young man without a wife and family, a job critical to national security, or a college deferment, was a likely target for the U.S. Selective Service and would have been drafted if he did not voluntarily enlist. Despite this, when asked years later why he joined the Army, he simply said, "I wanted to be in the service like my brothers were."[35] So on May 17, 1967, at the age of 18 years and four months, Calvin William Heath reported for duty to the United States Army.

---

[33] Life Magazine, *Remembering Martin Luther King Jr. 40 Years Later*, p. 139.
[34] Willbanks, p. 3.
[35] Bert Heath interview with author, October 24, 2013.

BASIC TRAINING

Calvin left Putnam, Connecticut on the morning of May 17, 1967.[36] His head was throbbing, and his brain was a little foggy as he boarded the plane heading to Columbia, South Carolina. The night before, he and his good friend Rob Authier decided to send Calvin off to the United States Army with a bang. Although illegal, securing alcoholic beverages was not a problem for the two 18-year-old, street-savvy young men. The night of celebration, 47 years later, still brought a smile to the 65-year-old Authier. During our interview in 2014, he quietly admitted, "Boy, we had a few that night!"[37]

The trip to South Carolina marked several firsts for Calvin, a local Connecticut boy with very little experience outside his small hometown. It was the first time he had ever left New England and the first time he had ever been on an airplane. Several months later he would add several more firsts to this list.

Calvin's flight landed at the Columbia Metropolitan Airport in the early afternoon of May 17, 1967. Upon arrival, a U.S. Army representative directed Calvin to a military bus waiting outside the terminal. The bus would take him the remaining 25 miles to Fort Jackson, South Carolina.

Upon arriving at Fort Jackson, Calvin was assigned to the U.S. Army Reception Station, (USARECSTA) where all new recruits began their training. The 12-day assignment at USARECSTA was a whirlwind of activity, the likes of which few of the young recruits, including Calvin, had ever seen. Calvin and the other confused 18 and 19-year old men were quickly organized, assigned barracks, and provided basic information about army life. Seemingly common tasks were now imperative to master if the men were to survive the next nine weeks. Simple items such as how to stand in a straight line, the more complicated "dress-right-dress," and how to properly address an

---

[36] Calvin Heath 201 File.
[37] Rob Authier interview with author March 28, 2014.

officer and a drill sergeant became matters of life and death... or so the recruits were made to believe.

The men's identities were stripped away, and they were assigned numbers and unflattering nicknames. Young men with names like Zmitikevitch became "Alphabet," tall recruits became "Beanstalk" or "Flagpole." Short soldiers became "Midget Shit," or something even less flattering. Calvin, with an easy last name, probably escaped the NCO's desire to rename him and he simply became "Heath." The weaker recruits, or those with excessive weight, became immediate targets for the drill sergeants and some would be deemed unfit for duty or even worse – recycled through a pre-Basic Training physical training class until they could meet the Basic Training requirements. Calvin, who was in good shape, was not singled out. The NCOs could easily see he would not have any problems keeping up with the intense physical requirements of Basic Training.[38]

Over the next few days, Calvin and the rest of the young men received haircuts, uniforms, medical examinations, shots, and their basic equipment. They were tested, questioned, scrutinized, and studied. Army experts administered aptitude tests to determine in what area the men could best serve their country and the U.S. Army. After the testing and examinations were completed, the recruits were assessed by psychiatric counselors and were assigned their Military Occupational Specialty (MOS). Calvin, despite signing up and requesting to be a heavy equipment operator, was assigned as an 11B10 – an infantryman. He asked the counselor if he would learn how to operate heavy construction equipment and was told, "Sure, every 11B gets to operate heavy equipment. Next!"[39]

On May 29, 1967, the recruits packed their new uniforms and gear and were transported to a different part of the base where they would begin U.S. Army Basic Training (BCT). Upon arrival, they

---

[38] Author's note: I was a five-foot-seven-inch, 125-pound recruit when I joined the service in 1974 and understand the drill sergeants' wrath when it came to making soldiers out of the less physically gifted. I graduated BCT among the top of my class and added an inch to my height and more than 30 pounds to my frame. Many my size were recycled.

[39] Calvin Heath interview with author, March 2013.

were quickly and abruptly introduced to the Army's most feared man – the drill sergeant.

The U.S. Army drill sergeant is the best of the best. The requirements and training to become one are among the toughest in the armed forces. At the end of the day, these men – and women – can out-run, out-shoot, and out-soldier anyone in uniform. They are the masters of discipline and the leading authority on creating soldiers out of young naïve recruits.

As soon as Calvin's bus arrived at his new company area – A Company, 5th Battalion, 2nd Training Brigade,[40] a very large, and angry drill sergeant jumped on the bus screaming. He looked like he was ready to rip someone's head off. Few of the new recruits noticed his impeccably starched olive-green uniform, his brightly shined Corcoran jump boots, or the unusual "Smokey the Bear" hat he wore; they were too busy vacating the bus with their gear hoping not to be the last person off. Outside the bus were several more drill sergeants yelling and screaming for the men to take their places along a painted line in the street. The recruits' efforts were of course well below the drill sergeants' standards and they were made to repeat the process several more times. Once the men met an acceptable level of performance, they were made to stand at attention while the drill sergeants introduced themselves.

Jaysus H. Christ! How in God's holy name am I expected to take such a bunch of mamma-loving maggots like you and make you soldiers in my beloved United States Army! You can't even get off a goddam bus in an acceptable and expeditious military manner without tripping all over your goddam happy sticks! Never in my entire life have I seen a bigger load of whale shit!

Selecting an especially nervous recruit, the red-faced D.I. moved to within an inch of the recruit's face and screamed, "Do you know why you're whale shit recruit?!"

"No sir!"

---

[40] Note: Calvin's 201 File was unclear as to which brigade.

"No sir! Are you shitting me? Do you see these stripes on my sleeve, dip shit? These are sergeants' stripes. I work for a goddamn living! You will address me as Drill Sergeant! Do you understand me?"

"Yes sir! Um... Yes, Drill Sergeant!"

"Now answer the goddamn question you pot-smoking-bag-of hippie dung! Do you know why you're whale shit?"

"No, Drill Sergeant!"

The D.I. backed off the now sweating recruit and addressed the entire formation, "Because there is no form of excrement lower than whale shit!"

Once the preliminary antics subsided, and the drill sergeants clearly had the men's attention, curt introductions were made. It probably went like mine, which was:

My name is Drill Sergeant Williams! There are only two things in this world I like – my mother and my dog. This here is Drill Sergeant Johnson – he doesn't like anything! For the next eight weeks, your heart might belong to your sweetheart, who is now home in East Where-Ever-the-Hell you're from, playing ass-grab with Jody, but your ass belongs to me!

For the next eight weeks, Calvin and the men of his basic training company were subjected to a rigorous routine that none of the men had ever experienced or were prepared for, especially the privileged and coddled. But Calvin was neither privileged nor coddled and was used to running and working hard. Growing up on a farm, rising each morning at 5:00 a.m. was something very familiar to Calvin. The exercise, long runs, and the quick-paced environment were not much of a physical challenge to him and he viewed the activity as comparable to what he was already doing at home.

On June 1, 1967, Calvin attended a briefing given by an airborne-qualified non-commissioned officer (NCO). The NCO was trying to recruit men for the Airborne and his descriptions of the exciting life of an Airborne Ranger greatly interested Calvin. He stated, "When I was going through Basic Training, they had a [sergeant] from the 26th

Infantry Division… and he was talking about [going] airborne. From that point [on], my interest [level] was going up."[41] Calvin was captivated by the sergeant's advice on how to avoid punji sticks, how to maneuver down dangerous jungle trails without being seen, and what they could expect in Advance Individual Training (AIT) and Jump School. Calvin considered his Native American heritage and what he felt it would take to become a worthy warrior. He also thought about his brother Bert and the time he served with the 101st Screaming Eagles and he soon decided to "go airborne."[42] "I just wanted to see if I could do it."[43]

The eight weeks of BCT were a blur to Calvin and the new recruits. They learned everything, including simple items they should have learned as young children like how to properly brush their teeth, make a bed, fold their clothes, dress, and care for their gear. The lessons were taught and retaught over and over again until they got it right. Nothing was left to chance. They were issued weapons and taught how to move as a unit. Above all else, they learned that attention to detail would save lives.

Every Saturday morning, general inspections were held. Any item not meeting the Drill Sergeant's high standard, or found out of order, was thrown on the floor and the recruits made to do it again and again, until they met the drill sergeant's rigid standards. The recruits who excelled were expected to help those who did not, and they were all evaluated as a team. If one man failed, they were all punished. The Drill Sergeants' expectations were high and their scrutiny unforgiving.

When they weren't learning, sleeping, eating, or being inspected, the men ran. They ran to breakfast, lunch, dinner, supply, training – hell, they ran everywhere. While the men performed other daily exercises to improve their strength and agility, it was the hundreds of miles that they ran that made them soldiers. During a 2009 interview,

---

[41] Adam Piore interview with Calvin Heath, 2009. Note: The actual unit could have been the 25th Infantry Division.
[42] Calvin Heath 201 File.
[43] Calvin Heath interview with author, May 2014.

journalist Adam Piore asked Calvin, "You did well in Basic Training?"

"Yeah, I did very well," replied Calvin.

"What was it that made you do very well?" asked Adam.

"It's a lot of physical stuff. I was able to do all of that. You know everything is running and I can run forever. I grew up on a farm chasing cows!"[44]

The initial physical pain of the first few weeks of Basic Training subsided, and the men could feel themselves getting stronger. They became acclimated to the D.I.s and their harsh criticism, and most of the men responded appropriately. They were slowly becoming soldiers.

By week three, the men began basic rifle training. They were trained on both the M-14 and the M-16 rifles, but it would be the M-16 that would be the Army's weapon of choice in Vietnam, and the weapon the men were required to eventually master. Calvin was a quick learner and mastered both weapons.

During the last five weeks of Basic Training, the men were trained in basic first aid, hand-to-hand combat, how to react properly to a gas and chemical attack, basic radio communications, how to properly toss hand grenades, etc. They finished their training with a two-day bivouac and forced-field march where they would apply basic small-unit tactics learning how to move and maneuver under combat conditions.

On July 26, 1967, those long-haired, disorganized young boys who had fallen all over themselves simply trying to get off a bus eight weeks earlier were now marching down the parade grounds in perfect unison. They were now well-trained United States Army soldiers. Calvin was especially proud the day his training battalion marched passed the reviewing stand and he had good reason. He excelled in virtually everything he was taught and graduated in the top three of his company, earning him a promotion to E-2 Private. It's easy to

---

[44] Adam Piore interview with Calvin Heath, 2009.

imagine Calvin's big broad smile as he marched past the saluting senior NCOs and officers.[45]

That afternoon, right after the BCT graduation, Calvin packed his things, said his goodbyes to the other men, and boarded a bus heading to Fort Gordon, Georgia. As he looked out the window of the bus leaving South Carolina, he smiled. Life was going very well, and he was proud of himself – and his new stripe.

Above: Calvin at Fort Jackson, South Carolina, during Basic Training. The flight to Ft. Jackson was the first time he had ever been in an airplane and the first time he had been out of New England. Paul Duquette photo.

---

[45] Calvin Heath interview with author, April 26, 2013.

ADVANCED INDIVIDUAL TRAINING - AIT

Calvin was assigned to E Company, 2nd Battalion, 3rd Training Brigade, United States Training Center (Infantry).[46] His reception at Fort Gordon, Georgia was much different than the reception he received at Fort Jackson. Here, the instructors were only interested in making the new soldiers infantrymen and they trained their new charges with a great deal less yelling and screaming.

As Calvin settled into at his new barracks at Fort Gordon, he met Paul Allan Conner from Fort Lauderdale, Florida, formerly of Becket, Massachusetts.[47] Paul Conner was the same age as Calvin, but was a draftee, not that it mattered to Calvin. The Army encouraged new recruits and soldiers to pair up with another soldier in what they called the "buddy system." This way each man could look out for the other. Paul and Calvin hit it off right away and they quickly became the best of friends.[48] They were soon exchanging every detail about themselves and after the first week of AIT, they knew more about each other than many of their own family members did. It was a friendship that would last until Paul's death in 1968.

On August 7, 1967, Calvin began eight weeks of advanced infantry training. Like BCT, Calvin excelled in AIT and was very proud of his accomplishments there. He was extremely comfortable in the woods and excelled in every exercise he was given. Later in 2009, Calvin shared a few stories with Adam Piore:

> *I could see well at night. I used to have 20-15 vision, so I could see really well. They had this sloping hill, and on this hill, they had seven bunkers hidden... and they said, "What*

---

[46] Calvin Heath 201 File.

[47] Nathan Conner interview with author, September 10, 2014. Note: Paul Conner's 201 File shows him enlisting on May 22, 1967 and attending Basic Training at Ft. Jackson, SC. He was assigned to Echo Co., 2nd Bn., 3rd Training Brigade, the same AIT Company as Calvin. Upon completing AIT, both men were assigned to jump school together.

[48] Nathan Conner Interview with author, September 10, 2014. Special Orders Number 136 dated August 30, 1967.

you're going to do is walk up this trail and as you see the bunkers point them out to the sergeant." [This was] to see how close you get before you can see them. Well, I'm standing there in the field looking at the ridgeline where they were talking about. I picked out all seven before we even went on the trail. You know they wondered, "How the hell did he see that?" I grew up on farm. I was always out, and you can tell unnatural things. You know, I can see square boxes. You know it wasn't right. Everything was green but [these things were out of] shape, it just wasn't natural.[49]

During his eight weeks at Fort Gordon, Calvin also received additional training in map reading, escape and evasion, and camouflage and concealment, all skills that would serve him well in Vietnam. The final test for this portion of the training was a grueling event that placed three-man groups in the middle of a large swampy wooded area with nothing more than a knife, a compass, and a map. From their landing zone, they were required to traverse a large area undetected, arriving at a pre-determined coordinate within a specific amount of time. To further complicate the task, the exercise was held at night when the soldiers could see very little in the dark Georgia swamps. Calvin continued:

They had Green Beanies (Green Berets) *playing NVA* (North Vietnam soldiers). *[They] were [positioned] in the line... and if you headed in the heading you got, you wouldn't run into them, but if you went off course you would run into them and they would mess with you. We had this one guy... They told us, "When you're going in there, if you get bitten by a snake or something... if you have a problem just yell out. And somebody will come and get you." Well we had this one guy and we were about half way through it and this guy is yelling and screaming out there. It's like one o'clock in the morning. He's yelling, so you could hear all the sergeants yelling back*

---

[49] Adam Piore interview with Calvin Heath, 2009.

*at him, "We're coming! We're coming! What's the matter?
What's the matter?" And he yells back, "I'm scared!"*

Calvin laughed and finished with, "The sergeant yells back,
"When I get there, you're going to know what scared is!"[50] Calvin
hesitated, thought, and then proudly added, "We didn't get caught."[51]

On August 25, 1967, both Calvin and Paul Conner qualified as an
expert marksman on the M-16 Assault Rifle. Five days later, Calvin
also qualified as an expert on the M-60 Machine Gun.[52] These two
qualification medals were in addition to the sharpshooter's badge he
had already earned on the M-14 during Basic Training. Once again,
because of his outstanding performance during training, Calvin was
promoted, this time to Private First Class – E-3. He was quickly
becoming a highly trained instrument of war.

AIT finished on October 3, 1967, and Calvin's class graduated in
a ceremony that did not have the same level of fanfare as did their
Basic Training ceremony but was every bit as meaningful to the men.
That evening, Calvin, once again, packed his belongings. The
following day, October 4, 1967, he said his goodbyes to the other men
of his AIT class and reported to Fort Benning, Georgia for Jump
School. Calvin Heath, who previously had only ever been in one
airplane in his life, would soon find himself jumping out of them.

---

[50] Adam Piore interview with Calvin Heath, 2009. Author's note: I completed an Advanced
Tactics course in 1974 at Fort Leonard Wood, MO that had the same final test. Navigating
through the swampy gauntlet in the pitch-black night without being caught was a difficult
and challenging affair.
[51] Adam Piore interview with Calvin Heath, 2009.
[52] Calvin Heath 201 File, Special Order 136.

AIRBORNE SCHOOL

The U.S. Army Airborne Jump School, located at Fort Benning, Georgia, is a grueling three-week program that can test even the very best of soldiers. Calvin's primary reason for changing his initial MOS to airborne infantry was the opportunity to follow in his older brother Bert's footsteps. Bert, a 40-jump former airborne trooper with the 101st Screaming Eagles, later stated "... [Calvin] always wanted to follow me and I don't mean that to be a bad thing. If I was in the 101st then that's what he wanted to do. But I said, Calvin it doesn't come easy, and he said, 'That's what I want to do.' And sure enough that's what he did."[53]

Another reason for attending Jump School was Calvin's father. During AIT, Wayland sent his son a letter that deeply bothered Calvin. In the letter, Wayland told his son that Calvin's brother Bert was the only one in the family who had the "balls" to go Airborne. Years later Calvin admitted, "I had something to prove to him and me."[54] Calvin's good friend Rob Authier later agreed with that recollection and also noted that, "He had something to prove to his father, his brother, and himself."[55] On October 6, 1967, Calvin began Jump School.[56]

The U.S. Army Airborne School was originally founded in 1940 in anticipation of the need for airborne troops for the United States' eventual involvement in WWII. The school has since become the finest in the world, and while primarily used by the United States Army, it's also used for training by the U.S. Air Force, U.S. Marines, U.S. Navy, and the armed forces of other countries looking to both train their airborne troops and to learn about the U.S. Army Airborne teaching methodologies.

---

[53] Bert Heath interview with author, October 18, 2013.
[54] Adam Piore interview with Calvin Heath, 2009.
[55] Rob Authier interview with author, March 28, 2014.
[56] Calvin Heath 201File.

By the time Calvin arrived at the U.S. Army Airborne School, the U.S. Army had refined and perfected the training and classes into a model of efficiency. While the equipment technology had changed significantly over the previous 20-plus years, the overall three-week class that Calvin took in 1967 changed little. It remains among the three most grueling weeks in military training.

Much like the feared drill sergeants in Basic Training, the airborne school has its famed "Black Hats." Also like the U.S. Army drill sergeants, they are the most highly skilled specialists when it comes to jumping out of aircraft. They take to their craft with the same intensity and professionalism as the Basic Training drill sergeants and for the next three weeks, Calvin and his classmates were in their hands.

Jump School is broken into three major phases; 1.) Ground Week, 2.) Tower Week, and 3.) Jump Week. During Ground Week, the men are physically tested to ensure they are prepared for the rigorous training of the next few weeks. An unfit soldier typically meant injury or worse – death. During week one, the men also learn how to properly wear a parachute harness and how to safely land on the ground after a jump. Properly dissipating the energy, a man can generate falling at 23 feet per second is very difficult and can mean the difference between an uneventful jump and a severely injured soldier. The men were required to master the parachute landing fall (PLF) before they could move to the next phase of the training. Those unable to complete the first week successfully were required to retake the training. Those who did not possess the grit or physical qualifications were simply released from the school and sent back to their old units.

During Tower Week, the Jump School used 250-foot towers with a mock airplane door to teach the soldiers the different phases of the parachute drop.[57] The men went through exercises that demonstrated parachute shock – the jolt when the chute opens – and how to steer

---

[57] Note: The towers where obtained after the 1939 New York's World Fair and re-assembled at Fort Benning.

themselves into a targeted landing zone. They were also taught how to use an emergency chute.

During Jump Week, the final week of training, soldiers are flown to 1,200 feet and jump from a C-130 or C-17 aircraft. During Calvin's day, the Army often used a C-119, an older post-WWII airplane, called the "Flying Boxcar." Students were required to complete five jumps under varying conditions which included "Hollywood style" – jumping with no load – to jumping with a full combat load that could weigh up to 60 pounds.[58]

Like BCT and AIT, Calvin completed the training at the top of his class and graduated on October 27, 1967. Later, Calvin added that he really enjoyed Jump School. "I always liked the idea of being a Screaming Eagle."[59]

Above-left: Paul Allan Conner from Fort Lauderdale, Florida during Jump School. Above Right: Paul shortly after Jump School, possibly during his leave home in

---

[58] Source: U.S. Airborne School, Fort Benning, GA, found at:
www.baseops.net/basictraining/airborne.html.
[59] Calvin Heath interview with author, April 26, 2013.

November 1967. Memories of his best friend more than 45 years later still evoked great emotion from Calvin. Nathan Conner photos.

After completing Jump School, Calvin attended a one-week course in Military Justice as well as a class on Chemical, Biological, and Radiological Warfare. He completed these courses on November 4, 1967. Finally, with all his training now successfully behind him, he was granted his first leave. On November 5, 1967, he said goodbye to Paul Conner and headed home for a well-deserved rest.[60]

Left: A current picture of the 250' tower at Fort Benning, GA. The 250' tower has changed little since 1967 when Calvin took the course. The tower is the culmination of Week Two training. According to the U.S. Army, "Parachute jumps from the 250-foot high tower culminate the second week of training and are the final transition from ground training to actual parachuting. Soldiers are strapped into a harness and lifted into the air at the top of tower. Their parachutes are opened, and they are left to drift down from the tower." Fort Benning digital archives photo.

As Calvin waited for the plane that would take him back to Connecticut, he glanced at the large plate-glass windows that served as the exterior wall of the airport. He did not notice the reflections of the soldiers and passengers moving by as they quickly made their way to and from the many planes parked outside the concourse. What he did notice, however, was the reflection the U.S. Army Airborne

---

[60] Calvin Heath 201 File.

trooper "standing tall and looking good" staring back at him. He studied the proud and confident young man in the window for a few seconds. It was easy for Calvin to see that this man was much different than the boy who left Putnam only a few short months ago. This man had a purpose and a future. He smiled and was very pleased with what he saw.

HOME ON LEAVE

Calvin returned home to Putnam, Connecticut on November 5, 1967, six months after he left for Basic Training.[61] He visited with his family and friends and quickly found himself in a very uncomfortable, and a somewhat unfamiliar place. At home, many of his friends were now voicing very negative opinions about the Vietnam War and the American government, something Calvin did not like. Initially it seemed like everything in Putnam, Connecticut had changed during the time he was away. After several days of listening to his friends, however, he realized that it was *he* who had changed, not his friends in Putnam. He was now focused, confident, and proud. He now saw things with a greater clarity and a higher degree of maturity than did many of his friends. He was also a proud United States Army Airborne Soldier – a Screaming Eagle, who now viewed many of the important issues of the day differently than his carefree friends – and he liked it that way.

In 1967, anti-war protests were in full swing all across the country and many young adults, even in small towns like Putnam, were opposed to the war. This presented several awkward situations for Calvin as many of his friends told him that they would rather leave America and go to Canada than be part of the "Vietnam travesty" in which Calvin was now part. At least one of his friends went AWOL after he came home on leave and went to Canada. Calvin stated, "He was two weeks behind me and he got drafted. He came home on leave and he had orders to go to Vietnam, but he took off to Canada."[62] The AWOL soldier's parents and brother even went to Canada to urge their son to do the right thing and finish his obligation to the U.S. Government. Calvin continued:

---

[61] Calvin Heath 201 File. Note: Calvin later stated that he had a 30-day leave, but his records, to include his 201 File, indicate it was more along the lines of ten days.

[62] Adam Piore interview with Calvin Heath, 2009.

28

Well, he took off to Canada and his mother and father and his brother went up to Canada to see him and they talked him [into] coming back and going to Vietnam. When his plane landed, I believe it was Saigon [where] he landed, and they were mortared, and he ran off the plane and before his foot hit the ground a mortar round went off. Right there at the base of the ramp – killed him instantly. He was dead before he was in country... hadn't even stepped in country. He was dead. He said he knew if he went there, he was [dead].[63]

Despite the anti-war input he received from his friends, Calvin returned to duty, reporting to Fort Benning, Georgia on November 13, 1967. There, he was reunited with Paul Conner and on November 14, 1967, the two men, along with several others, were transferred to the U.S. Army, Pacific Command (USARPAC).[64]

During the Vietnam War, most soldiers who graduated from Jump School were assigned to units in the United States. This allowed them time to become acclimated to their new units, their new command structure, and the new team with whom they would eventually fight. Calvin and Paul however, possibly due to their high qualification scores during training, and the urgent requirements of a massive American buildup, were assigned directly to the 173rd Infantry (ABN), 101st Airborne, already stationed in Vietnam.[65] According to Edward Murphy, author of the book, Dak To, the 173rd suffered great losses in the Battle of Dak To, November 3-22, 1967, and immediately requested replacements for their severely depleted ranks.[66]

---

[63] Adam Piore interview with Calvin Heath, 2009.

[64] Author's note: Several of Calvin's family members have suggested that Calvin volunteered to go to Vietnam in place of his older brother Glen who was also serving in the U.S. Army. Glen was scheduled to go to Vietnam, but was instead transferred to South Korea, possibly due to Calvin taking his place. There was nothing, however, found in his military files that could corroborated this.

[65] Calvin Heath interview with author, April 26, 2013.

[66] Murphy, p. 325.

Several days after reporting to Fort Benning, the two men found themselves on a plane heading to Southeast Asia. During the flight, unbeknownst to Calvin and Paul, another set of orders were cut transferring them from the 173rd to the 3/187th Infantry (ABN), also of the 101st Airborne Division.

187TH AIRBORNE INFANTRY
"THE RAKKASANS"

The 187th Infantry Regiment was constituted on November 12, 1942, at Camp Mackall, North Carolina and was activated on February 25, 1943, as a Glider Infantry Regiment (GIR) assigned to the 11th Airborne Division.[67] Once the regiment was fully trained, the 187th was reassigned to the Pacific Theater of Operations.

By all accounts, WWII Glidermen were a special breed of soldier that received little of the accolades they so justly deserved. Paratroopers volunteered for the dangerous duty of jumping out of airplanes and could quit if they felt the duty too hazardous. In return, for the additional dangers, they rightfully received an extra $50 per month "jump pay." The "Glidermen, on the other hand, were given no hazardous duty pay and no choice about whether or not they wanted to be tugged aloft in rickety, motorless aircraft made of frames of pipe and covered with canvas." The gliders on which they flew crash landed on open fields in order to deploy the men, oftentimes killing or severely injuring many of the soldiers in the glider.[68]

In 1944, the regiment was sent to Dobadura, New Guinea. There, they established a base of operations and trained for another six months.[69] Major General Joseph M. Swing, a man determined to have all his men dually qualified as glidermen and paratroopers, conducted jump training and within six months, 75% of the enlisted men and 82% of the officers of the division were qualified jumpers.[70] By the end of 1944, the 187th was among the highest qualified units in the U.S. Army when it came to airborne assault.

The 187th saw action in New Guinea, Leyte, and Luzon in 1944 and was "the first Airborne Regiment... to conduct a combat amphibious landing on enemy-held shores..." in the Pacific. During

---

[67] Fort Campbell site found October 13, 2013 at: www.campbell.army.mil.
[68] Flanagan, p. 5.
[69] Ibid, p. 14.
[70] Ibid, p. 15.

WWII they also fought at Purple Heart Hill, Tagtay Ridge, Nichols Field, Manila, and Mount Macolod, Philippines. They were the only unit in the Pacific to repel and destroy an enemy airborne assault.[71] They also led American troops in the liberation of Manila and were given the honor of garrisoning the city to clear it of enemy stragglers and the death squads roaming the streets.[72]

After the war, the 187th Regiment spearheaded the occupation of Japan and, on August 30, 1945, became the first foreign troops to enter that country in over 2,000 years.[73] After Japan was secured by the Allies, the 187th continued their training and it was during training jumps in Japan that Japanese civilians named the regiment the "Rakkasans," which loosely translates to "Umbrella Men."[74] Some have suggested it translates literally to "falling down umbrella" or "falling umbrella man." Whatever the exact translation, the men of the 187th kept the nickname.

Above: Men from the 187th c.1946. The Rakkasans were the first foreign soldiers on Japanese soil in many centuries. Photos compliments of Alton Orlomoski.

In January 1949, the 187th started the long process of returning home to Fort Campbell, Kentucky where, in August 1950, they were designated the 187th Airborne Regimental Combat Team. For the next year, they trained at Fort Campbell and in September of 1950, only 20

---

[71] Fort Campbell site found October 13, 2013 at: www.campbell.army.mil.
[72] Ibid.
[73] Ibid.
[74] Flanagan p. vii.

months after they returned home, they were redeployed to Korea to fight in the Korean War.

While in Korea, the 187th was instrumental in the United Nation forces success with the Inchon landings by clearing the Kimpo Peninsula of enemy between the Han River and the Yellow Sea. In the months that followed, the 187th defeated an enemy force of more than 3,000 soldiers, performed a textbook parachute assault and heavy drop at Sukchon-Sunchon, and defeated the Chinese in the Battle of Wonju. The Rakkasans performed another airborne assault into the Munsan-ni Valley, fought battles at Inje, Kumwha, Wonton-ni and quelled prison-camp riots at Koje-do.[75]

After the Korean War, the Pentagon reviewed the success of the 187th and its future role in air mobility. As a result, the 187th was assigned to the 11th Airborne Division as a test unit for new concepts in air mobility. In February of 1964, they were reassigned to the 3rd Brigade of the 101st Airborne, "The Screaming Eagles," where their air mobility expertise was used to train the rest of the 101st Airborne Division.[76]

On December 13, 1967, command and control elements of the 187th Infantry (ABN), 101st Airborne Division, reported for combat duty in the Republic of Vietnam. More recently, the Rakkasans served in Operations Desert Storm, Desert Shield, Enduring Freedom, and Operation Iraqi Freedom.[77]

> *Up to 1997, the Rakkasans earned four Medals of Honor; 26 Distinguished Service Crosses; 411 Silver Stars;[78] 3,841 Purple Hearts; 917 of its brave soldiers died as a result of combat; The Rakkasans proudly display twenty-three battle streamers, fifteen combat citations, including five American and three foreign Presidential Unit Citations.[79]*

---

[75] Fort Campbell site found October 13, 2013 at: www.campbell.army.mil.

[76] Flanagan, p. 264.

[77] Fort Campbell site found October 13, 2013 at: www.campbell.army.mil.

[78] Note: This did not include Calvin's Silver Star.

[79] Flanagan, p. 374. Note: Having seen combat in Iraq and Afghanistan many times since 1997, the Rakkasans have added many more medals to Flanagan's total.

Notable Rakkasans include General William Westmoreland, General David Petraeus and General Norman "Stormin Norman" Schwarzkopf. It also includes Medal of Honor recipients Captain Paul Bucha (Vietnam), Calvin's company commander, later discussed in this book, Corporal Lester Hammond (Korea), Corporal Rodolfo P. Hernandez (Korea), and Private First Class Richard G. Wilson (Korea).[80] Also included among the notable Rakkasans is Command Sergeant Major Basil L. Plumley (WWII, Korea and Vietnam,). Plumley was the hard-nosed sergeant major made popular in the movie *We Were Soldiers Once and Young,* the story of the 1st Battalion, 7th Cavalry, that held despite being surrounded and attacked by superior numbers during the Battle of Ia Drang in November of 1965.[81]

Calvin would be joining the best, most experienced, and most distinguished airborne unit in the United States Army, and the best in the world.

---

[80] Flanagan.

[81] Moore, *We Were Soldiers Once and Young.* Note: Many of the men I interviewed for this piece suggest First Sergeant Austin Harjo, Delta Company, 3rd Battalion, 187th Infantry (ABN), Calvin's first sergeant in Vietnam, was cut from the same cloth as Sergeant Major Plumley.

Above: U.S. Army paratroopers of the 187th Regimental Combat Team jump out of U.S. Air Force C-119 Flying Boxcars of the 403rd Troop Carrier Wing during a maneuver near Taegu, Korea, on November 1, 1952. USAF photo.

DELTA COMPANY, 3RD BATTALION

Lead elements of the 3rd Battalion, 187th (3/187th), 101st Airborne Division arrived in Vietnam in early December of 1967, with their command and control structure arriving on December 13, 1967. They were not expected to deploy until the early part of 1968, "…but due to intelligence reports that the enemy was planning an offensive, General Westmorland asked for, and received the 3rd Brigade, 101st Airborne Division months earlier."[82]

Less than six months earlier, Delta Company, the men with whom Calvin would eventually fight, was nothing more than a line-item entry on a battalion Table of Organization and Equipment (TO&E). Sometime before September of 1967, the battalion commanders of the 187th Infantry, 101st Airborne Division, Fort Campbell, Kentucky, were ordered to add another rifle company to their commands. The September 5, 1967 Daily Morning Report (a report that records the daily disposition of each unit), for Delta Company, 3/187th Infantry Regiment (ABN), showed only two names on the company roster – First Lieutenant Paul Bucha and Second Lieutenant Eugene Smith. Fifty-two days later, on October 27, 1967, the Daily Morning Report showed that the company was fully formed with more than 100 soldiers.[83]

Delta's first company commander, Paul Bucha, was an all-American swimmer and a 1964 graduate of the U.S. Army Military Academy at West Point. "On May 12, 1962, he was one of two cadet athletes who, because of a big water polo meet, were excused from the mess hall the day General Douglas McArthur was to visit West Point and make his "Duty, Honor, Country" speech, quite possibly the greatest speech by a military man in the nation's history."[84] Unfortunately for Bucha, the water polo meet ultimately proved to be much less memorable than McArthur's speech.

---

[82] Daugherty, p. 124.
[83] Daily Morning Reports, National Archives.
[84] Smith, p. 200.

Bucha graduated from West Point in the top five percent of his class and was offered a two-year stint at Stanford University where he earned an MBA. In 1967, after completing Jump School and Ranger School, and with little more than a few months experience as an Army leader, he was sent to Fort Campbell, Kentucky, first as a platoon leader for 30 days, then as a company commander ordered to put together the last rifle company of the last battalion of the last brigade of the 101st Airborne Division.[85]

Bucha had great difficulty in filling his ranks. Jones, in his book, *History of the 101st Airborne Division; Screaming Eagles, The First 50 Years,* reports, "...the 2nd and 3rd Brigades were fighting a losing battle in their efforts to fill their ranks and prepare for possible deployment to Vietnam in 1968."[86] He goes on to state that, "Levies from the Republic of Vietnam caused a continuous drain on the 101st as the 173rd Airborne Brigade and the Division's own 1st Brigade attempted to maintain a fresh source of airborne replacements to overcome losses due to rotation and battlefield casualties."[87] This left Bucha few options as there were no excess unattached men in the 101st. Some of his men would later comment that he emptied the jails and recruited every misfit, criminal, and oddball he could find just to fill his TO&E. According to Bucha, Delta Company quickly gained a reputation as being a unit of "Clerks and Jerks." Years later, Mike Rawson, one of those Clerks and Jerks, stated, "We had no infantry training other than Basic Training. I was a mechanic and he (pointing to Dave Dillard) was artillery."[88] Bill Heaney, a member of the 82nd Airborne, volunteered to go to Vietnam and was reassigned to Delta Company, 3/187th. He stated, "I was a cannon cocker (artillery) in the 82nd, as soon as I got to Delta, I was instant infantry."[89] Dillard adds:

> *Captain Bucha, no wait, he was a First Lieutenant at that time, actually went out and emptied the stockades. We were*

---

[85] Smith, p. 200.

[86] Jones, p. 137.

[87] Ibid.

[88] Calvin Heath interview with author, April 26, 2013.

[89] Heaney interview with author, September 10, 2014.

like the dirty dozen. We had these guys from the inner city...
there were the Blackstone Rangers, from Chicago, and men
from Watts, Detroit, Whitehall-Philadelphia... and oh boy
they were undisciplined.[90]

Jones agreed with Dillard and reported, "... the Division collected airborne qualified personnel from wherever they could be begged, borrowed, stolen, or scrounged."[91]

It should be noted that many of the Delta men, with whom I met, were all highly qualified airborne troopers and many noted that "I was neither a clerk nor a jerk." Whatever their backgrounds, they would quickly become part of the most highly decorated airborne unit to fight in the Vietnam War.

Establishing a combat company worthy of the Screaming Eagle patch in a very short months, was impossible without a good First Sergeant. Not knowing what to do, Bucha was finally approached by fellow West Pointer, Fred Smith. Smith advised Bucha that he needed to find the "right" First Sergeant, not just a "good" First Sergeant, if he was to be successful. Bucha asked if he had any suggestions. According to Bucha, Smith replied, "Yes I do. Austin Harjo is in brigade because he beat up a Sergeant Major and I think he'll work for you, if you can get him out of brigade."[92] Bucha followed Smith's suggestion and requested Harjo as his top sergeant. It was one of the best decisions the young company commander made.

Harjo, a member of the Muscogee Creek Nation was born on May 24, 1924 growing up in a small house on Native American land. In 1948, after he finished school, he joined the 82nd Airborne and was reassigned in 1951 to the 101st Airborne as a jump school instructor. He served two combat tours with the 187th, 3rd Brigade, 101st Airborne in Korean and one combat tour with the 173rd, 1st Brigade, 101st Airborne in Vietnam. By the time he had arrived at Delta Company in 1967, Harjo was a 44-year-old, 19-year, hardened and

---

[90] Dillard, Heaney, Rawson interview with author, October 9, 2013.

[91] Jones, p. 137. Note: Some of the men like Bill Heaney, an artilleryman from the 82nd Airborne, volunteered to go to Vietnam and was reassigned to the 101st Airborne.

[92] Paul Bucha, Pritzker Museum Interview, 2006.

experienced combat veteran.[93] According to his men, he was a hard-charging, "kick-ass" senior NCO who took no crap from anyone and gave plenty when he felt the need. "I'll tell you... First Sergeant Harjo was the perfect person... perfect [for getting us in shape]," stated Dave Dillard. Harjo's biggest challenge was time. Even the best first sergeants needed time to form a combat company and he only had a few short weeks. He jumped into his new assignment with a zeal his men remembered for the rest of their lives.

Bucha tells of a story about a soldier who disrespected him by refusing to call him "Sir." The soldier told First Sergeant Harjo "If I don't [call him Sir], are you sending me to the stockade so I don't have to go with some guy from Stanford University to Vietnam?" Harjo said, "No! Then, bam! He hit him."[94] Another member of Delta Company, Bill Heaney stated, "Harjo calls us into formation one day and yells, 'Ten-hut!' A guy in the back yells 'Fuck you, you big, red-pie-faced mother fucker!' [We] never saw him again."[95] Years later, during a 2013 interview, this particular story made the men smile. I asked, "What happened to the man?" All the men shrugged their shoulders and said, "Who knows?" And then they laughed as if they were all in on a well-kept secret.

All the men spoke about Harjo as being larger than life. Bill Heaney said, "He was like six-foot-five when we first saw him... when in all actuality he was only about five-foot-eight. He just seemed bigger!"[96] "Nobody could have done to Delta what Top did – nobody."[97]

During their brief time together in the United States, Bucha and Harjo trained the men relentlessly. Being combat tested, Harjo understood that whipping these "Clerks and Jerks" into a fighting machine would take extraordinary efforts and measures, and he wasted little time. They would learn how to become an effective combat team, or it would kill them – either here or in Vietnam. Dave

---

[93] Harjo, Teresa, telecom with author February 15, 2019.
[94] Smith, p. 201. Bucha Pritzker Museum Interview, 2006.
[95] Dillard, Heaney, Rawson interview with author, October 9, 2013.
[96] Ibid.
[97] Heaney interview with author, September 10, 2014.

Dillard stated, "He was an absolute disciplinarian. He ran us to death, he pounded us, he treated us like we were all shit under his boot and that was the way it was."[98]

Bucha also understood the importance of training his men and giving them a sense of who they were and who they needed to become. Bucha recalls an instance where he was teaching the men survival skills. He had one of his platoon sergeants, Dickie Quick, Calvin's eventual platoon sergeant, secure a number of chickens. Bucha asked the inattentive crowd of soldiers, "How do you kill a chicken?" Few paid attention, so he whacked off the head of several chickens with his bayonet and threw them into the crowd. He now had the attention of a few men. Then he asked, "How does an airborne trooper kill a chicken?" Again, after a few mumbled replies, he wrung the chicken's neck and pulled off its head, and once again threw several decapitated chickens into the middle of the seated men. Now he had most of the men's attention. Then he asked, "How does an airborne ranger kill a chicken?" Again, after few more replies he bit off the heads of several chickens and threw them into the crowd. This time, he had the men's undivided attention.[99] By the time the men left for Vietnam, they were a well-oiled machine – almost ready for combat.[100]

---

[98] Dillard, Heaney, Rawson interview with author, October 9, 2013.

[99] Smith, pgs. 203-204.

[100] Note: Tracing the birth of the term "Clerks and Jerks" has been a challenge. The first recorded use of the term was in March 1968 in an article written by Raymond Coffey, Chicago Daily News Foreign Service. The article was titled, "Clerks and Jerks; Ft. Campbell Heroes due for Medals." Source: Paul Buch interview, 2006, Pritzker Military Museum.

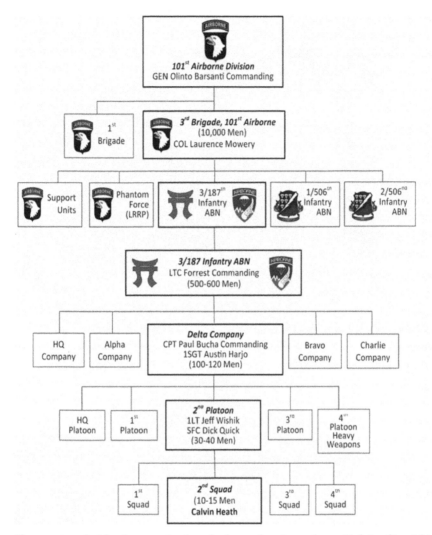

Above: An abridged organizational chart showing where Calvin fit within the different elements. Note this chart does not list all the supporting units that fought with the 3rd Brigade, 101st Airborne Division. The 173rd, the unit to which Calvin was first assigned, was part of the 1st Brigade already stationed in Vietnam. Joe Lindley chart.

JOSEPH LINDLEY

Above: Outside the headquarters of Delta Company, 3/187ᵗʰ Infantry (ABN), 101ˢᵗ Airborne Division 1967-1968, Phuoc Vinh, Vietnam. Rakkasan Delta photo. Below: Delta Company's 3/187ᵗʰ Infantry (ABN) orderly room 1967-1968. Phuoc Vinh, Vietnam. Rakkasan Delta photo.

IN-COUNTRY

Calvin and Paul Conner arrived in Vietnam on November 22, 1967, several weeks before the 187th arrived. Calvin's first recollection of Vietnam was the heat and the "stench." "It stinks! [There was] a bad odor from them burning human waste. As soon as you opened the doors from the plane, the smell would come right in and you would go like... Wow! Skunks smelled better."[101]

The two men were assigned to a holding unit and furnished with orders transferring them and several other newly arrived airborne soldiers to the 187th Infantry (ABN). The 3rd Brigade, 101st Airborne Division was on its way to Vietnam from Fort Campbell and despite Bucha's "recruiting" while stationed in the States, Delta Company, 3/187th was still short a few men and looking for qualified airborne soldiers to fill their ranks. Calvin added:

> *We reported directly to Vietnam. I was actually assigned to the 173rd and I got 30-day leave and I left for Vietnam three to four days before Thanksgiving. When I got there, they told us that we weren't going to the 173rd anymore that they were putting us on hold in that the [3/187th] 101st Division was coming over and [we were] going to get transferred to [them].*[102]

Elements of the 101st Airborne Division, more specifically the 1st Brigade, had been in Vietnam since July 1965, but it wasn't until 1967, during Operation Eagle Thrust that the balance of the division was ordered there from Fort Campbell, Kentucky, under the command of Major General Olinto Barsanti. The first transport planes left Fort Campbell on December 6, 1967, with the final load of men landing in Vietnam on December 18, 1967. Barsanti and his staff arrived on

---

[101] Adam Piore interview with Calvin Heath, 2009.
[102] Ibid. Note: Calvin's 201 File indicates he actually only had a two week leave.

December 13, 1967.[103] With "10,024 troops and over 5,300 tons of supplies, it was the largest and longest military air lift into a combat zone ever attempted by the U.S. military." The first unit to arrive was 3rd Battalion – Calvin's new unit.[104]

While in Vietnam waiting for their new unit to arrive, Calvin, Paul, and two other men, who were also reassigned to the 3/187th, were approached by a Brigadier General, who arrived with the 101st Airborne's advanced party. He informed the men that if they needed anything while waiting for their new unit, they could contact him. They thanked the General, never expecting to take him up on his offer, but the opportunity came several days later.[105]

When assigned to a war zone, few commanders want to deal with transient soldiers who do not belong to their TO&E. Not knowing what to do with temporary charges, most are assigned "shit details." The term "shit detail" can mean several things, especially to those in a combat zone. They can be those items on the bottom of a long list of necessary, but menial duties, or they can literally be "shit details." In Calvin's case it was the latter instead of the former, and he and Paul were assigned the worst of all jobs, removing the human waste of hundreds of soldiers from the latrines and burning it.

After a few days of "shit detail," Calvin and Paul, fed up with the disgusting job to which they were assigned, took the General up on his offer and asked for help. After hearing the complaint, the General, according to Calvin, sent the men to Long Binh, Vietnam to participate in a Long Range Reconnaissance Patrol (LRRP) class.[106] For the next week they learned the finer points of moving undetected through the jungles and rice paddies of Vietnam.

In his 2009 interview with Adam Piore, Calvin told Adam a comical story about transportation, possibly while being transferred to Long Binh for the LRRP class. He recalled:

---

[103] 101 Airborne, 1968, Vietnam, p. III. Note: Dave Dillard reports that the men of Delta Company left Fort Campbell on December 3, 1967 and arrived on December 5, 1967.

[104] Flanagan, pgs. 269-270. Note: Barsanti, on page III of the 101st Airborne 1968 Yearbook Barsanti reports the number of men to be 10,356.

[105] Adam Piore interview with Calvin Heath, 2009.

[106] Calvin Heath interview with author, April 26, 2013.

We flew out of Phan Rang[107] and they flew us in a C-130. We lifted off the runway, and they were climbing, and I happen to look out the right-side wing and it was smoking. The motor was smoking and there was just oil shooting over the top of the wing. I said, "That can't be right!" So, I yelled over to the Air Force guy that was in the payload deck with us and said, "Hey there's something wrong!" He said, "They all leak..." and I said, "You gotta take a look at this!" Well he went over, and he took a look and he went running back, and he climbed up the ladder, because you have to go up the ladder to get where the pilots were, and they made an emergency landing. Something was definitely wrong with [the plane]. So, they got us off, and now we're scared as hell anyway, they put us in this other airplane and we're going down the runway to take off and part of the fucking motor fell off! So, we come to another screeching halt! Now we're all bent out of shape we didn't want to go. We wanted parachutes if we fly these crazy-ass airplanes.[108]

After the second aircraft made it safely back to the tarmac, the men were offloaded and given something to eat. They were then put on their third aircraft of the day, this time a DHC-4 De Havilland Caribou. Luckily, they made the flight without any further incidents. The memory of that day was still fresh in Calvin's mind 45 years later. In May 2013, Calvin was planning to attend his unit's reunion and I asked him how he was getting there. He quickly replied, "It sure as shit isn't going to be in an airplane!"[109]

Soon after completing the LRRP class, Calvin, Paul Conner, and the other two men assigned to the 187th, were transferred by helicopter from Phan Rang to Phuoc Vinh, located in the Binh Duong Province. Calvin stated, "There were four of us that went to the 187th. [We] were on the buddy system and me and Paul Conner we went to

---

[107] Note: Phan Rang was an airbase used by the 101st as their divisional headquarters.
[108] Adam Piore interview with Calvin Heath, 2009.
[109] Calvin Heath interview with author, April 26, 2013.

D Company, and the other two guys went to B Company, and that's how I ended up with them."[110]

There are questions all soldiers ask when assigned to a combat area. They include, "Will I die?" and "Will I get wounded?" Calvin never worried about dying in Vietnam. He later stated that both he and his brother Glen had premonitions that Calvin would survive the war.[111] Calvin jokingly noted, in a 2013 interview, that in 1967, his brother suggested, "That I was going to get hit in the ass. And he wasn't far off!"[112] Calvin then added:

To say that anybody is not afraid of combat is lying. The difference between a hero and a coward is [there are some] people who can deal with stress and work [through it] and then there [are] other people who get hurt and they just curl into a ball. And in combat that's what happens. Everybody is scared, but some people react and can do things and other people can't... I was lucky that I could [do things].[113]

When asked about what frightened him most about being in Vietnam, he added:

Just wondering what the future was. I wasn't so much [afraid] of dying, because dead is dead, what I was scared of was fucking up and getting somebody else killed. That's what I was more scared of than anything. I [was afraid I] wasn't going to stand up to it. Am I going to be a warrior, am I going to be a man, or am I going to be scared and run? And until that happens you just never know. I know now![114]

On December 16, 1967, while Calvin and Paul were finishing their LRRP class, Paul Bucha and the men of Delta Company landed at Bien Hoa Airport. Their company was picked up by two-and-a-half-ton trucks and transported to their new camp at Phuoc Vinh,

---

[110] Adam Piore interview with Calvin Heath, 2009.
[111] Ibid.
[112] Calvin Heath interview with author, April 26, 2013.
[113] Adam Piore interview with Calvin Heath, 2009.
[114] Ibid.

located about 30 miles north of Saigon.[115] Upon arrival, they were assigned barracks and quickly began in-country briefings and small-unit tactics training with seasoned NCOs and officers of the veteran 1st Infantry Division. "A new life for the Rakkasans that would prove sometimes hazardous, sometimes boring, had begun."[116]

According to Calvin, on December 18, 1967, a few days after their new unit arrived, Calvin and Paul Conner arrived at Phuoc Vinh and reported to the 3/187th. Both were assigned as riflemen to Delta Company, Calvin to 2nd Platoon, under the command of Second Lieutenant Johnny D. Rusin[117], shortly thereafter First Lieutenant Jeffrey Wishik, and Platoon Sergeant Dickie Quick. Paul Conner went to 1st Platoon.[118]

Calvin's first impressions of First Sergeant Harjo, or "Top," matched the stories later told by other Delta men including Dave Dillard, Bill Heaney, Billy Ford, Mike Rawson and others – that Harjo was an intimidating and formidable man. Calvin later stated that, "All of us remember him as this big strapping guy, but at the reunion, he was like five-foot-six-inches tall."[119] Harjo's personality, demeanor and character made the man much larger than life.

Calvin tells of one of his first memories of Top.

...this big... guy out of New York wanted to fight [him]. Wanted to fight. Wanted to fight. Finally, Top had enough, and he said [to the guy], "You go talk to the CO, and if he says OK then we'll do it." [The soldier] went to talk to the Company Commander and he came back and said. "I got permission!" And we [ran] across the street [to see the fight]. Well when they got to the back of the building, Top

---

[115] Flannigan. Note: Information shows Delta Company actually arrived closer to December 6, 1967.

[116] Flanagan, p. 270.

[117] Note: Many of the men with whom I spoke indicated Rusin was wounded soon after arriving in Vietnam

[118] Note: Based on Calvin's input Paul was assigned to 2nd Platoon, but other evidence suggests he might have been assigned to 1st Platoon.

[119] Adam Piore interview with Calvin Heath, 2009. Note: The reunion Calvin speaks of was held in 2003.

was already coming back. He beat that guy up so bad they had to medevac him back to the States. He broke the guy's collar bone. Oh yeah, he tore him up.[120]

When the new men arrived at the Delta barracks, introductions were made, and Calvin and Paul settled into their new platoons. Calvin tells of one of his first recollections with his new assignment.[121]

We were in basecamp... one of the [funny stories] was I bought a pillow, but they told you that you had to watch out. If you drank your soda, they [the Vietnamese] had crushed glass and stuff to kill you and stuff like that, and they told us to watch out if you were getting anything from [them] that they don't do something. And anyways, I bought a pillow and had it on the bed, and I woke up I could hear this ticking noise. And I thought there was this freaking bomb [in it], and it was just my watch ticking through the pillow...[122]

Calvin then went on to tell about the first time he heard the sound of a live mortar. "The first time I heard a mortar round it was going out. I hit the floor," much to the amusement of the other men. "But then you learn really quickly what's incoming and what's outgoing. You learn all that stuff pretty fast."[123]

Within days of arriving at Phuoc Vinh, the 187th was patrolling the villages and jungles of War Zone D and the Iron Triangle and soon had their first taste of enemy fire. When not in the field, the men trained and worked at further securing their base perimeter. The tedious task of sandbagging became a familiar and unwelcomed, albeit very necessary, activity for all the men.[124]

---

[120] Adam Piore interview with Calvin Heath, 2009. Note: Some of the men indicated this was another first sergeant with whom Harjo had issues.

[121] Note: Paul and Calvin had technically been in-country longer than the men of Delta.

[122] Adam Piore interview with Calvin Heath, 2009.

[123] Ibid.

[124] Note: 3/187th also conducted missions in the Parrots Beak, Tran Rang, and the Hobo Woods.

As December turned into January, the men of the 187th received combat missions that were further and further away from the base. According to Dave Dillard, most of the missions were "search and destroy." When I asked Dave to explain further, he simply stated, "Find the enemy and kill him."[125]

Above: A Christmas card used by the men of the 101st Airborne, to include Calvin, during Christmas 1967. Thousands of families all over the country received these from their loved ones serving with the 101st in Vietnam. Compliments of Jerald Berry.

Calvin's first kill came less than two weeks after arriving at Phuoc Vinh, but, like many of Calvin's personal stories, this one also has a comical twist to it. For a time, the Viet Cong (VC) were very active in the Phuoc Vinh area and constantly sought ways to harass the American base. When I asked Bill Heaney how many times did the enemy try to breach the perimeter he responded, "All the time... Every night someone was trying to get through the wire."[126] This required the men to be on constant alert and they were never able to completely let down their guard. During the evenings, the VC sometimes probed the U.S. lines, seeking weaknesses. These probes ranged from several-man, lightly-armed teams to small unit attacks

---

[125] Dillard, Heaney, Rawson interview with author, October 9, 2013.
[126] Heaney interview with author, September 10, 2014.

accompanied by supporting mortar fire.[127] On or around Christmas 1967, the men of Delta Company had just returned from a patrol and were preparing for possible action that evening. Whether the following events were planned based on suspected enemy movement in the area that day is unknown, but at midnight, according to Calvin, the 187th planned to throw hand grenades into a mine field that protected a specific area of the base and then fire their weapons into that same area, a common tactic in perimeter defense. Calvin recalled:

> *I had to go to the bathroom, and I was sitting on the toilet and gunfire erupted hot and heavy. And I said, "Fuck! They're shooting without me!" So, I hurried to get out of the bathroom and bullets are going over my head and I say, "What the fuck is that?" I get out and the Gooks were shooting at us. I shot up one that was trying to hide behind a tree. I saw him and I fired him up.[128]*

Calvin ran down to the perimeter yelling "I got one! I got one!" Excited, and forgetting everything he was taught about fire discipline, Calvin emptied an 18-round burst into the man. By morning the blood trails confirmed that the VC who were trying to penetrate the perimeter were badly beaten and had at least one man dead – the one Calvin dispatched.[129] It is unknown how many men Calvin killed during his time in Vietnam, but it is with some certainty that this was his first.[130]

---

[127] Note: According to Jeff Davis and Richard Shoup, the attacks on the base became less and less as the frequency and efficiency of the patrols around the base increased. This was, in large part due, to the brigade LRRP team.

[128] Adam Piore interview with Calvin Heath, 2009.

[129] Ibid.

[130] Note: Calvin, while giving a talk many years later to local students about the war, was asked how many men he killed in Vietnam. Calvin would only say, "Too many, and not enough."

Left: Men of the 3/187th moving outside the Phuoc Vinh perimeter. The areas outside the fenced areas are mined. The men spent most of their time "outside the wire, moving at night." Jon Jakeway photo.

Above: Troopers of the 173rd Airborne landing in a hot LZ, 30 miles north of Saigon, in War Zone D, South Vietnam. The LZs' size varied depending upon the mission and the number of helicopters that were required. The men were expected to offload in seconds when approaching a hot LZ. Photo compliments of the Glenn Helm Collection, The Vietnam Center, Texas Tech University. U.S. Army photo.

Soon after arriving in Vietnam, the men of Delta Company found themselves training to perfect a new method of air assault. The concept of air mobility quickly evolved after the helicopter was first introduced during the Korean War. On December 11, 1961, 32 U.S. Army H-21 helicopters arrived in Vietnam and 12 days later were committed to combat actions.[131] By 1966, the 1st Brigade of the 101st Airborne Division developed training programs for rappelling from helicopters, but the dense jungles made this method problematic and they quickly developed other methods and techniques that permitted large amounts of men to arrive in landing zones (LZs) in a very short period of time. This new assault method oftentimes required the LZ to be "prepped" with artillery fire, aerial bombardment, or helicopter gunships. Then slicks, Bell UH-1 Huey helicopters, which were specifically designed to carry air-assault troops, would land and quickly deposit a large force in a hostile area. This new method allowed the U.S. Army to move troops without expending the energy, time, and resources necessary to hike or drive to the mission location.[132]

The slicks were armed with two M-23 or M-24 armament systems that featured an M-60, 7.62mm machine gun in each door. The number of slicks dispatched was based on the size of the operation and the size of the unit conducting it. They were often accompanied by heavily armed gunships that were used to "soften" target areas and LZs, and to protect the men as they landed. Men dropped into a "hot" LZ were given only seconds to disembark. Any longer and life expectancy of the chopper and men would decrease exponentially. Also, a Huey caught on the ground prevented other slicks from dropping their loads of men.

---

[131] Tolson, p. 3.
[132] Tolson, p. 114.

Above: Troopers from the 1ˢᵗ Brigade, 101ˢᵗ Airborne exiting a Huey during an air assault mission. The 1ˢᵗ Brigade arrived in Vietnam in 1965 and were among the first in the U.S. Army to use helicopter assault tactics. U.S. Army photo.

This new tactic also allowed the Army to rapidly cover a large area of operation with greater support using less men. The lessons learned by the 1ˢᵗ Brigade and other air assault units were passed onto the men of Delta Company and they soon mastered the new techniques.

It is important to note that helicopter air assault, now considered common, was only in its infancy when Calvin and the men of Delta Company were being dropped all over War Zone D and other areas in South Vietnam. They were among the first men to help perfect something that is still widely used today by the U.S. Army and Marines.

Left: A map of Vietnam showing the 3/187th's home base at Phuoc Vinh, South Vietnam. Phuoc Vinh is located approximately 30 miles north of Saigon. Also shown is War Zone D and the Iron Triangle, the main operational areas for Delta Company, 3/187th. Calvin and the men of Delta were transported to LZs (landing zones) aboard Bell UH-1 "Huey" helicopters. The Huey was known as an aerial workhorse for the American military and its allies. Missions could last anywhere from one day to more than a week depending on the objective. Many of the missions were conducted in enemy held areas. Map compliments of www.vietvet.org

January 1968

Calvin's first taste of heavy combat occurred during the first few days of January 1968, shortly before the Tet Offensive, while on a search and destroy mission in the Iron Triangle.[133] When the choppers approached the LZ, they immediately received incoming hostile fire. The Huey's door gunners opened fire, spraying the surrounding area with hot lead. While Calvin and the other men were trained and highly proficient in helicopter assault, nothing can prepare a man for his first landing in a hot LZ. Typically stuck in the open, they were places no soldier ever wanted to be. Calvin later remembered being "...really nervous, because you're thinking about getting hit, but then once you land, you're doing what you're told. You just don't want to fuck up. That's the thing. You're not even thinking about dying. You don't want to fuck up."[134] Asked how he felt he could have "messed up," Calvin replied:

Freeze. Don't shoot. If you get ambushed, you have to attack whoever it is. If you initially get shot at and you stand the line, well they already set up their ambush and they're going to just wipe you out, because they are going to have you on the sides. As soon as you get hit you've got to attack. You attack right at them, because you're going to lose less people by going right at them, than if you sit back and exchange fire with them.[135]

The scene at the LZ was absolute chaos. It could only accommodate a few aircraft at a time and all the aircraft landing and departing were receiving incoming fire. Men poured out of the choppers as they landed and those already on the ground were maneuvering and firing in every direction. The door gunners opened

---

[133] Calvin Heath interview with author, April 26, 2013.
[134] Adam Piore interview with Calvin Heath, 2009.
[135] Ibid.

up with their machine guns laying down suppressing fire and it was very difficult for the soldiers on the ground, or those exiting the aircraft, to determine the direction and source of the incoming fire. To the American soldiers, especially green troops like Calvin, the entire perimeter, because of the incoming and outgoing fire as well as the turbulence created from the choppers, seem to be alive as if it was one huge living creature. It appeared as if the enemy was all around them and in vast numbers.

As Calvin exited the helicopter, he felt the unmistakable whiz of a bullet as it passed him. It went through the door opening from which Calvin jumped and caught the man exiting the opposite side in the back. Life, death, or serious injury was determined by inches. Calvin, at the young age of 19, and after only seven months in the Army, survived his first hot assault, by mere inches. The other man, returned to base on an outbound chopper, badly wounded with a bullet hole in his back – he survived.[136]

While landing in a hot LZ was commonplace, the men did not come under fire every time they landed. Bill Heaney stated, "About half of the LZs [in which we landed] were hot."[137] The VC/NVA often found it futile to engage a landing American assault force and if they did, often did not sustain the attack, especially during the daylight hours when American artillery and air power could be used. As a result, most LZ ambushes were short-lived affairs, with the VC/NVA withdrawing before supporting fire could be brought to bear.

Most of the air assault missions, however, were tenuous dances in a variety of unpleasant environments between the VC/NVA, who did not want to be found, and the Americans who were determined to find them. Calvin stated, "Sometimes we'd jump off and there'd be a lot of contact at first, but they quickly left because they didn't want to screw with us. So, we would chase them for a few days."[138]

---

[136] Calvin Heath interview with author, April 26, 2013. Adam Piore interview with Calvin Heath, 2009.
[137] Heaney interview with author, September 10, 2014.
[138] Ibid.

Asked about those assaults, Calvin said, "You're always nervous... but, looking back I think I felt more comfortable in the field [than I did on the base]. There was just too much chicken shit back at the base. Out in the field we could just be us."[139] In 2009, he added:

I am not [afraid] of the dark, I grew up on a farm and we would work out in the dark. I'm aware of things in the dark. A lot of people are scared of the dark and they can't function. I wasn't scared because the way I looked at it was it was as much in my favor as it was theirs. If I can't see them, then they can't see me either. The jungle itself didn't scare me. The critters in it... yeah... the snakes and the spiders, they had spiders that big around. Nasty stuff![140]

During one mission Calvin obtained a taste of an oftentimes deadly VC/NVA tactic used to infiltrate American lines. Every American on the line understood an enemy soldier *close* to your lines during an evening operation could be dangerous but having an enemy soldier *inside* your lines could be catastrophic. Calvin recalled:

We went out on an ambush, now this was later on, but we went out on a 12-man ambush and we set up for the night in the ambush site and you do a roll call to make sure everyone was there, and we ended up with 13 guys. We had a VC in among us at first and when they counted heads, we kept coming up with 13 and we only went out with twelve. So, the guy at the end (the VC) he ended up taking off.[141]

The enemy soldier positioned himself on the end of a line hoping to work his way down, killing as many Americans as possible before being detected.

Another, more comical story Calvin was willing to share was about an unfortunate soldier who was literally caught with his pants down while on an operation in the jungle.

---

[139] Calvin Heath interview with author, April 26, 2013.
[140] Adam Piore interview with Calvin Heath, 2009.
[141] Ibid.

We were setting up a night defensive perimeter, and our company commander was real smart. We'd set up just before dark... and have the NVA... anybody that's watching... because a company going through the jungle makes a lot of noise. We would set up and just as it got dark, we would slowly work [our way] out of it and we'd actually set up somewhere else and use that as an ambush site. Anyway we're setting up and we are on top of this hill and we had been getting sniped at all the time, and this one guy, I don't remember his name, except that everyone called him Polar Bear [because] he was a big white kid.[142] He went outside the perimeter, he had to go take a shit, and so he walks away maybe 50 yards from the company into the wood line. All of a sudden a single shot rings out and here he comes running back up the hill with his pants down and he's yelling "Mother fuckers don't shoot! Mother fuckers don't shoot! It's me!" We tackled him as he went through the lines because he was hollering. I can't believe the sniper... I think the sniper was trying to scare him, I guess. He didn't hit him, but he scared the living shit out of him. That was pretty funny.[143]

Another story Calvin liked to tell was:

We were working with the 11th Cav. I saw a big old tree and I wanted to get the coconut out of it so I'm climbing up the thing because the tree got a big bend like this. So, I'm 90 percent of the way up the tree and 'ping, ping' over my head. I look down and the guys are looking at me... so I say "Hey, knock it off!"
"Knock off what?'"
"Throwing stones at me!"
"We ain't throwing stones at you!"

---

[142] Author's note: The soldier of which Calvin speaks is possibly Michael J. Pulitano, but this was never confirmed.
[143] Adam Piore interview with Calvin Heath, 2009.

"Yeah right!" I go up a little bit and 'ping, ping' again. "Come on guys!" Then a ping again and [once I realized what it was] I dropped right out [of the tree] ... it was a sniper shooting at me from across the rice paddies. I bailed right off this freaking tree as soon as I realized I was being shot at...[144]

Calvin finished the story with how the men dispatched the enemy sniper.

Like I said we had the 11th Cav with us and they had one of their big tanks. They could see he was in this big fucking tree. And the tank just turned on the [tree] and let go with the main cannon and took that tree... and that tree went straight up in the air, did a complete flip, and came back down and landed on the base of it and fell over. What it did was a complete flip; the Gook was in it and he was dead. He was all splintered up. I guess you have to have a sense of humor.[145]

By the end of January 1968, the men noticed a significant change in their first sergeant. Harjo, the heartless "son of a bitch" was transitioning from the hard-nosed disciplinarian who treated the men like "shit under his boot," into a father figure. Dave Dillard stated, "The minute we got to Nam his twin brother took over."[146] In the States, Captain Bucha and First Sergeant Harjo had to train a new company of "Clerks and Jerks" in a very short period of time. Harjo, especially, knew what a well-trained company could accomplish, and he witnessed, while fighting in Korea and during his first tour of duty in Vietnam, the fate of those untrained when facing a determined enemy. Now that the State-side training was behind them, the men of Delta needed leaders who cared about their welfare. Harjo knew each of his men intimately and he understood that most were just boys; boys with mothers, fathers, sisters and brothers; a few had wives,

---

[144] Adam Piore interview with Calvin Heath, 2009.
[145] Ibid.
[146] Calvin Heath interview with author, April 26, 2013.

many had sweethearts. Whomever they left behind, Austin Harjo, a combat-hardened senior NCO, would do everything in his power to ensure that every single man would make it back to them.

"Harjo was not like other first sergeants. He ran his office in the field, while many stayed behind. He would go around and make sure the men got what they needed."[147] He was the voice of reason, and a source of confidence for the men. Before a mission, when the men were developing doubts, they would look to him for a reassuring word. Harjo, recognizing they needed encouragement, would tell the men in a confident fatherly manner, "It's OK men; we're going to go out there and kick their ass and then we're going to go home." And the men would always say, "OK Top," and always, somehow feel better.[148]

Unlike First Sergeant Harjo, Captain Paul Bucha was not a combat veteran and he knew he had to learn, and learn fast. Many, who dismissed this Stanford University graduate, failed to see Bucha's greatest asset – his brains. Bucha, who graduated from West Point among the very top in his class, was sent to Stanford because the Army recognized something very special with this young officer; they saw a future senior officer. He was also a man of incredible character and strength who was rapidly becoming a great leader. He used his exceptional intellect to become the best leader he could be. If any of the men had any doubts about Paul Bucha when they left the United States in December 1967, there certainly weren't many by the end of January 1968.

By February 1968, the men were getting used to their environment both inside the relatively safe perimeter of their huge basecamp – Phuoc Vinh, and outside the gates in the villages and jungles of South Vietnam. The basecamp housed thousands of soldiers, many from the 101st, but there were also several other units and support elements located there as well. While the basecamps were different from military bases back home, the Army went to great lengths to make them as comfortable as possible. Phuoc Vinh had a

---

[147] Dillard, Heaney, Rawson interview with author, October 9, 2013.
[148] Ibid.

medical center, church, PXs, and bars. The men could play basketball and baseball, but outdoor activities were usually limited to the cooler times of the day.

The men's barracks were simple wooden structures that were approximately 16 feet wide by 40 feet long. They had racks (beds) that had thin mattresses and pillows, but few soldiers complained, especially after a week in the field. Many of the men found the standard issue living supplies inadequate and supplemented what the Army provided with items they purchased at the PX.

Above: One of Delta Company's Phuoc Vinh barracks in 1967/68. Squads and platoons were usually grouped together. As sparse as the barracks appear in this photograph, they were welcomed sights after a few days in the bush. Compliments of the Rakkasan Delta web site.

Each of the men had their own individual storage above, at the side, and below their beds. Weapons were stored in racks at the entrance of the barracks. Each unit was assigned defensive positions in the event of an attack and each platoon and squad assigned their section. Buildings were heavily sandbagged to protect against random enemy probes, sniper fire, and mortar attacks. The barracks usually housed up to two squads of men. All the buildings could be reached by well-placed enemy mortar rounds.

The problem for the men of Delta is they were seldom at Phuoc Vinh to enjoy what little comforts the base provided. With the number of missions rapidly increasing, Delta saw their basecamp less and less. Bill Pray later stated, that at one stretch, "…we went 62 days straight in the field. All the time we were there we probably got 10 hot meals, the rest was all "C" rations." Sam Spencer added, "After Christmas, I don't think we ever saw Phuoc Vinh again." Pray added, "We were in the field for such long stretches, the clothes used to rot right off of us and they'd fly in new uniforms."[149]

Above: Picture of Phuoc Vinh from a U.S. helicopter. Delta did not spend much time in base and were always in the field. Picture from Calvin Heath. Original source unknown. Below: Delta Co. arriving at Phuoc Vinh on November 30, 1967. Billy Pray Photo.

---

[149] Pray, Callahan, Spencer interview with the author, April 13, 2016.

TIME IN THE FIELD

During Calvin's time in Vietnam, major battle strategies and offensive operations were created by General William Westmorland, Military Assistance Commander – Vietnam (MACV), and his staff located at Tan Son Nhut Air Base, near Saigon. Orders were then disseminated to individual commands located throughout Vietnam. War Zone D and the Iron Triangle, located north/northeast of Saigon, were the 187th's primary area of operations. When a mission was planned, individual units received Warning Orders – general orders that started the cycle of preparation. Warning Orders included a general description of the overall mission, general instructions, expected uniform and equipment, and a tentative time schedule for the mission. This was usually followed by an Operation Order that provided more detail such as the overall size of the organization participating, the current situation, friendly forces in the area, suspected enemy location, other units providing fire support, expected methods of execution and maneuver, and anticipated obstacles. Any changes to these orders would come to the line units in Fragmentary or "Frag" Orders.

Once Delta Company received their Warning Orders, Captain Bucha and First Sergeant Harjo would first brief the platoon leaders and platoon sergeants, with Bucha and his officers concentrating on the tactical side of the mission, and Harjo, the platoon sergeants, and the squad leaders concentrating on prepping and equipping the men. Personal equipment and weapons were checked and double checked, ammunition issued, canteens filled, and the men given their final instructions.

Other elements such as scout dog units – soldiers with dogs specifically trained to find and alert the men of enemy soldiers, forward artillery observers, LRRPs, Combat Engineers, and interpreters were often attached to the units going out to the field. The missions varied from a single platoon to battalion or brigade size actions. Grid coordinates were distributed, and order of battle and situational briefings were held. Radio call signs were assigned, and maps issued and reviewed. According to the men of Delta Company, Bucha and Harjo, by habit, disseminated as much information as possible to the men in their chain of command so that every man knew his job as well as the job of the man to his right and left. If a sergeant or lieutenant fell during battle, the next man in line was prepared to assume command. This became a weekly routine for the men of Delta and by the end of February 1968, they were becoming a well-disciplined, experienced combat team.

Above: Men of Delta on Company Street prepping for a mission. According to Bill Heaney, during most missions the men were given few details and simply ordered to "Saddle up!" Compliments of the Rakkasan Delta web site.

For his first two months in Vietnam, Calvin was assigned as a rifleman in the second platoon under the command of Sergeant First Class (E-7) Dickie Quick and First Lieutenant Jeff Wishik. With an 11B10 MOS and expert badges on the M-16 and the M-60 machine gun, as well as his excellent ability to see at night, Calvin must have been an extremely effective soldier. By the end of February, however, Calvin began to cross train in a secondary MOS as a Radio-Telephone Operator (RTO). Calvin stated:

> *I was a light weapons expert, an M-60 machine gunner. That was my primary MOS. My secondary MOS was RTO, so I decided I'd rather carry the radio. If you carried the [M-] 60 you carried ammo [and] you're really 100 pounds heavier – easy. If you carried the radio that's all you had to carry. I carried the radio, two spare batteries, four canteens of water and I walked around with seven bandoliers of ammo for the M-16, seven magazines in each bandolier.[150]*

---

[150] Adam Piore interview with Calvin Heath, 2009.

The PRC-77 (Portable Radio, Communications) or "Prick-77," as the men called it, entered service in Vietnam in 1968. Its solid-state components and encryption capabilities made the older PRC-25 obsolete. It weighed 13.7 pounds (versus the M-60's 23 pounds, not including ammunition), although several batteries were also taken into the field. Both radios had several types of antennae to include a three-foot and ten-foot whip antennae, which the RTOs avoided using in combat whenever possible as it always attracted enemy fire. The company commander's radio was usually preset to the battalion air support and/or command net, while the platoon radios, like the one Calvin carried, was usually preset to the company and/or platoon net.[151]

During a 2013 ceremony in Hartford, Connecticut, Dave Dillard, Delta Company's RTO, described the RTO's job as "...a job with major responsibility..." It required, "...unquestionable confidence by the leader."[152] The job also came with incredible danger and the life expectancy of an RTO was less than that of a regular line soldier as the enemy always knew the man to the front or rear of the radio was an officer. Because of this, the RTO became primary targets for enemy snipers and ambushes.[153]

The dangers of wearing a radio were not just confined to the battle field. Calvin, in February 1968, while exiting a chopper on a hot LZ, barely avoided disaster. As he was exiting the chopper, a strap from his radio got caught on a cross bar located above the door gunner's position. Calvin quickly found himself dangling precariously outside the aircraft by his shoulder strap. The pilot, anxious to leave the area, was screaming at the crew to cut him loose, threatening to climb with Calvin hanging outside the chopper. The door gunner, not knowing what else to do, was now kicking Calvin screaming, "Get out! Get out!" Finally, the strap gave way and Calvin fell to the

---

[151] Note: A "net" was a group of radios that were capable of communicating directly with each other on a specific channel or frequency. The company net for example, was the preset frequency used on company-level radios. There were also command nets, used by battalion staff and command.
[152] Heath Memorial Ceremony, October 10, 2013, Hartford Connecticut.
[153] Ibid.

ground. Years later, he said laughing, "That was pretty funny. It was a hot LZ and [the pilots] don't like to stay there too long."[154]

Also, by February 1968, the men of the 187th had developed a great respect for their enemy. During the early years of the war, many in the United States military underestimated the skill, resolve, and creativeness of the North Vietnamese soldier and the Viet Cong. They failed to recognize the importance of their four decades of experience gained by fighting the Japanese and French. The VC and NVA developed and perfected fighting methodologies that were unfamiliar to the Americans. During my October 2013 interview, Dave Dillard noted, "I had great respect for the Vietnamese. They learned how to beat the French and they learned how to beat the Americans." Mike Rawson adds, "The respect we had for the North Vietnamese soldier was profound."[155] Calvin added, "Anyone who says they didn't know how to fight weren't there. These guys were good."[156]

The great respect the Americans had for their adversary was best illustrated by the quickly-changing nicknames they gave their opponents. Using the phonetic alphabet, V and C (VC-Viet Cong) became "Victor-Charlie." This was soon shortened to "Charlie." As the war progressed "Charlie" became "Charles" and then "Sir Charles."

The enemy's ability to adjust to varying situations was impressive. Soon after the Americans introduced their new air-assault tactics, the NVA/VC adjusted and countered with extremely effective guerilla tactics. Using a network of spotters, the enemy could determine where the Americans were landing and then quickly initiate highly effective hit-and-run raids against the landings. Calvin stated, "We had no idea what to expect when landing. When artillery and air support was light, they [the enemy] seemed to be everywhere."[157] At other times, "...once you're coming in, they're just sniping at you, and then they just take off."[158]

---

[154] Adam Piore interview with Calvin Heath, 2009.
[155] Dillard, Heaney, Rawson interview with author, October 9, 2013.
[156] Calvin Heath interview with author, June 2013.
[157] Calvin Heath interview with author, April 26, 2013.
[158] Adam Piore interview with Calvin Heath, 2009.

Above: Men of the 101st (possibly the 187th) while on patrol. Here they inspect the body of a dead VC. While gruesome, it was not the most disturbing photo in Calvin's collection and it clearly depicts what the men were subjected to on a daily basis. Scenes like this haunted Calvin for most of his life. Earl Vanalstine, U.S. Army photo.

Another very effective tactic used by the enemy during the war was the building of vast networks of tunnels and bunkers. First used against the French in the 1940's, the Viet Cong and NVA perfected the art of living underground. Some underground complexes were several stories deep and often included hospitals, large barracks, headquarters, storage areas, and tunnel systems that could extend for miles. This required the Americans to quickly develop a special breed of men who were willing to enter the tunnels alone. Calvin's battle mate Mike Rawson, one of the smaller men in Delta Company, was one such man. Soon after arriving in Vietnam, Rawson became one of the company's first "Tunnel Rats." In 2013, Dave Dillard stated that, "We didn't even know there were tunnels [out] there," an obvious flaw in U.S. Army training. The Americans, and Mike Rawson, were forced to learn on the job. During an interview in 2013, Dillard, pointing to Rawson said, "Mike was one of the godfathers of tunnel rats."[159]

Left: A young Michael Rawson eating a slice of pineapple after one of Delta's missions. Rawson provided much input for this book and contributed several poems. Note the blood stains on his pants. He now lives in Livingston, Texas. Earl Vanalstine, U.S. Army Photo.

Armed with only a .45 caliber pistol, and a flashlight, men like Rawson entered the dark tunnels alone to flush out the enemy and eliminate booby traps, or to set explosives to destroy the passageways and shafts. Years later, Calvin gave his input about the job and emphatically stated, "There was no fucking way I wanted that job!"[160]

From 1965 until the end of 1967, more than 485,000 American troops were sent to Vietnam to stop the "dominoes from falling."[161] With the growing manpower on the ground in Vietnam, General Westmorland conducted "large scale operations designed to find and destroy VC and PAVN (People's Army of Vietnam) forces." He foolishly believed that the American's overwhelming force could win the war through attrition. He reasoned that the far-superior air power of the United States combined with strategic ground action would

---

[159] Dillard, Heaney, Rawson interview with author, October 9, 2013.
[160] Calvin Heath interview with author, April 26, 2013.
[161] Willbanks, p. 3.

quickly wear the enemy down and eventually destroy his will to fight.[162]

Hanoi, on the other hand, "adopted a strategy of protracted war designed to exhaust America's determination to continue its commitment to South Vietnam... much as the Viet Minh had done against the French."[163] By the summer of 1967, according to Willbanks, "...the war in Vietnam had denigrated into a bloody stalemate" and Hanoi was busy constructing plans to break the stalemate and destroy *America's* will to fight.[164] A major factor in their decision to conduct a large scale offensive was undoubtedly the growing resentment for the Vietnam War in the United States. It would be the anti-war sentiment, and not military defeat, that would eventually become the most important reason the Americans returned home.

In April of 1967, in spite of General Vo Nguyen Giap's opposition, the Communist government approved "Resolution 13, which called for the 'spontaneous uprising in order to win a decisive victory in the shortest possible time.'"[165] Planning for the operation began immediately, and by January 1, 1968, the VC/NVA were ready to launch their offensive.

"The Tet Offensive began in full force shortly before 3:00 a.m. on January 31, 1968 when more than 80,000 Communist troops – a mixture of PAVN regulars and VC main-force guerrillas – began a coordinated attack throughout South Vietnam."[166] Their intense, well-planned attacks included the key American targets of Khe Sanh, a U.S. Marine combat base, the ancient city of Hue and MACV headquarters (Military Assistance Command Vietnam), located at Ton San Nhut Air Base, Saigon.

The Communists' planning and secrecy of TET was like nothing the Americans or their allies had ever seen. At Tan Son Nhut Air Base, the suddenness and ferocity of the attack caught the Americans

---

[162] Willbanks, pgs. 3-4.
[163] Ibid, p. 4.
[164] Ibid, p. 5.
[165] Ibid, p. 10.
[166] Ibid, p. 30.

by complete surprise. Much of the full-time Vietnam Airforce (VNAF) was on leave for the TET holiday and had to be immediately recalled. U.S. and VNAF security police held off the initial attacks while reinforcements could be sent.[167]

The Viet Cong's main objectives for this particular segment of the overall plan was the air strips and MACV headquarters, located on the southeastern part of the airbase. General Westmorland seeing that his security forces were struggling to hold, and fearing more attacks, ordered Delta Company to assemble and be immediately airlifted via helicopter from their current position in the field to MACV, where they would help secure the southern perimeter of the massive airbase. Westmorland specifically requested Captain Bucha and his company, possibly due to his familiarization with Captain Bucha while he attended West Point, or possibly because of Delta's rapidly growing reputation as a hardened combat team. Whatever the reason, according to the men, they were specifically requested. "We were Eagle Shit that day alright," stated Bill Pray with a smile.[168]

After two months in the field, the men of Delta Company had become experts in air-assault. They were frequently transported via helicopter from one hot location to another. This often-used method gave birth to a nickname used by the men to describe their unit, one that still gets a chuckle from the men today. Pray explained; "They'd come out and pick us up and then drop us off somewhere else. It would happen all the time. [On January 31st, when TET began,] they pulled us right out of the field, because we were in the middle of no-man's land and sent us to MACV"[169] The thought of these Screaming Eagles being frequently picked up and deposited in another hot location from above, made the men laugh. Pray finally added, "We used to call it Eagle Shit."[170]

When the men arrived at Tan Son Nhut, they quickly established temporary defensive perimeters and unexpectedly inherited a civilian trying desperately to avoid incoming fire. His departing Braniff flight

---

[167] United State Airforce, After Actions Report (RCS: MACV J3-32) (U), March 9, 1968
[168] Pray, Callahan, Spencer interview with the author, April 13, 2016.
[169] Ibid.
[170] Ibid.

did not make it off the ground and was shut down during the attack. One of the Delta men later suggested that plane was hit by enemy mortars. It did not take long before the men recognized the civilian as the famous actor, Sebastian Cabot – Mr. French from the TV show Family Affair. Bill Pray continues:

> He was freaked out. Braniff was flying troops in and out of Tan Son Nhut at that time. I think his aircraft was hit – not sure, my memory isn't that clear... and I remember him asking Bucha, 'What am I going to do? What am I going to do?' Bucha turned to him and said you have two choices. Yan can stay here or come with us to MACV headquarters. 'Well I'm coming with you guys!' So, we had several flak jackets, but one wouldn't fit him, so we had to put one on this arm and one on the other and tie them. The steel pot wouldn't fit either because the liner was too small, so we put a steel pot without the liner on him.[171]

The men all laughed as they recalled the sight of the heavy-set actor trying to make his way across the base with two tied flak jackets and a bouncing steel pot on his head. Sam Spencer later stated, "He signed my helmet and told me, if you ever get hit, I hope you get hit above my name! I had that helmet on the day I was wounded."[172] Cabot's hope that Spencer would stay safe did not come to fruition. On March 16, 1968, he was severely wounded in the leg and spent months in the hospital and rehabilitation.

Bill Pray stated that when the men arrived at MACV, they quickly found they "...had to secure the back part of the base - part of it had been overrun"[173] and MACV had no defensible area from which to properly fight. "They had these bunkers... sandbags mixed with cement, they were all white washed. Well, we had to tear them down because we couldn't fight from them," states Pray.[174] The

[171] Pray, Callahan, Spencer interview with the author April 13, 2016.
[172] Ibid.
[173] Ibid.
[174] Pray, Callahan, Spencer interview with the author April 13, 2016.

bunkers were constructed as protective positions against mortar attacks not as fighting positions against a ground assault. Sam Spencer adds, "They were the prettiest bunkers you'd ever want to see, but you couldn't fight from them!"[175] Within minutes, the men of Delta dismantled the bunkers and rebuilt fighting positions.

Above: Sebastian Cabot "Mr. French," during his trip to Vietnam. U.S. Army photo.

Calvin later recalled that he and his unit received incoming sniper fire, but there was no major action in Delta's sector of the base. However, he did recall an enemy attempt to overrun a section of the air base. Calvin stated, "... they didn't make it through. We were watching the gunships hover and turn, and they were standing still,

---

[175] Pray, Callahan, Spencer interview with the author April 13, 2016.

and then they would dive and when they opened up the mini-guns, the chopper would stop and actually go backwards."[176]

Bill Mullholland, a childhood friend of Paul Conner's was stationed at Tan Son Nhut with the U.S. Air Force when Delta arrived. Mullholland recalls:

> *I was assigned as backup for the base security police. We had more than 200 122mm rockets and a number of satchel charges hit the base and we were close to losing the whole thing. The [South] Vietnamese were out celebrating TET and we didn't have that many guys at the base to protect it... If it wasn't for those guys [101st ABN] we would have lost the whole thing, and that would have been a big deal with MACV there.[177]*

The Tan Son Nhut Airbase perimeter was penetrated multiple times in several locations by VC forces. Each time the Americans and Vietnamese Air Force pushed them back. More than 50 allied soldiers were killed and 165 wounded defending the airbase. Enemy casualties exceeded 1,000 dead and hundreds more wounded and evacuated.[178] American aircraft sustained heavy damage or were destroyed, but the VC failed to hold any of their objectives.

Soon after the attack, Delta was sent on patrols to the west of the airbase. Their mission was to catch the remnants of the withdrawing enemy forces before they could reach safe havens in Cambodia. Bill Pray describes the next few days:

> *We started going out of town, we didn't have trucks to come and pick us up... we didn't have choppers we just kept walking until we were out in the villages of the outlying areas. Our mission was to chase those Gooks all the way to Cambodia and I'll never forget how many dead bodies there were. I remember dogs eating*

---

[176] Adam Piore interview with Calvin Heath, 2009.
[177] Mullholland interview with the author, November 4, 2016.
[178] United State Airforce, After Actions Report (RCS: MACV J3-32) (U), March 9, 1968

*the Gooks in the street and the other gooks weren't
doing anything about it. And Stunk? I couldn't breathe
I thought 'Oh my God I can't make it.' It was the
worse smell I ever smelled in my life. There was so
many dead bodies out there. They were laying there for
days...*

The bloated, partially dog-eaten bodies were dead enemy soldiers
who have been baking in the hot sun. Calvin later stated, "The stench
[of rotting humans] is something you never forgot."[179]

*Above: Viet Cong killed January 30-31, 1968 during the TET attack.
(Photo compliments of Vietnam Virtual archive, LT E.B. Herr Neckar
A.V. Platoon, 69th Signal BN)*

---

[179] Calvin Heath interview with the author, April 2013. Note: Paul Conner's letter to his Aunt
Claire Mowery, dated February 15, 1968, suggests Delta was at Tan Son Nhut until February
17, 1968.

Above: The 3/187th would often be assigned as the infantry support for the 11th Cavalry. Above is a M114 APC possibly with men from Delta. The picture shows the jungle thickness found in War Zone D. U.S. Army, Earl Vanalstine photo.

By most accounts, the Tet Offensive was the Communists' greatest defeat. It was also their greatest victory. Politically, it destroyed President Johnson and further encouraged the rapidly growing anti-war movement. More and more people in cities and towns all over America took to the streets in protest of the war. On February 27, 1968, Walter Cronkite, "The most trusted man in America," after returning from Vietnam while covering the news of the Tet Offensive, filed this report on national television:

> *To say that we are closer to victory today is to believe, in the face of the evidence, the optimists who have been wrong in the past. To suggest we are on the edge of defeat is to yield to unreasonable pessimism. To say that we are mired in stalemate seems the only realistic, yet unsatisfactory conclusion.*[180]

---

[180] Cronkite report, February 27, 1968.

North Vietnam General Giap commented, "Until Tet they had thought they could win the war, but now they knew they could not."[181] Despite this statement, however, it was clear that militarily the defeat of the Communist during the Tet Offensive was undeniable. Communists' casualties were staggering and estimated at more than 40,000. Further, they "failed to hold on to any of the major objectives that they had attacked."[182] Dave Dillard added, "The VC ceased to exist as a fighting force. We annihilated them. They were done. Giap was going home, he had had enough."[183]

Above: A dead VC. Soldier. This soldier appears to be missing his head, most likely a result of automatic fire from an M-16 rifle. Calvin could describe several of these scenes with extreme clarity 45 years after they occured. U.S. Army, Earl Vanalstine photos.

---

[181] Olsen and Roberts, *Where the Dominoes Fell*, p. 186
[182] Willbanks, p. 81.
[183] Dillard, Heaney, Rawson interview with author, October 9, 2013.

Immediately following Tet, more than 65,000 enemy soldiers were making their way back to their safe havens in Cambodia and Laos. American troops throughout South Vietnam set out to intercept and destroy what little remained of the enemy. U.S. intelligence suggested that a large enemy force was maneuvering south of Phuoc Vinh. The 187th was, once again, helicoptered into the jungles of War Zone D with a simple mission – locate the enemy, converge on their locations, and destroy them.[184] Many of the men suggested that units like 187th and other ground units, were simply used as bait in order to draw out the enemy often taking on much larger units. Once contact was made, the men would then call in artillery and air support to annihilate the enemy. For the balance of Calvin's time in Vietnam, this was his job.

Hunting human beings, especially those trained to hunt you, can be an extremely stressful affair that oftentimes results in the death of civilians caught in the crossfire. During the war, an estimated 195,000-430,000 South Vietnamese civilians were killed, many by American soldiers.[185] Many soldiers returned from the war never coming to grips with the knowledge that they willingly, or unwillingly, were responsible for the death of innocent civilians.[186]

During my interviews with Calvin, he would sometimes talk about civilian casualties. It was apparent that it was a subject that greatly bothered him. During our discussions, just before he would offer any details, he would stop and move to a different topic. I could sense he was extremely guarded about relinquishing any particulars or thoughts he had about the subject.

After Calvin's death in 2013, one of his combat buddies offered the following. During an operation in early 1968, Calvin was involved in securing a water hole to replenish the troopers' water supply. The men heard rustling in the bushes near the water supply and ordered the people hiding in the bushes to come out. Having been in contact

---

[184] David Dillard, Calvin Heath Memorial Ceremony, October 10, 2013, Hartford, Connecticut.

[185] Jeffries, W. *Trap Door to the Dark Side*.

[186] Note: Bond notes several incidents involving children. One of the most heart breaking is about a child playing in the dirt next to her dead mother, p. 109.

with the enemy for days and having sustained a number of casualties, the men took no chances and fired upon the site after repeated requests for the hidden persons to surrender. After the firefight, the men moved to the water hole and found VC soldiers and the bodies of two children. It was a very difficult discovery for Calvin.

Whether the deaths of the children were a direct result of Calvin's or his fellow troopers' fire is unclear. They could have easily come across the waterhole deaths after the fact and the official records do not indicate any incidents of this nature. What is undeniable though is that civilians were often caught in the crossfire and few units, on either side, could avoid inflicting non-military casualties. It is also highly likely that Calvin saw many dead children, elderly, and women during his time in Vietnam, most of whom wanted nothing to do with the war.

Above: A 1968 photo of Nick Goudoras (left) and Dave Dillard (right) while stationed at Phuoc Vinh, Vietnam with Calvin. Dillard was a major contributor to this piece and was a long-time friend of Calvin Heath. Dave Dillard photo.

MARCH 1968

During the balance of February and into March of 1968, Delta Company and other American combat units were on the hunt for retreating enemy all across South Vietnam. Delta and other air mobile units were dropped in LZs all over their areas of operations where they would offensively maneuver until they located enemy units or strongholds. Airpower and/or artillery were then called in and the enemy destroyed.

Years later, Calvin remembered two specific events from this time period. The first was a river assault, most likely across the Song Be River. The men came across a large, rapidly moving river they needed to cross. Crossing without the aid of ropes would have been both dangerous and tactically foolish as any man washed down stream could alert the enemy to the American's presence and potentially cost the man his life. After at least one failed attempt by another soldier, Calvin, possibly relying on his experience gained from swimming the rapidly flowing Five Mile River in his hometown of Putnam, volunteered to try and cross. He stated:

> We made a combat assault across the river and the first guy tried swimming across and he couldn't make it. I took my clothes off and I went up river along the bank and then I swam up [diagonal to the far shore] so it would carry me back down. I got to the other side and on the banking and pulled the rope across and then the rest of the company came across.[187]

Calvin goes on to suggest that it was the first combat river assault performed by the Rakkasans in Vietnam.[188] In an article titled *Two Rescued from Swirling River*, found in the March 8, 1968 edition of the Screaming Eagle newspaper, reporter SP4 Douglas Harrell

---

[187] Adam Piore interview with Calvin Heath, 2009.
[188] Ibid.

80

describes such an assault. He writes, "For what seemed like an eternity, the paratroopers of the 2nd Plat., D Co., 3rd Bn. (ABN), 187th Inf., pushed toward their objective beyond the Song Be River." Harrell reported, "The river was nearly 100-yards wide" and required a safety line for the men to cross the "fast waters." He goes on to note that at least one man nearly drowned and had to be rescued as he struggled across the river.[189] In September of 2014, Bill Heaney admitted, with a smile on his face, to be "…one of the guys who got pulled out."[190] Once the men of Second Platoon reached the other side, they reassembled and rested on the far shore and then moved on with the operation.

On March 3, 1968, the men were choppered into suspected enemy territory located in War Zone D. There, in triple canopy jungle, they clover leafed (moving forward in three directions), searching for enemy strongholds. Soon into the mission, the men came upon a tunnel complex. Not understanding the size of the complex, or for that matter, what to do with it, the position was reported to headquarters back at Phuoc Vinh and a chopper was sent with intelligence personnel to investigate. Determining it was a fresh, large complex – size undetermined – a more detailed report was sent to Phuoc Vinh and more choppers were dispatched, this time, according to Calvin, with "55 gallon drums of gasoline and this other stuff that smoked like hell…"[191] The plan was to pour the fuel mixture down the discovered tunnel, seal the hole, and place a fan over the opening, forcing the smoke through the underground complex and out other entrances and exits. Calvin later stated:

> *…they said to look for smoke coming out of the ground to find where the exits are and stuff, and Jesus man, smoke started popping up over here, popping up over there. We were in the middle of a major complex like four stories deep. A hospital complex. It was… that was a big, big find. They thought [it was] the basecamp and they called in a B-52*

---

[189] Screaming Eagle, March 8, 1968, p. 1.
[190] Heaney interview with author, September 10, 2014.
[191] Adam Piore interview with Calvin Heath, 2009.

strike. We had to get out of the area and I can remember – I don't know how many clicks away that we were – but the ground shook where we were.[192]

Calvin also reported, "It was the most awesome firepower I ever heard."[193] When the men returned to the area and investigated the damage caused by the B-52s, they heard unfamiliar sounds. As they closed on the bombed site, the low murmurs they first heard turned to the unmistakable groans of men who were injured and buried alive in the underground complex. Calvin continued:

And then when we went back to sweep the area you had 500-pound bomb holes... you could put this house in it... 40-50 feet deep. And I can remember... me and this other guy we looked into this one hole and we saw a boot, so we went down to it and the foot was still in it. And then we could hear moaning and groaning underneath in the tunnel complex. The tunnels had collapsed, but we didn't dig them out, but we could hear them moaning and groaning under the ground.[194]

By the beginning of March 1968, the men of Delta Company found themselves caught in a hazardous routine. Enemy leadership, understanding they could not match American military power, adopted "the elephant and the tiger" strategy of fighting which had worked successfully against the French. This meant there were no front lines and the battlefield remained fluid. An area cleared one day could become a VC/NVA haven the next. To combat the ever-changing battle lines, Delta would be airlifted to suspected enemy areas where they would conduct search and destroy missions lasting from several days to a week. During these missions, the men were on constant watch for enemy soldiers, strongholds and supply caches. When the enemy made contact, the men of Delta would immediately

---

[192] Adam Piore interview with Calvin Heath, 2009. Note: A "Click" = 1,000 meters. Follow-up conversations with Calvin suggested that the men were positioned more than a mile away.
[193] Calvin Heath interview with author, May 2013.
[194] Adam Piore interview with Calvin Heath, 2009.

engage and destroy what they could. When caches of supplies were found, the weapons were inventoried and destroyed, and the food flown to local villages. The environment in which they fought varied from open villages to triple canopy jungle so thick the men were forced to hack their way through it with machetes.

Above: Men of the 101st Airborne while on a mission circa 1968. This photo might be the men distributing VC/NVA captured rice. U.S. Army photo.

The elements in which they fought were also a formidable enemy. The weather was always hot and humid, and the men contracted all sorts of illnesses and ailments due to the humid environment. Heat exhaustion was one of the most common problems. Also, biting ants, snakes, leeches, etc. were always present and seemed to exist solely to make the men's life miserable. The missions were exhausting and draining. Once a mission was completed and the area cleared, the men would return to base where they were given a few days' rest before the cycle would start all over again.

During a particularly long mission, possibly on March 9, 1968, Captain Bucha had his men establish their night defensive perimeter

(NDP) centered on two hills split by a valley that ran into rice paddies. The NDP had the main element established on one hill, an ambush element on the other, and listening posts to the front of both positions. Bucha hoped to catch the enemy in the valley, the most likely funnel point, and then destroy any who came through.

Calvin, as RTO, Paul Conner, and Sergeant Bobby Dietch were assigned to be one of the listening posts for the unit's NDP. Listening posts were placed up to several hundred meters to the front of the unit's NDP. Their job was to listen for approaching enemy and warn the main body of their approach – it was one of the most undesirable jobs in combat. After moving to the assigned location, they came across a trail where they stopped and established a camouflaged and concealed position. From here, the three men sent Captain Bucha hourly situation reports.

At approximately 11:00 p.m. that evening, the men saw an unfamiliar site. Calvin stated, "At first I could see these fire flies way off in the distance, but they were all in a straight line… so I hit Dietch and I said, 'What the hell is that?' And he's looking and looking and he says 'Shit, that's torches!'" What Calvin spotted was a long line of enemy soldiers walking down a hillside path coming right towards them. Calvin continued:

> *[They were] walking down the other hill coming towards us. So, we called back to the company and Bucha was on the phone and we told him we had movement coming our way. So, he says when the first enemy goes by you click the radio and when the last one goes by click again. In the meantime, these guys are sitting on this ridge and they're going to go right by them. They're going to ambush them. And they had a rookie second lieutenant with them, and he said, 'Get ready to fire.' and the sergeant that was with him said to wait a minute… 'Listen! There are too many of them…' they would have been wiped out [if] they had opened up fire on them. We're watching them and they came down the hill and came across the rice paddy. When they were coming, they looked like there was one behind the other. The torches they*

carried... there were like seven or eight guys between each guy with a torch... and they walked right by [us]! We could have reached out and grabbed them [but] they didn't even see us. And it took them the better part of three hours for that line to go by.[195]

When asked how many enemy soldiers passed their position that evening, Calvin replied, "There was a shit load; well over 2,000! We all think that they were the guys we ended up fighting five days later. It was like a whole battalion of NVA and they walked right passed us."[196] A letter found on a dead enemy soldier several days later, suspected to be part of the same unit that was now passing Calvin, Conner and Dietch, was identified as a soldier from the Dong Nai Regiment.

The Dong Nai Regiment traced its history back to 1948. They were based in War Zone D and consisted of three maneuver battalions to include the Phu Loi Battalion, the unit Calvin and the men of the 187th would eventually fight. After years of fighting the French, the men of the Dong Nai were deeply familiar with the jungles in which they fought and were regarded by the Americans as one of the more tenacious and dangerous enemies to face. They had a reputation of never relinquishing a stronghold without a fight.[197] It was well known that the Americans owned the skies, but the jungles in which Calvin now found himself firmly belonged to the men of the Dong Nai Regiment.

As hundreds of men from the Dong Nai passed, Calvin, Conner, and Dietch, only feet away, laid motionless. Any noise or movement, a squelch from the radio, a stumbling enemy soldier or an unlucky glance in their direction, would mean certain death. Calvin later reported that the enemy soldiers were so close they could smell the fish they ate that day. "We were scared shitless! They were right there, only a few feet away! All we had to do was move and we were

---

[195] Adam Piore interview with Calvin Heath, 2009.
[196] Calvin Heath interview with author, June 2013.
[197] Tonsetic, p. 11.

dead!"[198] Possibly expecting a profound response from Calvin about his inner thoughts during that particular moment when he was so close to death, Adam Piore asked him in 2009, "What were you thinking?" Calvin without hesitation said, "Let's get the fuck out of here!"[199]

Calvin and the other two men had several tense moments during the few hours it took for the enemy to pass. One NVA soldier stopped on the narrow trail just opposite the men's position. None of the men knew at that time why he stopped, and all thought that they had been discovered. Fighting the urge to run, they remained motionless as the enemy soldier, now with his back to them only yards away, seemed to fumble with what they thought was a weapon or hand grenade. The fumbling soon stopped, and it finally became apparent he was urinating on the opposite side of the path. Had he decided to urinate on the side of the path on which Calvin, Conner and Dietch were hidden, their location would have most certainly been discovered.

The following morning, after the enemy passed, Sergeant Dietch gave Lieutenant Wishik and Captain Bucha a full report to include estimated supplies and arms the enemy was carrying. The VC/NVA, according to Calvin, had bicycles and ox carts loaded with food and weapons, including Chinese .51 caliber machine guns used against Delta several days later.

Calvin recalls thinking, "There were an awful lot of them! We just said, 'Holy shit!' We're chasing them and we got 100 guys and we just saw hundreds and hundreds of them going by us."[200] He went on to say:

> *[If] we run into these guys we're in deep shit. If they surprised us that would have been bad shit. But they didn't, and they went on. We let them go. We came back in the morning and we told [Wishik and Bucha] it took three hours for that whole group... there were hundreds and hundreds of them... [to pass]. As it turns out there were thousands of*

---

[198] Calvin Heath interview with author, June 2013.
[199] Adam Piore interview with Calvin Heath, 2009.
[200] Ibid.

them. But they were going to where they set up their basecamp. And we kept clover leafing trying to find them. [201]

---

[201] Ibid.

MARCH 15, 1968 - THE NIGHT BEFORE

By March 15, 1968, Calvin "Willy" Heath had been a soldier in the United States Army for more than 300 days, 94 of which had been in hostile areas. Due to his assignment to the Rakkasans, he had seen more action than the average American serviceman, and more than most who had served in units stationed throughout Southeast Asia. He was an airborne soldier specializing in small weapons, jungle warfare, and he was LRRP trained. He was able to set a variety of explosive devices and booby traps and was an expert in hand-to-hand combat. He had drawn enemy blood and had many near-death experiences – all in less than one year from enlisting. Now the 19-year-old from Connecticut was preparing for his last battle in Vietnam, one that would cost Calvin a heavy and long-lasting price.

Contact with the enemy continued throughout the next few days and it was evident that large numbers of enemy soldiers were still operating in War Zone D. American intelligence reported large unit activity ten miles to the south of Phuoc Vinh, just south of the Song Be River in an area that many referred to as "the testicles," (as the two bends in the river resemble testicles). American military planners reasoned that if they could get a sufficient force behind the enemy, they could push them to what the U.S. Army referred to as the "blue line" – the Song Be River – where, trapped and nowhere to run, they could easily be destroyed by American artillery and airpower. A plan was developed and on March 15, 1968, the men of Delta Company were once again preparing for another mission.

While Delta Company was refitting and prepping at Phuoc Vinh, other elements of the 3rd Brigade continued to scour War Zone D. LRRPs made contact with the enemy on March 14th outside a village west of the Phuoc Vinh airstrip. As a result, four VC soldiers were confirmed killed.[202] Alpha Company was maneuvering in the field and shortly after midnight on the 15th, they linked up with the LRRPs

---

[202] Note: According to Dillard, the LRRPs were a brigade commanded unit established by Colonel Mowery. The LRRP team mentioned above could have been Phantom Force.

so they could assist in their extraction. The LRPPs, searching for a "Mortar team that had been targeting the base,"[203] had been in contact with the enemy for some time and required the assistance of gunships and reinforcements, "to allow [the] LRRP to get out of the area."[204]

At the same time, a platoon from Charlie Company, call sign "Silent Post Charlie," complete with a dog team, was on an ambush patrol about a mile and a half from the Phuoc Vinh airstrip. They established their ambush site at 6:00 p.m. on March 14 and completed that assignment at 7:00 a.m. on the morning of the fifteenth. By 12:35 a.m. March 15, 1968, most elements of the 187th were returning to base and by 9:50 a.m., all units of the 187th were back at Phuoc Vinh, with the exception of B Company who had a small number of men on assignment with the 11th Armored Cavalry Regiment.[205] During that same night, seven ARVN units and one unit each from 1/506th and 2/506th, set up night defensive and ambush positions around the base and did not make enemy contact.

At 12:15 p.m. on March 15, the 187th received an intelligence briefing indicating that they had finally found the location of the Dong Nai and the 141st Regiments. Shortly after the briefing, Lieutenant General Bruce Palmer, Westmorland's second in command arrived in the Rakkasan area. While the specific reason for Palmer's visit is unknown, what is known is that shortly thereafter, at 5:13 p.m., The Rakkasans received Operation "Order (OPORD) 8-68" for "Operation Rakkasan Chaparral," a battalion-sized operation designed to locate and destroy a large enemy force located nine and a half miles south of Phuoc Vinh, whose headquarters had been identified within grid coordinates XT 938372.[206] Other intelligence sources had also reported that elements of the 7th NVA Division, and the 165th Regiment, were believed to be in the same area of operation with an estimated strength of 1,300 men.[207]

---

[203] Davis correspondence with author, September 12, 2016.
[204] Daily Staff Journal, March 15, 1968.
[205] Note: According to the Daily Staff Journal, B Company returned at 5:04 p.m.
[206] Daily Staff Journal, March 15, 1968.
[207] Bond, p. 23.

Once OPORD 8-68 was in place, Calvin and the men of Delta Company made preparations. They had been in the field for a number of days and they undoubtedly needed to refit. This included stripping and cleaning weapons, replacing any lost or damaged gear and equipment, showering, eating, and most importantly, resting.

Suddenly, at 9:20 p.m., preparations were interrupted when the base "…received four incoming [mortar] rounds from the northwest from about 2,500-3,000 meters out. Two rounds hit on each side of the [main] road approximately 300 meters from the gate."[208] The Tet Offensive was still fresh in the minds of all the soldiers at Phuoc Vinh and no one could determine whether or not the mortar rounds were simply harassing fire or the prelude to a larger assault. The 187th was placed on "Red Alert," requiring them to gear up and man their defensive positions or be prepared and hold in place so they could move rapidly to vulnerable areas.[209] Gunships were dispatched, and the men could hear the choppers searching nearby for the enemy mortar sites, but they were long gone. Thirty minutes after it began, the Red Alert was called off, the base went to "Condition White," and all the men returned to their mission preparations.

When asked in June 2013 what his thoughts were on the night before Operation Rakkasan Chaparral, Calvin sat back, thought for a moment and replied, "I'm sure I thought about it [the upcoming battle], but we had been in the field for so long that every day and night just sort of ran together. I don't remember thinking of much the night before."[210] In other words, for the men of Delta it was "just another day in paradise."

---

[208] Daily Staff Journal, March 15, 1968.
[209] Ibid.
[210] Calvin Heath interview with author, May 2013.

MARCH 16, 1968 - HOT STUFF

Hot Stuff

We hit the LZ,
Dropped by a chopper,
Sun was a 'blazing, hot ball of copper.

Dust a 'flying,
Lungs a 'choking.
Red hot lead, barrels a 'smoking.

No place to hide,
Running for cover.
No time to think, of wife or lover.

The chopper left,
Those taxis from hell.
I remember the taste, I remember the smell.

Explosions a 'many,
That ripped the air.
Nature in hiding, with untold despair.

I saw the rocket,
In dead slow motion.
Coming for me, in a timeless ocean.

Many were hit,
Dropped all around.
The dead and wounded, littered the ground.

I jammed the radio,
Called in the planes.
Many explosions, in multiple rains.

The 60 went silent,
Stopped spewing its lead.
The man with the ammo, lost half of his head.

We fired that gun,
Till the barrel melted down.
And noticed the ants, as they covered the ground.

Drawn by the smell,
In their unending trains.
They sought out the dead man, and covered his brains.

We patched up the wounded,
And bagged the dead.
I can't stop remembering, that half of a head.

Michael Rawson
Delta Co., 3/187th Infantry (ABN)
101st Airborne Division

At 6:00 a.m. on the morning of March 16, 1968, the men of the 187th rose, ate, and made their final preparations for the mission. Aircraft maintenance personnel were up throughout the night prepping the choppers. The pilots had been up since 4:00 a.m. to review the operation and to conduct their pre-flight preparations.[211] Calvin rose with the other men of his platoon and after finishing breakfast, he went to the communication's building, otherwise called the commo shack, where he requisitioned a PRC-77. possibly an older model PRC-25, radio with two spare batteries from Dave Dillard, the communication's sergeant. For this mission Calvin was assigned as Platoon Sergeant Dickie Quick's RTO. After securing the radio and performing a communications check, Dillard and Calvin ran through the signal operating instructions (SOI). SOIs included the assigned frequencies, call signs, code words, and special radio signals that might be needed during the operation.

The 3/187th Infantry's mission was simple. Fly four combat loaded companies, the Brigade LRRP Platoon, and several dog teams to two landing zones located approximately 12 miles southeast of the Phuoc Vinh. Then find and destroy the enemy. Combat Engineers, under the command of 1LT Mike Blalock, were assigned to the mission if the men found enemy bunkers or other enemy strongholds that required destroying.

The mission was to be conducted in three phases.

---

[211] Meacham, *Lest We Forget.*

PHASE 1

The LZs were prepped with 105mm artillery and supporting gunship fire. Alpha Company, under the command of Captain William Barron, and Charlie Company, under the command of Captain Robert Halliday, along with a reconnaissance team, would land into LZ Eagle located at grid coordinates XT 923354. They would be joined by the battalion executive officer, Major Colby. Delta Company, under the command of Captain Paul Bucha, supported with a brigade LRRP team designated "Phantom Force," commanded by 2LT Floyd "Jeff" Davis, would land at LZ Falcon located at grid coordinates XT 937343. They would be joined by the battalion commander, Lieutenant Colonel Forrest. Both Colby and Forrest would be flying above the men in command and control (C&C) helicopters. The two LZs were located seven miles northwest of the Song Dong Nai River and the Village of Tan Uyen, five and a half miles south of the Song Be River and were approximately one and one-quarter miles away from each other. They were also located approximately three miles southwest of suspected enemy strongholds reported to exist at grid coordinates XT 938372.

PHASE 2

Delta Company would maneuver to LZ Hawk, located approximately two miles northeast of LZ Falcon. There, on the following day at noon, they would secure the LZ for the arrival of Bravo Company under the command of Captain John Dowling.

Once on the ground the units were to head in a north/northeasterly direction in two large clover-leafing columns pushing the enemy against the Song Be River. Axis 1, the West Column, was assigned to Alpha and Charlie Companies. Axis 2, the East Column, was assigned to Delta and Bravo Companies. Phantom Force was assigned to advance between the two columns protecting Delta's left flank and Alpha and Charlie Companies right flank. Each paired set of companies were to mutually support each other in the case of serious enemy contact. Artillery support was available, but due to the somewhat remote location, the men could only expect support on a limited basis since many of the smaller batteries where located out of range. Air support was available in a variety of forms.

PHASE 3

Once the mission was completed, and the enemy destroyed, 3rd Battalion would then move to their extraction points, LZs "Boa" and "Cobra," located approximately four and one half miles northeast of LZs Falcon and Eagle.[212]

The terrain in which they had to operate had been identified by a 1966 U.S. Army Engineer map as dense forest or jungle with a number of large and small swamps.[213]

Also assigned to Delta Company was a support squad of Combat Engineers under the command of First Lieutenant Mike Blalock of the 326th Combat Engineers Battalion, 101st Airborne. The Combat Engineers were there to clear mines, destroy enemy bunkers and other assets and fight alongside Delta. Blalock later commented that he joined this particular mission in order to evaluate his men's performance in the field. By all accounts, they did well.[214]

At 8:30 a.m., March 16, 1968, approximately 90 men from Delta Company assembled on Company Street, the main drag outside the basecamp barracks for weapons and equipment checks. Alpha and Charlie companies were doing the same thing. Squad leaders and platoon sergeants moved up and down the ranks of men checking to insure they had the required equipment. Calvin did not recall this mission being any different than the dozens of other missions in which he participated. From Company Street they moved to the Phuoc Vinh airstrip where they were assigned their transport helicopters. The men approached the choppers and boarded like they had dozens of times before. They didn't need instruction on how to load, but there was a Crew Chief on each aircraft to insure the men loaded properly. When the men were secured in the chopper, the Crew Chief gave the pilots the thumbs up. At precisely 9:35 a.m. the first helicopters left

---

[212] Daily Staff Journal, March 16, 1968.
[213] 1969 U.S. Army Corp of Engineer, Tan Uyen Map number 6331-II, Series L7014.
[214] Mike Blalock telecom interview with author February 9, 2019.

their pads and within minutes, a dozen aircraft were airborne and the men from Delta Company were heading southwest to LZ Falcon.

The 12-mile flight lasted approximately 20 minutes. With the noise of the aircraft, the men were unable to converse without yelling, so most sat quietly and watched the passing countryside. Below them, the beautiful lush green jungle sporadically gave way to abandoned Vietnamese villages and rubber tree plantations, some destroyed by the allies, others destroyed by the enemy. The men, including Calvin, knew that below them, hiding under the thick green canopy, were VC and NVA soldiers watching the helicopters, calculating the size of the force flying overhead and where that force would be landing. Because the men landed during daylight hours, the VC/NVA in the area avoided contact. For now, they would simply watch and fade away into the jungle as the Americans advanced. Their time would come after dark. By 11:15 a.m., all the American units reported landing in their designated LZs without incident.

Shortly after arriving at LZ Falcon, Tim Smith, 1LT Jeffrey Wishik's RTO, fell off a log bridge into a river taking his radio and combat load out of commission.[215] Calvin reported that Smith requested Calvin's radio, but refused knowing if you signed for a piece of equipment, you're responsible for it. Calvin later stated, "I wouldn't give up my radio. He wanted me to go to the rear area, back to the company area to get another radio… and I didn't want to go back. I signed for this radio and I keep it, so they sent him back and I was [LT's] radio guy for the next [few] days."[216] It should be noted that Calvin may have this part of the story incorrect. According to PLT SGT Dickie Quick and Smith, when Smith was taken out of action, Quick reassigned Calvin to 1LT Wishik, where he remained for the balance of the mission.[217] Smith returned to base.

Also, during the initial stages of the mission, First Sergeant Harjo was ordered back to Phuoc Vinh in order to prepare the company for an upcoming Inspector General inspection. Harjo was furious. He

---

[215] Tim Smith interview with author March 11, 2019. Note: Smith was Wishik's assigned RTO.
[216] Adam Piore interview with Calvin Heath, 2009.
[217] Dickie Quick message to author, March 11, 2019.

loathed being in the rear while his men were in the field. "Harjo was a first sergeant who ran his office in the field. He didn't like being at the base when we were out there," stated Dave Dillard.[218] Ray Palmer added, "Top being with the men would have definitely helped. He could just smell when things weren't right."[219]

The bottom line for Delta Company was shortly after the mission began, Harjo and Smith, two key members of the company, bordered a helicopter heading back to Phuoc Vinh.[220]

Thirty minutes after the last choppers landed, Charlie Company, located on Axis 1 to the west, found six enemy bunkers with overhead protection located approximately 1,800 meters north/northeast of LZ Eagle. They relayed this information to battalion headquarters and resumed their mission. According to the Daily Staff Journal (DSJ), forty-five minutes after that, Phantom Force surprised two VC, possibly manning a listening post (LP). They exchanged fire and the enemy "fled leaving rucksacks behind."[221] The equipment was sent back to the battalion intelligence section (S-2) for evaluation. Jeff Davis added:

> The platoon [Phantom Force] was moving as one unit, in column. If these two NVA/VC were operating a listening post, they were doing so while taking a break. We surprised them as they were sitting in the middle of a trail eating lunch. They only left one rucksack. I called in a report to Captain Bucha. Shortly thereafter, I received instructions to find a place for a helicopter to land. There was room at our location, which we had secured. Soon, an observation helicopter arrived, landed, and I ran out to it and passed the rucksack.

---

[218] Dave Dillard telecom interview with the author February 16, 2019.
[219] Ray Palmer interview with author, February 19, 2019.
[220] Note: This was the recollection of several of the men.
[221] Daily Staff Journal, March 16, 1968.

Once it departed, we continued to move cautiously up the trail.[222]

As the two columns carefully advanced, they uncovered more and more evidence that a very large enemy force was in the immediate area. At 2:15 p.m., after travelling approximately one and half miles through the jungle, Bucha and his men found an abandoned enemy basecamp located at coordinates XT 938352. The company-sized camp was complete with "…large bunkers, chairs, tables, and cooking utensils." It was apparent to the men that the site had been recently used, and whoever was there had obviously left in a hurry. Thirty-five minutes later, less than 500 meters away from the discovered enemy camp, the men found another large bunker complex "…situated along both sides of a trail; three meters apart with six-inch overhead cover."[223] Some of the men inspected the complex looking for booby traps and intelligence while others established a defensive perimeter. The reinforced overhead protection on the bunkers were an indication that the enemy was either there or had planned on staying there for a long period of time. First Lieutenant Blalock recalled, "On day one, we were hit by a sniper. One of our guys shot him and he fell out of the tree tied to his safety rope. He was hanging out of the tree."[224]

At 3:36 p.m. Captain Bucha reported his first casualty. While trying to disarm a butterfly bomb, Private First Class Robert L. Meyer was severely wounded and evacuated by helicopter back to Phuoc Vinh.[225] Meyer survived, but he would not return to the mission. I later asked Mike Blalock if this was one of his Combat Engineers and he stated, "I don't think that was one of our guys because we would have blown in place." Few Combat Engineers, even today, would have risked disarming an anti-personnel mine in the field while on a search and destroy mission. [226]

---

[222] Davis correspondence with the author dated September 19, 2016.

[223] Daily Staff Journal, March 16, 1968.

[224] Mike Blalock telecom with author February 10, 2019.

[225] Daily Staff Journal, March 16, 1968.

[226] Mike Blalock telecom with author February 10, 2019.

For the balance of the afternoon the men moved toward their objective uncovering bunker after bunker, some of which were supplied with large caches of rice and other supplies. Shortly after 4:05 p.m., the men received word that a personal letter was among the contents of the VC rucksack found earlier by Phantom Force. The letter was translated and identified as being written by a soldier named Binh of the Dong Nai Regiment. This confirmed that Bucha and Delta Company had found what they were looking for.[227] The letter read:

My Dear Mother,

Today, Hai has a mission in your village, and I sent a letter to you through him. Since the day I was wounded I have not received any letters from you. I miss you, sister, and the children very much. Now I am with my unit. Do you have any cigarettes, if so please send me some. I don't have any cigarettes because I am in the jungle. Being in the jungle is very bad. I wish you and sister anything you want. I can't write anymore. Your boy.[228]

Humping the Vietnamese jungles, even under the best of circumstances, is an arduous and difficult task. The jungles are among the oldest and densest on earth, with most experts agreeing they are more than 70 million years old. For thousands of years, man has traversed the dark tangle of confusion, but always at his own peril. If the vegetation didn't get to you, the animals and insects would. In a triple canopy eco system, large trees can reach several hundred feet high with their green crowns struggling for the crowded space high above the jungle floor. This competition for space oftentimes blocks sun light from ever hitting the ground. The large trees are covered with thick vines that use the trees in a twisted symbiotic dependency to complete their own photosynthetic needs. Emergent trees stuck in the middle of this three-level madness struggle to quickly grow for

---

[227] Bond, p. 24. Note: According to Bond the unit to which the soldier belonged was "HT 61/343 VT – K5."
[228] Ibid.

height, endlessly competing with the higher vegetation for light, and the dense undergrowth for position in this complicated system. Ground-level trees and shrubs with their large leaves struggle for whatever light remains and are often so thick that a man has to hack his way through or be swallowed in its depths.

Over the millennia, the Vietnamese have slashed and chopped trails through these dense environments in an effort to make the trips between villages relatively easy, but in 1968, these trails were often booby trapped with a plethora of horrible devices specifically designed to kill and maim, and the Americans often avoided the trails forcing them to pursue their enemy through dense virgin jungle. This became incredibly stressful as the VC/NVA were experts in camouflage and concealment and could hide undetected within inches of their enemy.

Above: Sam Spencer patrolling the type of jungle in which Delta Company fought during March 1968. Sam's wife Ann stated during a September 2017 reunion that, "I never knew what Sam went through until I read your book (1ˢᵗ Edition- 2015). He just would not speak about all this." Delta Rakkasan photo.

Throughout its history, the American Army developed training programs based on lessons learned from previous wars and battles to better prepare its soldiers in jungle warfare. As a result, it had produced some remarkable jungle-ready units. The 5307th Composite Unit (Merrill's Marauders), a WWII long-range special operations and jungle penetration unit operating in Burma was extremely successful. But no matter how much training was provided, no American was as skilled in these particular jungles as the soldiers of the Dong Nai Regiment.

As the afternoon of March 16th dragged on, the men of Delta Company cautiously advanced, clover leafing through the dense jungle in a northeasterly direction. With every new piece of ground they covered, they found more evidence that they were in the midst of a very large enemy force. Lead elements understood that any lapse of concentration or a moment of inattentiveness could cost them their lives through a booby trap or a well-hidden enemy soldier. It could also result in them leading the entire unit into an enemy ambush.

Second Platoon Leader, 1LT Jeffery Wishik, along with Calvin, his RTO, were positioned in the middle-front of the 25-man platoon so that Wishik could maintain control and contact with his men.[229] Since Calvin was monitoring the radio traffic, he heard incoming reports from the other platoons and from Dillard, the company RTO, of further discoveries. The entire battalion area, in both columns, was full of enemy bunker systems that were vacated only seconds before the Americans arrived. Unable to find the enemy's elusive main body, the men advanced with ever-increasing caution.

During the balance of the afternoon, Delta Company maintained continuous contact with the withdrawing enemy and found 11 more bunkers. At approximately 6:00 p.m. they stumbled into a basecamp and exchanged heavy fire with VC/NVA troops. Bucha reported to battalion command that his men were receiving heavy automatic machine gun fire and M-79 grenade fire from a squad-sized unit. More of his men were injured and at least one, Sergeant Jeffrey Hein,

---

[229] Note: It is uncertain how many men Wishik had at this point.

possibly spelled Hines, was sent back to Phuoc Vinh via dust off (medical evacuation helicopter) due to serious wounds.[230]

By the end of the day on March 16, according to the Daily Staff Journal, the men of the 3rd Battalion, 187th located and destroyed 27 enemy bunkers and two tunnels. They also found two rucksacks, located one large basecamp and another bunker complex, and confirmed at least one enemy killed in action. [231] The action reported to Lieutenant Colonel Forrest by his company commanders indicated that his men had indeed located their intended target and that a major engagement was imminent.

Above: A 240th Assault Helicopter Company resupply chopper with inbound food and outbound mail. This would have been similar to the resupplies Delta received on March 16-21, 1968. The above photo was taken by Specialist 4th Class Richard McLaughlin for the January 31, 1968 edition of the Screaming Eagle. U.S. Army photo.

---

[230] Daily Staff Journal, March 16, 1968.
[231] Note: The Daily Staff Journals were detailed reports that recorded all the activities and radio calls from the field.

With darkness rapidly approaching, Bucha had to quickly find a defendable position in which to establish a company NDP. With such a large body of enemy in the area, every man understood the importance of getting this right. Once the NDP was established, machine guns were positioned, fields of fire were determined, anti-personnel mines were set, and listening posts established. The men settled in for whatever little rest they could get. Since landing 11 hours earlier, the men of Delta Company had moved northeasterly from LZ Falcon 1,850 meters, a little more than a mile. Calvin later noted, "You knew they were there. You could just feel it. When we set up that night, I knew we were in deep shit."[232]

---

[232] Calvin Heath interview with author, May 2013.

MARCH 17, 1968 - HEAVY CONTACT

Throughout the night of March 16th and early morning hours of the 17th, the enemy probed for weaknesses and fired mortar rounds throughout the 3rd Battalion area. Approximately 2,000 meters from Delta Company's position, Charlie Company was receiving heavy 60mm and 82mm mortar fire from nearby enemy positions. Several men were reported killed and a number more wounded.[233] Bucha also reported heavy fire to the west which turned out to be Charlie Company engaging the enemy as they began a cat and mouse game with the enemy's mortar units. This engagement would last most of the early morning hours of March 17th.

Hearing the mortar fire in the distance, Calvin and the other men of Delta Company glanced to the sky more than once that evening as they heard the distinctive "*phoomp*" of the mortars, wondering if the next shell would be dropping on them. No one would be sleeping tonight.

At 2:45 a.m., Lieutenant Colonel Forrest reported to Phuoc Vinh the possible location of an enemy mortar site at grid coordinates XT 947354. He requested a forward air controller (FAC) to investigate.[234] The FAC eventually located the enemy mortar unit and U.S. artillery was brought to bear and the mortar fire ceased.[235]

As daylight approached on March 17th, the men of the 3/187th readied themselves to continue with their mission and by 8:45 a.m., things were already getting "testy." Alpha Company, located to the west of Delta Company, reported finding a large enemy basecamp that had just been vacated. They reported the camp was complete with shower facilities as well as an eating area with fresh food still on the tables.[236]

---

[233] Daily Staff Journal, March 17, 1968.
[234] Ibid.
[235] Ibid. Note: Despite what is stated in the DSJ, none of the men recall any artillery support.
[236] Ibid.

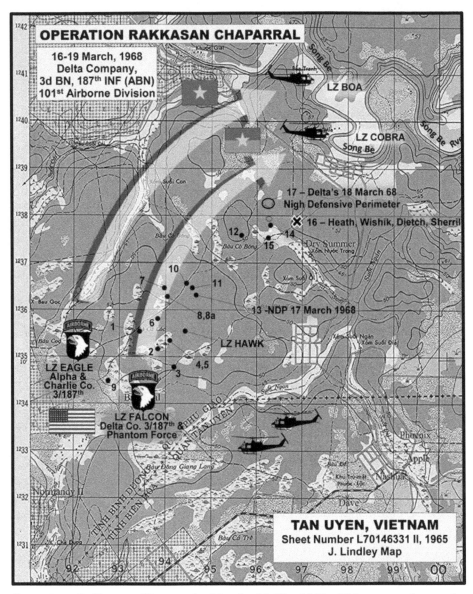

Operation Rakkasan Chaparral, March 16-19, 1968. This map shows the movements of Delta Company 3/187. Alpha, Bravo, and Charlie Company, along with other support groups, also participated in this operation and took heavy casualties. Grid coordinates determined from the Daily Staff Journals March 16-19, 1968. Detailed information provided on the next page. Map – Joe Lindley.

Detail Explanation for 16-19 March 1968
Tan Uyen, Vietnam, Sheet No. L70146331 II

Item	Coordinates	Date - Time	Comment
LZ Falcon	XT937343	16 Mar 0935	Initial landing zone
LZ Eagle	XT923354	16 Mar 0935	Initial landing zone
1.	XT934355	16 Mar 1230	Phantom Force found rucksack
2.	XT938352	16 Mar 1415	D. Co. found basecamp
3.	XT942348	16 Mar 1440	D. Co. found basecamp
4.	XT941352	16 Mar 1536	PFC Meyers wounded
5.	XT941352	16 Mar 1617	D. Co. found bunkers
6.	XT939358	16 Mar 1800	D. Co. "stumble into" basecamp, J. Hein evacuated
7.	XT940364	17 Mar 0900	Phantom Force hit with mine, 3 men wounded
8.	XT941363	17 Mar 0940	Phantom Force contact with estimated SQD size element
8.a	XT941363	17 Mar 1101	D. Co. destroyed one bunker
9.	XT927344	17 Mar 1120	D. Co. destroyed one bunker
10.	XT945365	17 Mar 1925	D. Co. found six fresh, bullet-riddled VC bodies in grave
11.	XT946364	17 Mar 2040	Phantom Force and D. Co. establish NPD
12.	XT957375	18 Mar 1405	Contact with 5-6 VC, moving in pursuit, bunker found
13.	XT947363	18 Mar 1540	COL Mowery & LTC Forrest evacuate heat stroke victims
14.	XT963378	18 Mar 1815	Contact with one VC, lost contact, LRRP moving forward. Approximate position of LZ
15.	XT962375	18 Mar 1850	D. Co. in firefight with "reinforced squad"
	XT962375	18 Mar 1920	D. Co. reports under heavy fire from all directions
	XT962375	18 Mar 1920	Bucha reports pulling all elements into tight perimeter
	XT962375	18 Mar 2010	Bucha reports 3 WHA, all serious condition, 4 persons isolated on the trail - Wishik, Heath, Sherrill, Dietch
	XT962375	18 Mar 2025	All elements in tight perimeter 25 meters across
	XT962375	19 Mar 1920	Contact with Heath
16.	XT969379	18-19 Mar	Location of Wishik, Heath, Sherrill and Dietch
17.	XT962382	18-19 Mar	Last NDP

Five-hundred meters to the west, Phantom Force once again made enemy contact. At approximately 9:00 a.m. the small group was hit by a Claymore mine (grid coordinates XT 940364). AK-47 fire from what appeared to be the "same elements [they had been] pursuing for past two days" immediately followed the mine detonation.[237] Phantom Force member, PFC Dennis Cunningham, was seriously wounded, and evacuated back to Phuoc Vinh by helicopter, he died later that day. Monte Cooley was killed in action and several other LRRPs were seriously wounded.

Forty minutes after the initial contact, Phantom Force re-engaged the same enemy element approximately 100 meters to the southwest (grid coordinates XT 941363) as the enemy was maneuvering to break contact. This firefight lasted for approximately ten minutes before the enemy, once again, broke contact. Phantom Force then moved into the area vacated by the enemy and found additional bunkers and numerous tunnels. Approximately one hour later, Delta Company moved into the same area and found yet another bunker that they destroyed.[238]

Captain Bucha then ordered Phantom Force to join his column. Jeff Davis, Phantom Force Platoon Leader, recalls:

> *Later that morning Captain Bucha directed me to join his column. We moved eastward and linked up, and I discussed what we had seen. At some point, either upon arrival or later, we moved into 'point' position of the column. I assume that we were likely pulled in because he had more information about the suspected size of the enemy forces, and recognized, as I did, that an element of our small size was a bit exposed and*

---

[237] Daily Staff Journal, March 17, 1968.

[238] Note: The DSJ also shows that at 11:20 a.m., 19 minutes after their last find, Delta made another find at grid coordinates XT 927344. This was a curious entry and may not be accurate as it places the men 2,500 meters away (nearly 1.6 miles), an impossible distance to cover in a hostile jungle in this amount of time. Possible explanations include they could have been a detached element, the coordinates were wrong, or it could have been elements of A or C Company.

insufficiently close to other U.S. forces in case
someone needed to response to an (our) emergency.[239]

In accordance to the original OPORD, on the morning of March 17, Delta Company secured LZ Hawk (grid coordinates XT 946355). There, Delta Company left a small contingent to guard the LZ and moved on with their portion of the mission. At 12:15 p.m., Bravo Company, with approximately 90 soldiers, departed Phuoc Vinh and landed without incident at LZ Hawk. By 12:15 Delta's main body had advanced past LZ Hawk and was located approximately 900 meters to the northwest. The last elements of Bravo Company were on the ground by 2:00 p.m.[240]

Throughout the early afternoon of the seventeenth, there was constant contact with the enemy up and down the battalion lines. The firefights varied from small skirmishes to larger unit engagements that required artillery and air support to suppress. According to Dave Dillard, "We were hitting rice caches (large supplies of rice) all day that were heavily guarded by NVA soldiers, so we knew we were close to the enemy."[241] Mike Blalock added, "We ran across piles of rice so big that they were 10 high by 20 deep. Some of the rice was from the U.S.! When we blew that, it looked like it was snowing."[242]

Calvin, and the remaining men of Delta Company, had now been in pursuit for more than 24 straight hours. The constant enemy pressure and the extreme heat and humidity were taking their toll. The men were starting to run out of water, ammo and food. Unable to properly hydrate, men were beginning to collapse due to heat exhaustion and dehydration. Dave Dillard reports that, "By this time the numbers are shrinking... and we (Delta Company) don't have a 100 capable men."[243]

Many of the wounded and fallen men needed to be immediately evacuated back to Phuoc Vinh which required a secured LZ for

---

[239] Davis correspondence to the author September 12, 2016.
[240] Daily Staff Journal, March 17, 1968.
[241] Dillard, Heaney, Rawson interview with author, October 9, 2013.
[242] Mike Blalock telecom with author February 10, 2019.
[243] Dillard, Heaney, Rawson interview with author, October 9, 2013.

supply choppers and dust offs to land. This was near impossible in their current location due to the dense vegetation and the close proximity of the enemy. Therefore, Bucha made the decision to move the wounded and ill men to the LZ used earlier that day. Dillard continued, "So we move to the last LZ and we start having strange happenings. We heard chickens and we see rice droppings, so we knew we were close [to the enemy]."[244]

Calvin, as RTO, had more information than the other soldiers, but he did not need the radio to tell him that they were in the middle of a large enemy force. At 2:50 p.m., Battalion Intelligence (S-2) reported that the 7th NVA Regiment was reported to be in grid 9236, only a half mile from Delta's position.[245] Initial intelligence reports that suggested the 7th, 165th, 141st NVA, and the Dong Nai Regiment,[246] 2,000 to 3,000 enemy soldiers, were operating in the area were proving correct, and Delta Company was located *right in the middle of them*!

In 2009, when Calvin spoke about that day, he said, "We were losing people like crazy... no water, so I knew we were getting in serious trouble."[247] Bill Heaney added, "You have to remember we were in triple canopy. There were attempts to resupply us. Choppers [came in and] attempted to drop bladders of water, but they broke."[248] Water was now becoming a serious issue for Delta Company.

Later in the afternoon of March 17, 1968, at approximately 4:09 p.m., Phantom Force once again came under heavy attack and suffered several more casualties.[249] Davis states, "We were moving in a column, LRRP platoon in the lead. Our two-man point element discovered a rice cache next to the trail. As we continued to move forward and probe, they were taken under fire from a position perhaps 30-40 yards ahead. Both [lead] soldiers were wounded."

---

[244] Dillard, Heaney, Rawson interview with author, October 9, 2013.

[245] Daily Staff Journal, March 17, 1968.

[246] Note: The specific unit the Americans faced was the Phu Loi Battalion of the Dong Nai Regiment, and the 7th NVA.

[247] Adam Piore interview with Calvin Heath, 2009.

[248] Calvin Heath interview with author, April 26, 2013.

[249] Daily Staff Journal, March 17, 1968.

Davis continued, "One other soldier and I moved up to them and then leap-frogged past to lay down a base of fire. Others moved up to the wounded men and pulled them back to relative safety. The fire from the front soon ceased and the commander was able to call in a medevac.

Colonel Mowery's command and control chopper immediately moved in to drop supplies and evacuate the seriously wounded men. Several men of Delta Company suggest that Mowery's C&C chopper received heavy enemy ground fire and was shot down. Davis later stated that the chopper "suffered a blade strike against a tree as the pilot tried to maneuver to land in an extremely small place."[250] Whether or not the aircraft was hit by ground fire is unknown, what is certain, is the blade strike witnessed by Davis and the other LRRPs would have been catastrophic. What is also known is another chopper was sent to retrieve the colonel, and what few wounded men they could load.[251] Operation Rakkasan Chaparral was quickly deteriorating and the officers of the 3/187th were scrambling to maintain mission control, but they were rapidly losing that fight.

While some of the men were now dealing with a downed aircraft and seriously wounded LRRPs, other Delta men found 11 more bunkers in the same proximity of the basecamp located earlier, further suggesting the size of the camp was massive, possibly holding more than one battalion or regiment. Calvin stated, "When we saw all those bunkers, we knew we were in trouble."[252] He then added, "We heard chickens..."[253] Puzzled about that particular comment, I later asked him about the significance of the chickens and he replied, "The enemy don't carry chickens around when they're on a mission. They only have them in their basecamps."[254] The chickens were a sign of the enemy's position, size, and strength.

With darkness rapidly approaching, Bucha had the men established their NDP. While doing so, several of the men found a

---

[250] Davis Correspondence with the author September 12, 2016.
[251] Bond, p. 26.
[252] Calvin Heath interview with author, April 26, 2013.
[253] Ibid.
[254] Ibid.

trail with deep fresh ox-cart tracks. Calvin later recalled, "Captain Bucha called the LT on the radio and wanted him to see these tracks going into the woods. So, me and [Wishik]… I was the RTO… went and there were these deep tracks heading into the jungle. That meant we were pushing a big unit."[255] This was most likely the same unit they encountered a week earlier between the two hills carrying torches. By this time, the sun was setting, and supplies were inbound, so Bucha decided to wait until the following morning to further investigate the trail area and the ox-cart markings. Bucha's decision most likely saved a lot of lives because as Calvin later suggested, had the men proceeded down that trail that night, they would have walked straight into a well-concealed ambush site located on both sides of the trail. In 2013, Calvin added, "Joe, nobody would have walked out of there that night if we went in. They would have wiped us all out."[256]

Shortly after sunset, Delta found additional evidence that they were closing in on the enemy and at 7:15 p.m. Bucha reported to headquarters that his men found "…six fresh graves with VC bullet-ridden bodies at XT 945365."[257] Immediately before this, the men of Bravo Company reported smelling tear gas (CS) in the area.[258] The use of CS gas in the field was a common tactic used by the VC and NVA to cover a withdrawal. Bill Heaney added, "We detected a smell of gas… The North Vietnamese were notorious for throwing CS gas to cover their retreat or their movements."[259]

Meanwhile, Delta Company and the remaining LRRPs, established ambush sites, rigged mines, set up listening posts, and finally settled into their NDP at 10:25 p.m. around coordinates XT 946364, 100 meters off the main trail. The area was so dense that most of the men could not see more than a few meters into the deep thick jungle. They relied on their hearing to detect approaching enemy, but even this began to betray them as there seemed to be sounds of enemy soldiers emanating from every direction.

---

[255] Calvin Heath interview with author, May 2013.
[256] Ibid.
[257] Bond, p. 26.
[258] Ibid.
[259] Dillard, Heaney, Rawson interview with author, October 9, 2013.

I asked Calvin how he felt that night. He replied, "I don't know… I know I felt different. This time seemed different and I think we all knew something big was going to happen."

"Were you frightened?" I asked.

"We were always a little scared, but I was more concerned about getting some sleep. The jungle was so thick we couldn't see too much. We were beat… I wasn't scared of getting shot or anything."

"What was Lieutenant Wishik doing?"

"Part of the night he was working with Bucha on what they were going to do the next day, those tracks were a real big deal. He also worked with Sergeant Quick to make sure the men were OK. Quick did most of that."[260] I quickly found that my questioning was not going to produce anything that would become literarily notable. Calvin was a soldier's soldier and he lived by Tennyson's words, "Ours is not to reason why, ours is but to do or die."[261]

At the end of the day on March 17, 1968, the 3/187th's Daily Staff Journal stated that the 3rd Battalion, 187th reported 49 VC KIA, with another 58 possible KIA. They also had one enemy prisoner, 650 pounds of rice, found eight semi-automatic weapons, two anti-tank mines, ten anti-personnel mines, 27 bunkers, two tunnels, five bicycles, two basecamps, and one large bunker complex.[262]

As nighttime fell, Calvin and the men of Delta settled into a quiet uneasiness that few of them would ever forget. They realized that if they were not attacked that evening, they certainly would be the following morning. At that moment however, there was little any of them could do but to grab as much rest as they could. As they settled down for a tense night in the dark jungle, they knew that much of the mission's ultimate success or failure lay in Paul Bucha's hands, and the men trusted Bucha completely, but they also trusted one another. They understood that the outcome would completely depend on how strongly they held together.

---

[260] Calvin Heath interview with author, May 2013.
[261] Note: From Alfred Tennyson's poem, *Charge of the Light Brigade*.
[262] Daily Staff Journal, March 17, 1968.

111

MARCH 18, 1968 - ISOLATION

At 4:11 a.m., two hours before sunrise, on March 18, 1968, Calvin and the men of Delta Company heard heavy gunfire and explosions to their southwest. Bravo Company, located approximately 1,000 meters from Delta's position, came under heavy attack as the enemy continued to probe for American weaknesses. Up and down the line, and now *behind* the advancing Americans, the VC/NVA sent out small teams to gather intelligence to establish the size of the American forces they were facing, find the weaknesses in their lines, and then determine the best way to exploit those weaknesses. Bravo Company was able to push the enemy probe back, sustaining one casualty, but the action resulted in the entire Rakkasan line being alerted for possible heavy hostile activity.[263]

By 4:30 a.m., the men in Delta's NDP were very uneasy. As daylight approached, the morning mist seemed to grow thicker by the minute, further limiting their already restricted view into the jungle. Everyone knew that the optimal time for the enemy to attack was just before sunrise and the men of Delta Company were preparing for the worse. Calvin looked into the jungle around him. He understood from the previous day's intelligence that they were dangerously close to the enemy and that there could be thousands of them. He later recalled, "That morning, I just knew we were in deep trouble. I could just feel it. The day before we had been uncovering stuff all day, and we all knew we were close to the enemy."[264]

By 5:35 a.m. the first bright rays of sunlight poked through the thick mist. The attack for which the men had prepared did not come. They ate quickly, eyes always toward the jungle, checked their equipment and weapons, and prepared to continue with the mission. Bucha and his lieutenants reviewed maps, reported to base, and briefed their men. The sergeants went to each man in their section of the perimeter and checked personal equipment and ammunition.

---

[263] Daily Staff Journal, March 18, 1968.
[264] Calvin Heath interview with author, April 26, 2013.

Calvin, who was with 1LT Wishik, was prepared and ready to move. The men of Delta Company were now 44 hours into their mission and 14 hours away from, what Dave Dillard would later call, their "defining moment."

At 8:35 a.m., with Phantom Force in the lead, the men were silently and cautiously clover-leafing in the direction of the trail discovered the previous evening, searching for the enemy who left the deep ox-cart tracks,. They were extremely fatigued, but exceptionally vigilant. Bill Heaney stated, "We were all pretty scared. We knew something big was coming."[265]

As the men moved silently through the jungle, they searched for enemy strongholds and concealed booby traps, and found neither in the immediate area. Any ambush established by the enemy the night before had long-since moved on and the cat and mouse game continued, but now the men were wondering, "Who was the cat and who was the mouse?"

Around 12:40 p.m., approximately 1,500 meters from Delta Company, Alpha Company stumbled upon 2,000-3,000 pounds of rice (grid coordinates XT 930378). They also found more recently abandoned bunkers. Shortly thereafter, they made contact with ten enemy soldiers believed to be NVA resulting in one enemy KIA and one WIA. These ten men were most likely a rear-guard action protecting the main body as it tried to maneuver away from the Americans. Contact reports were sent to battalion headquarters further confirming the previous day's intelligence that the Rakkasans faced a very large enemy force. Additional documents captured at the newly discovered bunkers indicated that the enemy they now faced also included the "81st Rear Detachment, supporting the Dong Nai and 7th NVA Regiments,"[266] approximately 100 to 200 additional men.

At 1:35 p.m., Delta found another 2,200 pounds of rice, some rotted, that they destroyed in place (grid coordinates XT 957375). Twenty-five minutes later, they made contact with five or six enemy soldiers resulting in two probable kills. The Daily Staff Journal noted

---

[265] Heaney interview with author, September 10, 2014.
[266] Daily Staff Journal, March 18, 1968.

that men from Delta Company were "moving in pursuit" of the enemy survivors.[267] By this time, Delta Company had only moved 1,600 meters, one mile, in a north/northeasterly direction from their last NDP. Around 1:40 p.m., Delta was once again in contact with five or six VC/NVA and exchanged gunfire with them until 2:25 p.m., when the enemy finally broke contact.

Throughout the balance of the afternoon, the men found more booby traps, tunnels, abandoned supplies, and additional bunkers in the area. Several of the complexes were so large that according to the Daily Staff Journals, "it would take three or four days to destroy [them]."[268] Minor skirmishes and contact with the enemy continued throughout the balance of the day. The men were running critically low on supplies and water, and more men dropped due to heat exhaustion and dehydration and needed to be evacuated.

At 3:14 p.m., Bucha had his men move to a small opening in the jungle to secure a temporary LZ. Calvin noted that he only had, "...a few hours of sleep over the past two days and we were beat."[269] At 3:40 p.m., the men were resupplied with ammo, food and water, and that several of the men, suffering from heat exhaustion, were evacuated by Lieutenant Colonel Forrest's and Colonel Mowery's command and control (C&C) choppers.[270] The food was especially memorable. Forty-five years later, Calvin recalled the food being a "...delicious dinner of steaks with peppers, mashed potatoes, with all the trimmings." Calvin added, with delight, "Boy, it was great!"[271] It would be Calvin's last meal in the field. Years later, Calvin and the other men suggested that the helicopters flying in food and supplies that evening were what ultimately saved Delta Company from complete annihilation. Calvin later explained:

The Gooks are counting choppers coming in and out. Well between... that first chopper was the mail, it takes off and ends up coming back and going to take the mail out, so that

---

[267] Daily Staff Journal, March 18, 1968.
[268] Ibid.
[269] Calvin Heath interview with author, June 2013.
[270] Daily Staff Journal, March 18, 1968.
[271] Calvin Heath interview with author, April 26, 2013.

chopper comes back. The four choppers that brought in the food, they leave and then they come back and flew the food back out or what's left over. And then the brigade commander, I think the brigade commander came in... so there were maybe 10 or 12 choppers that came in. Well, the only thing that makes sense to us, was they [the enemy] had to think that another company landed with us. They absolutely had to think that there were more of us than there really was.[272]

After the men ate, they continued with their mission. Calvin later said, "The whole day was crazy. We kept finding shit and the NVA kept moving back and then they were shooting at us." He went on to say, "We never knew where the next attack was coming from, and every minute we felt like we would be attacked by that huge force we saw a few days earlier."[273] Bill Pray adds, "I knew we were going to get hit."[274]

Bucha moved Phantom Force to cover the column's western flank. At approximately 6:15 p.m., they were alerted by their supporting dog team that the enemy was in the area. Almost immediately, they spotted an enemy water carrier. The Americans opened fire. The startled enemy dropped the water and ran. In 2016, Jeff Davis, Phantom Force Platoon Leader stated, "We had been following enemy signs, to include commo wire, for three days and when we came across that water carrier... The dog immediately alerted, and we fired. We then cautiously advanced." Davis reported that his team then carefully maneuvered through dense thick "scrub brush" until they came to a tree line where the thick vegetation gave way to a heavily treed area with opened ground. Davis sent two two-man groups right and left. The men then heard an explosion to their right and then all hell broke loose.

"...we had been doing reconnaissance for nearly four months as a small element, often operating alone miles

---

[272] Adam Piore interview with Calvin Heath, 2009.
[273] Calvin Heath interview with author, June 2013.
[274] Pray interview with author, April 13, 2016.

away from U.S. forces, so recklessness was not our modus operandi, and I was in direct communication with Captain Bucha as soon as my point men fired on the watercarrier. Movement had been slow and methodical, and this naturally continued forward from the point of engagement with the watercarrier…slow and deliberate in order to avoid an ambush, while determining exactly what we had in terms of enemy troops in the vicinity. It turns out that there were quite a few. [275]

What Davis and his men had found was the edge of a large base camp.

Order of Battle

Delta Co. 3/187th, 101st ABN
18 March 1968, 1800 Hrs.
Source: Colonel Mowery Narrative March 1968

Phantom Force (16 Men) [276]

2LT Jeff Davis

1st Platoon (25 Men)

SFC Kuykendal

2nd Platoon (23 Men)

1 LT Wishik (PFC Heath RTO)

Company HQ (8 Men)

CPT Bucha (SGT Dillard RTO)

4th Platoon (7 Men)

Heavy Weapons PLT

3rd Platoon (30 Men)

2LT Sherrill

---

[275] Col. Floyd "Jeff" Davis phone interview, January 29, 2016.
[276] Note: There has been some disagreeing information as to the total number of LRRPs during the mission. Jeff Davis, Rick Shoup and others from Phantom Force confirmed they began the mission with seventeen and went into the battle with sixteen.

326th Combat Engineers (3 Men)[277]
1LT Mike Blalock

TOTAL: 110 Men

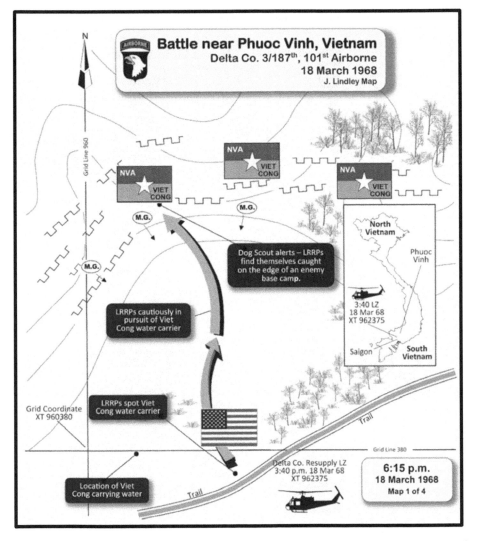

Above: 6:15 p.m. March 18, 1968. Phantom Force spots VC/NVA water carrier and cautiously gives chase. They soon find themselves inside the enemy's basecamp

---

[277] Note: Speculation on the author's part.

receiving heavy fire. According to Calvin, all the members of Phantom Force were killed or wounded. Conversations with Phantom Force members later proved this was not correct. Several were not wounded and were able to engage the enemy. J. Lindley map.

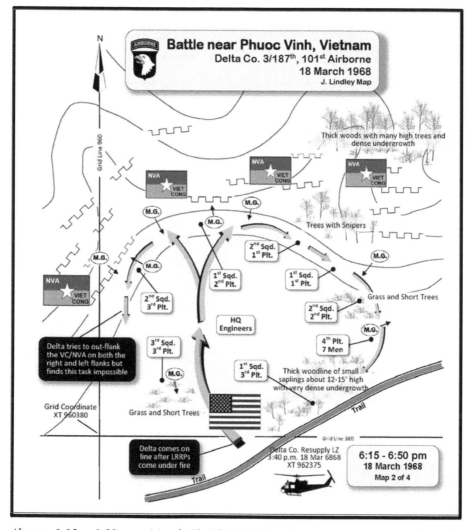

Above: 6:15 – 6:50 p.m. March 18, 1968. Delta advances and tries to outflank the VC/NVA positions only to find that the enemy lines are much too large to out-flank. Many men are wounded and killed. Calvin's best friend Paul Conner was killed,

most likely at the head of the column in the 2nd Squad-1st Platoon area. The gunfire, according to Calvin, "Just never stopped." J. Lindley map.

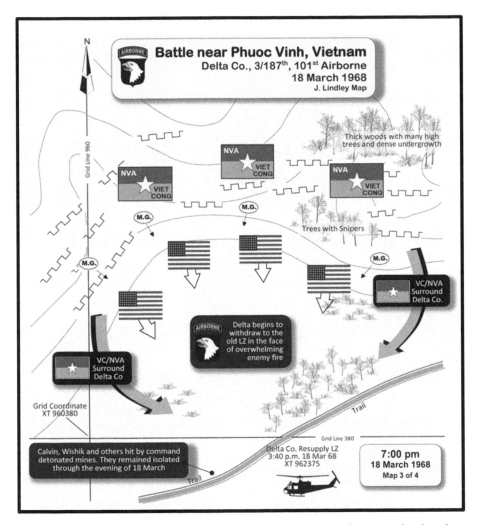

Above: 7:00 p.m. March 18, 1968. Captain Bucha, now knowing he faced an overwhelming enemy force, pulled his men back to consolidate their lines and evacuate the wounded. Rakkasans, including Calvin, Wishik, and Dietch, were sent to the old LZ to secure the area. They were met by an overpowering VC/NVA force who had moved behind the men in an attempt to surround Delta Company. J. Lindley map.

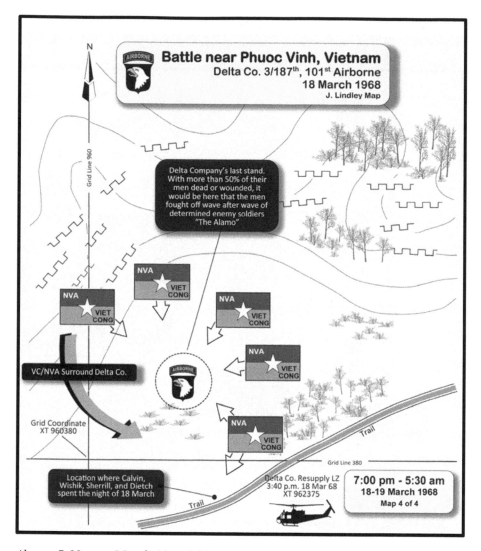

Above: 7:00 p.m. March 18 – 5:30 a.m. March 19, 1968. Delta moves to a small perimeter. Many Americans are caught outside Delta's main lines with several KIA and WIA. Calvin, Wishik and Dietch were the only men outside the lines for the entire night who survived. The VC/NVA attacked in wave after wave. J. Lindley map.

Captain James Bond, an officer with 3/187th later noted, "It appears at this point, that Company D had been led by the VC into an ambush and then surrounded by the VC/NVA forces."[278] This assessment of Delta's situation at this time of the battle would later prove to be a sensitive issue for Calvin and the other men, one addressed later in this piece.

Dave Dillard, located in the center of the column with Captain Bucha stated, "Then all of a sudden the jungle exploded." Bill Heaney added, "We were used to seeing eight to nine guys, now it's 80 to 90, maybe 1,500 to 2,000. We just didn't know."[279] Shooting quickly intensified and Phantom Force was taking serious incoming fire. Calvin later stated, "We could hear the guys in the front had pushed right into a big force. Shit was flying everywhere!"[280] He also added that of "…the 18 LRRPs [in the lead group], I believe that all but maybe two of them ended up getting killed. I remember Bucha on the horn telling them to attack and he radioed us to come on the run… to support them and so we ran across the field (LZ)."[281]

Delta Company's "Battle of all Battles" began at 6:50 p.m. on March 18, 1968. After the company had run straight into the VC/NVA basecamp, Bucha reported to LTC Forrest that his men were in a quickly developing firefight with an estimated "…VC reinforced squad at XT 962375."[282] His report severely underestimated the number of enemy they faced by many hundreds, perhaps thousands of men.

As the men scrambled and maneuvered, the small arms fire reported by Bucha to headquarters a few minutes earlier quickly escalated to "…heavy automatic weapon, heavy machinegun, rocket-propelled grenades, Claymore mines, and small-arms fire."[283] One of Delta's men was hit almost immediately and was killed. Less than

---

[278] Bond, p. 27.

[279] Dillard, Heaney, Rawson interview with author, October 9, 2013.

[280] Calvin Heath interview with author, May 2013.

[281] Adam Piore interview with Calvin Heath, 2009. Note: All records indicate there were 11 LRRPs, several, to include Jeff Davis, were seriously wounded.

[282] Daily Staff Journal, March 18, 1968.

[283] Bucha's Medal of Honor Citation.

five minutes later, Bucha reported having six more men down.[284] Clarence Jones, one of the men moving forward to help Phantom Force, stated, "I saw Sgt Estrada hit by a machine gun on our right flank, and the medic that went to get him also went down; several members of my platoon went down also." [285] Things were quickly getting out of hand and LTC Forrest scrambled a light fire team – helicopters equipped with machine guns – for air support.[286] Some of the wounded men were brought to a make-shift company command post near the center of the rapidly developing perimeter. Dave Dillard, who was with Bucha stated, "The wounded men looked like a book of names. And [now] we know we are in the middle of it."[287] Bill Pray was hit with a Claymore mine and received serious wounds. The force of the explosion knocked off his helmet. "The guys swore my head was decapitated, because they saw my helmet rolling around."[288]

Bucha knew that he and his men were now in serious trouble. His entire lead element was either wounded or dead and his main body was pinned down. He also knew that if he did not move quickly, his entire company could be trapped, surrounded and overrun. Calvin, who was listening to the company radio traffic stated, "Bucha kept on the phone calling the first platoon up front, 'What's going on? What's going on?' Well everybody got hit. So, he didn't know what was going on so he went up there."[289] Bucha moved to the front to see if he could personally gain control of the rapidly deteriorating situation. What he found, when he arrived, was utter chaos,

Within minutes of Phantom Force making contact with the VC/NVA lines, Delta's first platoon, who were advancing behind the LRRPs, moved forward to help extract the wounded men. They quickly became pinned down under extremely heavy machine-gun fire. A concealed bunker, located approximately 40 meters to their

---

[284] Daily Staff Journal, March 18, 1968.

[285] Jones, Clarence, letter dated April 22, 2001 for the recommendation of 1SGT Harjo for Medal of Honor.

[286] Daily Staff Journal, March 18, 1968.

[287] Dillard, Heaney, Rawson interview with author, October 9, 2013.

[288] Pray interview with author April 13, 2016. Note: Pray was thought to be KIA. Seriously wounded, he was able to crawl and rejoin the line some time later.

[289] Adam Piore interview with Calvin Heath, 2009.

front, stopped the men dead in their tracks and poured crushing machinegun fire into them, ripping them to pieces. Men were dropping everywhere, some literally exploding apart. Other men who had been hit were clutching their wounds trying to stop the bleeding.

Seeing many of his men in the lead element dead or wounded, Bucha reacted. Without consideration for his own safety, he ran forward, located the concealed machine gun, and "crawled through the hail of fire to single-handedly destroy the bunker with grenades." During this heroic action, Bucha was "painfully wounded by shrapnel," but it would be some time before he had the wounds treated.[290] Calvin added, "[He] really shouldn't have done that. The Company Commander... shouldn't have been out in front of the company, but he did, and he made all the right decisions that night. All of them!"[291]

One of the men hit in the initial action was acting 1st PLT Leader, SFC Stephen Kuykendal. Calvin reported that Bucha, after reaching the front, instructed Wishik to move forward to take command of the lead element. "He radioed us to come on the run... to support them so we ran across the field." Colonel Mowery, in his after-action report stated, "The Company Commander next directed Second Platoon Leader, 1LT Wishik, to leave his element in command of his platoon sergeant and to move forward and take command of the First Platoon."[292]

During this phase of the battle, Senior Aidman SP5 Dennis Moore also distinguished himself by leaving...

> *...the security of the company headquarters element voluntarily to go to the aid of the wounded in the front element. As he approached the first of eight wounded comrades, he was seriously wounded in the leg and stomach. Completely ignoring his own wounds and safety he pushed ahead into the enemy fire. He discarded his personal weapon so as to better aid the wounded. In the course of moving from*

---

[290] Jones, p. 151. Paul Bucha Medal of Honor citation.
[291] Adam Piore interview with Calvin Heath, 2009.
[292] Bond, p. 45.

the first to the sixth man who lay only ten feet from an enemy machinegun bunker, Specialist Five Moore was wounded repeatedly. Not once did he stop to tend his own wounds but continued to crawl to the front, treating the wounded as he moved. He courageously moved to the lead man and began treating him, when he was mortally wounded by machinegun fire.[293]

For his actions that day, Moore was posthumously awarded the Distinguished Service Cross, the second highest award for valor.

After destroying the bunker, Captain Bucha, understanding the dire situation of his lead elements, ordered second, third and fourth platoons up front to quickly fill the large gaps in his developing defensive line. Bucha knew if he did not get men on that line, and fast, the enemy would break through and his whole perimeter would quickly collapse, spelling disaster for his entire company.

The ferocity of the firefight was like nothing Calvin and the men had ever experienced. Cut and shredded vegetation stripped from the trees and bushes by machine gun fire, fell to the ground like snow. Overwhelming enemy fire seemed to be coming from every direction and many of the Americans were now lying dead or wounded. The NVA understood they needed to get close to the Americans and pour withering small-arms fire into their lines before they had the chance to use their far-superior artillery and air support.

Second platoon ran the entire 300 meters to reach the company's ad-hoc command post, situated near the front of the rapidly developing battle. As the second platoon reached the main body, Captain Bucha, having just returned from neutralizing the machine-gun bunker, was organizing the deployment of the arriving men. The American lines to the front were already beginning to collapse and the threat of being overrun was almost inevitable. According to Calvin, Bucha placed the arriving second, third, and fourth platoons, who were originally in the middle and rear of the advancing American column, into positions along the front and sides of the American position in an attempt to first establish a stronger defensive line and

---

[293] Moore, Dennis, Distinguished Service Cross Award.

then, to push the enemy back. This was proving extremely difficult for Bucha and his men because of the heavy enemy fire from well-established positions within their own basecamp, and the rapidly rising Delta casualties.

Calvin said later, "It was absolute chaos. We ran a long way to try and help the other platoon and the bullets and shit were just flying everywhere. I could see wounded guys everywhere, but we couldn't stop, or we'd be dead."[294] Calvin continues:

When we went there [Bucha] was in this little clearing. He said, "Go over and reinforce first platoon, and try to push through the [enemy]." Well, when we got up there was no way we could push. So Wishik decided we were going to try and outflank them. We went left, Second Lieutenant Sherrill was over here (looking at the map and pointing to Sherrill's position) *and he took some guys and he went to the right trying to find [a way to move around their flanks].*[295]

The men moved in several directions in an attempt to outflank the enemy, but as Calvin related:

...we went maybe a couple hundred yards and we were on a dead run. And as we're running [there was] a little bit of a clearing maybe every 20 yards – you can see where a trail shoots this way... as we came to [the NVA/VC] we would be firing down [the trails] and you could see the Gooks firing back at us.[296]

It became quickly apparent to Wishik that the VC/NVA lines were far too extensive to outflank. No matter how far down the line they went they encountered more and more NVA and VC soldiers. Bill Heaney added, "We probed to get flanks out there and the [lines just] kept going and going and we kept finding more and more enemy."[297]

---

[294] Calvin Heath interview with author, May 2013.
[295] Adam Piore interview with Calvin Heath, 2009.
[296] Ibid.
[297] Dillard, Heaney, Rawson interview with author, October 9, 2013.

The continued thinning of the Delta lines by attempting to outflank a superior and well-established enemy could have been disastrous, as thinning lines when facing a vastly superior enemy, seldom hold. The men's tenacity and audacity, however, had the opposite effect. The enemy assumed that the American unit they faced, because of their rapid flanking maneuvers, was much larger than it actually was. "We just kept going down, hoping we would find the end of the lines, but we didn't, they were everywhere," stated Calvin.[298]

Back at the Delta Company CP area, Dillard was busy calling in air support and relaying information from the individual platoons to Captain Bucha and to Battalion Headquarters. There was no doubt by everyone in the chain of command, that Delta had stumbled into a major basecamp and was in very serious trouble. In less than 15 minutes after the battle began, Dillard estimated that of the 89 men remaining in the field, 40 were now dead or wounded. "I could hear, 'I got four men down,' 'I got three men down,' etc. So, we had to clear an LZ. Bucha tells me, 'You have to stay here and get these men out of here!' The Alamo was established."[299]

Sergeant First Class Stephen Kuykendal, the first platoon sergeant, later wrote a narrative explaining the actions up to this point:

Unbeknownst to us, they (NVA/VC) *lay in wait while we cautiously proceeded toward the north. Evidently, they did not realize that the approaching element was of company size, and when the 11 members of the LRRP came upon the first signs of impending contact they stopped and dispersed their men. The enemy opened fire with a significant and overwhelming amount of fire power. The fact that the carefully planned ambush had been sprung by them prematurely allowed the company to deploy to its greatest*

---

[298] Calvin Heath interview with author, May 2013.
[299] Dillard, Heaney, Rawson interview with author, October 9, 2013. Note: 89 was the number of men from Delta. This did not include the remaining members of Phantom Force, Combat Engineers, forward observer, etc.

advantage. The call came from the LRRPs for reinforcements, and an element from the company was able to take up positions and form a perimeter around them within minutes. The LRRPs had taken 100% casualties. The enemy was attempting to overrun this position and the company commander [Bucha] called in artillery and air to overwhelm the enemy.[300]

Around 7:35 p.m., seeing the situation further deteriorating, Captain Bucha began to consolidate his perimeter.[301] At the same time, Dillard was still on the radio frantically seeking air support and requesting dust offs. Calvin and the men of second platoon who tried to outflank the enemy, were now under heavy fire, trying to desperately fight their way back to the main company area. According to Calvin, the scene was so chaotic, that several NVA soldiers actually mistook Calvin and the other American soldiers running *toward* the American lines as their fellow soldiers and jumped out and ran in front of the Americans, thinking they were joining an attack. These enemy soldiers were quickly killed by Calvin and the other Americans from behind. A few seconds sooner, Calvin and his small band would have been the ones who were shot in the back.

As Calvin, Wishik and the other men continued to move back to the company area, the enemy detonated anti-personnel mines and fired RPG rounds into the trees to maximize the shrapnel raining down on the men. The men of Second Platoon, including Calvin with a radio strapped to his back, crouched down and ran for their lives through a hail of bullets, shrapnel and debris. Some of the men carried and assisted wounded soldiers. Calvin later reported that, "If I stood up we would have caught [bullets or shrapnel] in the chest," As they moved closer to Bucha and their own lines, Calvin and Wishik were suddenly caught by several exploding mines. Calvin stated, "I remember they were going down through us [blowing mines]. I stopped for a quick second because of my legs. I rubbed them... I can remember [thinking] 'God damn, fucking fire ants!' That's what it felt

---

[300] Bond, pgs. 28-29.
[301] Daily Staff Journal, March 18, 1968.

like, and it turned out it was actually shrapnel I had taken in the legs."[302] Calvin's legs were peppered with small shrapnel wounds and they were now bleeding badly. He knew, however, that if he slowed down or dropped because of his wounds, it would mean certain death for him and any soldier stopping to assist him. Wishik's actions that day eventually earned him the Distinguish Service Cross. His citation described this part of the battle:

> *The fierce enemy onslaught of small arm, automatic weapon, claymore mine, and grenade fire inflicted heavy casualties on the point platoon, including the platoon leader. Charging through the storm of bullets, Lieutenant Wishik took command of the stricken lead element. While exposed to the hostile fire, he positioned the men and carried the wounded back to the defensive perimeter.*[303]

Calvin reported that Wishik and the rest of the uninjured men continued to exchange fire with the enemy as they feverishly rolled back their dangerously extended lines. As the two men passed the next man in line, they would kick the soldier's feet yelling "fall back!" One after the other the American line began to withdraw in order to consolidate at the main company area. As Calvin withdrew, he came to the next man in line, one of the company's M-60 machine gunners, his best friend, Paul Conner.[304]

Conner had been experiencing his own brand of hell. He was among the lead element attempting to extract Phantom Force when the lines exploded with enemy gunfire. His Silver Star citation states, "A large enemy force attacked the company, hitting hardest at the lead element. Private First Class Conner, along with the rest of his squad, was engaged by a numerically superior enemy force while attempting to lay down a protection base of fire for the lead

---

[302] Adam Piore interview with Calvin Heath, 2009.
[303] Jeffrey Wishik Distinguished Service Cross Citation. Note: Calvin was at Wishik's side during this part of the battle.
[304] Paul Conner letter to Claire Mooney dated February 15, 1968.

element."[305] While other elements were rapidly moving forward to reinforce the lead elements, Conner and the other men of his platoon were desperately trying to lay down covering fire. Enemy machine guns were ripping the American lines apart and Conner and the rest of his platoon knew if the enemy gained the advantage the entire company would be overrun. His citation goes on to state:

> *Upon spotting the enemy fire coming from a fortified bunker, Private First-Class Conner unhesitatingly and with complete disregard for his own safety single-handedly assaulted the enemy position with automatic rifle fire until he was only a short distance away. He then silenced the position with a hand grenade. As he was returning to his squad, he noticed one of his companions lying in an open position, seriously wounded, and calling for a medic. Private First-Class Conner immediately moved to the site of the wounded man, administered first aid and courageously carried him back to a more secure area.[306]*

When Calvin reached Paul, he was in the prone position laying down covering machine-gun fire to keep the enemy's head down long enough for the other men to pull out the wounded and fall back. Without Paul's supporting fire it is with great certainty that more men in that sector would have perished during the withdrawal. Calvin kicked his best friend on the foot and screamed "Paul! Time to go! Pull back!" Conner turned and was pleased to see that Calvin was still alive. He nodded and gathered his equipment and began to move.[307]

Calvin moved to the next man in line to tell him to withdraw, but there was a sudden flurry of bullets hitting behind him and he knew instantly something was horribly wrong. He turned back to see his best friend on his knees, badly wounded, looking down in horror as

---

[305] Paul Conner Silver Star citation dated August 3, 1968. Note: Calvin recalls Paul manning an M-60 machine gun. His citation suggests he had an M-16. Paul could have been an assistant gunner and manned the gun after the gunner was injured or killed.
[306] Paul Conner Silver Star citation dated August 3, 1968. Note: According to Jeff Davis, this was possibly SP4 Clark Karrell, a member of Phantom Force caught behind the enemy lines.
[307] Calvin Heath interview with author, May 2013.

his insides began to pour out, his right hand trying desperately to hold his entrails in place. According to Calvin, Conner had taken a machine gun blast that nearly cut him in half. Calvin later recalled, "He was right on the side of me and how he got it I don't know. He cried, 'Help me!'"[308] Calvin scrambled back to help his friend, but he had seen enough death by that point to understand that there was absolutely nothing he could do. Conner's last words to Calvin were, "I don't want to die." Calvin later remembered telling his friend, "I got you buddy." At great risk to himself, Calvin tightly held his friend as the life quickly drained from his body. To Calvin, it seemed like hours, but in fact was only a few short seconds. The last thing Paul Conner saw before he passed away was the face of his close friend Calvin Heath holding and comforting him. For the rest of his life, Calvin had hoped that being there at that moment was somehow enough for his friend.

Calvin was now covered in Paul's blood. He gently laid him down on the ground and continued to move up the line to make certain the others, especially the wounded on line, were pulled out.[309] For Calvin, there would be more time later to process what had just happened to his friend. At that moment there were other men to save. Under intense fire, and despite losing someone close, Calvin continued to assist Wishik in conducting an organized withdrawal. Delta Company was now outnumbered nearly 20 to one.[310]

After the other men were pulled off the line and headed back to the main company area, Calvin held back and found another American soldier dragging Conner's body by the web gear back to the company area.[311] Calvin became suddenly enraged and smacked the

---

[308] Dr. Schweitzer report, August 27, 1997. Author's note: This is Calvin's version of Paul's death. The official reports, and the report the Conner family received, indicate that Paul was killed by a fragmentation wound. I offer that this is incorrect because it was Calvin who was one of the men with Paul when he was killed.

[309] Adam Piore interview with Calvin Heath, 2009.

[310] Note: This number is derived using 1,500 VC/NVA to 89 Delta men. Some estimates place the actual number faced at 2,000 which would place the ratio at 22:1.

[311] Author's note: Web gear is the belt and shoulder straps that hold the soldier's back pack, ammo, canteen, etc. It is a modular system that allows the soldier to add or remove equipment based on the mission.

guy in the back of the head with his hand. "I don't know who the guy was. I don't remember his name. He was dragging [Paul] and I got really pissed. I remembered that I said, 'Don't drag him!'" Under heavy and constant fire, Calvin picked up the body of his best friend and carried him back to the company CP area where he placed him among the other dead and wounded men.[312] He stared at his friend for a few seconds, absorbing the enormity of the moment, regained his wits, and then quickly returned to the battle. When asked later how he felt at that very moment, Calvin would only say that he was, "Really fucking pissed off."[313]

When Calvin and Wishik returned to the company area, Bucha ordered them to make their way back to the main lines and assist with the wounded so they could be medevac'd back to Phuoc Vinh. The minutes ticked by as if in slow motion as the men tried to reestablish their lines and recover the wounded and dead. The scene was total chaos. Mortar rounds were landing all around them and men were lying everywhere dead or dying. When I asked Calvin how many were wounded by that point of the battle, Calvin replied, "Just about everybody![314] As the men began organizing the wounded, it became painfully apparent that the jungle area in which they were now located was too thick for a helicopter to land.

As things continued to deteriorate, Dave Dillard was at the company command area trying to help control the Alamo. The incoming choppers were still unable to land, and they were under heavy enemy fire from all directions. Still, they flew in low over Delta's command post trying to drop supplies and gurneys for the wounded. During the early phase of the battle, the men at the Alamo managed to get a few of the seriously wounded, to include 1LT Jeff Davis, Phantom Force Leader, on a medevac.[315] Dillard later reported:

A few choppers flew in and gave us gurneys. We had a chopper hovering about ten feet off the ground and we were

---

[312] Adam Piore interview with Calvin Heath, 2009.

[313] Calvin Heath interview with author, May 2013.

[314] Ibid.

[315] Jeff Davis interview with the author January 29, 2016.

trying to get this wounded guy on, and I could hear ping, ping, ping as the chopper was getting hit [by enemy fire]. So, we had to wave him off. God help us if that chopper ever came down on top of us. He was getting fire from the south, so I knew we were surrounded.[316]

Dillard, understanding what the incoming enemy fire from the south meant, turned to inform Bucha that they were now surrounded. Before he could relay the information, however, Dillard was suddenly attacked and covered with swarming fire ants. He later stated, "Then all of a sudden I'm hit with fire ants, and I needed to tell Bucha that we were getting fire from the south, but I had the ants I had to deal with."[317] Anyone that has ever been attacked by fire ants knows the immense pain inflicted by these aggressive insects. Their bites are sudden, ferocious and sometimes deadly. Dillard, with the help of another soldier, quickly stripped off his clothes and dealt with the fire ants as best he could. Finally, just as he turned to Bucha to report the incoming fire from the south, the CP was hit with a grenade. Dillard continued:

I was then hit by a grenade and the concussion threw me back, but by this time we were already in motion moving south. We were walking into an ambush. We pulled back as many as possible into the CP area while circling the wagons. We had 4-6 people that did not make it back.[318]

What Dillard didn't mention in his account above was the concussion from the grenade blast severely damaged his eardrums, making it nearly impossible for him, as an RTO, to assist his commander. After a few minutes, Dillard, now seriously wounded from the grenade concussion, badly shaken by the blast, and eaten up by the ants, returned to the Alamo to do what he could.

---

[316] Dillard, Heaney, Rawson interview with author, October 9, 2013.
[317] Ibid.
[318] Ibid. Note: According to Mowery's narrative, Captain Bucha was able to get three medevacs in. One of the men evacuated was 2LT Jeff Davis.

In the meantime, Calvin and other men returned to the company CP area with some of the wounded, Bucha ordered all his men to fall back to the old LZ to the south (the one used at 3:40 p.m.) so they could evacuate the rapidly growing number of wounded, hunker down and call in artillery and air support.

On their way to the old LZ, the lead element, likely led by Jimmy Sherrill, encountered an overwhelming number of VC/NVA who were attempting to surround the Americans. According to Calvin, his small group encountered members of the lead group withdrawing in a near panic screaming. "They're coming and nothing's stopping them! There are hundreds of them! They're everywhere!"[319] Clarence Jones added:

We organized the remaining Troops and they began to move down the trail towards the LZ. Captain Bucha, his RTO, myself and a couple of others remained to form a rearguard on our back trail. Suddenly, we heard a hail of fire breakout on the trail. I moved toward the firing only to meet the remains of our Company moving back up the trail towards the clearing. They had been ambushed as they had tried to move towards the LZ. My heart sank. We were cut off. A large enemy force to our front, another to our rear. We had more wounded than we could carry out and our KIAs were mounting. My Platoon Leader was gone.[320]

Just as the men from the first group passed, the VC/NVA hit Calvin's small group with command-detonated anti-personnel mines killing several men and seriously wounding Calvin and Wishik. "I remember that vivid as all hell. I can remember [Wishik] flying over the top of me. I was thinking that he got blown up while I was standing. But I got blown off my feet too."[321] Calvin later recalled, "...we went about 50 yards down the trail, the NVA blew mines to our left front and opened up with machinegun fire, hitting Lieutenant

---

[319] Dillard, Heaney, Rawson interview with author, October 9, 2013.
[320] Jones, Clarence, letter dated April 22, 2002 recommending Harjo for Medal of Honor.
[321] Adam Piore interview with Calvin Heath, 2009.

Wishik, myself, and killing the man directly behind me."[322] Calvin and 1LT Jeffery Wishik now lay severely wounded on the trail cut off from the main body with nowhere to go, several other men including a photographer were now dead.[323] In a report to a psychiatrist in 1997, Calvin further explained:

> *I was wounded in my left arm, both legs, [my] back, and left side of my head with little pieces of shrapnel. I saw the Lieutenant get blown over my head. Four men ran toward [me] from the front and said, "You're all dead men!"*[324]

Within a few minutes of the mine detonation, Calvin and Wishik were joined by 2LT Jimmy Sherrill. Sherrill was part of the first group of men moving toward the old LZ when their group was hit by mines and small-arms fire. Juan Nazario and Steve Messerli were killed and Sherrill seriously wounded. Bill Pray, Sherrill's point man during their movement to the old LZ, stated, "I turned around and all the men were gone! I asked Sherrill, 'Where are the men?'" Pray knew the answer. Sherrill and Pray were the only ones left standing. Pray added, "Sherrill was hit. He was holding his stomach with his left hand. I yelled, you're hit! He said, 'Don't worry about it.'" Pray continued, "We lost the radio, so continuing to the site [old LZ] was fruitless, because we couldn't call in any air support or choppers." Pray was then hit and lay seriously wounded 100 meters outside Delta's lines for several hours before making his way back. Sherrill, most likely thinking he was the only one in his small group left alive,

---

[322] Calvin Heath affidavit, February 12, 1997.

[323] Author's note: According to Calvin, David Smith, a photographer from 3rd Brigade PIO, was killed instantly from a round that ricocheted off the trail surface. Captain Robert D. Williams 3rd BDE, PIO, in a letter dated April 16, 1968, to 1LT Jeff Davis states: "Things have been so quiet since the action last month that my people are really chomping at the bit. They have been told that they are not to be with the point element and to be careful. I believe that Smith's death made an impression on them. It is a very bad way to learn a lesson, but I keep reminding them, SP4 Harrell and SSG Vanalstine will be with the 3/187th."

[324] Dr. Schweitzer report, August 27, 1997.

was making his way back to the lines when he came across Calvin and Wishik.[325]

The VC/NVA had now maneuvered around the right flank of Delta's lines and within minutes had Delta completely surrounded. Within a few short moments, Calvin and his small group of badly wounded men found themselves caught approximately 100 meters outside their own lines, among the enemy who clearly had the advantage. Calvin understood the gravity of the situation and recognized their window of opportunity to return to the relative security of main lines was closing rapidly. As the main body of enemy soldiers continued to surround Delta, a small VC/NVA element spotted Calvin and the other isolated Americans and opened fire. In spite of being seriously wounded, the men quickly organized themselves and returned fire. They were not about to go down without a fight. Wishik's DSC citation picks up the action:

> *As they made their way to the [LZ], the communists exploded a command detonated mine, injuring three members of the party and killing the others. As he staggered to his feet, bleeding profusely from multiple fragmentation wounds, Lieutenant Wishik was assaulted by six screaming enemy soldiers. Dropping to one knee, he switched his rifle to fully automatic and shot the assailants with one long burst.[326]*

In spite of dropping the six charging VC/NVA, it was painfully obvious to Wishik, Sherrill and Calvin, the only survivors from their small group of volunteers that they were in severe trouble. It was only a matter of time before more VC/NVA would spot them, converge, and annihilate them. Wishik and Sherrill were severely wounded and bleeding badly, Sherrill taking several shots to his stomach.[327] As Calvin, the least wounded of the three, was formulating a plan to withdraw the other wounded men, he spotted another American crawling toward them. He immediately recognized him as SGT

---

[325] Bill Pray interview with author, November 2, 2014. Note: According to Bill Pray, the radio was lost when Messerli, who was carrying the radio, was hit.
[326] Jeffrey Wishik Distinguish Service Cross citation.
[327] Calvin Heath interview with author, May 2013.

Bobby Dietch. Dietch was with the lead element and was severely wounded and temporarily blinded. Following the sounds of the Americans, Dietch was attempting to crawl back to the company lines. Calvin stated, "I can remember grabbing him and he was all fucked up."[328] The April 22, 1968 edition of the *Screaming Eagle* newspaper reported Dietch's harrowing experience. It reads:

> *A group of NVA regulars surrounded the badly wounded, young American paratrooper down on his knees praying. They touched his head and hands lightly and began to talk among themselves. "Suddenly I became aware that they were leaving. I knew they had been talking about me," said 19-year-old Sgt. Robert Dietch, Philadelphia. "When they saw my wounds and blindness, and that I was praying, they figured I was no threat and nearly dead anyway." Dietch crawled in an attempt to get off the trail. He suddenly felt "the cold muzzle against his head." The owner of the weapon asked Dietch who he was, Dietch recognizing the voice "of a lieutenant," said "It's me sir, Sgt. Dietch." There he lay in silence as the NVA moved all around him.[329]*

Bucha was immediately on the radio trying to reestablish contact with his lost and isolated men. After several long minutes, Calvin finally responded and gave the handset to Wishik. Bucha asked Wishik "How far are you?" Wishik replied that they were "… about 50 yards outside your perimeter."[330] With most of the men now dead or seriously wounded, and now completely surrounded himself, there was little Bucha could do to help the trapped men. Based on the amount of fire they were receiving from all sides, Bucha knew that they were facing a vastly superior enemy and any rescue attempt would be disastrous for his remaining men. This was soon confirmed by the amount of enemy fire that an approaching helicopter received

---

[328] Adam Piore interview with Calvin Heath, 2009.
[329] Screaming Eagle Newspaper, April 22, 1968.
[330] Smith, p. 208.

while trying to resupply the men. Bucha thought, "Holy shit, that's a big unit that's shooting at the helicopters."[331]

Bucha quickly understood that the only way for the remaining men of Delta Company to survive the night was to establish a "status quo," much like William Travis did in Texas at the Alamo 132 years earlier, Bucha continued to consolidate his lines, hoping to hold until reinforcements could arrive. Delta Company's small defensive perimeter had now truly turned into their own form of the Alamo.[332]

In the meantime, approximately 100 meters from the company's perimeter, Calvin, Wishik, Sherrill and Dietch coped as best they could. Calvin later stated, "Wishik was hit real bad, Sherrill was hit real bad, Dietch was hit real bad. I just had the shrapnel wounds in my legs and when they blew the mines, I had got a big chunk in my leg, my arm and my head with all small little pieces..." But at least Calvin could still move.[333]

The wounded men exchanged gunfire with the enemy, and each went through several 20-round magazines. When the gun exchange finally subsided, Wishik considered his options. He quickly realized that he, Dietch and Sherrill, had no chance of returning to the company perimeter under their own power, but Calvin, despite being severely wounded might – if he left immediately. Wishik, knowing he was signing his own death warrant, turned to Calvin and said, "Calvin, get out of here. Get back to Bucha..." Without hesitation, Calvin told his commanding officer, "I'm not going to leave you!" Wishik, not to be deterred, then told Calvin, "That's an order!"[334] To which Calvin replied, "Sir, I'm not going anywhere... I'm not going to leave you guys behind."[335] When asked years later why he disobeyed a direct order from a commanding officer, Calvin said, "I couldn't have lived with myself if I did that. I was not going to leave

[331] Smith, p. 208.

[332] Ibid.

[333] Adam Piore interview with Calvin Heath, 2009. Author's note: By this point of the battle, Calvin still did not completely comprehend the severity of the recently acquired wound to his back.

[334] Calvin Heath interview with author, April 26, 2013.

[335] Ibid.

a man behind to die. In the Airborne you just don't do that. You don't leave anybody behind." He faded off and then added, "You just don't do it."[336]

Many heroes are created when an average person who is facing a life or death situation acts instinctively in a courageous manner. The clear difference between that type of hero and Calvin Heath, however, was that Calvin made a conscious decision to stay with the stricken men instead of saving himself. Calvin's older brother Bert later said, "[Calvin] was just a kid [when that happened]. He was told that they would come and get him in the morning, but he knew what that meant. He was on his own and [knew that he] may not survive the night."[337] Nineteen-year-old Calvin Heath decided to put the lives of the other men ahead of his own. He understood that he and the small group were completely cut off and had little chance of surviving more than a few hours. But, despite this, he stayed with his wounded comrades.

---

[336] Calvin Heath interview with author, April 26, 2013.
[337] Bert Heath interview with author October 24, 2013.

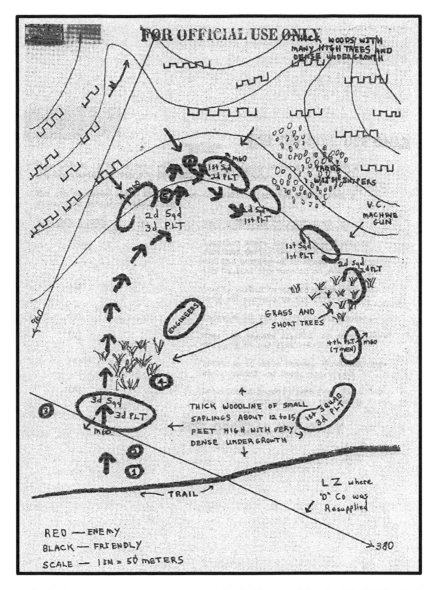

Above: Delta's perimeter at approximately 7:00 p.m. March 18, 1968. Calvin, Wishik, Sherrill and Dietch were located between where the 380 line crosses the trail and the "LZ where "D" Co. was resupplied." Official U.S. Army Records.

At some point during the chaotic battle, the VC/NVA had captured several American radios and now had Delta's radio frequencies so they could hear much of the company and platoon communications. Bucha called Calvin on the radio and asked for a situation report. Calvin reported his approximate position and Bucha told Calvin, "Stay right there. I'll be right up to get you." Calvin immediately radioed back and informed his commander, "Don't come up, they're all around us. There're hundreds of them, they're everywhere. They're waiting, don't come out. You'll never make it."[338]

Bucha then instructed the trapped men to play dead and he would come for them at first light. In spite of this, men from Delta Company, probably unknown to Bucha, made four attempts to try to rescue Calvin and the other men, all four attempts failed.[339] Bill Heaney later recalled the feeling of utter frustration after he had been unable to reach the wounded men.[340] Everyone within the company main lines who were aware of the isolated men now knew the group had little to no chance of surviving the night. Some of the men felt that they should have done more to rescue the wounded men and this horrible feeling stayed with them for the rest of their lives.[341] Calvin later stated that "There was absolutely nothing they could do."[342]

At 7:20 p.m., Bucha reported to headquarters that Delta Company was still under heavy fire from all directions and that they were now completely surrounded and pinned down. Five minutes later, he reported that he had ordered his men into a tight perimeter approximately 25 meters across; an area not much bigger than a regulation sized basketball court.[343] Five minutes after that, Bucha reported that Delta had suffered very heavy casualties with at least 50 WIA and five KIA.[344] This brought his effective strength to approximately 39 men against an estimated 2,000 enemy. The middle

[338] Adam Piore interview with Calvin Heath, 2009.
[339] Dillard, Heaney, Rawson interview with author, October 9, 2013.
[340] Ibid.
[341] Author's note: This is based on conversations Calvin had with some of the men during his first few reunions.
[342] Calvin Heath interview with author, May 2013.
[343] Daily Staff Journal, March 18, 1968.
[344] Bond, p. 30.

of Delta's command area was full of wounded and dead men, many of the wounded incapable of defending themselves if the enemy penetrated their perimeter. Things were rapidly going from bad to worse. Calvin noted, "Based on the number of NVA that kept passing us, we knew that they were in trouble – *real* trouble."[345]

Calvin, now knowing there was no way the men of Delta Company could come to their rescue, contacted Bucha and requested permission to get rid of the radio. "I didn't want to have that on me because if I had a radio they'd kill me for sure."[346] He added, "The CO said, 'Stay where you are, turn the radio off and we'll do our best to get you at dawn, [so] I took the radio off....[347] Bucha later stated, "I couldn't think of anything else to do. I heard the radio go off and that was it."[348] With so few abled-body troopers, and reinforcements fighting for their own lives elsewhere, Bucha knew that any rescue attempt outside their ever-shrinking perimeter would mean total obliteration of the entire company. Forced with absolutely no options, he decided to fight through the night and attempt a rescue at daylight.

Back in the small company perimeter, Bucha looked around and suddenly realized that if his men fired indiscriminately from within their tiny perimeter, the enemy, using the muzzle flashes from the American weapons, would be able to quickly establish the American lines and easily determine just how small a unit they really were. Bucha's plan therefore was to fight back with indirect fire. "We threw grenades at random times in different directions..." stated Dillard. "[As a result] the NVA had no idea how large our unit was, and we were determined to keep it that way."[349]

Throughout the night, according to Dillard, other men from Delta Company continued to perform heroic acts that also helped save the company. "Dickie Quick crawled out to set up Claymores, but he armed it before he went out. No one does that! But he did! He gave the clacker (detonator) to one of his guys and said, 'If I call out you

---

[345] Calvin Heath interview with author, May 2013.

[346] Adam Piore interview with Calvin Heath, 2009.

[347] Calvin Heath affidavit, 1997.

[348] Smith, p 208.

[349] Dillard, Heaney, Rawson interview with author, October 9, 2013.

hit it!'" Dillard thought for a moment and continued, "No one arms a Claymore first – no one."[350] Platoon Sergeant Dickie Quick was willing to give his life for his men. Dillard continued, "In the meantime, I'm trying to keep the wounded under control. I could see the muzzle flashes from the NVA guns and I can see their faces! That's how close they were."[351] 1LT Mike Blalock, also in the Alamo at that time, stated, "We were throwing grenades 5-10 yards out. If we hadn't they would have overrun us."[352] Years later, the men of Delta would all agree, that had the enemy realized just how few abled-bodied men Delta Company actually had left, there would have been no question – the Company would have been overrun and every man killed.

It was now 7:25 p.m. and the sun had set an hour earlier. The men of Delta were now utterly alone in the dark jungle surrounded by several thousand enemy soldiers. Green and red tracers were splitting the black sky everywhere. Explosions erupted throughout the jungle from all directions as the Americans and VC/NVA detonated mines and lobbed grenades at each other. Helicopter gunships and Tactical Air Control (TAC) arrived and dropped their deadly loads of bombs and fire power from above in an attempt to keep the advancing enemy from overrunning Delta Company. The noise at times was deafening. Through the explosion flashes, Calvin could see the silhouettes of hundreds of VC/NVA soldiers as they advanced through the area probing for Delta's weaknesses and trying to locate any Americans caught outside their lines. He could hear branches snapping, the enemy talking, VC/NVA leaders directing their troops, all of whom were hell-bent on maximizing the rapidly developing opportunity. The Communist officers knew that completely overrunning and destroying a company from the prestigious 101st Airborne would be a feather in all their caps, and this was one time they would not fail.

After shutting down his radio, Calvin and the other men attempted to consolidate their position as best they could. He stated, "I grabbed Lieutenant Sherrill off of the trail and brought him into the

---

[350] Dillard, Heaney, Rawson interview with author, October 9, 2013.
[351] Adam Piore interview with Calvin Heath, 2009.
[352] Mike Blalock telecom with author February 10, 2019.

jungle part. He was bleeding from his stomach and his legs were all shot up. I didn't know [at that time that] he was gut shot. He never said a word."[353] Calvin then grabbed Wishik and Dietch and dragged them approximately five to ten yards off the trail into the thick vegetation.

Above: The M-18A1 Claymore mine fires approximately 700 eighth-inch ball bearings in an arcing pattern up to 100 meters. It is known for its brutal effectiveness and lethality. Some describe the mine as a "Big, badass shotgun."

Shortly after Bucha instructed Calvin to turn the radio off, Dave Dillard heard voices through his handset. He later recalled, "I remember listening and hearing the radio coming back on, and hearing Vietnamese voices. I always thought they hollered at us or said something, but I think in retrospect we just heard them talking on the radio and it was our radio on our net!"[354]

Around 7:30 p.m., things started getting worse for the isolated men. Through the waning light, the men saw the dark shapes of enemy soldiers approaching. They stuck with their original plan of feigning death. They knew that they could not win a gun fight with so

---

[353] Adam Piore interview with Calvin Heath, 2009.
[354] Dillard, Heaney, Rawson interview with author, October 9, 2013.

many enemy soldiers. Calvin urged the wounded men not to make a sound and he himself rolled face down on the ground hoping the enemy would pass by them assuming they were dead. As the VC/NVA soldiers approached the men, however, Calvin heard the distinctive click of one enemy soldier switching his weapon to fully automatic. He braced himself for what was to follow. The enemy soldier then sprayed the men with 20 rounds of 7.62mm bullets. All the men were hit, with Calvin taking point blank rounds to the hip and to his right groin area. He immediately knew the round to the hip found its mark and later stated that it was "like getting kicked by a cow,"[355] but it would take hours for him to know whether or not he had lost his genitals. All he could do for now was lay motionless, bleed, and pretend he was dead.

The VC/NVA soldiers then moved closer and poked the severely damaged Americans with their rifle barrels. Calvin's, Sherrill's, Wishik's and Dietch's blood-soaked and motionless bodies convinced the enemy soldiers that they were dead.[356] Calvin later stated, "[Moving or wincing] meant my life, so I didn't make a sound. [The shots] picked me up and I landed right on top of my rifle. I never said a word. Didn't yell… Nothing… None of us yelled."[357] The pain was excruciating. Convinced the Americans were dead, the VC/NVA took Calvin's radio and moved on.[358]

Dillard later remembered that, "…after a hail of small arms fire, I heard the squelch [of Calvin's radio] break again and the voice of a NVA soldier telling me, in broken English, that they were going to find us and kill us all."[359] The voice Dillard heard was most likely from the group who shot Calvin, Dietch, Wishik and Sherrill.

At 8:10 p.m., Bucha radioed Lieutenant Colonel Forrest stating that he now had three seriously wounded men and they needed immediate evacuation. He also reported that he had "…four persons isolated on a trail of the initial contact." The Daily Staff Journal goes

---

[355] Adam Piore interview with Calvin Heath, 2009.

[356] Calvin Heath affidavit, February 12, 1997.

[357] Adam Piore interview with Calvin Heath, 2009.

[358] Note: Speculation based on the time line provided by the men.

[359] Dillard narrative for Harjo.

on to report that Bucha "…does have contact with these persons, [and] instructed them to hold position and try to resist contact."[360]

Back inside the company perimeter the remaining men of Delta Company were living their own nightmare. They repelled wave after wave of determined enemy soldiers and were now running dangerously low on ammunition. Bucha was busy trying to coordinate incoming air support and resupplies, but it was impossible for a chopper to land in such a small perimeter, now being assaulted by three enemy .51 caliber heavy machine guns. By 8:12 p.m., it started to look like all was loss, but then suddenly more air support began to arrive. This wave included the greatly-needed "Spooky," also called "Puff the Magic Dragon," a C-47 air cargo plane converted to a heavily armed air support system. Bucha had ordered his men to throw out bean bag lights and place helmets near them. The lights would give the Spooky gunners an idea of the perimeter, the pings off the helmets allowed Bucha to direct fire.[361] Their incredibly effective and accurate mini guns opened on the quickly advancing VC/NVA, decimating their ranks, quickly suppressing the attack, and providing Delta badly needed breathing room.[362] Calvin, lying in the jungle approximately 100 meters away, could see the air attack. He later recalled:

We were laying there, and the gunships would come in and I remember hearing [what] sounded like rain coming. So I looked up in the sky and I could see the stars through the tree tops and then I looked over from where I heard it coming from and I could see this yellow sheet coming… and that was Puff the Magic Dragon.[363]

What Calvin saw approaching through the trees was Spooky's 7.62mm General Electric mini guns "lighting up" the area. The three mini guns could each fire at a rate of up to 6,000 rounds per minute for a total of 18,000 rounds per minute – 300 rounds per second. At

---

[360] Daily Staff Journal, March 18, 1968.

[361] Bucha interview with the Pritzker Museum, 2006.

[362] Bond, p. 25.

[363] Adam Piore interview with Calvin Heath, 2009.

the time, it was the deadliest close-air support system in the American arsenal. To help the gunner direct fire, the ammunition belts included "tracers" placed every 10-15 rounds. This allowed the gunners to "walk" their fire around bean-bag lights and onto the target area. The "rain" Calvin heard was the mini-gun's bullets cutting through the jungle canopy. The "yellow sheet" he saw approaching was the guns' tracers. Thousands of friendly rounds were hitting within a few feet of the isolated group and Delta's perimeter.[364] Calvin adds:

> *We watched as they fired right over the top of us. But Bucha knew right where we were, so they got within five feet of us... firing... so that kind of kept the NVA off of us and every time they would mass up, to make their charges, our gunships were just chewing them up.*[365]

Calvin could hear the unmistakable dull thuds of bullets as they found their marks, especially when they found center mass, or the skull of the enemy soldiers. The sounds oddly reminded Calvin of someone hitting a side of beef with a baseball bat. The muffled thuds, as the bullets found their marks, were always followed by a blood curdling scream of a badly injured man or the soft, almost unperceivable sound as a man expended his last breath. Bill Heaney stated, "I was very surprised that Calvin and the others didn't get wiped out. Puff came right up to our lines."[366]

As Spooky left the area to rearm, the men within Delta's lines heard the screams of dying men outside the lines. Some thought the screaming was Calvin, Wishik, Sherrill, and Dietch being tortured by the VC/NVA. Several of the men, infuriated with what they thought they heard, wanted to leave the relative security of the new perimeter to try to save the men, but they were held in place by more rationally

---

[364] Note: Some might suggest that it was a matter of luck that the men were not killed by friendly fire. During our interviews, Calvin was adamant that it was Bucha's skill and not luck that they were able to walk supporting fire in that close. Bucha later stated he had his men arranged bean-bag lights so the pilots could zero in on the enemy attempting to break through.

[365] Adam Piore interview with Calvin Heath, 2009.

[366] Heaney interview with author, September 10, 2014.

thinking comrades.[367] What the men inside the lines were actually hearing was the VC/NVA dying a slow painful death after being shot up by Spooky's Gatling guns.

Other Rakkasans within the American lines, including Bill Heaney, thought that everyone outside their lines were now dead. "Once we settled into that [new perimeter] we didn't try to get out to them anymore. By the time we set up our perimeter, anyone who would have gone out would have been wiped out easily."[368]

The short break from the enemy fire allowed Calvin to test his badly injured body and assess his situation. He looked over to Wishik and Dietch and they were not moving at all, and Calvin now wondered if they were dead. Five feet away, Sherrill was leaning against the same tree on which Calvin had placed him earlier. He was visibly alert and extremely agitated. Calvin stated, "We were listening to [the enemy] yelling, screaming and dying. And that's when Sherrill was up against the tree and he started yelling at the NVA."[369] Elated with the overwhelming American fire support, the severely injured Jimmy Sherrill, knowing that he was dying, threw all caution to the wind and started to yell at the enemy all around him. When asked his thoughts as to why Sherrill yelled out at that point, Calvin replied, "I think he knew he was dying. He was shot up pretty bad. He had gunshot wounds in the chest and the stomach and fragmentation wounds all over." Calvin went on, "They were yelling at us and he was yelling at them. Those guns tore them up so bad that he was yelling, 'Come on you mother fuckers, come and fuck with us some more!'"[370]

Concerned that Sherrill would give away their position, Calvin, who still lay face down on the ground due to his back and hip wounds, whispered to Sherrill to be quiet. Calvin reasoned that any attention to their area would be the end of them all. Calvin continued:

And I was lying down that way and I turned over and I was going to tell him to be quiet and an NVA was standing right

[367] Dillard, Heaney, Rawson interview with author, October 9, 2013.
[368] Heaney interview with author, September 10, 2014.
[369] Adam Piore interview with Calvin Heath, 2009.
[370] Calvin Heath interview with author, May 2013.

there and shot him right in the head… killed him. So, I just laid back down and didn't move. He stood there for a few [seconds] then he left.[371]

Lieutenant Jimmy Sherrill was shot several times in the head and died instantly. Calvin, after watching Sherrill take the rounds to the head, slowly laid his head back on the ground and continued to play dead hoping the NVA/VC soldier who shot Sherrill did not see him move. He closed his eyes and waited for what seemed like an eternity for the next round to find its mark into his own head. Years later when Calvin told the story about Sherrill, it was easy to see that he held great admiration for the way in which Jimmy Sherrill died. "He went out basically telling the enemy to kiss his ass. It doesn't get much better than that!"[372]

Three days later, Sherrill's mother, Loretta Moore received a Western Union Telegram that simply read:

The Secretary of the Army has asked me to express his deep regret that your son, Second Lieutenant Jimmy L. Sherrill, died in Vietnam on 18 March 1968 from wounds received while on a combat operation when [he] engaged a hostile force in firefight. Please accept my deepest sympathy. This confirms personal notification made by a representative of the Secretary of the Army. Signed: Kenneth G. Wickham, Major General USA, the Adjutant General.[373]

Shortly after Sherrill was killed, more VC/NVA soldiers moved through the area, policing up their own dead and wounded. Thinking that the badly damaged Americans lying among the VC/NVA were dead, one soldier stopped at Calvin. Calvin, sensing and hearing the man, completely froze. He didn't dare to even breathe, and he hoped the darkness would conceal the fact that he was still alive. Lying face down, he understood he had very little chance of surviving a hand-to-hand battle with a healthy man hovering above him. Even if he could,

---

[371] Calvin Heath interview with author, May 2013.
[372] ibid.
[373] Western Union Telegraph dated March 21, 1968, Sherrill Family Collection.

he realized that there were undoubtedly many other enemy soldiers nearby who would hear the fight and come and finish off Calvin and the other men.

Left: Second Lieutenant Jimmy Sherrill, Delta Company, 3/187th, 101st Airborne Division. Sherrill was part of the small group of men cut off from the main body. He was killed during the evening of March 18, 1968. Jan Sherrill Hampton photo.

The VC/NVA soldier stooped over Calvin and placed his rifle across his lap and began to rummage through Calvin's pockets looking for items that could be used or later sold. Once he picked the low-lying fruit, the soldier went through Calvin's pants pockets. When he reached into Calvin's right-hand pants pocket, he touched Calvin's recently-acquired bullet wound. Unable to control his reflexes, Calvin flinched in pain, startling the enemy soldier. The surprised NVA soldier staggered back and quickly grabbed for his rifle to finish off Calvin. As he turned his weapon on Calvin, he fell slightly back toward Jeff Wishik. Wishik, although severely wounded, near death, and falling in and out of consciousness, came to just when his RTO needed him most. Seeing that Calvin was in desperate trouble, he gathered what little strength he had left, grabbed his knife and reached up and grabbed the man from behind. He then quickly and silently slit the man's throat, immediately killing him and saving Calvin's life.[374] The enemy soldier, his head now nearly severed, fell

---

[374] Calvin Heath affidavit, February 12, 1997.

across Calvin and bled to death.[375] Calvin, incredibly grateful for Wishik's actions, said nothing and continued to lay silently.

Meanwhile, the number of wounded within Delta's perimeter continued to grow. At 8:22 p.m., 3rd Brigade Commander, Colonel Mowery, informed the 3rd Battalion Commander, Lieutenant Colonel Forrest that he had requested four medics and two doctors to be inserted into Delta's area to assist with the seriously wounded.[376] This was extremely good news to Delta Company medic Ray Diaz. Throughout the night, Diaz worked feverishly doing what he could to save the men within the quickly diminishing perimeter. Early in the battle, Diaz himself received fragmentation wounds to the neck and chest. He patched himself the best he could and moved on to the men who needed his help.[377] He undoubtedly saved several lives that evening.

The Americans and the VC/NVA were now engaged in an ugly dance of death. TAC Air and helicopter gunships were in and out of the area attempting to destroy the enemy with accurate and deadly gunfire. When they left, the enemy would quickly renew their attacks on the American lines. At 8:35 p.m., Lieutenant Colonel Forrest, flying overhead in his C&C helicopter, came on site with a light-fire-support team from Phuoc Vinh and Bien Hoa. Four minutes later Delta's CP came under heavy enemy attack from the northeast and west and the light-fire-support team was deployed to those areas to keep the enemy from overrunning the American lines.

At 9:22 p.m., the enemy once again made an attempt to penetrate Delta lines and Bucha called in TAC Air to drop their bomb loads north of Delta's perimeter. The enemy was so close to the American lines, Bucha was forced to walk the deadly ordinance within a few feet of his own men. At 10:10 p.m., Lieutenant Colonel Forrest requested a Chinook helicopter to evacuate the wounded but was told by headquarters that none were available for the mission. At 10:24 p.m. a second wave of TAC Air arrived on station and deployed their ordinance to the north and northeast of the Delta lines. Twenty

---

[375] Calvin Heath interview with author, April 26, 2013.
[376] Daily Staff Journal, March 18, 1968.
[377] Diaz interview with author, February 5, 2014.

minutes later, Bucha reported that all movement in the area had stopped and there was nothing left but "burning trees."[378] The fierce onslaught from above was the only thing keeping the Americans alive.

With a slight lull in the action, a medevac helicopter was able to hover above Delta's small CP area, and under heavy enemy fire off-load Dr. William Schultheis and several medics and evacuate some of the more seriously wounded men. For at least a few of the men, the horror of the night in the deadly jungle was over.[379]

For more than four hours, the enemy attacked Delta Company in wave after wave, oftentimes running right over the top of Calvin, Wishik and Dietch. The human traffic was so high at one-point, enemy soldiers were tripping and falling over the wounded men. Calvin later reported:

For the rest of the night, the NVA were running away on both sides of us, to get away from the gun ships, I believe that the size of the NVA forces had to be in the thousands because it would not take hundreds of men four or five hours to move away from us. We could hear the company still being attacked throughout the night.[380]

Around midnight, as one of the waves of enemy soldiers moved through Calvin's area, one soldier made the fateful decision to stop and once again search through the men's belongings. This time it was Calvin and not Wishik who would respond with deadly force. Calvin, still lying on his stomach and soaked in blood, was rolled over onto his terribly painful back wounds by an enemy soldier. Knowing there was no way to prevent from wincing in pain and hiding the fact he was still alive, Calvin, in that split second, decided his course of action. As he was rolled onto his right side toward the VC/NVA, he drove the large survival knife he had hidden in his left hand into the man's right rib cage.[381] The sharply honed weapon sliced into the

---

[378] Daily Staff Journal, March 18, 1968.
[379] Ibid.
[380] Calvin Heath affidavit, February 12, 1997.
[381] Note: Calvin suggest this was a Bowie knife.

man's chest cavity, cutting muscles, colon, liver, and puncturing the man's right lung. The attack was so violent and so precisely and quickly executed, that the soldier was caught entirely off guard and could not respond. He silently stared at Calvin in utter disbelief, thinking, *how could I have made such a foolish mistake?* He died within seconds as his sliced organs ceased to function.[382]

Calvin now had two dead enemy soldiers lying with him, the last man lying face-to-face as he quickly bled out. Calvin watched as the man, only inches away, took his last breath. Calvin then took a deep breath and prayed for this hellish night to be over. For the second time that night, a man looked directly into Calvin's eyes as he died. The first was his best friend; this time it was someone else's.

Calvin later recalled the man's final moments with vivid detail. He described the dying enemy's emotions as they moved rapidly from shock to disbelief to acceptance and then finally to peace.[383] Calvin also noted his own conflicting emotions. He did not hate this man, even though a piece of him felt he should. He was a soldier just like him, doing his duty. He was someone's son, brother, husband and possibly father. For the rest of his life, Calvin often thought about that man.

Soon after Calvin killed the second enemy soldier, another group of approximately six NVA silently advanced towards their position. Calvin watched as they methodically moved from one dead soldier to the next. The sounds of the battle were all around him. He was fighting from going into shock, and he could not quite make out exactly what they were doing. VC/NVA, moving through wounded Americans, bayonetting them to insure they were dead, was a common practice in the jungles of Vietnam, and Calvin half expected to soon feel the cold steel of his enemy's blade. Questions began to run through Calvin's mind, *should we make a last stand? Are Wishik and Dietch even alive or conscious? Do we have any ammunition? Do the other men have weapons, and can they bring them to bear quickly enough if I make a move?* After thinking long and hard on the

---

[382] Adam Piore interview with Calvin Heath, 2009. Calvin Heath interview with author, April 26, 2013.
[383] Calvin Heath interview with author, April 26, 2013.

prospects, Calvin realized that they were in absolutely no shape to fight back. Any attempt to defend themselves would be futile. He knew he might have a chance to escape, but he also knew that any movement would bring attention to Wishik and Dietch.

Calvin remained completely still, wondering when that last bayonet thrust to the chest or bullet to the head would finally come. Miraculously, it did not. This new wave of enemy soldiers moving through the area were not interested in American plunder – they were there to retrieve their dead and wounded comrades.[384] They collected what they came for and, much to Calvin's relief, left the immediate area. Calvin, Wishik and Dietch had once again escaped death.

Above: The Douglas AC-47 Spooky with its three miniguns. It was guns like these that provided the "yellow sheet" and the "rain" Calvin saw and heard during the evening of March 18th. Their incredible fire power was a key reason Calvin, Dietch and Wishik survived. Source: Vietnam Conflict Aviation Resource Center.

---

[384] Adam Piore interview with Calvin Heath, 2009.

Calvin noted that during the first four hours of the battle, the gun fire and explosions were continuous. He later said, "Joe, it just didn't ever fucking stop. It was steady heavy shooting and stuff from seven o'clock until way past midnight."[385] He could feel the concussions of the hand grenades and see the explosion flashes. Vegetation fell like rain, and several times, supporting fire was so close he could feel the hot flying fragments peppering his body. Life or death inflicted by both sides was literally measured in inches, but despite the chaos, Calvin and the other men did not panic and continued to lay silently, using what little cover they could.[386]

By 11:42 p.m., Bravo Company had maneuvered within 300 meters of Delta's lines and could advance no further. Dealing with heavy enemy contact of their own, they reported that they were in no position to assist Delta Company during the evening and would proceed to their location at first light. Delta would have to hold their rapidly shrinking lines until morning. Calvin and the other isolated men, who were now presumed dead, were on their own.[387]

Left: Men of the 3/187th, 101st ABN DIV maneuvering through the thick jungle. The 187th spent most of their time in Vietnam on search and destroy missions. Many of the men stated they were often used as bait to draw the enemy into the open. Bill Pray photo.

[385] Calvin Heath interview with author, May 2013.
[386] Ibid.
[387] Daily Staff Journal, March 18, 1968.

MARCH 19, 1968 - HARJO ARRIVES

Greater love has no one than this:
To lay down one's life for one's friends.
John 15:13[388]

While the men of Delta Company were fighting for their lives, Colonel Mowery, the 3rd Brigade commander, ordered all other elements of the 3rd Brigade back at Phuoc Vinh to stand by to relieve the beleaguered men. He requested a rapid reaction force be assembled and be ready to assist. That mission was assigned to the 1st Battalion, 506th Infantry (ABN). In addition, First Sergeant Harjo, with the help of 1LT William Lechner, Ray Palmer and other NCO's located at Phuoc Vinh, mobilized what remaining men they could from Delta Company to first, quickly load the resupply helicopters, and then second, to be ready to fly in, support, and relieve Bucha and the surrounded men in the field. Palmer later wrote:

> *We organized a reaction force made up of Delta guys who happened to be in the rear at the time plus some cooks and drivers and we were ready to go into Delta's position that night, but we could never get helicopters to fly us in. So, we just listened helplessly to the radio transmissions. [It was] a bitter night.[389]*

Listening to the radio transmissions of the embattled men was a painful experience for the relief force assembled at Phuoc Vinh. 1LT Lechner stated that over the radio, they could hear the gun fire, explosions and screams of their comrades as they were viciously cut down one after another. They desperately wanted – *needed* – to be there with them, especially their first sergeant. As the battle progressed, Harjo's and the men's separation anxiety grew. Harjo was

---

[388] Note: During his communication with the author, Bill Mulholland, Paul Conner's hometown friend used this passage when describing his old friend.
[389] Palmer email to author March 21, 2014. Lechner interview with author March 7, 2019.

155

previously ordered back to Phuoc Vinh to prepare the company for an upcoming Inspector General (I.G.) inspection, and he loathed being in the rear when his men were in the field. Now he thought, *I should be with them, not here loading these goddamned helicopters!* Richard Cunnare, crew chief for one of the eventual relief choppers stated, "It was fast getting dark, and the sounds [over the radios] of battle were heartbreaking. Men dying while on their radios screaming as they were executed trying to rally their men. The NVA were running through them shooting the wounded."[390]

Shortly after midnight, on the morning of the March 19, the men were running critically low on ammunition and were virtually out of water. Many of the men began questioning whether they would or could survive the night. At 12:15 a.m., a resupply chopper loaded with ammunition and food was en route to Delta Company and arrived on site 15 minutes later. Receiving extremely heavy ground fire, the chopper veered as it attempted to drop supplies into Delta's CP area but failed to hit the mark by 100 meters, dropping the supplies in an area held by the enemy. The Daily Staff Journal reported that, "Gunships were immediately instructed to destroy the last supply [drop] so the VC would not get it."[391] Calvin wrote:

> *I was able to see what was happening to the company. The NVA had surrounded our company and were attacking them in human waves. In a short time, I heard, then saw choppers coming in over our company perimeter. The NVA were opening fire on the choppers that were coming in. I could tell the choppers were getting hit because the tracers that were going up would change directions.*[392]

All the helicopters that attempted to land during the early hours of the 19th were shot up badly. There was no suitable LZ and the men could not be pulled from the rapidly shrinking defensive perimeter to hack a make-shift landing area. Calvin added, "The NVA had heavy

---

[390] Cunnare, Richard, letter of support for Austin Harjo's Medal of Honor.

[391] Daily Staff Journal, March 18, 1968.

[392] Calvin Heath letter in support of Harjo's Medal of Honor, December 8, 1997.

machine guns and they were shooting the shit out of any incoming choppers, they really took a beating."[393]

By 12:30 a.m., First Sergeant Harjo had had enough. When he heard that the last helicopter missed the drop zone, he made up his mind that he would be on the next outbound chopper to personally manage the next drop. Bucha stated, "My first sergeant, Harjo, is back at basecamp, and I call him and say. 'Top, we got trouble. The resupply missed us!'" Unable to wait any longer, the battle-seasoned Harjo said, 'I'm coming!'"[394] Calvin stated:

The NVA had forced the choppers away... As the choppers left, the NVA came at the company even harder. More waves of the NVA went by us heading straight toward the company. With the resupplies landing into the enemy hands, the NVA had to know the company was really low or even out of ammunition and were getting set to overrun the company. I then heard choppers coming back.[395]

Richard Cunnare, the rescue helicopter crew chief adds:

He [Harjo]had driven up in an Army ¾ ton truck that had 55 boxes of 40mm for the M79s along with several boxes of small arms ammo. Also, boxes of medical supplies and 5-gallon cans of water. 1st SGT Harjo approached me and in the nicest way possible, asked me to help him get this resupply to his men. At first, I was a little shocked because we had already been in that hell hole twice and the request started my fear welling up again and my mouth got really dry. 1st SGT Harjo explained that the first resupply aircraft had almost been shot down and dropped the supplies into the enemy hands short of the landing zone where the 101st unit was located. He further explained that no one else would help him because they considered the mission a suicide.[396]

---

[393] Calvin Heath interview with author, May 2013.
[394] Smith, p. 210.
[395] Calvin Heath letter in support of Harjo's Medal of Honor, December 8, 1997.
[396] Cunnare, Richard, letter of support for Austin Harjo's Medal of Honor.

To insure the next helicopter would hit the mark, the embattled Rakkasans set off flares to mark their perimeter. Dillard later reported, "We set off flares and below it looked like day; above it was black."[397] The flares, however, also helped the enemy locate the American positions and better determine Delta's actual perimeter. Also, with the destroyed resupply of ammunition now in their midst, they knew the Americans were running out of ammo. The enemy reasoned that, "*Now* was the time!"[398]

With his men low on ammunition and the amount of wounded growing, Bucha understood the next load of ammunition could not miss its mark or the men would all die. Looking around and seeing no other options, he grabbed his flashlight, stood in the middle of the small company perimeter, completely exposing himself to enemy fire from all sides, and guided the next chopper to Delta's CP area. Dillard years later stated:

> *You're talking about a guy* (Bucha) *that in the midst of all this chaos and darkness, he's holding a flashlight. He stands up in the middle of the perimeter and he's holding a flashlight... and he's pointing it at the gunships so they could see our position and he's bringing hell in all around us. I mean bullets were [hitting everywhere], but it didn't matter. I liked all the heat I could get. If they wanted to walk that thing right in front of me, I didn't care. He was standing there with this flashlight in the middle... I mean this guy was amazing.[399]*

To give the situation proper perspective, Bucha stood in an area smaller than a basketball court while being shot at by hundreds of enemy soldiers. He later remarked that one of the thoughts going through his mind that night was, "What a terrible place to die. I don't even know where I am! I know where on the map, but there's no

---

[397] Dillard, Heaney, Rawson interview with author, October 9, 2013.

[398] Note: There was at least one report that indicates the ammunition was not recovered by the enemy.

[399] Dillard, Heaney, Rawson interview with author, October 9, 2013.

name. 'Where was your son killed?' 'He was killed... at grid coordinates [such and such].' What a shitty thing."[400]

Hearing that the last resupply missed the drop area, Brigade Command dispatched two more helicopters to resupply the men and to evacuate the wounded. First Sergeant Harjo made certain that he was onboard the next chopper outbound. Major Nelson E. Luce, pilot of that helicopter, call sign "Dust Off 46," explains the overwhelming fire power they encountered as they attempted to land in Delta's perimeter. He stated, "We approached the LZ and were informed of three 50 cal. enemy machine guns at gun pits triangulating our position by a forward air controller flying above our position." [401] Not only was the aircraft under heavy small-arms fire, they had to contend with three heavy machine guns. Others on "Dust Off 46" were Co-pilot W01 Thomas Murphy, Crew Chief Richard Cunnare, Medic Sp4 Dennis Telischak. All from the 45th Medical Company, 4th Flight Platoon. These men bravely flew into a maelstrom of hell to help save Delta.[402]

Bucha later recalled, "On the next helicopter, I see this nut standing on the skids as the chopper descends. He's standing on the skids, kicking out the boxes [of ammo], and then he jumps down beside me and he says, *I missed the last Alamo!*"[403] Bill Heaney added, "[Harjo] walked off that chopper like he was having lunch."[404] Richard Cunnare later added, "Ground fire was coming from everywhere... As I handed 1st SGT Harjo the last box he reached up and shook my hand. He then turned and jumped a considerable distance to join his men."[405]

Mike Rawson, who was back at Phuoc Vinh recovering from a fragmentation wound to the arm, also jumped on the next chopper out

---

[400] Smith, p. 208.

[401] Luce, Nelson E., undated letter in support for the Medal of Honor for Austin Harjo.

[402] Cunnare, Richard, undated letter in support for the Medal of Honor for Austin Harjo

[403] Smith, p. 210.

[404] Dillard, Heaney, Rawson interview with author, October 9, 2013.

[405] Cunnare, Richard, letter of support for Austin Harjo's Medal of Honor. Note: the helicopter crews who aided the men that evening deserve their own story.

with Harjo. Rawson stated, "If I couldn't be there, I was going to get on that chopper and at least help. Things were pretty dicey."[406]

After the battle, rumors quickly developed regarding the method Harjo employed to secure the last resupply chopper, load it and get to his men. While some of the survivors' stories may not be consistent, they all recalled a very determined Harjo brandishing a .45 Caliber Colt Model 1911 pistol. According to Calvin, the division chiefs at Phuoc Vinh had shut down all out-going flights for the evening, reasoning that any further rescue attempts were far too risky. Harjo jumped on a helicopter winding down only to be informed by the pilot that they were grounded for the night. "I can't fly out there, Top! I've been ordered to stand down," said the pilot to a determined Harjo. "…but if somebody put a gun to my head, I can't turn that down. I'd have to go then." Calvin's version continued:

So that's basically what [Harjo] did – he pulled a .45 so if anyone ever said anything, [the pilot] could say he was ordered to do it. Because Top, there was no way in hell that he wasn't going to be in a fight with his men. And so, they loaded up the ammo on [the helicopter] and they flew out over the top of the company and kicked out the ammo and grenades and shit and then at tree top level he jumped into the perimeter. And the guys, they all told me they thought they were dead until Top was in there. When Top got in there, they all said, "You know what? We're all going to make it out of here."[407]

Rawson continued, "While we hovered, it looked like a psychedelic light show. Red and green tracers firing in every direction. There were no defined battle lines."[408] Watching the helicopters attempt to land, Dillard once again thought, "If they dropped the chopper we're done. But I see this old man jumping off in the middle of it with only a .45 caliber handgun."

---

[406] Dillard, Heaney, Rawson interview with author, October 9, 2013.

[407] Adam Piore interview with Calvin Heath, 2009.

[408] Dillard, Heaney, Rawson interview with author, October 9, 2013.

The men, by this time, were in contact with the enemy for more than two days and in the battle of their lives for more than six hours. Most of their senior NCOs and all their officers with the exception of the Company Commander were severely wounded or killed. They were running out of ammunition, men and water. All the remaining men were rapidly developing a fear that there was no hope.

Dillard continues, "[Harjo] went around and talked to everybody – Calvin used to say how much Harjo meant to us."[409] Rawson added that, "It was like having Sitting Bull at the party!" Heaney agreed and added, "When he arrived, we knew we would be okay, that we weren't going to lose another man. The whole attitude changed and from that point on, we had no more wounded, no more dead, and nothing more happened to us."[410] Dillard added, "They always said that having Napoleon was like having a thousand extra soldiers on the field, that's how it was with Harjo."[411] "He was the hardest man I [have] ever known in my life and at that moment we all knew we could turn this nightmare into hope."[412] Calvin added:

At the time I didn't know it, but Top Sgt. Harjo was on the resupply ship to the company. The NVA at this time opened up with everything they had. It seemed like it was directed at the resupply ship. I could see tracers coming up from all around the company perimeter hitting the chopper. Again, the reason I know the chopper was being hit is because the tracers were changing direction in the sky. At the time, I didn't know it but Top 1st Sgt. Harjo was standing on the skid of the ship kicking and throwing supplies into the company perimeter. All the time the NVA were shooting the hell out of the resupply ship. He then jumped from the chopper which was 40 or more feet from the ground into the company perimeter to be with us, knowing we were outnumbered and would in all likelihood be overrun and annihilated. I have no

---

[409] Dillard, Heaney, Rawson interview with author, October 9, 2013.
[410] ibid.
[411] Ibid.
[412] Dillard narrative. Bond 39.

doubts that if Top 1st Sgt. Harjo had not made the resupply to our company that night all of us would have been killed. After the resupply, the NVA could not get through company lines.[413]

The stories from all the men speak volumes about Harjo's character and bravery that day. While it seems impossible that Harjo would have survived a 40-foot (four-story) jump into the confused jungle from the hovering helicopter without serious injuries, all the men there agree he jumped 30-40 feet to be with his men. The men thought so highly of this five-foot, eight-inch Creek Indian that he and his actions that day became legendary. Harjo, by all accounts, was all over the perimeter motivated, placing and instructing the men, most times at his own peril. He distributed ammunition and help to organize the wounded. Many years later, Calvin, who was by this point a man into his mid-60s, still thought Austin Harjo was one of the greatest and bravest men that ever walked the earth.

At 1:30 a.m., Bravo Company, who had maneuvered to support Delta, came in heavy contact with the VC/NVA. Bravo's Commander, Captain Dowling, reported that the enemy that attacked his unit was the same unit attacking Delta Company. At 1:55 a.m. Lieutenant Colonel Forrest ordered both Bravo and Delta Companies to stay in place and for Bravo Company, at first light, to proceed to Delta's location and rescue any men that remained.[414]

For the next few hours, Calvin, Dietch and Wishik floated in and out of consciousness. Sometime between 1:00 a.m. and 4:00 a.m., while the VC/NVA were still probing Delta's, and now Bravo's perimeters, the trapped men heard a soldier calling out for help. Calvin stated:

We were lying quietly, and they were still attacking the company and they were around us and I can remember hearing this guy [shouting] "Hey man bring me water. I need water." Talking in English, but he had a funny accent

---

[413] Heath, Calvin, Letter in support of Harjo Medal of Honor dated December 8, 1997.
[414] Daily Staff Journal, March 18, 1968.

and I started to crawl toward him and Wishik grabbed me by the ankle and said, "What are you doing?" I said, I'm going to go get him. He said, "That ain't one of ours. Listen to that voice. That ain't one of ours." I was listening and listening, and he was right. I didn't recognize the voice. So, we just laid there and [the soldier] kept it up for maybe 15 minutes to 20 minutes and then he quit talking and he started talking Vietnamese. I think it might have been a Russian. That's what we think it was. We think it was a Russian advisor.[415]

It was the second time that night that Wishik saved Calvin's life.

Calvin had now gone two and a half days with little or no sleep, food and water. He was seriously wounded and was fighting shock. There was little activity in his immediate area for the last half hour and he was hoping it would all soon be over. It was not.

Around 4:45 a.m. several enemy soldiers once again made their way into the isolated men's tight perimeter.[416] Thinking the Americans were dead, they sat down and ate their breakfast, with one of the enemy soldiers actually sitting on Wishik. Once again, the Americans knew that if they moved even slightly, they would be instantly killed. Calvin later said, "Well, they ate breakfast – I don't know what their idea was eating around the dead. I don't know what the hell they were thinking. They were talking among themselves in Vietnamese and we just laid there, we didn't move and they [eventually] moved off."[417] One can only imagine the incredible difficulty Wishik had trying to lie completely still while a man sat on his horribly mangled body and ate his breakfast.

As daybreak approached, Wishik, checked on the remaining men. He later recalled reaching to his right and touching Calvin's leg, thinking that he had felt him move earlier. When he found no response, he reached to his left and did the same to Dietch, but again nothing. Wishik tried to process the enormity of the situation. He knew he was too badly damaged to crawl back to the American lines

---

[415] Adam Piore interview with Calvin Heath, 2009.
[416] Note: Estimated time based on the evidence available.
[417] Adam Piore interview with Calvin Heath, 2009.

and he had little hope that others would find him before he died. Just when the situation seemed hopeless, Calvin, who was unconscious when his lieutenant touched him, came to and sensing movement to his left, said in a low voice "LT you alive?"[418]

Wishik and Calvin could hear the helicopters and gunships moving in as daylight was about to break. Wishik quietly asked Calvin, "Can you move? Do you think you can make it back to the company and get help?"[419] Calvin, knowing Wishik was too badly wounded to move, replied, "Yes sir." Calvin later stated, "The LT and Sergeant were hurt really bad and needed immediate help."[420] Calvin knew that he was the only one who had any chance of returning to Delta Company's lines. Wishik later stated, "One thing was for sure – we would not be making that journey together."[421]

At approximately 5:00 a.m., March 19, 1968, PFC Calvin Heath, then severely wounded in the back, ribs, legs, face, arms and head by anti-personnel mines, as well as being shot in the groin and right hip point-blank by an AK-47, locked and loaded his M-16 rifle and, with a useless right leg, began to crawl the hundred or so meters back to the company. It would be the longest distance he ever had to traverse alone.

Before he left the other two men, Calvin looked around the area one more time. He thought; *How in the hell did we make it through the night?* First, he crawled to Lieutenant Jimmy Sherrill still leaning against the large tree Calvin had placed him against hours earlier. He could only see the side of Sherrill that had not sustained any injury and hoped that what he remembered from the previous evening was only a bad dream. Calvin stated, "I checked Sherrill out and he was leaning up against the tree and I could see this half of him and his eye was open so I nudged him and he didn't move and as I crawled by him, I looked over at him and this side of his face was gone where they had shot him."[422] Years later, Calvin met Jimmy Sherrill's sister

---

[418] Wishik, Heath Memorial Ceremony, October 10, 2013, Hartford Connecticut.

[419] Adam Piore interview with Calvin Heath, 2009.

[420] Calvin Heath affidavit, February 12, 1997.

[421] Wishik, Jeffrey, Calvin Heath Memorial Ceremony, 10 October 2013, Hartford, CT.

[422] Adam Piore interview with Calvin Heath, 2009.

Jan. When she asked, "Was he shot up that bad?" Calvin replied, "No." He went on to say, "You don't tell the family he got shot in the face - you leave that out. They don't need to know that he suffered and getting shot that way…"[423] He gave his platoon leader and Dietch one last look, took a deep breath, and slowly and silently crawled away.

Calvin, covered with blood and mud and badly wounded, with survival knife and M-16 in hand, inched his way on his belly back through the jungle toward Delta's lines. Every movement he made, every inch he crawled was an agonizing ordeal. He was fighting to stay conscious and there was little left of his body that was not damaged and throbbing with pain. Calvin knew that he had to endure the torment a while longer; if he did not, he was certain Wishik and Dietch would not survive and everything they endured the night before would have been in vain. He was determined that was not going to happen.

As Calvin continued to crawl north, he thought about what he would find in the company area. There were no sounds other than the incoming helicopters and he was suddenly hit with the realization that Bucha, Dillard, Heaney, Diaz, hell all the men, could all be dead. He began to think that Dietch, Wishik and he would be the only survivors, and even that was not yet certain.

As he continued to crawl, Calvin could still hear the enemy moving about the area and he was forced to maintain the same level of silence he had throughout the night. He quietly thanked the hovering choppers for their covering noise. About 50 meters out from Delta's lines, Calvin observed an NVA sniper crossing the trail between him and Delta's perimeter. He knew the sniper was positioning himself to snipe at Delta while the main body of VC/NVA withdrew. Calvin put his head down for a moment and assessed the situation. He understood that dealing with the sniper might cost him

---

[423] Adam Piore interview with Calvin Heath, 2009. Author's note: I thought long and hard about adding this piece of information to this book. I ultimately felt it was part of the story the way Calvin told it and it needed to be added. I spoke with Jan Sherrill, Jimmy's sister, to get her thoughts and approval before adding it. I only hope the other members of the Sherrill family understand.

his life but doing nothing would cost another American soldier his. Calvin stated, "… [the sniper] went across [the trail] laid down, never saw me, or if he did see me, he thought I was dead."[424] Calvin, instead of trying to move away from the man, decided to eliminate the threat. At approximately 5:20 a.m., 15 minutes before sunrise, Calvin, calling upon what little strength he had remaining, quietly crawled to the man, surprised him, and a hand-to-hand battle ensued. Calvin, larger than the smaller Vietnamese soldier, struggled with his opponent as they fought in a life and death struggle. They rolled and wrestled as each man tried to gain the advantage over the other. Calvin, badly wounded, was tiring quickly. He understood that if he gave into the pain and exhaustion, he was dead. With his last ounce of energy, he found an opening and, like a lion killing his prey, he locked onto the man's throat with his teeth. This stunned his opponent long enough to allow Calvin to finally overpower the smaller man. Once again using his large survival knife, he stabbed the man repeatedly, finally killing him. The struggle seemed to last for hours, but in fact was over in less than 30 seconds.

Thirty-one years later, while speaking about the incident with Dr. Laurence Schweitzer, a psychiatrist from the West Haven VA Hospital, Calvin stated, "One thing that bothers me [to this day] is that I tore [the man's] throat out by biting him. I am not proud of that, but I didn't want to die."[425] It was the last life Calvin would have to take in the war.

It took Calvin several minutes to recover both physically and emotionally from killing the sniper. His energy levels were already on reserve when he left Wishik and Dietch, and even that was now gone. He wondered if any of the sniper's fellow soldiers heard the struggle and wondered if he would be the next casualty in this ugly and terrible place. By this point, part of him didn't care, as he was simply too exhausted. He wanted to scream, "Come on you mother fuckers! Kill me and get it over with!" He now completely understood why Jimmy Sherrill had yelled out the way he did.

---

[424] Adam Piore interview with Calvin Heath, 2009.
[425] Dr. Schweitzer report, August 27, 1997.

After a few more minutes, he collected himself, looked at the dead man lying in front of him, and in one brief thought apologized and crawled on. The thought of Wishik and Dietch lying badly wounded back in the jungle drove him on. He was their only chance of survival.

Less than an hour later, men from Delta would find the bodies of four NVA soldiers, through which Calvin had to crawl. Dave Dillard stated, "They were lying there like they were on guard duty. One of the men had an RPG. If he had hit us at that range he would have finished us off."[426] These NVA soldiers were caught between Calvin, Wishik and Dietch, and the Delta perimeter by a Spooky run. This is incredibly remarkable especially when considering the two groups were less than 100 meters apart. The last man Calvin killed was most likely part of this enemy group.

---

[426] Dillard interview with author, February 20, 2014.

Above: Paul Conner with his M-60 machine gun. Paul and Calvin met when they were training in the United States and became good friends. Calvin always hoped that being with Paul when he died was enough. Linda Hisert photo.

MARCH 19, 1968 - MAD MINUTE

Back inside Delta's small perimeter, Bucha and Harjo, fearing the enemy would try one last attempt to overrun the company before American reinforcements arrived and the sun came up, devised a plan. Dillard stated, "So at about 5:30 a.m., and I don't know who made this [decision], whether it was Bud (Bucha), I think it was Harjo. He said there is only one way to do this. And about 5:30 a.m., just before first light, we are going to have a 'mad minute.'"[427]

The "mad minute" is a tactic developed during WWI where all the soldiers in line would fire their weapons to clear infiltrators from a particular area. In the case of Delta Company, the men would fire in a 360 degree circle. Dillard stated, "We figured the morning comes and they're going to hit us. The first thing we wanted to get into their heads was that if you're going to come in, you're going to pay a [very high] price. Is that price worth what you're going to get?"[428]

Shortly before the "mad minute," at considerable risk to themselves, several men, including 19-year-old Bill Heaney, crawled outside the lines into "no man's land" to check the Claymores that were set the night before. The Americans had to make certain that the VC/NVA did not turn the mines around and point them at their lines during the night, a favorite enemy tactic.

Just after sunup, what remained of Delta Company silently locked and loaded full magazines, rounds, and belts into their M-16s, M-79s, and M-60 machine guns.[429] A few seconds later, the jungle exploded as every man who could physically squeeze a trigger, discharged thousands of rounds into the surrounding jungle. Hot 5.56mm and 7.62mm projectiles travelling at approximately 3,000

---

[427] Dillard, Heaney, Rawson interview with author, October 9, 2013.

[428] Ibid.

[429] Note: COL Mowery's narrative states the mad minute occurred at 7:00 a.m. Sunrise was 6:02 a.m. Calvin stated he called out immediately after the mad minute. The Daily Staff Journal reports contact with Calvin at 7:25 a.m. making Mowery's time of 7:00 a.m. more probable.

feet per second penetrated the forest with surprising efficiency, destroying everything in their path. Explosions from thrown hand grenades and detonated Claymore mines ripped trees apart. Bushes were stripped of their foliage and nothing, not even Mother Nature herself was going to survive the brutal onslaught brought to bear in that one short minute.

Unbeknownst to the men of Delta, Calvin was now only approximately 15 meters away from their lines. As soon as he heard the first rounds go off, he knew exactly what was happening. He hugged the ground hoping it would protect him from the incoming onslaught. He later stated, "I kissed the ground and stayed there until it was done." He hesitated, and then added, "That would have been a real bitch, getting shot by your own men after all that!"[430]

When the mad minute finally finished, an eerie silence fell over the jungle. Within Delta's tiny perimeter, the only sounds were the metallic clicks of the Americans ejecting dozens of spent magazines and reloading their weapons. Outside the perimeter, Calvin, dazed due to his loss of blood, and now dumbfounded by the sudden and utter silence, gazed in amazement as he saw what appeared to be a supernatural fog rising from the damp jungle floor. Strange shapes rapidly formed in the thickening mist, and for a moment Calvin thought his Native American ancestors, led by tribal elders, were emerging to guide him to the place where all dead warriors go. *Am I dead?* He wondered. *How could my vision have been wrong? I am not supposed to die here!* Suddenly, off in the distance, a familiar voice broke through the deafening silence. Calvin, quickly recognizing the voice, realized that his time in this world was not yet done. Those who waited for him on the other side would have to wait a while longer. Dave Dillard added:

> *The mad minute finishes – and you know the thing that impressed me the most was the quiet – awesome quiet – and you see rising from the jungle floor all of that gun smoke. So, all that gun smoke is rising and you're waiting for the next step. Everybody's ready. We're all locked and loaded. We're*

---

[430] Calvin Heath interview with author, May 2013.

already to go and we're sitting there waiting and what happens? We hear one voice come from outside the perimeter. "Quick!" he called, "Sergeant Quick!" And Sergeant Quick goes, "Heath! Is that you Heath?" "Yes!" Oh man we tore ass out there and God damn, the first words out of his mouth were "Go get the Lieutenant – he's still alive down this trail, but there are [NVA] still around... go get him." And so, Heaney and a group of us went down the trail and got to them."[431]

Calvin called out to the voice he had recognized, "Quick! Sergeant Quick!" After 13 hours of absolute hell and doing all that was humanly possible, Calvin finally collapsed. He later wrote:

I moved to about 15 yards from the company when I heard Top and Sergeant Quick talking, so I yelled to them not to shoot, that it was me. Top and Sergeant [Quick] recognized my voice, they came right out to get me. We were still being sniped at, at this time. I told Top that Lieutenant Wishik and Sergeant [Dietch] were still alive back down the trail, about a hundred yards... and that they needed help bad. Top said, "Don't worry, I will go after them right now and bring them back," and he did.[432]

Several men inside the perimeter immediately grabbed a gurney, went to Calvin, loaded him and brought him into the company CP area. The men were absolutely amazed that he had been able to crawl back to the perimeter given the wounds he had sustained. Dillard and Heaney further describe the moment; "Calvin had crawled back in from his position on his belly. His back was opened up like a watermelon..."[433] They continued, "He had a back wound from the base of his spine to midway up his back exposing rib bones and his spinal column."[434] Mike Rawson added, "He was out there all by

---

[431] Dillard, Heaney, Rawson interview with author, October 9, 2013.
[432] Heath, Calvin, affidavit February 12, 1997.
[433] Dillard, Heaney, Rawson interview with author, October 9, 2013.
[434] Bond, p. 40.

himself all night…"[435] Heaney sat back and reflected for a moment and then sadly added, "They didn't [even] have morphine or anything." Dillard continued, "…and he crawled, low-crawled, it had to have been absolutely excruciating."[436] Nick Goudoras, another Delta survivor later stated, "That he survived the night is nothing less than a miracle."[437]

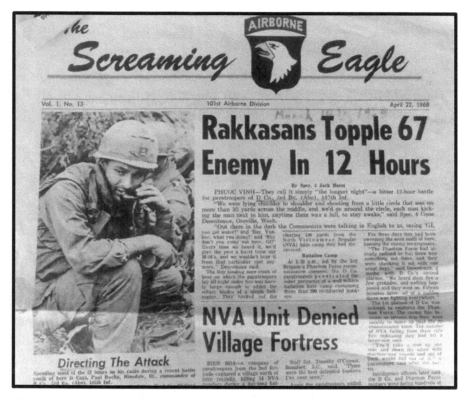

Above: A picture of the front page of the Screaming Eagle dated April 22, 1968, describing the battle of March 18-19, 1968. Shown on the front page is Captain Paul Bucha. The article, written by Specialist 5 Jack Hurst, started with, "They call it simply 'the longest night' – a bitter 12-hour battle for paratroopers of D Co., 3rd Bn.' (ABN), 187th Inf. 'We were lying shoulder to shoulder and shooting from a little circle that was no more than 30 yards across the middle, and we'd go around the

---

[435] Dillard, Heaney, Rawson interview with author, October 9, 2013.

[436] Dillard, Heaney, Rawson interview with author, October 9, 2013.

[437] Goudoras Email to author, September 21, 2014.

circle, each man kicking the man next to him, anytime there was a lull, to stay awake," said Spec 4 Gene Descoteaux, Orville, Wash." Descoteaux survived the war. Screaming Eagle Newspaper, Jerry Berry collection.

MARCH 19, 1968 - WISHIK AND DIETCH

As soon as Calvin informed the men of Wishik's and Dietch's location, First Sergeant Harjo organized a rescue squad that included Harjo, Dave Dillard, Dickie Quick, Clarence Jones, Bill Heaney, Mike Holland and Peter Colantuoni.[438] Dillard stated:

I was behind the First Sergeant when I heard him start firing. The First Sergeant killed three [enemy soldiers] within the first 15 or 20 meters, and three or four more before we reached Lieutenant Wishik and Sergeant Dietch, who were still alive. But he didn't stop there. I saw him continue to attack with speed and accuracy. He kept going and he kept firing until he reached the last of our dead who had led the way down the trail the night before.[439]

Like the sniper that Calvin killed, the NVA soldiers that Harjo killed were on the trail so they could harass Delta while their own forces withdrew. Their leaders did not want their main body of soldiers to be caught in the open by American gunships and they were quietly slipping away into the jungle. Harjo, determined to reach his own wounded men, kept running and firing at the stunned NVA soldiers, killing most of them as he made his way to the wounded Dietch and Wishik, and then up to his last dead troopers. Dave Dillard credited Harjo and others with punching a hole through the enemy line, allowing Bravo Company to advance and provide relief for the beleaguered men. After they secured their men, Harjo asked Dillard, "Did you see their faces?"[440] Dillard noted, "I knew what he meant. The NVA were stunned that we attempted such a rescue. The [First Sergeant's] tenacity overwhelmed them and they retreated."[441] Bill Heaney accompanied Harjo during his deadly assault and then

---

[438] Harjo's Medal of Honor request narrative dated January 16, 2004.
[439] Harjo narrative found in Bond p. 40.
[440] Dillard narrative found in Bond p. 41.
[441] Ibid.

established a make-shift, one-man perimeter allowing the evacuation of the wounded and dead.[442] As it turned out, many of the men Harjo and the others killed were the same men through whom Calvin had to crawl in order to make his way back to Delta.

As Harjo, Quick, Heaney and the other men moved south along the trail, Calvin was carried back to the company perimeter where Delta's medics, including Ray Diaz, Frank Parham, Ron McMurry, Michael Doyle, and Dr. William Schultheis, who had flown in the night before, immediately went to work on Calvin's wounds. Diaz cut away Calvin's clothes so he could properly clean, assess, and field dress Calvin's injuries. There was so much blood, mud, and other matter all over Calvin, that Diaz had no idea where to start. His first impressions were not good and once Calvin was rinsed off, all were amazed the man that lay before them was still alive.

Later, Diaz, a 33-year U.S. Army veteran, remembers Calvin's back being "laid wide open." He continued, "I had to cut away his clothes, cleaned him up the best I could in the field. I dressed his wounds and started an IV."[443] Calvin remembered Diaz backhanding another soldier, possibly another medic for scaring Calvin. Calvin recalled:

> *They kept telling me "You're going to make it. You're going to make it. You're going to be all right." I can remember the medic when he ripped open my pants and he looked and he went, "Oh my God!" So now he scared the living shit out of me and the other medic punched him to snap him out of it.[444]*

Calvin later stated, "I don't remember being scared until that moment. I really had no idea how bad I was. And before, all I could think about was helping Wishik and Dietch."[445] Years later when I asked Ray Diaz about the slapping incident, he stated, "I don't

---

[442] Dillard, Heaney, Rawson interview with author, October 9, 2013.

[443] Diaz interview with author, February 5, 2014.

[444] Adam Piore interview with Calvin Heath, 2009.

[445] Calvin Heath interview with author, April 26, 2013.

remember that specifically. We had so many guys wounded and dead, but he was a mess, so I don't doubt it."[446]

Above: Calvin lying face down on a stretcher shortly after returning to the company perimeter. The caption from the "Screaming Eagle" newspaper dated April 22, 1968, read "TO SAVE A LIFE – Working to save the life of a soldier following a heavy firefight near Phuoc Vinh are 101ˢᵗ Airborne Troopers [R-L] SP4 Frank

---

[446] Diaz interview with author February 5, 2014 and interview at Ft. Campbell, October 2017.

Parham, SP4 Ronald A McMurry and SP4 Ray Diaz, all of the 3rd Brigade's 3rd Battalion, 187th Infantry. Earl Vanalstine, U.S. Army photo.

Above: Calvin, Dietch and Wishik being loaded on a chopper. Far left with helmet Ray Diaz, second from left Audrey Perkins, far right, in the flak jacket, Captain Paul Bucha. Notice the broken chopper glass. Most of the choppers were hit with enemy fire. Earl Vanalstine, U.S. Army photo.

As Diaz, Parham and McMurry dressed Calvin's wounds, other men of Delta Company arrived with two more stretchers carrying Wishik and Dietch, both severely wounded and near death. Diaz covered Calvin with a poncho to keep the bugs away from his wounds and went on to treat the other two men. Calvin, unaware of Wishik's and Dietch's current condition, kept inquiring about their location and condition. But through the confusion and noise of the hovering choppers, as well as the medics yelling instructions, it would take a while before he would get an answer.

Dr. Schultheis quickly determined that Calvin, Wishik, and Dietch were among the most critically wounded and had to be evacuated immediately if they were to survive. With no dust offs available in the immediate area, Colonel Mowery ordered his pilot to land in the crude LZ the men on the ground hacked out of the woods with machetes. Dave Dillard reported that the LZ was so small, "… that the chopper blades were cutting foliage as it landed"[447] Mowery was determined not to allow any more of his troopers to die that day.

Above: SGT Dietch, 1LT Wishik and Calvin being loaded on Colonel Mowery's Chopper. Ray Diaz is in the front holding the I.V. The ammo boxes located to the left-front of the chopper may have been those kicked off by First Sergeant Harjo the night before during his daring resupply. Earl Vanalstine, U.S. Army photo.

Calvin later reported:

> *They got Wishik and that's when they loaded us up, and when they needed a chopper to get us out.... It was still considered too hot of an LZ. Division radioed down not to come pick us up, to wait a while. And we had a surgeon that dropped in that night and he said, "If you don't come and*

---

[447] Dillard interview with author, February 2014.

get them out, they're going to be dead." So, this helicopter disobeyed a direct order from a superior officer. That Colonel, he never made any rank above that and he should have.[448]

Whether or not Mowery disobeyed a direct order, as Calvin suggests above, is uncertain. The chain of command contains few people who can tell a colonel (brigade commander) what to do. What is certain, however, is that Colonel Mowery ordered his chopper to land at considerable risk to himself and his flight crew in order to evacuate the three critically wounded men, and for that, Calvin was forever grateful.

Above right: Raymond Diaz (right) talking with Captain Paul Bucha (left with flak jacket) loading the wounded. Colonel Mowery can be seen inside the helicopter, wearing a fatigue hat, helping to load the wounded men. Most helicopters resupplying the men the night before sustained serious damage.. Earl Vanalstine, U.S. Army photo.

---

[448] Adam Piore interview with Calvin Heath, 2009. Note: The assumption that Colonel Laurence Mowery did not earn any further promotions because of this action was speculation on Calvin's part.

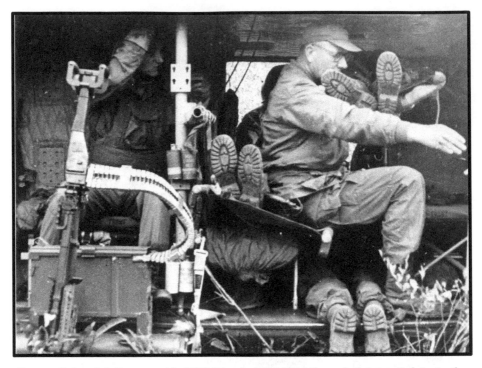

Above: Colonel Mowery with SGT Dietch, 1LT Wishik and Calvin. Calvin is the soldier with his feet pointing down underneath Colonel Mowery. Mowery is in the fatigue hat, holding one of the men's stretcher. Helicopters like the ones used as command and control, were not set up as medevac choppers. Earl Vanalstine, U.S. Army photo.

Calvin was feeling the full effects of the morphine as Mowery's helicopter lifted off the ground. He was in less pain, and for that he was extremely grateful. He glanced out the open side door of the helicopter as it banked north. He looked out over the lush green landscape of War Zone D below and marveled at its beauty. How could such a land produce so much heartache and misery he wondered? It was a question with no answer. He closed his eyes and felt the cool morning air blow against his face. It felt so good. Knowing there was nothing more he could do, Calvin quietly slipped into unconsciousness.

BATTLE AFTERMATH

On April 30, 1968, Colonel Mowery submitted his after-action report to Division Headquarters. It read:

On 16 March the 3d Battalion (Airborne), 187th Infantry conducted Operation BOX SPRING in southern section of Binh Duong Province from 16 March to 22 March 1968. The area of operation included long-time enemy sanctuaries in the western section of War Zone D. Numerous small unit actions to include airmobile assaults, reconnaissance in force, and Bushmaster-type operations were conducted throughout the area of operation. Participating units experienced light but steady contact with major action beginning the afternoon and early evening hours and continuing into the night, the employment of night operations in conjunction with the use of scout dogs kept the enemy off balance; often catching him by surprise and forcing him to fight a brief but tenacious battle in an effort to break contact. The persistence of friendly forces forced the enemy to move his position constantly which apparently resulted in the permanent relocation of some of the enemy units. Basecamps, which had been considered sanctuaries by the enemy, were cleared and destroyed. At 1650 hrs. 22 March the last Company was moved by air to Phuoc Vinh Base and Operation BOX SPRINGS terminated. 16 US personnel were killed, 62 wounded of which 52 were evacuated from the battlefield. Enemy losses were 147 killed.[449]

---

[449] After-action Report, Colonel Mowery, dated 30 April 1968. Author's note: I believe "BOX SPRINGS" was the overall brigade operational name for the mission. Operation "Rakkasan Chaparral" was the 187th's portion of the overall mission. COL Mowery's after-action report also includes casualties for units other than just Delta Company.

The men of Delta Company, many of whom were injured themselves, worked feverishly to treat and evacuate the more seriously wounded men and then prepare the dead for transport back to the base. It took several hours and a number of choppers to accomplish this task. Between 9:00 a.m. and 10:00 a.m., the balance of the Delta's men, most of them walking wounded, all exhausted and emotionally drained, boarded a helicopter and left the un-named place in the dense jungle near Phuoc Vinh. Dillard and Harjo were among the last men to leave the company perimeter.

The pilot of the last helicopter, after attempting to leave with the last load of men, told Harjo the aircraft was too heavy, and that one man had to get off. Harjo was not about to leave one of his troopers behind after the night they had experienced, and he made it perfectly clear to the pilot that leaving a man behind was not an option. Dillard states, "[The pilot] had to back the aircraft up so he could get a running start to clear the LZ... [Harjo] made darn sure we were all getting out of there."[450]

One group that does receive enough credit in this piece is Phantom Force. They sustained thirty-eight percent casualties during Operation Rakkasan Chaparral. Dennis Cunningham and Monte Cooley lost their lives in this action. First Lieutenant Jeff Davis, Platoon Sergeant Forest Messer, Squad Leader Rick Shoup and Clark Karrell were all wounded in action. Gene Hobson, Don Lescault, John Hunt, Roger Elling, James Martinez, Doug Pinder, Ed Crowley, Jerry Brown, Bill Graham[451], Sammy Washburn and Peter Gliha completed the mission. Those not evacuated to the U.S., healed and returned to their duties, always taking the point position. Rick Shoup's son David produced the film titled *Phantom Force Revisited*.[452] It was masterfully done and depicts what Phantom force endured during the war.

In the aftermath of the battle, the Rakkasans found "147 NVA/VC bodies lying strewn throughout the area of the battle and

---

[450] Dillard interview with author, February 2013.

[451] Note: Jerry Brown and Bill Graham and were assigned to the LRRP platoon at that time, but I was unable to verify if they participated in the mission. It is likely they did.

[452] *Phantom Force Revisited* is found at: https://www.youtube.com/watch?v=tDS-p036meg

huge blood trails and other tangible evidence [that] suggested [a] tremendous number of enemy casualties."[453] PLT SGT Dickie Quick stated that one of the pilots stated, "...they could see the enemy pulling dead away by the dozens."[454] While the exact number of enemy dead and wounded will never be known, many involved in the battle place enemy casualties at 400 to 500 men. Based on Calvin's report about several waves of VC/NVA coming through his area to recover bodies and the amount of air support that came to the Americans' aid, these estimates make sense.

Left: Paul Bucha during the morning of March 19, 1968. This picture gives the reader a sense of the environment in which the men fought the night before. Earl Vanalstine, U.S. Army photo.

As far as the American casualties were concerned, Bond reported that between March 16 and 22, 1968, the 3rd Battalion sustained 14 killed in action and 97 wounded, for a total of 111 casualties. Mowery's after-action report lists 16 dead and 62 wounded, for a total of eighty-six. The U.S. Army Itemized Report, declassified in 1994, states there were 158 confirmed enemy killed with another 30 possible and 18 Americans killed with 95 wounded for a total of 113

---

[453] Colonel Mowery's report found in Bond p. 47. Note: Jones, p. 152, suggests 156 enemy killed. It is uncertain which is correct.

[454] Quick interview with the author, November 8, 2016.

casualties. The Vietnam Memorial, in Washington, D.C., lists the dead from Delta Company, 3rd Battalion, 187th Infantry (ABN), 101st Airborne Division during that operation as PFC Michael Carroll, PFC Paul Conner, SGT Cecil Davis, SGT Roy Estrada, PFC Larry Green, SP4 Steven Messerli, SP4 Juan Nazario, and 2LT Jimmy Sherrill. The men's names are listed on Panel 45E.[455] Other men who supported Delta during that mission, to include Phantom Force and the combat engineers, also became casualties – some of their names are also listed on the Vietnam Memorial.

Above: "The Morning After." According to Calvin, as the men were getting ready to evacuate the dead, one of the ponchos blew off 2LT Jimmy Sherrill's face. It was too much for the exhausted commander, Captain Paul Bucha. Earl Vanalstine, U.S. Army photo.

The exact number of Delta casualties during those two days has been difficult to determine. Dillard and some of the other men who fought, later reported that most of the remaining men of Delta were

---

[455] Source: Virtual Wall found at: www.virtualwall.org/units.htm.

wounded and they estimate that they had sustained nearly 80% casualties. If this is correct, of the 89 men who started the battle on March 18, 1968, fewer than 20 were unscathed on March 19.

After the evacuation of Delta Company, reinforcements were flown in, and the battle with the Phu Loi Battalion of the Dong Nai Regiment and other VC and NVA elements continued for several more days. In a 1997 narrative Buch reported that "A company size [enemy] unit fleeing the battle area was ambushed by C Company a few hundred yards from the D Company battle location."[456] Fleeing enemy soldiers were not the only things found after the battle. The Americans continued to find several more tons of rice, as well as additional bunkers, basecamps, and other evidence that they were in pursuit of a very large force.[457]

After the epic battle, the rifle company known six months earlier as the "Clerks and Jerks," painstakingly assembled and trained by Bucha and Harjo, ceased to exist. Some of the men, like Dave Dillard, recovered from their wounds in-country, but many were sent home badly injured or in flag-draped coffins. After the battle, Dillard and many of the other survivors were "infused" into the 101st Airborne Division's 1st Brigade. Bill Heaney remained with Delta Company, 3/187th and was badly wounded on August 3, 1968 by a hidden booby trap while on an ambush mission near the Hobo Woods. After eight months of fighting, he was sent home badly injured.[458] Bucha was transferred shortly after the battle and what little remained of Delta Company was now under the command of Captain Ron Nelson. The men who replaced Calvin and the other fallen Rakkasans were not all airborne qualified, creating considerable problems for both the new men and the few remaining airborne troopers from the original roster. Of the more than 120 men from Delta Company who arrived in Vietnam in December 1967, only 32 remained after the battle.[459]

---

[456] Bucha, request for Harjo's CMH narrative dated September 15, 1997.
[457] Daily Staff Journal, March 19, 1968.
[458] Heaney interview with author, September 10, 2014.
[459] Dillard interview with author, February 19, 2014.

Upon arriving at Phuoc Vinh, Bucha and his remaining officers were debriefed. The wounded were attended to and those very few who were not wounded went to their barracks to clean up, change uniforms, and get something to eat. Walking past the bunks of the men who would not return was extremely difficult for the survivors, and a few of them broke down. Two of those bunks belonged to Calvin Heath and his best friend Paul Conner.

Dave Dillard, who stayed in Vietnam with the 1st Brigade, later stated:

We were in lots of firefights. In 1970 I was shipped back [to Vietnam] again and I went through more, but nothing would ever compare to the intensity of this night in March of 1968. It was not like any... Most firefights were like this - rat-ta-tat- tat-tat, rat-ta- tat- tat-tat, rat-ta- tat- tat-tat, back... back, back and forth. They ran and it's over. We had a lot of those. Sometimes it was glorious, I can remember getting in a firefight and we had three tanks with us. My God! Three tanks! I mean give me a shot in there somewhere. These things are throwing hell out there you know, and we knocked out an NVA company in a matter of 20 minutes and we're walking over there picking up the pieces. Great! Now, I remember it, but did it affect me? No... it was a win-win. [The battle of March 16-19] was a lose-lose. This was different. We loss so many men.[460]

Dillard went on to state that "It wasn't a night [that history] will remember. But to us, it was *the* major [event] in our lives, because it shaped our lives. And there is never a day that goes by that I don't think about that day."[461] Bill Heaney added his thoughts. "I was with Sherrill the whole night until the end. I should have been with him that night. We got separated after we cut the LZ." Heaney sat back and it was easy to see he was transported back in time for a few seconds. Looking down, he sadly added:

---

[460] Dillard, Heaney, Rawson interview with author, October 9, 2013.
[461] Ibid.

Unless you were there that night, you can't understand the feeling. You don't know what we went through, no matter [what]. It was not the biggest battle of Vietnam. It wasn't the biggest battle the 187th was ever in! But it was something that shaped the rest of our lives. We have to carry that now with us forever. There was nobody there that night that doesn't have PTSD.[462]

Jeffery Wishik, the man who lay with Calvin gravely wounded that night, and saved his life by killing an NVA soldier would later write:

It is my strongest conviction that sound leadership by soldiers like Captain Bucha, First Sergeant Harjo, and Sergeant First Class Quick, unselfish devotion to duty to their soldiers, luck, a timely and critically needed resupply of ammunition, plus the protecting light of God are the reasons that Americans like myself and the rest of D Company lived through hell to tell about it.[463]

In May of 2013, I asked Calvin what bothered him most about the battle. Without hesitation, he replied, "Losing Paul. Having your best friend die in your arms was the toughest. After that I was fighting mad."[464] I'll never forget the image of Calvin sitting in my kitchen, taking a sip of coffee and wiping away tears as he recalled the death of his friend. Forty-six years later, it still bothered my 64-year-old friend greatly that he did not save Paul.

In 2009, reflecting on the battle, Calvin told Adam Piore:

I'm Native American. [Earlier that night] I got visited and I knew that I was going to make it out alive. My spirit told me I was going to make it. When I was lying there, that was right after I got hit and that's before they overran us that first time, before I had any hand-to-hand combat – I was

---

[462] Dillard, Heaney, Rawson interview with author, October 9, 2013.
[463] Wishik narrative in support of Harjo found in Bond, p. 42.
[464] Calvin Heath interview with author, April 26, 2013.

lying there and this ah – People are going to think I talk to the wind, but this voice talked to me. And it said, "You're going to be all right, you're going to make it." My spirit told me, "You're going to make it out. You're going to be OK." I heard it plain as day and it wasn't out loud, but it was in my head. I was calm. I really was. The only thing I was [afraid of] was... I wasn't scared of dying... it was being captured. Or, you'd rather be dead than lose an arm or leg. That was our mentality back then anyway. And that's stupid. Being alive, even if you lose an arm, is lot better than being dead. When you're 19 years old, 18 years old, you're not thinking that at all. You know you don't want to be messed up when you go back home. [465]

Calvin reiterated that one of his greatest concerns during the battle was the well-being of Wishik and Dietch. "All I wanted to do was get back and get help." He went on to state, "Years later, I found out from the guys that they would not have been mad at me if I just left them and got back to our lines, but I just couldn't do that."[466] He stated:

I just wanted to get back... to get help for the other guys. That was pretty much what I was thinking. He was my First Lieutenant, but we were on a first name basis. You end up getting close and when they are hurting that's what you are thinking of. You're trying to save them, you're not thinking about yourself. I know now that if I had [gone back earlier when I had the chance] that, nobody would have found fault with that at all, but they would have been dead for sure... [467]

Calvin later added, "How we made it through that night, I don't know. I was all torn up, and the Lieutenant and Sergeant Dietch were in worse shape than me."[468] When reflecting about the wave after

---

[465] Adam Piore interview with Calvin Heath, 2009.
[466] Calvin Heath interview with author, April 26, 2013.
[467] Adam Piore interview with Calvin Heath, 2009.
[468] Calvin Heath interview with author, May 2013.

wave of VC/NVA that came through their area shooting, tripping over and even sitting on them, Calvin added, "Why they didn't just shoot us in the head is beyond me."[469]

Above: The names of the last 32 men from the original roster of Delta Company, 3/187th Infantry (Airborne), 101st Airborne Division. According to Bill Pray, this list was given to him by First Sergeant Clifford Funk his last day in Vietnam. "1st Sgt Funk gave me this list of those rotating home... When we deployed to Vietnam in 1967, there was close to 150 of us. This was all of the original 150 left to rotate

---

[469] Ibid, April 26, 2013.

home together. The list was written on the back of a Sick Call slip. The name Chambers was later crossed out. Compliments of the men of Delta Company.

Other soldiers who survived the battle still reflect over what SP5 Jack Hurst would call "the longest night." Mike Blalock stated, "For the most part we were used as bait. Once we found the enemy then artillery and air power were brought in."[470] During a 2013 Hartford, Connecticut memorial service honoring Calvin, who had just passed away, Jeffrey Wishik stated:

Calvin, severely wounded, struggled to crawl for help. I am not sure of much after that, but I thank God he was successful. There will always be a lot that I am not sure of, when it comes to Vietnam. But there is one thing which I am absolutely certain – My Native American RTO, and battle friend, saved the lives of Dietch and his LT [that day].[471]

According to Bond, during their time in Vietnam (1967-1968), the 3rd Battalion, 187th Infantry (Airborne), 101st Airborne Division became the United States Army's most highly decorated airborne battalion. They received:

- 1 Medal of Honor, Captain Paul Bucha (Note: four other men, Corporal Michael W. Langer, Specialist Fifth Class Dennis F. Moore, First Sergeant Austin Harjo, and Colonel Robert L. Friedrich were also recommended)
- 5 Distinguished Service Crosses
- 95 Silver Stars[472]
- 259 Bronze Stars with "V" Device
- 720 Bronze Stars for Meritorious Service
- 3 Air Medals with "V" Device
- 560 Air Medals
- 87 Army Commendation Medals with "V" Device

---

[470] Mike Blalock telecom with author February 10, 2019.

[471] Heath Memorial Ceremony, October 10, 2013, Hartford Connecticut.

[472] Note: Bond lists 95, which did not include Calvin's awarded in 1999 and does not include any awards that may have been awarded after 2006.

- 573 Army Commendation Medals and
- 202 Purple Hearts[473]

Many more men earned and were recommended for medals during the battle of March 16-18, 1968 but did not receive them due to command's failure to properly follow up. Calvin Heath and Austin Harjo, recommended for the Silver Star, were among those not properly recognized, despite their heroic efforts.[474] For his actions on March 18-19, 1968, Bill Heaney and others should have earned the Bronze Star, but like Calvin's medals, it never made its way to the men who were willing to give everything for their friends. The lack of proper recognition by the U.S. Army was only one of the many injustices the men of Delta Company endured.

---

[473] Bond, p. M.

[474] Note: Calvin's was finally recognized in 1999, 31 years after the battle. Heaney, and many others, still have not received the awards they so justly deserve.

Above: Paul Conner's parents Marie and Nathan Conner receiving his Silver Star in August 1968. It's easy to see the utter sadness on the Conners' faces, even five months after the death of their son. It is unfortunate that the Conners never got the chance to speak with Calvin about their son's heroic role in the battle. Nathan Conner photo.

This portion of the book would not be complete without addressing the following: James Bond, in his 2006 book titled, *Rakkasans; A History and Collection of Personal Narratives from Members of The 3rd Battalion (Airborne), 187th Infantry, 101st Airborne Division, Republic of Vietnam*, reported that when Phantom Force and Delta Company's lead elements found themselves in the VC/NVA basecamp that it appeared "...that Company D had been led by the VC into an ambush and then surrounded by the VC/NVA forces."[475] While there was no doubt that Delta Company was

---

[475] Bond, p. 27.

surrounded, isolated, and nearly destroyed, the men of Delta to include Calvin, strongly disagreed with Bond's assessment of the battle. Years later, this topic still provoked great emotion with Calvin and the other men from Delta. Several times during our 2013 interviews, Calvin stated, "The enemy does *not* lead you into an ambush into their own camp! They just don't do that."[476] Colonel Floyd "Jeff" Davis, Phantom Force's platoon leader, agreed with Calvin and later stated:

> *...from the perspective of the NVA/VC commanders: They had put a lot of effort into building their camps. They had recuperating soldiers. They had no reason to lure U.S. forces into their base camp when we could have attempted to fight earlier and elsewhere.* [477]

Others, to include Phu Loi Battalion soldiers Nqyuen Trong Quac, Thanh Nguyen and Nguyen Ngoc Duong who fought that day against the Americans, have suggested that after TET, the 7th NVA, the Dong Nai Regiment, and their support units established this base camp to refit and resupply. They had no intention of taking on the Americans in an all-out battle, one they could not have won when considering the American air and artillery power.[478]

It is not my place or intent to question Bond's assessment. The one undeniable fact, however, was that Delta Company successfully completed their mission. They located the enemy and despite being vastly outnumbered, they held their ground, and were able to direct "hell from above" to destroy a large portion of the enemy they sought.

On March 21, 1968, Calvin and most of the men from Delta Company were awarded the Purple Heart, "For Wounds Received in Action on 19 March 1968."[479] On November 5, 1968, the Adjutant General's office also issued General Order 9029 awarding 53 men

---

[476] Calvin Heath interview with author, April 26, 2013.

[477] Davis Email dated January 22, 2016.

[478] Phantom Force Revisited by David Shoup, 2017 Version. Found at: https://www.youtube.com/watch?v=tDS-p036meg

[479] General Order 59 dated March 20, 1968, Purple Heart Citation, Headquarters 24th Evacuation Hospital.

from Delta Company, 3/187th Infantry (ABN), 101st Airborne Division, most of whom fought in the battle, Bronze Stars "For meritorious service in connection with military operations against a hostile force" during the period of "01 January 1968 to 31 August 1968."[480] Conspicuously missing from the list was PFC Calvin Heath, who was nominated for a Silver Star, an award he would not receive for 31 years.

Operation Rakkasan Chaparral was an extremely costly affair. The 187th nearly lost an entire company, and two aircraft. After-action reports indicate that many of the military planners involved felt it was worth the price paid, but some of the men who fought there disagreed. The last elements of Alpha, Bravo, and Charlie Companies of 3rd Battalion, and elements of the 506th, later sent in for reinforcement and support, finally returned to base before midnight on March 22, 1968.[481] One hundred and sixty hours after it began, Operation Rakkasan Chaparral was officially over.

The remaining men of Delta Company did not stop fighting on March 18, 1968, at the place now known as Bau Co Bong.[482] By the end of March, the battered unit was refitted and their KHAs replaced. For the next eight and a half months, these young men, many of whom were only high school students a short time before, were back on combat patrol in the dark jungles, villages and rice paddies of South Vietnam. Sergeant Bill Pray, who was wounded in the battle, later recalled, "Delta didn't die on March eighteenth. That was just the beginning!"[483]

Throughout those remaining months, many more men of Calvin's old outfit would be added to the unit's overall casualty list.

---

[480] Calvin Heath 201 File.

[481] Daily Staff Journal, March 19, 1968.

[482] Author's note: Years later, Paul Bucha would refer to the battle location as the "place with no name." David Shoup, during his interview in 2016 with NVA Company Commander - Thanh Nguyen (Phu Loi Battalion, Dong Nai Regiment), identified the location of the battle as Bau Co Bong. Thanh confirmed that the NVA established a major base there that was used after TET to refit and replenish NVA troops. He pointed to the map where the men fought and stated to David, "This is where we fought your father." Source: *Phantom Force Revisited.*

[483] Bill Pray Email to author, April 16, 2017.

The 3rd Battalion, 187th Infantry (ABN) participated in some of the most horrendous, and costly, fighting of the war to include the Battle of Hamburger Hill (May 11–20, 1969). Pray added, "[That] one night didn't define the mission all of us remaining had to complete. March 18th in and of itself is a great story, but there were many more bad days & nights…"[484] But that's another story.

MILITARY MEDICINE

Medical personnel met Mowery's chopper as it landed at Phuoc Vinh. Calvin, Dietch and Wishik were quickly offloaded on the tarmac where nurses and doctors checked the men to ensure they were stable and had not gone into shock. They gave orders to immediately transfer the seriously injured men to the larger, better equipped medical facility at Long Binh, located 40 miles away.[485]

Calvin, now unconscious, was placed on the tarmac awaiting transfer to Long Binh. He awoke briefly to find a Catholic priest bent over him and crying.[486] Calvin stated, "I woke up with him bent over me with tears running down his face doing his thing. Well I thought he was giving me Last Rites. I was scared as hell [and yelled] 'I'm not dying! I'm not dying!'" The priest, who probably thought Calvin was in fact dying, was pleasantly surprised by Calvin's outburst. He looked at him and laughed, and with his hand gently placed on Calvin's head in prayer said, "I'm praying for you my son." The priest then continued, "Is there anything I can do for you?" Calvin, relieved he was not dying, now focused on his next priority, the most important for a 19-year-old young man. In great pain and unable to look for himself, he said to the priest, "Yes sir there is! Can you check them out and see if they're there?" The priest, amused by Calvin's request, laughed and said, "I don't know about you guys. I see you get all shot up and every last one of you, the first thing you ask me to do is to 'check them out!'"[487] The priest obliged and much to Calvin's delight, that particular part of his body was indeed intact. Calvin would later find that he had in fact been hit in the groin, but the wound was cauterized as the bullet passed through his flesh, missing

---

[485] Note: Calvin was unclear as to where the men were first flown, possibilities include Phuoc Vinh and Bien Hoa, or where he was flown for surgery. Calvin recalled Long Bien, but there were no records found to corroborate this.

[486] Note: According to Davis, the priest was possibly Captain Leo Metz, 2/506th. Metz was a WWII paratrooper who fought at Bastogne and later entered the priesthood. He was well respected by the men.

[487] Adam Piore interview with Calvin Heath, 2009.

the most crucial parts. Luckily, the round that hit Calvin was a tracer.[488]

Long Binh Evacuation Hospital was located approximately 40 miles to the south of Phuoc Vinh, just outside of Saigon. It was a massive modern military medical facility that was well equipped and manned by several U.S. Army medical units including the 24th and 93rd Evacuation Hospitals and the 74th Field Hospital. By 1968, the facility treated more than 10,000 admissions and more than 70,000 patients in its outpatient clinics. The surgical units stationed there were among the best in Southeast Asia.

Long Bien Hospital, 93rd Evacuation Hospital, circa 1968. The helicopter landing pads can be seen in the background. U.S. Army Photo.

---

[488] Calvin Heath interview with author, May 2013.

By the time the helicopter carrying Dietch, Wishik and Calvin landed, medical personnel were already at the landing pads waiting with litter carriers and gurneys to transport the men to triage units. Upon arriving at triage, they were quickly evaluated for internal wounds and moved to pre-op where what remained of their clothes was removed. From there, X-rays were taken, blood drawn, and a number of other tests were performed by the medical staff.

Due to the severity of his wounds, Wishik was immediately wheeled into pre-op and placed in a room directly across from where Calvin lay. Calvin thought, *At least he's still alive.* These thoughts, however, were quickly tempered when Calvin saw another Catholic priest approach Wishik and give him his Last Rites. Calvin stated:

They read him his Last Rites and they told me then they didn't think he was going to make it. He was really shot up – and they turned around and when they were talking to him about me, they said the same thing about me. They didn't think I was going to make it.[489]

Calvin and Wishik were then wheeled into surgery and Calvin later recalled, "When they operated on us and we were all drugged up, I don't remember seeing him anymore..."[490]

Once Calvin was placed under anesthesia, the doctors removed the field dressings and went to work. The most serious of the wounds was the bullet to his right hip, and the severe fragmentation wounds to his side and back which left his ribs and spine exposed. The surgeons first concentrated on the most serious wounds near his spine. The minor wounds to his face, head, chest, arms, and legs would simply have to wait.

After cleaning Calvin's back wounds and finding no serious damage to the spine or any internal organs, surgeons reconnected the damaged muscle tissue, and carefully sutured the wounds together. If the wound had been slightly deeper, he would have had serious damage to his spinal column causing possible paralysis. The surgical

---

[489] Adam Piore interview with Calvin Heath, 2009.
[490] Ibid.

team then moved to the hip wounds and removed what fragmentations they could but found that the AK-47 bullet deeply imbedded into the hip would require a more sophisticated medical facility. The decision was then made to close that wound and transfer Calvin, as soon as he was stabilized, to a better equipped hospital back in the United States.

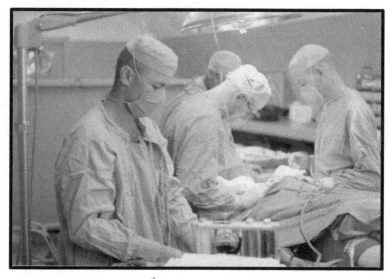

Above: A surgical team at the 24th Evacuation Hospital, Long Binh, Vietnam, circa 1968. Shown in the foreground is Ken Bopp a nurse anesthetist. The patient, most likely a wounded soldier, is being worked on in the background. Ken Bopp picture.

According to the U.S. Army Center for Military History, it was the Army's policy at that time to return as many soldiers to the field as possible. "Under this policy, it was possible to return to duty in Vietnam nearly 40 percent of those injured through hostile action and 70 percent of other surgical patients."[491] Calvin was among those who would not be returned to the field due to the severity of his wounds. His transfer back to the United States, in and of itself, was a definitive indication of the serious nature of his wounds. State-side Army officers, to whom Calvin would later report, should have understood

---

[491] U.S. Army Center of Military History Found at: www.history.army.mil/index.html, pgs. 69-70.

this, but did not, later sentencing Calvin to decades of unnecessary emotional, psychological and legal problems.

After his initial surgery, Calvin was sent to Recovery where he was stabilized awaiting transfer to the United States. A few hours later, an enemy soldier, also recovering from surgery, joined Wishik and Calvin in post-op.[492] Calvin later heard that Wishik, still under the influence of the anesthesia, tried to crawl out of the bed to kill the NVA soldier.[493] While they were usually separated from American soldiers, enemy soldiers were sometimes treated at U.S. hospitals, making it an extremely uncomfortable affair for both sides. Few enemy soldiers were able to ever get a good night's sleep fearing their demise from an American patient or possibly even a staff member.

While awaiting his return to the United States, Calvin was visited by Captain Bucha and some of the other men from Delta Company. Calvin stated, "Bucha came to see us there [with] some of the guys from the company. That's when I found more about what was going on."[494] It was at this point that Calvin began to process the brutal reality of the past few days. Many of his friends, including his best friend, would be making their trip home in a flag-draped coffin, several of the dead in pieces. He knew these men, their names, and their stories; Michael, Cecil, Roy, Larry, Steven, Juan, Jimmy, and Paul – especially Paul. Calvin felt that he knew everything there was to know about Paul Conner. They shared personal stories and hopes and dreams only the way close friends in combat can. Over their time together, they covered each other's backs in firefights; they shared food, water and their most inner and deepest thoughts. Now Paul was gone, and Calvin could still clearly see his face as he died in his arms. It was a picture that was now seared into his memory – a haunting snapshot in time that Calvin would see over and over again for the rest of his life – forcing him to think, *Why him and not me?*

---

[492] Note: Wishik recovered from his wounds and returned to active duty and Vietnam. He served until he retired as a Lieutenant Colonel. Calvin did not know he survived until he was informed by Dave Dillard in 1984.
[493] Adam Piore interview with Calvin Heath, 2009.
[494] Ibid.

On March 24, 1968, only five days after being wounded, Calvin was transferred via military ambulance the few miles to Tan Son Nhut Air Base and was loaded on a modified C-141 Star Lifter. The flight was manned with flight nurses and doctors who tended to the wounded men during their long flights home. From Tan Son Nhut, Calvin was flown to the U.S. Army Hospital, Camp Zama, Japan where he would be evaluated before being shipped back to the United States. Calvin recalled, "They flew me to Japan, from Japan to Hawaii, Hawaii to California. [From] California, they flew me to Houston. From Houston they flew me to Walter Reed Hospital..."[495] The entire trip would take several days.

Walter Reed Hospital, located in Washington, D.C., was the flagship facility of the U.S. military medical corps. Thousands of wounded soldiers and other military and government personnel, including several presidents, have been treated there. It was the best military hospital in the country. While at Walter Reed Hospital, Calvin immediately went through another surgical procedure on his hip. Unfortunately, the procedure to remove the bullet was unsuccessful. The decision was then made to leave it in place. The doctors reasoned that removing the bullet after he recovered and regained his strength would be less risky than trying to remove it now. Calvin would later note that it was too close to a nerve and they risked further, more serious problems by removing it at that time.[496]

After his second surgery, the Walter Reed medical staff developed a rehabilitation and recovery plan for Calvin. On April 3, 1968, just 15 days after being evacuated from the battlefield, Calvin was sent to Fort Devens, Massachusetts to complete his initial recovery. Sending soldiers to military hospitals closer to their homes was a common practice as the Army Medical Corps found that wounded soldiers responded better and faster with the help of their family and friends. Fort Devens was located approximately one hour northwest of Putnam, Connecticut, Calvin's hometown, and was the most logical place to temporarily assign him.

---

[495] Adam Piore interview with Calvin Heath, 2009.

[496] Calvin Heath interview with author, April 26, 2013. Note: Calvin's military records indicate he was only at Walter Reed for a few days.

When Calvin returned to New England, he was not greeted by throngs of well-wishers lining up at the airport to welcome home their returning wounded warriors. In fact, it was quite the opposite. Upon arriving at Westover Air Force Base, in Chicopee, Massachusetts, Calvin and other men were unceremoniously placed on stretchers and moved by military personnel to a medical transport bus waiting on the tarmac for the 90-minute drive to Fort Devens.[497]

The drive itself was uneventful, but what greeted the men at the main gate of Fort Devens was something Calvin would never forget or forgive. Anti-war protesters holding signs screamed at the sick and wounded soldiers to let them know just what they thought about their actions in Vietnam. Calvin recalled, "Outside the gates of Fort Devens, I was going through and there were people standing there calling us baby killers and shit... and throwing blood – big five gallon pails of blood [at the bus]."[498] Calvin, a man who only days before was covered in the blood of his friends and enemies, now had to endure the indignity of having animal blood being thrown at him. It was a scene that visited Calvin often in his dreams.

Left: Vietnam War protesters confronting MP's. Protests varied from peaceful demonstrations to those that resulted in death, like the one held at Kent State University in May 1970. Public Domain picture

---

[497] Note: The airport at which Calvin first landed is speculation on the part of the author based on the information provided by Calvin.
[498] Adam Piore interview with Calvin Heath, 2009.

There were, however, several pleasant things that greeted Calvin when he passed through the front gates of Fort Devens. While telling about the "baby killer" incident, Calvin's sense of humor poked through, as it often did. Anti-war protests were not the only thing to sweep the country while Calvin was away. He continued, "One of the nicest things about when we came back [was that] the mini skirt was out. We're lying there and the girls [were] walking by and we're like 'Whoa! We've been missing something!'"[499]

For the next five months, from April 4 to September 4, 1968, Calvin was stationed at Fort Devens, Massachusetts where Army doctors tried once again to operate on his damaged hip. This attempt, like the first two was unsuccessful and the bullet and fragments remained lodged deep in his hip. For several long, painful weeks, Calvin remained a patient at the Fort Devens Army Hospital where he recovered from the surgery and began a painful round of rehabilitation. At first, walking was a real challenge and it was doubtful he would ever again walk naturally or without constant pain.

During his stay at the Fort Devens Hospital, Calvin was often visited by his family and friends, many of whom were shocked at his transformation. The healthy young man who left Putnam, Connecticut only months ago was now a drawn and severely damaged specimen who aged 20 years. He was on crutches and needed help to move around. Brother Bert stated, "He was a mess the first time I saw him at Devens."[500] As disturbing as the visits were for Calvin's friends and family, they provided the only meaningful emotional assistance he had had since being wounded.

Sometime in June 1968, approximately eight weeks after the surgery, Calvin was granted a well-needed, and well-deserved weekend pass. His good friend, Rob Authier later stated, "When I first saw Calvin after Vietnam, he was on crutches and had to use a pillow when he sat because of his hip."[501] Authier went on to tell about a weekend adventure the two shared during this time, the most notable being the following. "We went up north and we only had like $20

---

[499] Adam Piore interview with Calvin Heath, 2009.
[500] Bert Heath interview with author, October 18, 2013.
[501] Authier, Rob, interview with author, March 28, 2014.

between us, so we bought some booze for some college students. They gave us some money and we went out and had a great time." The weekend of drinking and carousing was so enjoyable that both Calvin and Rob lost track of the time and Rob later reported, "When we came back, I can remember doing about 100 MPH just to get him back to Fort Devens on time."[502]

After Calvin returned from his weekend pass, he continued to receive further rehabilitation for his hip injury. The Fort Devens' doctors ultimately determined that there was little more they could accomplish with further surgery and they concluded that Calvin's wounds had resulted in permanent and inoperable damage. The attending physician met with Calvin and explained the bad news. The doctor reviewed what few options remained and informed Calvin that the only reasonable option was a medical discharge from the Army as he was now clearly unfit for duty. When asked in 2013 how he felt about the news, Calvin stated that, "…a big part of me felt like crap. I wanted to be back with the guys. I didn't want to be a cripple or anything, and at that point I really didn't even know if I would ever walk properly again."[503]

During his short time in the States, Calvin lost contact with the remaining men of Delta Company. Many were reassigned to other units, had returned home with serious wounds, or were simply discharged after serving their time. He wondered how his fellow Rakkasans were doing, whether or not Wishik and Dietch survived, and of course what became of Bucha, Quick, Harjo and the others. Those questions would not be answered at Fort Devens and the U.S. Army provided no help. Helping a wounded soldier find closure was not a priority for the Army in 1968, and it would take years before Calvin learned of their fate.

Once Calvin received word of his pending medical discharge, he began to consider his future prospects. He often thought about making the Army a career and breaking away from the inevitable future that awaited him in Putnam, Connecticut. He understood that without a

---

[502] Authier, Rob, interview with author, March 28, 2014.
[503] Calvin Heath interview with author, April 26, 2013.

high school diploma, his options on the outside were limited and he saw the Army as a way for him to contribute to something larger than himself. He was very good at his trade. The medals he earned, but had not yet received, proved that. He later stated, "If I would have stayed in Vietnam, I would have probably ended up staying in the service, because I made Spec-4 the day I got shot. I would have come back here to the States an E-6 (Staff Sergeant)."[504] This would have made all the difference in a life he was willing to risk for a future.

The doctor explained to Calvin that once he received his medical discharge papers, he would be sent before a disability review board that would determine his VA disability income. Disability assistance was based on the soldier's physical limitations, which the doctor felt in Calvin's case were very significant. A week later, the doctor confirmed to Calvin that he had approved his medical discharge and that he should have no issues being eligible for military disability income. This was also confirmed with several family members to include Calvin's older brothers Glen and Bert, sister-in-law Betty and Calvin's mother and father.[505] Calvin was upset over leaving the Army, but if there was a silver lining in this unfortunate story, it was Calvin would at least receive a monthly stipend to help reestablish his life "in the world." After considering all his options, Calvin felt he had no choice but to accept the doctor's recommendation, and he began to mentally prepare for a life after the army.

Calvin let the bad news set for a week and then made an appointment to meet with the doctor once again so he could begin the discharge process. For several hours, he waited anxiously as he considered his mixed feelings about leaving the Army. When he finally asked a clerk what was going on, he was told that no one at the hospital knew anything about his medical discharge. Absolutely stunned, Calvin demanded to see his doctor who had just approved the discharge only a week earlier. He was told that the doctor had been reassigned and could not be reached. Calvin was then informed that not only was he *not* getting his medical discharge, he was being

---

[504] Calvin Heath interview with author, April 26, 2013.
[505] Various interviews with Bert and Betty Heath.

transferred back to active duty in another infantry unit! Calvin was upset and confused by the news. He knew that his physical condition made it impossible to continue his life as a soldier and he felt that any physician could see that if they just reviewed his file! He could not help to think, *what they hell is going on?*

By June 1968, primarily due to the stress created by the U.S. Army's botched handling of his medical discharge, Calvin developed terrible and recurring nightmares. While the mishandling of his discharge was not the cause of Calvin's nighttime problems, it certainly accelerated its development. Multiple attempts to speak with medical personnel about his quickly developing psychological issues and discharge finally caught the attention of a sympathetic psychiatrist who quickly determined that aside from his physical issues, Calvin needed immediate assistance with his emotional state. Calvin stated, "[They] then sent me to see a psychiatrist at Devens. I [was having] nightmares and all that crap, and I saw the psychiatrist and he said, "Yeah you need help." And he even wrote it in my report, 'This man needs help!'"[506]

Army records suggest, that with the psychiatrist's help, orders were soon issued transferring Calvin out of the Airborne and into a unit stationed at Fort Devens. Here, the psychiatrist was able to keep an eye on him and continue to assist with his discharge. Calvin added:

> *So, I'm waiting for the medical discharge and they said to me, "You can't stay here, we have to send you to the airborne unit because you belong to them, unless you sign a waiver. If you sign the waiver then you give up being Airborne." I couldn't jump anymore anyway, my hip being all messed up. They said, "If you sign the waiver to get you out of Airborne then we can keep you here until you get your discharge." So, I signed the paperwork.[507]*

In a letter dated March 15, 1999, to Paul Bucha, Calvin later wrote:

---

[506] Adam Piore interview with Calvin Heath, 2009.
[507] Ibid.

At this time I was told that if I wanted to stay at Fort Devens [and wait] for a medical discharge, I had to sign a [waiver] to be released from airborne duty or be transferred to Fort Bragg waiting for the medical discharge. I chose to stay at Fort Devens because it was within driving distance for my family to visit me.[508]

Calvin was led to believe that if he signed this document, his medical discharge would quickly follow. Within a few days, however, still in great pain and unable to properly walk, he received disturbing news that he would *not* be discharged from the United States Army, nor would he be staying at Fort Devens. In fact, he had orders granting him a 30-day leave, after which he was to report to his *new* unit at Fort Carson, Colorado. Calvin protested and told the person in charge, "What the hell do you mean Fort Carson? I'm waiting for my fucking medical discharge!" The desk sergeant responded, "I don't know anything about a medical discharge. You have to see them when you get out there." In 2013, Calvin reflected on that moment 45 years earlier and added, "And that was the end of it. I had no choice."[509] When asked how he felt the day he received his transfer orders, Calvin stated:

I was pissed off. I had nobody I could talk to. Top and Bucha were still in Vietnam – and Wishik was gone – so there was nothing they could do from there. I had nobody trying to help me after that doctor retired. I was stuck. So, I went home. I didn't know what else to do.[510]

---

[508] Calvin Heath letter to Bucha, March 15, 1999.
[509] Calvin Heath interview with author, May 2013.
[510] Ibid.

THIRTY DAYS TO THINK

Unheard Cry

Vietnam is but a thought that splits the midnight air,
Bombarding me with memories, a never-ending nightmare.

The whistle of the mortar round, the silence now is broken,
We all run for cover, and not a word is spoken.

They're coming through the wire again, as one by one they fall,
The chaplain said that it's God's will, the lost ones have been called.

The lieutenant lost three out of four, two legs and an arm,
He talks and smokes a cigarette, with no fear or alarm.

The medics tie up every stump, and pat him on the back,
He talks and speaks of better days, and awaits the medevac.

Some lost their friends and family, some were maimed and blind,
I didn't lose my body parts, I only lost my mind.[511]

Michael Rawson
Delta Co. 3/187th Infantry (ABN)
101st Airborne Division

On September 4, 1968, Calvin's 30-day leave began. Calvin, now assigned to temporary barracks near the Fort Devens hospital, rose early, went to breakfast at the mess hall and returned to his room to pack. He only had a few possessions; many of his personal items, much like his paperwork and medals, were still in Vietnam or on their way home... or so he thought. As he packed, his mind was swimming with questions with no answers. He thought, *if Quick, Wishik, Bucha or Harjo were here they could help sort this mess out.* These were leaders who took care of the men under their command and made

---

[511] Note: The Lieutenant Rawson speaks about in the poem is Chad Colley, who was seriously wounded by stepping on a land mine on July 21, 1968. Colley eventually became the National Commander of the Disabled American Veterans.

certain their needs and questions were addressed. Here in the United States, it seemed to Calvin like "nobody gave a rat's ass!"

Calvin was met at the Fort Devens' main gate by his brother Glen. When Glen and other family members first saw Calvin, they were struck by how utterly heartbreaking he appeared. It was clear to them that Calvin's injuries, surgeries, and stress had taken a huge toll on their little brother. Calvin was a completely different person.[512]

On the ride home the brothers exchanged small talk. Glen knew that the Army telegram notifying his mother that her son was wounded in action only told a small part of the story. He understood the rest would have to come from Calvin himself and only when he was ready to talk.

In 2013, when thinking about that time, older brother Bert stated, "Calvin didn't even have time to be a soldier before he became a warrior. He never got to see stateside garrison. He was balls to the wall and he never got to see that part of the military – the spit and polish part."[513]

Bert, a combat veteran himself, understood that the Army rushed his little brother into the maelstrom that was the killing fields of the Vietnam jungles far too quickly. One day Calvin was a teenage boy working at the Highway Department in Putnam, Connecticut cleaning streets, the next he's brutally slitting the throats of other human beings in the jungles of South East Asia. Bert wondered, *how does a young man come to grips with that?*

It was only a few months since the battle near the trail, and Calvin had no closure to an overwhelming amount of life-changing pain and horror. In a matter of a few short weeks he was handed more challenges, more heartache, more stress, and had seen more ugliness than most people see in a lifetime. He was getting very little assistance from the Army and he was now on his way home, to visit friends and family who, with possibly the exception of Bert, Glen and Chet, had little to no understanding of the terrible things Calvin had seen and experienced.

---

[512] Betty Heath interview with author, October 2014.

[513] Bert Heath interview with author October 24, 2013.

As Calvin drove home, he knew there would be a lot of questions and he thought long and hard about how to answer them – his contemplation only resulting in more questions. *How can I possibly describe what happened? How could they understand?* When trying to get his mind around the last few months, Calvin was quite certain even he did not understand what had actually happened.

Some of the questions eventually asked emotionally staggered Calvin and provoked overwhelming memories. No one had prepared him for this, and he did not know how to react or how to recover. At first, he tried to answer the questions, but how could he possibly explain to someone who had never dealt with tragedy what it was like to kill another human being. How could he describe what it was like to run through a hail of bullets and explosions with the body of your best friend in your arms? Or the incredible hopelessness that you and your friends felt when you were surrounded by a far superior force hell-bent on killing each and every one of you in the most brutal of ways? How do you explain the dead and wounded whose screams still haunt your nights? Few people at home could ever imagine one man inflicting that level of cruelty on another man, so how could he possibly answer these incredibly naive and stupid questions? Worse, Calvin's typically casual answers led many to believe that his experiences in Vietnam were actually no big deal, or that he was just "full of shit." This, unfortunately, set the stage for a lifetime of problems.

When Calvin rose on the morning of September 5th, the first day of his 30-day leave, his first step out of bed sent sharp pains through his back and hip. He looked down as he sat on the edge of the bed and saw the scars that served as a reminder that this was no dream. He paused for a moment with his face in his hands, uncertain what lie ahead and what he should do next. Things were becoming so very complicated and he suddenly felt utterly alone. Taking stock of the situation, Calvin decided that at least for the next few weeks, he would rest, visit with his friends and try to forget. As he pondered his own situation that morning, he thought about the other guys back in Vietnam and wondered how they were doing. He wished he could talk to someone – anyone that would understand his predicament, but of course that was impossible.

The next 29 days of his leave were no better than the first. Calvin visited his friends, got drunk and for a short few hours each night he would forget all he had experienced. But each morning when he awoke, the horrible pain in his hip reminded him, once again, that there were no answers to his questions. His future was uncertain, and he had no closure to the events in Vietnam, especially the epic battle near the trail. He was not present when they removed the dead and dying men from the field; he was not present when they boxed up his friends in coffins and sent them home. He never had a chance to morn their death; he did not get that all-important opportunity to speak with his battle buddies to reconcile the horrific details and to make some sense of it all. He wished he could just hug those who survived and tell them, and have them tell him, "Things will be all right." Bill Heaney later explained, "We trained together, ate together, worked together, bled together, and died together, and then we came home alone – We just came home alone."[514] Calvin *was* alone. He later stated, "One morning I just sat there and cried like a baby. I felt like I had nobody."[515]

As his leave neared the end, Calvin found few answers with his family and friends. On the last day of his leave, his physical problems were unresolved, and his emotional pain was escalating. While he did not want to go to Fort Carson, he knew he had little choice. He called the Fort Devens' medical staff, but there was no one there who could tell him the status of his medical discharge. Calvin was becoming angry; angry with life, and more importantly – angry with the U.S. Army. Calvin's brother Bert later stated:

The Calvin I knew before Vietnam and the Calvin I knew after was not the same person. That night put so much stress on him as a youngster that it did a number on him mentally. [The enemy moved] back and forth, picking at him, taking his zippo lighter and their watches – taking whatever they

---

[514] Dillard, Heaney, Rawson interview with author, October 9, 2013.
[515] Calvin Heath interview with author, May 2013.

could, I can't even comprehend it. Have I been scared? Yeah. Have I pissed my pants? Yeah... but [what Calvin went through] that's a whole different ball game. They were hammered and were left [alone] and that's the hard part... they were left [alone].[516]

On October 4, 1968, the last day of Calvin's leave and 17 months after he had enlisted in the Army, Calvin woke, packed his military items and civilian clothes in a large duffle bag. With his new orders and paperwork from Fort Devens' in hand, he kissed his mother goodbye, drove to Hartford, Connecticut, where he boarded a plane heading west to Colorado.

---

[516] Bert Heath interview with author October 24, 2013.

FORT CARSON, COLORADO

Calvin looked out the window of the plane as he travelled west. He had never been to Colorado and there was a small piece of him that was excited to see another part of the country. He understood that he would have to deal with the question of his medical discharge when he reported to his new assignment, and right now, flying 30,000 feet above the country for which he so gallantly fought, he still held some hope that his paperwork would eventually catch up to him and this whole mess would soon be over.

Upon arriving at Fort Carson, Calvin reported as ordered to C Company, 1st Battalion, 10th Infantry, 5th Infantry Division (Mechanized).[517] He entered the company administration office and stated, "Specialist Fourth Class Calvin Heath reporting as ordered." He presented what little paper work he had to the company clerk and was assigned to a platoon and barracks. Throughout the first day, he met all the key people to include his new first sergeant, squad leader, platoon sergeant, and platoon leader.

What Calvin did not expect in October of 1968 was that his sealed personnel file (201-File) that he carried to Fort Carson from Fort Devens and presented to the company clerk was full of errors and omissions. His file did not list the medals he earned, with the exception of his Vietnam campaign medal and his Purple Heart, and it did not list the engagements in which he participated while serving with the 101st Airborne. It also did not list the brutal way in which he received his wounds. Further, his file did not include any of the medical records from Long Binh, Japan, Walter Reed, or Fort Devens; the surgeries he had, or the eventual recommendations of the doctors to medically discharge him based on his severe physical limitations. The file presented to the company clerk at Fort Carson showed the record of a soldier who had done very little in the Army since enlisting 17 months earlier. The administration and personnel system

---

[517] Calvin Heath 201 File.

213

of the United States Army, in Calvin's case, had failed miserably. As a result of these failures, Calvin would endure decades of mistreatment. But there was nothing he could do about it in October of 1968.

The brief medical report from Fort Devens Hospital listed Calvin's physical restrictions or his "profiles," but had no details as to why. The Military Physical Profile System (MPPS) was originally designed to help classify military personnel with regards to their physical and psychological limitations. However, key to this process is having accurate descriptions of a soldier's experiences, wounds, surgeries and treatments. Calvin recalled, "I had a profile C, D, E, F... I mean, they couldn't make me do anything. I couldn't stand more than ten minutes at a time, I could do absolutely no marching, couldn't walk for anything more than two or three minutes at a time."[518]

After reviewing Calvin's very limited file and suspicious about the medical report and profiles assigned, the company clerk questioned him in an attempt to fill in the gaps. Calvin gave him all the details explaining the last six months. The company clerk listened and then decided that no one in the U.S. Army could have possibly gone through so much in such a short period of time. He quickly became convinced that Calvin was most likely lying. Unclear what to do with Calvin, the clerk sent the file to Calvin's new Company Commander.

When Calvin's new commander reviewed his incomplete 201 File, he saw no mention of any medals, except his Purple Heart, and very little about Calvin's injuries, emotional state, or his recent battle experience. He only saw one note that said:

Fragmentation wound in the buttocks 18 Mar 68.[519]

Given the information provided in Calvin's file, his new Company Commander decided not to sit with Calvin to discuss his wounds or time in Vietnam or seek additional information. Instead he

---

[518] Adam Piore interview with Calvin Heath, 2009.
[519] Calvin Heath 201 File.

concluded that Calvin was wounded running *away* from the battle not to it! The new CO also concluded that a 19-year-old who had only been in the Army for 17 months could not have possibly experienced what Calvin stated he had experienced. He felt that any soldier who claimed to have completed Basic Training, AIT, Jungle School, Jump School, LRRP class, spent three months fighting in the jungles of Vietnam with the 101st Airborne, the finest fighting force in the United States Army, and then earned a Silver Star, was certainly not only a "slacker" and "malingerer," he was an outright liar! Profile or no profile this CO was going to show this young man what good soldiering was all about. Calvin later reported that his new CO told him straight to his face that, "... I was full of shit and that I was faking."[520] Bert also later added:

> *I remember Calvin having stateside problems... out in Colorado. When he was in [Colorado] they just thought he was a blow hard and they just couldn't see an 18-19-year-old kid going through what he went through.[521]*

Bert went on to state, "... that many REMFs (Rear Echelon Mother Fuckers), soldiers who never saw combat, had a case of the ass for guys who came back with a Combat Infantry Badge – that was also part of the problem."[522] It is highly likely Calvin's new CO was a REMF who felt this way.

With his new assignment at Fort Carson, Colorado, Calvin's time in the Army went from bad to worse. Without the support of his new leaders, word began to spread that Calvin was lying about his combat experiences. Many of the other men in Calvin's new outfit began to question his story and some of them began to joke that if he *was* really wounded, he was wounded in the *ass* –running away from danger – not toward it. Some of the men now considered Calvin a slacker, liar, and a *coward* – certainly not the hero he claimed to be.[523]

[520] Calvin Heath interview with author, May 2013.
[521] Bert Heath interview with author October 24, 2013.
[522] Ibid.
[523] Note: Speculation on the author's part based on his interviews with Calvin. In all fairness, seasoned soldiers whose filters told them that this was a man who paid a high price in battle

Once the CO convinced himself that Calvin was faking, he ignored the doctor's orders and placed Calvin on normal duty despite his severe pain.[524] In those first few weeks at Fort Carson, it had seemed to Calvin as though the Army had gone absolutely mad. He wondered, *why won't these idiots listen to me? Can't they see me limping and in pain?* Up until that point, Calvin had never disobeyed a direct order and by all accounts, was a model soldier. He followed every order given to him by SSG Quick, 1SGT Harjo, 1LT Wishik, and CPT Bucha, for that matter, every NCO and officers to whom he reported. Calvin didn't know what to do, but he knew the treatment he was now receiving was wrong and for the first time in his short military career, he began to fight back.

As it turned out, Calvin was not the only target of this particular commander. Calvin stated that another soldier who served with the First Cavalry in Vietnam and had earned the Congressional Medal of Honor, received the same sort of treatment. During a Class A inspection, the soldier was stripped of his CMH by the CO, disrespected in front of the men and made to do pushups for "illegally" wearing the medal. The soldier's records, like Calvin's, were incomplete and the CO apparently did not have the time to inquire about such an important matter. When the soldier protested, he was arrested. Calvin continued the story:

> *So, they arrested him, and he got his phone call and he called his father and his father's brother was a congressman, so they came down and they, it was like a week later, right out in front of the whole battalion that company commander had to apologize to him, for doing that to him. You don't do that to a Medal of Honor recipient. You don't pull that kind of a stunt.*[525]

---

and watched his friends and fellow soldiers pay the ultimate price, most certainly existed, but there were few in Calvin's life at this point.

[524] Calvin Heath interview with author, May 2013.

[525] Note: Research shows there were several men from the First Cavalry who earned the Medal of Honor and who could have been assigned with Calvin at Fort Carson during this time.

Unfortunately for Calvin, he did not have any high-level contacts to support and protect his honor. He was forced to suffer in silence, becoming more and more isolated and angry as time went on. His building anger coupled with his severe pain and his growing issues with nightmares and night scares became a ticking time bomb.

During the military buildup in Vietnam, stateside commanders were tasked with the mission of making their units combat ready. To assist with this task the Army sent combat veterans to help units supplement their inexperienced cadres. In November of 1968, the 10th Infantry, 5th Infantry Division was prepping for Vietnam and senior officers and NCOs were trying to convince their more experienced combat veterans to sign a waiver to return to Vietnam.[526] To assist with this effort, the division commander assembled the combat veterans in a large auditorium and attempted to sell them on the opportunity to return to Vietnam. Calvin stated:

The Division Commander had [assembled] all the Vietnam vets that had six months or more left in the service. He wanted to talk to us. So, they put us in this big auditorium, and there must have been two-three thousands of us that were inside this big-ass auditorium, just packed like sardines. He came out on the stage and he was doing his gung-ho crap. He says, "All you men here right now if you volunteer to go back to Vietnam every single one of you will be an E-5. No matter what your rank is now you will become a sergeant and if you are already a sergeant, we'll boost you up one grade." And he said, "So how many volunteers I got?" And he's standing on the stage with his arm up and shit, and not one fucking person volunteered. Not one! And was he pissed! He started calling us cowards. I said, "I'll go back to Vietnam, but you send me back to my old outfit. I don't want to go with these guys."[527]

---

[526] Calvin Heath interview with author, May 2013.
[527] Adam Piore interview with Calvin Heath, 2009.

Throughout his troubled time at Fort Carson, one item that *was* very clear on Calvin's 201 File, was his military qualifications and MOS. It clearly showed his infantry training, Jump School qualification, and the fact that he was a small weapons expert. In spite of that information, the CO, possibly out of spite, assigned him to heavy weapons, an area completely unfamiliar to Calvin. Calvin stated:

> *So, I'm sitting there one day, and they tell me I'm in the heavy mortar platoon. Joe, I don't know a fucking thing about mortars, and they want me to teach the other guys how to shoot it! I told the sergeant and the CO I don't know shit about mortars. But they kept me there anyways.*[528]

Even though Calvin was still recovering from his wounds, he was ordered by his CO to participate in the company's normal duties. When his platoon sergeant ordered him to gear up for a two-day field maneuver, Calvin finally had enough and refused. He told his platoon sergeant and his CO that he was not going to go – that he was in great pain and requested to go to sick call.[529] Calvin hoped that he could plead his case to a military doctor. Reluctantly, the CO granted Calvin's request.

Upon arriving at the medical facility he told the doctor about his assignment in Vietnam, the many patrols, the horrific battle near Phuoc Vinh, and the wounds he sustained. He told the doctor the difficulty the surgeons had in removing the bullet from his hip, the hospitals in which he was a patient, the discussions with the doctors at Fort Devens about a medical discharge, and the problems he was now having with his current CO. He also told the doctor that he was unable to stand for more than ten minutes at a time and how excruciating the pain was when he was forced to do any physical labor.

After an examination and several X-rays, the doctor quickly determined that Calvin was indeed telling the truth about his medical condition. The physician also understood that sending him back to the

---

[528] Calvin Heath interview with author, May 2013.
[529] Ibid.

company would only exacerbate his medical situation further, and so he granted Calvin a 14-day medical leave allowing the doctor time to request a complete set of records from Fort Devens.

When news of his two-week leave reached Calvin's CO, he exploded. Now the CO was even more determined to make an example of this contemptible excuse of a soldier. *How dare he run to the doctors and hide behind them. And who the hell was this idiot doctor keeping my soldiers away from their responsibilities?* Unfortunately, Calvin's plan to finally speak out to a doctor at Fort Carson did very little to help, and in fact, only made his life in the Army much more miserable.

On Wednesday, January 22, 1969, the day he received his leave from the doctor, Calvin found a flight heading east that was scheduled to leave within the hour.[530] He knew that if he rushed, he could make it on that plane and avoid any further contact or problems with his CO, so he quickly packed his things, gave his new medical leave orders to the company clerk, and rushed out of the company area. As he left, instead of walking on the cement walkway around the weed-infested lawn, Calvin cut across a corner, walking on the grass. He later stated, "When I went home, I crossed the grass. I cheated, to catch the airplane. I wanted to get out of there fast." Unfortunately, a second lieutenant happened to observe Calvin cutting the corner and called him over intending to discipline him. Calvin continued, "This second lieutenant was there and he's standing me at attention just being a jerk and the guys up in the barracks up on the second story were yelling down, 'Tell him what he can do! Tell him what he can do!'" Calvin, having had enough, did just that – he told the young officer, "Fuck you sir! I'm going home."[531] He bolted for the plane, boarded without further incident and sat back wondering what the next few weeks would bring.

When Calvin returned to Fort Carson on February 4, 1969, one day before his leave expired, he was immediately arrested by the MPs and was given an Article 15 for being AWOL. Calvin was caught off

---

[530] Calvin Heath 201 File.
[531] Adam Piore interview with Calvin Heath, 2009.

guard as he thought he was actually being arrested for disrespecting an officer.[532] The company commander, 1LT John W. Brauer, did not approve or recognize Calvin's two-week medical leave and in the Record of Proceedings dated February 5, 1969, wrote:

It has been reported to me, that on or about 0700, 22 January 1969, at Fort Carson Colorado, you did, without proper authority, absent yourself from your unit, to wit: Company C, 1st Battalion (Mechanized), 10th Infantry, 5th Infantry Division (Mechanized), located at Fort Carson, Colorado, and did remain so absent until on or about 4 February 1969.[533]

He was fined $32, given 14 days of extra duty, 14 days restriction to the company area, and worse, he was reduced in rank from specialist fourth class, something he earned on March 19, 1968, the day of the battle at Bau Co Bong, Vietnam, to private first class.

The problems he thought he left behind at Fort Carson two weeks earlier were now worse. The CO became more determined than ever to make an example of Calvin. He, according to Calvin, continued to ignore the medical limitations established by the doctors at Fort Devens and those now established by the doctor at Fort Carson. Calvin was forced to participate in activities well beyond his limitations, further aggravating his physical condition and emotional stress. After several weeks, Calvin returned to the hospital a physical and emotional wreck and was told by the doctor, "I'm going to put you in the hospital and if they mess with you, just come on sick call. They can't stop you from going on sick call."[534]

The CO, feeling his control slip away, reasoned that if he could not get this slacker to train, then he sure as hell could make his life

---

[532] Calvin Heath 201 File.

[533] Calvin Heath file, Record of Proceedings under Article 15, UCMJ. Note: It should be mentioned that a medical leave issued by a military physician does not automatically allow a soldier to leave base. Calvin, frustrated with the current situation, most likely did not understand the doctor's authority and assumed he could leave. Another possibility was the front office, after receiving the doctor's order, did nothing to convince him otherwise.

[534] Adam Piore interview with Calvin Heath, 2009.

miserable. To punish Calvin for going to the hospital, his weekend passes were revoked, and he was confined to base. Not knowing what else to do and getting even more frustrated with his situation, Calvin finally went to the Inspector General's office to file a complaint. According to Calvin, the IG's office determined that the CO's actions were against regulations and the CO was told to cease and desist and that Calvin deserved his weekend passes just like the other men. Calvin later stated that other combat veterans were similarly targeted, "They were trying to blackmail us into going [back to Vietnam] and there was no way we were doing it. I was standing up for most of the other combat vets that were in the company."[535]

Over the next few weeks, the battle between Calvin and the CO continued to escalate. At one point, Calvin was ordered to gear up and report for field exercises. Calvin requested he be allowed to return to sick call as the doctor instructed and was told that the option no longer existed for him. Regardless, Calvin disobeyed the order and went to the hospital to see his attending physician. This time the doctor, a Colonel, provided Calvin additional paperwork reminding the CO of his authority as a doctor and that he, the CO, did not have the authority to countermand his orders. Calvin, hoping the nightmare was finally over, brought the new paperwork to the CO who flew into a rage. According to Calvin, he "crumbled the order and threw it in the garbage." He ripped into Calvin screaming, "That ain't nothing! Where were you?" Calvin replied, "Down at the dispensary." Calvin continued the story:

> *Well he calls the dispensary and asks for the guy in charge. Well it just so happens that the full bird Colonel that was my doctor was at the dispensary. So, when my company commander asked for the guy in command, he thought he was going to get himself a sergeant or something. When [the colonel] came on the phone... I'm standing there in the company commander's office and he's just carrying on, "Who's the fucking idiot... this guy is [a] mal[content]... he's faking it, and he's just... the doctors are assholes down*

there. They don't..." And he's just carrying on. Finally, he [suddenly] stops and he goes... "Oh." The doctor said to him, "Do you know who you're talking to?" He said no. And he said. "You're talking to a colonel."[536] *[The CO] went from yelling and screaming to, "Yes sir, yes sir, no sir, yes sir, yes sir..." and all that shit. And when he got done, he said, "Go to the hospital!" So, I went to the hospital and they admitted me.*[537]

In April of 1969, six months after arriving at Fort Carson, Calvin once again went under the knife. The surgeons at Fort Carson felt that Calvin would benefit, in more ways than one, with another attempt to extract the bullet. For 13 months Calvin had experienced severe pain due to the deeply embedded bullet and the damage it caused as it fragmented and penetrated the hip joint. The pain Calvin experienced was due to the jagged edges of the shattered bones scraping at the joint. The surgeon felt he could mitigate Calvin's pain by surgically removing some of the fragments. He also felt that further surgery would help Calvin obtain the medical discharge he was told he had months earlier.

During the surgery, the surgeon found that he could not remove the deeply embedded bullet without risking permanent nerve damage. So, he scraped away and removed what fragments he could hoping this would alleviate at least some of the pain and prevent any further damage to his hip.[538]

In spite of the surgery, Calvin's CO was still not through with Calvin and the battle intensified. While Calvin was in the hospital, per the doctor's orders, the CO withheld Calvin's pay. In a letter to Paul Bucha in March of 1999, Calvin wrote, "While in the hospital, I was harassed by the CO who continued to tell me that while I was in the hospital I would not get paid. My doctor told me that what was happening was not right and he would take care of it."[539] It would

---

[536] Note: Calvin reported that the colonel was both a colonel and a lieutenant colonel.

[537] Adam Piore interview with Calvin Heath, 2009.

[538] Calvin Heath interview with author, May 2013.

[539] Calvin letter to Paul Bucha, March 1999.

take some time before Calvin's pay situation was corrected and another 30 years before the alleged injustices perpetrated by Calvin's commanding officer were rectified. Calvin's brother Bert said, "He went back out [on rehabilitation leave] again because they had to work on that hip again. And I think that's when he got disillusioned, more so than when I first met him at Devens [when he returned in April 1968]."[540]

After the surgery, the doctor decided to see what he could do for Calvin. Given that he only had one year remaining on his three-year enlistment and was of little use to the Army because of his physical limitations, he sent him home to recover. Calvin stated, "[The doctor said], 'You know what? I'm going to send you home on a 30-day hospital leave and I'm just going to keep renewing it until your time is done.' He said, 'They're not going to [mess] with you anymore.'"[541]

Calvin returned home to Putnam, Connecticut in May of 1969, fully expecting he that was done with the 10th Infantry and the "CO from hell." This, in Calvin's mind, was confirmed on June 4, 1969, when his mother received a phone call from Calvin's CO. Calvin stated, "... the CO called my home and told my mother that I didn't have to return to Fort Carson. Orders were being sent to me where to report."[542] Calvin was given the impression that his CO was sending him transfer papers, presumably assigning him, once again, to Fort Devens, this time to finish up what little time remained on his enlistment. Calvin also assumed the doctors would continue to renew his monthly rehabilitation leave. Calvin was elated, the end of this ridiculous nightmare was finally in sight.

On June 4, 1969, the same day as the phone call, Calvin was reported AWOL by his CO. One month later, on July 3, 1969, Calvin was listed as "Dropped from the rolls – *Deserter*."[543] This combat tested soldier whose exemplary conduct and gallantry in action earned

---

[540] Calvin Heath interview with author, April 26, 2013.
[541] Adam Piore interview with Calvin Heath, 2009.
[542] Calvin's letter to Paul Bucha March 1999. Note: Bert indicates that Eva did not have a phone at that time and the call could have gone to Eva's next-door neighbor.
[543] Calvin Heath 201 File.

him the Purple Heart and the Silver Star, was now listed in one of the Army's most detestable categories.

None of this news reached Calvin at home in Putnam and he remained convinced that the doctors at Fort Carson would continue to automatically renew his leave orders, per their discussions. Calvin naively thought everything was taken care of and he simply stayed in Putnam. He later stated, "I never went back. I waited in Putnam for them to send me notification that I was either transferred or discharged."[544] Calvin spent the next five months at home trying to recover, hobbling around on crutches. He received no pay and no communication from Fort Carson, the hospital, the doctor, or the Army. Receiving no further instructions and not knowing what else to do, he foolishly did nothing. Sixty days after being reported as a deserter, a federal warrant was issued for his arrest.

On October 2, 1969, there was a loud knock at the front door of Calvin's parents' home. Calvin's mother answered the door and found two men dressed in dark suits standing there. Eva Heath asked, "Yes? Can I help you?" The man at the door responded, "Is this the Heath residence?" She noticed the other man standing behind him scanning the area as if he was looking for something. "Ma'am we're with the FBI. We are looking for Private First-Class Calvin Heath." Before his mother could respond, Calvin limped to the front door and said, "I'm right here." The federal agent at the door said, "Private First-Class Heath, you are under arrest for violation of Article 86 of the Uniform Code of Military Justice. You've been AWOL for four months. Please come with us." Ironically, Calvin was not surprised. He assured the agents he would not be a problem and grabbed his clothes. The agents, seeing that he was in no physical condition to run, waited patiently.[545]

Calvin was then driven to Fort Devens, Massachusetts by the federal agents where he was turned over to the Fort Devens' Provost Marshall. There, he was processed, and placed in a confinement area awaiting the military legal system to process his charge. Within a day

---

[544] Calvin Heath interview with author, May 2013.
[545] Ibid.

or so, he was brought before a Judge Advocate General (JAG) officer to answer the desertion charges. Calvin explained to the officer his side of the story – how he was wounded in Vietnam, how there was no paper trail from Vietnam, how he was treated at Fort Carson, the surgeries, how his CO had sent him home to await transfer orders, and how the doctors from Fort Carson planned to renew his 30-day leave so he could eventually be discharged from the service, but it was all for naught. Without the proper paperwork and orders, the officer thought Calvin's story was just that – a story.

Calvin was processed using non-judicial proceedings and found guilty of desertion. This process allowed penalties and punishments to be assigned without having to go before a Court Martial hearing. He was fined and assigned to a detention company at Fort Devens, where he was confined to barracks and ordered to perform menial work around the base. Many soldiers who went AWOL and were incorrigible were simply granted a general discharge, processed out of the service and sent on their way. But like the CO at Fort Carson, those at Fort Devens seemed to want to set an example with Calvin.

On October 24, 1969, after three weeks of detention and restricted duty, Calvin was finally released and granted a weekend pass. Once again, he returned home, naively thinking his medical discharge, which was bound to catch up to him at some point, would take care of this whole ugly business. He made inquiries and those with whom he spoke told him they would check on his medical status; they of course did not.[546] By Wednesday of the following week, three days after his required return date had passed, Calvin was once again listed as "Dropped from rolls – Desertion."[547] He was again arrested on November 26, 1969, and sent back to Fort Devens, there to once again be held in confinement. This sad process repeated itself five more times, each resulting in Calvin's arrest. Calvin later recalled, "At Fort Devens, I was put in a holding company for AWOL's, deserters and the like. Because I didn't have any paper work with me,

---

[546] Calvin Heath interview with author, May 2013. Calvin Heath 201 File.
[547] Calvin Heath 201 File.

the profiles were not recognized."[548] Calvin had to make the choice of doing what he was told and risk permanent damage to his hip or go home and take his chances with the military legal system.

Research for this project found no reasonable advocacy on Calvin's behalf and the longer the process continued, the deeper in trouble he got, and the more disillusioned he became. What little legal defense he did receive was appointed by the Army's JAG office and even they were unwilling to listen to Calvin's story, buying into the version suggested by the deplorable records that followed him from Vietnam. There was still no mention of his role in the battle near Phuoc Vinh or the medals he earned, no mention of his medical discharge, and no mention of the other mistreatments he endured since Vietnam. Still feeling dejected 30 years later he sadly stated in a letter to Paul Bucha, "I received no help. I was treated like a lowlife."[549] During my interviews with him in 2013, he sadly added, "How could they have done that to me? I was treated like absolute garbage."[550]

To add to the already miserable state of affairs, since April of 1968, when Calvin was initially screened by psychiatrists at Fort Devens, he had received no counselling support or psychological help. No one believed his story, and no one evaluated him or recommended any psychological treatment. No one up his chain of command ever bothered to sit with Calvin to develop an understanding as to what was happening to this once exemplary soldier. A simple phone call by an interested officer to Bucha could have cleared up everything. Thirty minutes of someone's time could have saved Calvin 30 years of heartache and grief, but like Barsanti, Calvin's commanding general in Vietnam, they were too busy.

Throughout his post-Vietnam time, Calvin only wanted one thing – someone to listen to him; someone who would believe his side of the story, but not one person stepped forward. A knowledgeable advocate would have easily found the Fort Devens surgical records,

[548] Calvin Heath letter to Paul Bucha, March 15, 1999. Note: Calvin's 201 File shows 13 AWOLs and seven incarcerations.
[549] Calvin Heath letter to Paul Bucha, March 15, 1999.
[550] Calvin Heath interview with author, May 2014.

and the Fort Devens psychiatric reports. They would have found and spoken with Bucha and Harjo and tracked down the missing paperwork for his Silver Star and his other medals. He would have been exonerated at the military hearing and he would have secured the medical discharge he was promised and the benefits he earned. A few minutes of someone's time and this entire mess would have been behind Calvin shortly after it began. Unfortunately, none of that happened and he was rapidly becoming one of the military's worst examples of mistreatment and abuse.

As Calvin's disillusionment with the Army grew, so did his personal problems. The terrible memories of March 18 and 19, 1968, were rapidly turning into full-fledge nightmares and night terrors. Stuck with nowhere to go and nowhere to turn, Calvin quickly slipped into a state of depression. The once happy-go-lucky kid that once played on the Ciconne's farm was now a pissed off, beaten and depressed young man of twenty. He felt that he had given his country everything when they needed him most, and now he was sick, wounded, damaged and was being treated like a common criminal instead of the hero he was.

Back in Putnam, Connecticut, people close to Calvin, due to his growing difficulties with the Army and arrests, now began to seriously question his accounts of Vietnam. Many reasoned that the United States Army does not arrest its heroes and send them to jail. Calvin had no paperwork, no orders, no medals, and so no proof. Doubt began creeping in and many close to him now believed the worse. Calvin was becoming very isolated and few people at home wanted anything to do with him.

Calvin's older brother Bert agreed that his brother was being mistreated, but he advised him he had to "make it good with the Army" or he'd never be free. Bert states:

They lost all his records, he wasn't getting any pay and he just said, "Piss on them," and he asked me "What do I do?" and I said, "Calvin you can't have the [authorities] coming up here and picking you up because they're going to find your records. And in all honesty, unless you have a

champion on your side you're not going to get anywhere.
You're just one [man] in a big pot full [of men]."[551]

---

[551] Bert Heath interview with author October 24, 2013.

BAD CONDUCT DISCHARGE

By 1970, Calvin tried to get his life back on track and with the help of his brother Bert, he secured a full-time job in Southbridge, Massachusetts.[552] Within months, however, the Army caught up with Calvin again and the job didn't last long. Any employer who knew he was having trouble with the federal government avoided him like the plague. In 2013, Calvin sadly remembered, "I bounced around from job to job and I couldn't hold on to anything."[553] He continued, "I would get odd jobs, but I couldn't hold anything full time because I couldn't be in a mill or around anyone with authority. I just couldn't do it. And being with a lot of people bothered me. It was like..."[554] Calvin faded off, the thoughts of that time were still unsettling to him.

Calvin's last arrest for desertion and AWOL was in September of 1971, after which the Army seemed to lose interest in him. For several years, Calvin heard nothing. In July 1973, Calvin had learned of a large fire at the National Personnel Records Center, located in St. Louis, Missouri which resulted in the loss of millions of military records. Calvin assumed that his records were among those lost and once again, foolishly felt his problems were behind him. Bert added, "I don't think he was in contact with the Army any more [after that]. The Army kind of ... from what I understood, the records were either burnt in a fire or something happened to them. Anyway, the records got lost."[555]

For several years, Calvin floated aimlessly around from one odd job to the next, unable to land anything permanent. As the weeks turned into months, his difficulty with life increased and he was now

---

[552] Bert Heath interview with author, October 24, 2013.

[553] Calvin Heath interview with author, May 2013.

[554] Ibid.

[555] Bert Heath interview with author, October 24, 2013. Note: On July 12, 1973, there was a major fire at the National Personnel Records Center and more than 16M records were destroyed. The destroyed records were from those people serving from November 1, 1912 to January 1, 1969. It is unlikely, however, that Calvin's records were among those lost in the fire.

having considerable problems sleeping and coping with day-to-day life.

The issues he had with the Army, while serious, were nothing in comparison to the quickly-evolving devil he now wrestled with each and every night. Calvin's reoccurring nightmares about the battle at Bau Co Bong, the horrific death and destruction he saw, the loss of his best friend who died in his arms, had become so vivid that he was terrified to sleep. "For a while I didn't want to go to sleep at night because of the dreams. Every night I would have them."[556] Every time he fell asleep, he found himself back in the jungle – on that trail. Every night, visions of Paul Conner dying in his arms, the shadowy silhouettes of the approaching enemy, the NVA soldiers that picked through his bloody and damaged body, and the two men he killed up close and personal with his survival knife, plagued what little rest he could find.[557] Every night his nightmares relived the horrors of his first kill at the 187th base perimeter and the faceless ghosts of all the other people he killed after that. Calvin related that the nightmares were relentless and each and every night, shadowy figures pursued him, all seeking vengeance. When he did sleep the figures seemed to lurk in every shadow, behind every door. He woke most mornings startled, scared, sweating and often crying. Sometimes it would take several minutes before he realized he was no longer in the jungles of Vietnam.

Unlike today's soldiers who often see counsellors within hours of a battle, Calvin had no one to teach him the skills necessary to battle the nightly demons he now fought. His older sister Joyce, with whom Calvin lived for several months in Plainfield, Connecticut during that time, confirmed Calvin's story. She stated, "You could never touch him while he was sleeping. We had to call his name to wake him up. He was always afraid that he would hurt someone."[558]

Even when not sleeping and in the perceived safety of the daylight hours, Calvin continued to fight other demons. He reported, "For a while I couldn't even look at a piece of raw meat. Going by a

---

[556] Calvin Heath interview with author, May 2013.

[557] Ibid, April 26, 2013.

[558] Joyce Lefevre interview with author, March 30, 2014.

butcher shop, seeing the blood used to make me puke." He went on, "Loud noises or a car backfiring, things like that would set me off. How do you [go through life and] avoid shit like that?"[559]

In 1970, Calvin met and married 17-year-old Maryanne Richardson. Maryanne had lived next door to Calvin's brother Glen and his sister-in-law Betty. The two hit it off and were soon married. Calvin and Maryanne rented a small house trailer in East Killingly, Connecticut and for a while, things seemed to be going well. Maryanne became pregnant and gave birth to a son, whom they named Calvin William Heath Jr, or "CJ." Calvin had a few months of happiness, but because of all his unresolved issues, the marriage was doomed before it began.[560]

Left: One of the few pictures of Calvin, Maryanne and Calvin Jr. "CJ." Shortly after this picture, according to Calvin's family, Maryanne left for Indiana. Calvin later stated that he wished he could go back, "I would have done things differently." With Calvin's unresolved issues, the marriage had little chance to succeed. Picture circa 1971. Paul Duquette photo.

---

[559] Calvin Heath interview with author, May 2013.
[560] Authier, Rob, interview with author, March 28, 2014.

By the time CJ came along, Calvin was still having difficulty holding a steady job and he continued to battle nightmares and flashbacks. The dreams soon became so bad that Maryanne became frightened of Calvin whenever he slept. He later admitted to thrashing about at night thinking he was back in the jungles of Vietnam and she was an enemy soldier. But the enemy he fought existed only in his mind. He later sadly added, "I scared the hell out of my [first wife]. I [once] grabbed her by the throat, because..." Not knowing how to properly finish the sentence he simply said, "I was really bad then..."[561] Soon after, the marriage began to falter.[562]

In August of 2014, Calvin's sister-in-law Betty stated that Calvin was "... locked in time. He couldn't get past Vietnam. Maryanne was growing intellectually and Calvin couldn't handle the responsibilities of a family."[563] Approximately two years after the wedding, Maryanne had enough and she packed up the baby and left Calvin. She moved to Indiana, met another man and asked Calvin for a divorce. Shortly after that, she asked Calvin to sign adoption papers allowing her new husband to adopt CJ. Calvin's good friend, Rob Authier stated, "That really bothered Calvin for a very long time, and he wasn't going to sign the papers."[564] He eventually relented, most likely feeling Maryanne's new husband was able to provide a better life for his son than he could. For the next 17 years, Calvin had little contact with his son.

During our meetings in 2013, Calvin always found the topic of his first marriage and his son extremely uncomfortable. It was easy to see that he was heartbroken about the way things turned out and he wished that things were different.[565] When telling me this part of his story, it was abundantly clear that Calvin felt Maryanne was forced to

---

[561] Adam Piore interview with Calvin Heath, 2009.
[562] Ibid.
[563] Heath, Betty, interview with author, August 25, 2014.
[564] Authier, Rob, interview with author, March 28, 2014.
[565] Note: Calvin was uncomfortable with this topic and is one I agreed with him not to further explore.

face challenges that most new wives do not have to face. Calvin stated, "If I could go back, I would have done things differently."[566]

During the 1970s and 1980s, Calvin did find refuge in several areas. The first was with his one and only true love – athletics. Back in Connecticut, Calvin played basketball and softball in every league where he could find a spot. Being one of the better athletes in Northeast Connecticut, few teams refused his talent. He was always happiest when on a softball diamond or a basketball court. Retrospectively, it's easy to suggest that subconsciously Calvin viewed these new teams as a substitute for the comradery he once felt with the men of Delta Company. It would take him many years before he understood the futility of that expectation as there was no substitute for the deep bonds he developed with men with whom he had bled and suffered.

Another area of refuge for Calvin lay deep inside a bottle. When he wasn't working or playing sports, Calvin drank. As he relayed to me in 2013, "You remember me from back then Joe, I drank a lot just trying to drown my sorrows..."[567] Like millions of soldiers returning from war, he attempted to find a solution to his problems by self-medicating with alcohol, but there were few answers to be found there, and of course, only more heartache. The more Calvin drank the angrier he got, and the angrier he got, the more he fought. By the mid-1970s, Calvin was rapidly gaining a reputation for being a little crazy and fighting anyone at the drop of a hat.

During his heavy drinking days, Calvin often became paranoid and felt that people were always talking about him. "Everybody back here [was saying] I was shot on the back side and everybody was saying, 'You were running... That's why you ain't got this and you ain't got that...'"[568] Everywhere he went, people seemed to have an opinion about the terrible mess he single-handedly made of his life, but few had the courage to voice those opinions to his face. When they did, it usually resulted in a fight.

---

[566] Calvin Heath interview with author, June 2013.
[567] Calvin Heath interview with author, May 2013.
[568] Adam Piore interview with Calvin Heath, 2009.

Calvin noted, "It used to be that I'd go into a place and they whispered as I went by, you know… you could hear them saying shit; people that I grew up with. I ended up getting in fist [fights with everyone]."[569] He was also quickly gaining a reputation for being the worst kind of person to take on in a fight. No matter how badly beaten up he was, he just never went down. He would not stop until the other person was badly hurt or he could no longer stand. He later told Adam Piore in an interview, "If [I] get really angry at somebody… really, really, really get upset… I'd have no qualms in killing [him]."[570]

Sometime during the late 1980s I witnessed such a fight. After a softball game, Calvin, the guys and I were in the parking lot drinking a few beers, as was typical after a game. Someone from the other team had a few too many drinks and started teasing Calvin about his time in Vietnam, accusing him that his stories were all bullshit. I warned the man to knock it off, but he continued with his abuse. After taking what he could, Calvin completely lost control and went after the man in a rage. When we finally managed to pull Calvin off the verbal assailant, the crazed look in his eyes convinced me he would have killed the man, or at least seriously hurt him, had we not intervened. The badly beaten man left the park, and nothing ever became of the fight.

As time went on, and Calvin's drinking and fighting became worse, he became more and more isolated. Everywhere he went people avoided him.

I'd go to the [high school] football games and I would be in the bleachers or if I was up on this knoll – people would talk to me, but they'd shy away from me. I'd go to the high school basketball games. When I sat in the bleachers, there'd be a gap [around me] from the other people. I don't know. I guess they were scared of me. They thought I was loony tunes.[571]

---

[569] Adam Piore interview with Calvin Heath, 2009.
[570] Ibid..
[571] Ibid.

Sadly, many people who knew Calvin as the happy-go-lucky kid "...who would not hurt a fly as a kid,"[572] now saw him as a volatile, unpredictable and dangerous young man. After a couple brushes with the law, Calvin began to realize that "taking on the world" especially those who thought of him as a screw up, coward, or liar was completely futile. He was a trained soldier and knew that he was fighting an enemy he could not defeat. He began to reason on his own that the best tactic in this case was something he learned in LRRP class in 1967 – "escape and evade." He added, "I was getting into too many fights and I was hurting people. And then I just got to the point where I [wouldn't] fight anymore and I just stayed away from everybody."[573]

To add to his rapidly growing misfortune, the U.S. Army did not forget about Calvin, nor did they lose his records in the 1973 National Personnel Records Center fire. In November 1974, six years and eight months after the battle at Bau Co Bong, and seven years and six months after enlisting, the U.S. Army sent Calvin a notification, requiring him to report to Fort Benjamin Harrison, Indiana, for discharge. In a 1999 letter to Paul Bucha, Calvin wrote:

> In 1974, I got a letter from the military telling me to go to Fort Benjamin Harris for discharge. Once there I was told I could either go back in the Army or be discharged. With all the ways I was being treated, I chose the discharge. When I was going through the discharge procedure, I was told to just sign the papers and I would be out in a day or two. If I didn't sign the papers, I could be there for at least a month.[574]

Calvin, under extreme duress and without understanding the significance of the papers placed in front of him, simply signed everything presented to him by the JAG officer. As a result, a Court Martial hearing consisting of five officers, two Army and three

---

[572] Bert Heath interview with author, October 1, 2014.
[573] Adam Piore interview with Calvin Heath, 2009.
[574] Calvin Heath letter to Paul Bucha, March 15, 1999.

Marines, was immediately convened. Calvin was upset and confused. Instead of going home, like he thought he would be, he now found himself in front of a U.S. Military Court of Law alone, unprepared and poorly represented. The Board reviewed the evidence of Calvin's case and Calvin's incomplete 201 File, the reports from 1LT John W. Brauer, his commander at Fort Carson, and his arrest records from the JAG office and the civilian authorities. They found insufficient evidence to support Calvin's accounts of 1968 and 1969, and in spite of his pleas and requests for the Court Martial Board to conduct further research, the Board felt the case did not warrant the time it would take to seek additional first-hand accounts from First Sergeant Harjo and Captain Bucha. As a result, there would be no further investigation of Calvin's military history. Considering only the evidence they had in hand, the Board quickly found Calvin guilty of multiple violations of Article 86 of the UCMJ – finding that he was in fact guilty of:

> *Failure to go to appointed place of duty; that a certain authority appointed a certain time and place of duty for the accused; that the accused knew of that time and place; and that the accused, without authority, failed to go to the appointed place of duty at the time prescribed.*[575]

Instead of throwing him in jail once again, however, the Board did agree that Calvin's service in Vietnam and his Purple Heart did carry some weight into the matter and they granted him the option of a discharge or returning to duty to finish his remaining time. Calvin adds:

> *I was given the choice of a discharge or return to service... because of the Purple Heart and combat in Vietnam, I had my choice. I told them I wanted out. They told me because I couldn't prove that I had the Silver Star they would not give me an Honorable Discharge. The two Army officers voted to*

---

[575] Uniform Code of Military Justice found January 3, 2014 at: www.ucmj.us/. Note: The quote used is current language. The language used in 1974 might have been slightly different.

give me an Honorable Discharge and the [three] Marine officers voted to give me a Bad Conduct Discharge. Result: BCD.[576]

A BCD is a punitive discharge that is one step above Dishonorable Discharge. BCDs typically follow incarceration in a military prison. All benefits, to include VA disability compensation, and all future medical assistance are completely forfeited. The BCD also prohibited Calvin from ever working for any federal and many State agencies. He was now officially a branded man.

With few options, confused and anxious to leave Fort Harrison, he chose to put the Army behind him and signed the discharge papers without further review or legal assistance. He later stated, "I signed everything. I didn't realize that I was signing my rights away."[577] By signing those papers, Calvin forfeited all future rights to any and all veteran benefits. He was left with unresolved physical and psychological issues, recurring nightmares, and no hopes of any future financial or medical assistance from the Veterans' Administration.

In addition to the BCD, stories later persisted as to why Calvin initially left the Army and did not return as ordered. Calvin later told the men of Delta Company that he was extremely upset over the fact that the Army docked his pay for the value of the Army property that was taken from him by the enemy during the battle of March 18-19, including the PRC-77 that he was ordered to shut down and discard by CPT Bucha. In a 2013 discussion, Bill Heaney stated, "Calvin ended up getting a dishonorable discharge because of that radio." While this wasn't the only reason for his BCD, it was certainly part of the picture. Calvin himself mentioned the radio incident and he believed it was why he received so little money from the Army in 1969. Dave Dillard, the company Communications Sergeant at that time added:

---

[576] Calvin Heath letter to Paul Bucha, March 15, 1999.
[577] Adam Piore interview with Calvin Heath, 2009.

That's what I understand, but I'm not sure of that whole story, but that's what I understand. The radio was lost, and he was charged. Here's the way it was, he lost the radio and our supply sergeant who evidently done some things and needed to cover his ass, so he went out and put in what we call a Reporter's Survey. A Reporter's Survey means they go out and investigate the loss and if you are found responsible for the loss, they attach [your pay], charge you for it. And this guy had evidently forged Calvin's name saying that he had lost the radio... and eventually while he was down here at that sub base, or wherever he was assigned, in Connecticut (probably Fort Devens), he had to pay for it. [They] took his money so Calvin went AWOL. He was married at the time... and he went AWOL because he couldn't pay for it. And when he came back, they discharged him dishonorably. And that created a stir with his tribe too... [578]

On December 2, 1974, Calvin returned home from Fort Benjamin Harrison emotionally drained and deeply depressed over the continually deteriorating course his life had taken. His personal honor now lay in ruins, few of his friends and family believed his story about his Silver Star, and now, the only paperwork he had to show for his time in the Army and his heroic efforts in Vietnam was a BCD. Utterly dejected and feeling completely dishonored, this once proud Screaming Eagle of the 101st Airborne, a member of the famed Rakkasans and Native American warrior, returned to Putnam, Connecticut in total humiliation and shame. Dave Dillard later reflected on what must have been Calvin's frame of mind:

You're dishonest? And you're a warrior? You see what I mean Joe? That whole idea that when he came back that

---

[578] Dillard, Heaney, Rawson interview with author, October 9, 2013. Note: There is a great deal of speculation on this particular topic and no official records were located to corroborate this story. Based on comments from several sources, it is the author's opinion that this was in fact a piece of Calvin's problems with the Army and he was charged for the radio that was taken from him by the NVA while he lay gravely wounded on the jungle floor.

nobody believed him. He told me that he went before his company commander and said, "I didn't lose that radio. It was taken off of me by the gooks in Vietnam, when I was lying out there all night [wounded]." And he told the story to the company commander and the company commander said to him, "That's the biggest bunch of bullshit I ever heard..." But it was all true.[579]

Several weeks after Calvin returned to Putnam in 1974, he still did not fully grasp the full ramifications of the BCD and the paperwork he had signed at Fort Harrison. Triggered by his trip to Fort Harrison, his nightmares and pain worsened and eventually became unbearable. He felt himself slipping deeper and deeper into what seemed like a bottomless pit. He had no full-time job and therefore no medical insurance. Not knowing where else to turn, he contacted the VA for help. Calvin still did not understand that the U.S. Army and the United States government had completely abandoned him.

The VA, after reviewing his records, immediately rejected all requests for service and callously turned Calvin away. Whether or not his physical and psychological problems were a direct result of his honorable combat service in Vietnam didn't matter. As far as the VA was concerned Private First Class Calvin W. Heath, 2nd Platoon, D Company, 3/187th Infantry (Airborne), 101st Airborne Division, was persona non grata. As he stated, "I was so bad in 1974 that I applied to the VA for benefits. But because of the AWOL they wouldn't give me any and I had nowhere else to go."[580]

In 1975, Calvin's untreated pain and nightmares were getting worse. He had no professional help and he had not spoken with any of the survivors of the battle. As a result, he began to lose the details of March 18-19, 1968 and even he now began to question his own recollections of the battle. Many nights he lay in bed thinking, *maybe those around me are correct and I am a coward. Maybe I was running away.*

---

[579] Dillard, Heaney, Rawson interview with author, October 9, 2013.
[580] Calvin Heath interview with author, May 2013.

Further, with no training nor understanding of her son's problems, Calvin's mother Eva tried to provide comfort in the only way she knew how. Calvin's brother Melvin would later say, "When Calvin looked for a little [understanding], my mother would just tell him he had to let it go and move on."[581] Eva did not comprehend the extent of her son's pain. She could not help him with his physical wounds, the emotional damage, or the demons he now fought. She had no idea how to provide her son any sensible advice.

Calvin's father Wayland was another source of great despair for Calvin, as even he now began to question his son's version of his time in Vietnam. How can a son feel good about the doubts of his own father? Calvin often fell asleep, sometimes drunk, trying to sort out which version of the story was closer to the truth, the one everyone believed or the one he thought he remembered. This feeling of utter confusion and hopelessness oftentimes led to suicidal thoughts. "There were a lot of nights I just felt like ending it. I really don't know why I didn't."[582]

In April 2014, while sitting in my kitchen, Calvin stared into the bottom of his coffee mug, obviously transported back in time when all seemed lost. He told me that he had contemplated suicide many times during this period. I could not help but feel saddened by the fact that he had no one at the time who completely understood the pain and anguish he combatted on a daily basis. I was saddened by the fact that America had turned its back on him and wondered how many more Calvins were out there.

Calvin's self-doubts about the facts of those horrific days, however, always disappeared as soon as he fell asleep. Nightly visits from the maimed and dead men of Delta Company and the ghostly figures of NVA soldiers long-dead, hauntingly approaching as he lay helplessly on the blood-soaked jungle ground, reminded Calvin, in the cruelest of ways, that *his* memory of the battle was indeed correct. And then there was Paul Conner; his badly torn body, his eyes always staring – burning unceasingly into Calvin's soul, telling him, "Don't

---

[581] Melvin Heath interview with author January 13, 2014.
[582] Calvin Heath interview with author, April 26, 2013.

you dare forget about me! Everything you remember is true! Don't let those bastards wear you down!" Calvin always woke with a stir, drenched in his own sweat. It took him a while to gather his wits, but when he did, he would agree with Paul… for the moment he was determine *not* to forget – not to let the bastards wear him down.

1970s - Carving Out a Life

There were a few bright spots in Calvin's life during the mid to late 1970s. He had a good relationship with his mother and other members of his family. He did have friends who accepted him unconditionally, several of whom were veterans with high functioning military "bullshit filters." They could tell which military stories were true and which were not. They could see through those who bragged about deeds they never performed, and they provided a sympathetic ear for those who had truly "danced with the devil." They immediately knew that Calvin wasn't full of shit and some of these veterans defended his honor at the risk of their own. I would like to think that I was among this group of friends.

Above: Calvin with two of his dogs Thor and Boo. Calvin Heath photo.

Another group of loyal friends that never questioned Calvin's deeds or his service, who loved him unconditionally, and who were always there when he needed them most, were his dogs. From the

1970s and through the balance of his life, Calvin always had an extraordinary relationship with his canine companions. There were a number of them, and several stuck out through the years as special friends to Calvin including his German Shepherds, Thor and Boo. They stayed with him through thick and thin and, on at least one occasion, fought side-by-side with him, but that story a little later. For Calvin, Andy Rooney's quote, "The average dog is a nicer person than the average person," definitely applied.

During the mid-to late 1970s, Calvin supplemented his income by becoming a bouncer at a local bar in Dayville, Connecticut. It was never clear during my interviews with Calvin why he chose this line of work. Possibilities include his training and qualifications, a way to deal with his anger, or simply the chance to earn a few extra dollars and get free drinks. Although a hazardous profession, all indications suggest Calvin was very good at it.

Calvin later recalled several incidents, including one night when he was forced to contend with a belligerent drunk at the bar. He stated:

> *The guy was drunk and big. He was like 6'5" and well over 200 pounds and we were trying to get him to go out the door. He braced [himself against] the door and I tried to grab him, and he went like that* (showing a punch) *and he threw a back hander at me and all he caught was the end of my nose. And the blood just shot out and I flipped right out. I spun right around, and I chopped him into the knee, and I had my boots on and I slit him all the way down. I caved in his knee. I shattered his knee, dislocated it, and then ripped his skin going all the way down into his ankle. He bent over and I kneed him in the face, flipped him on his back, and stopped right there... stopped at that.*[583]

The rage that had been building in Calvin for several years nearly spilled out that evening and for a moment he had entered a place he hadn't been for many years. It was a place so dark that it nearly cost

---

[583] Adam Piore interview with Calvin Heath, 2009.

the other man his life. Luckily, Calvin was able to rein in his anger before he crossed a line over which he would never have returned. He walked away from the fight shaking, leaving others to deal with the drunk, and uncertain about what had just happened.

He told another story:

When I [finally] had enough [with bouncing] – I was working Sunday night by myself at the bar. We had to throw this guy out of the bar, and he left with his buddy. Then towards closing time, I was getting ready to leave and a guy came in and he said, "Watch out! There's two guys out in the parking lot and they said they're going to nail one of the bouncers when he comes out for throwing them out... they're going to beat him up." So, I was the one who went out and I looked around and I didn't see anybody. I had a '55 Chevy and I walked over to my car, and I had a German Shepard, 105-pound German Shepard – snow white, blue eyes, pink nose, pink ears – and he was lying on the front seat. I opened up the door – well I looked around and didn't see anybody. I unlocked the door. I opened up the door and somebody behind me says, "Hey!" So, I turned around. When I completely turned around, he had already thrown the punch and he caught me right in the forehead. Well, when he hit me in the forehead, my head snapped back and my '55 – the roof line – I hit it with the back of my head and it stunned me and I went down onto my knees, and as I went down onto my knees he came in and he was going to do whatever he was going to do and my dog came in right over the top of me. Got him right on the shoulders and right on the face and wrestled the guy down to the ground and bit him right in the face, just tearing this guy's face up and the other buddy that was with him took off running and they called the cops. I pulled the dog off of him and had him back in [the car]. A State cop came and the State cop that came had a dog with him – and he asked what was going on and he's taking statements and I thought I was going to lose the dog for sure for attacking the guy. I told him, and the witnesses all said the same thing, he was getting beat up and his dog came to his rescue. The cop looked at me and told me "Get the hell out of here. Get your dog and get out of here. Don't worry about it." And they arrested him (the attacker) *for assault. I'll bet that guy had over 100 stitches in his face. That dog just chewed his face up bad.*[584]

On October 8, 1977, Congress enacted Public Law 95-126, which stated:

An act to deny entitlement to veterans' benefits to certain persons who would otherwise become so entitled solely by virtue of the administrative upgrading under temporarily revised standards of other than honorable discharge from service during the Vietnam era; to require a case-by-case review under uniform, historically consistent, generally applicable standards and procedures prior to the award of veterans' benefits to persons administratively discharged under other than honorable conditions from active military, naval, or air service; and for other purposes.[585]

The newer restrictions upset veterans' groups all across the country. They rightfully felt that Vietnam veterans deserved more assistance from the government, not less! The law further isolated those wounded combat veterans who remained on the fringes of the system. Less veterans would be receiving benefits, and for combat veterans like Calvin, the new law moved any chance of help further and further away. His only hope now was to try to convince the Army to upgrade his BCD to an Honorable Discharge, something he knew was nearly impossible.

In March 1978, having nothing to lose, Calvin contacted the VA and inquired about the discharge upgrade process. He was told by a VA staff member that he would have to fill out a number of forms, including a Request for Administration and Adjudicative Action. These forms were to be completed and submitted along with any other

---

[584] Adam Piore interview with Calvin Heath, 2009.
[585] Public Law 95-126 enacted on October 8, 1977.

supporting evidence Calvin might have, such as independent medical reviews, psychological evaluations, letters of recommendations, and support-for-change affidavits from men *with* whom, and *for* whom he had served. Everything would then have to be submitted to a review board for a final decision. A week later, a package with the paperwork from the VA office arrived. Calvin spread the contents on the kitchen table and stared at the pamphlets, forms, and complicated explanations. Within a few minutes, he once again became incredibly overwhelmed and discouraged. The mound of paperwork that lay before him was not deliverance and hope but was rather another insurmountable road block. To Calvin, had the information been written in Latin, it would have made as much sense.

According to many veterans' groups at the time, the process to seek benefits for those who had none, was humiliating and degrading. It forced many deserving combat veterans to beg for help that they rightfully deserved. Many former combatants viewed the process as futile as they saw a vast majority of the applicants immediately turned down. With little help, and again no legal advice, Calvin filled out the questionnaires the best he could, supplied what supplemental information he had gathered, and submitted the forms to the return address provided. It took him days to complete the paperwork and he undoubtedly did a less than adequate job presenting his case. Once the forms were submitted, all he could do was sit back and wait. Two months later he received his answer from the Army Discharge Review Board (ADRB). It read:

> *On May 23, 1978, the ADRB voted, in a 3 to 2 decision, not to affirm the applicant's upgrade characterization of service under uniform standards. The ADRB considered the applicant's initial excellent service, however, it did not consider that to be of sufficient magnitude to outweigh his acts of indiscipline which led to his discharge.* "[586]

---

[586] U.S. Army, Board for the Correction of Military Records Proceeding Summary, dated August 14, 2003, Docket Number AR2003086947, p. 6.

Had just one person of the three who voted to reject Calvin's case voted in his favor, his nightmare would have ended, and he would have been finally able to seek the medical and psychological help he so desperately needed. Once again discouraged, but unsurprised, Calvin set the file aside. It would be several years before he attempted any further requests to the VA for help. For now, he would have to continue as best he could, getting through each day on his own.

Above: Calvin's 1955 Chevy. During the late 1970s and through the 1980s, Calvin always found a little peace under the hood of a classic car. Calvin Heath photo.

SEARCHING FOR HELP

Wounded and traumatized Vietnam veterans returning to civilian life oftentimes had to deal with conflicting and contradictory emotions. Battle-wounded soldiers like Calvin dealt with diametrically opposing feelings of wanting to avoid going back into war at all costs, while the same time, battling an intense need to return to their units and their fellow soldiers. Soldiers who were shipped home within hours of being wounded, became PTSD-worst-case scenarios. The more detached they became from their fighting comrades, the worse their psychological issues became. Calvin, who never had the chance to sit and talk with the men about the battle, was forced to deal with his rapidly developing PTSD alone.

Unbeknownst to Calvin, many of the men with whom he had fought alongside in Vietnam were also living their own brand of personal hell. Many turned to drugs and alcohol, most experienced unsuccessful marriages, and some were homeless for years. Like Calvin, these soldiers returned to an ungrateful country that had little sympathy for them or their problems. To many of the returning combat veterans, it seemed that no one appreciated the sacrifices they made. They returned to a VA system that was broken for most, and ambivalent at best, for the rest. PTSD was still an undefined psychological condition even though the results were abundantly clear and obvious. Very few professionals had a complete understanding of the far-reaching effects of PTSD and the isolation these men felt.

Bill Heaney, one of the men who made numerous attempts to save the men isolated near the trail during the battle of March 18-19, 1968, later said that the most difficult part about being a Vietnam veteran was, "We had to hide the fact that we were Vietnam veterans. We would go for job interviews and people would ask, 'What did you do in the army?' And I would say 'I killed people.' What else could I say?"[587] Mike Rawson, another member of Delta Company stated, "I

---

[587] Dillard, Heaney, Rawson interview with author, October 9, 2013.

248

got to a point where I couldn't live in my own skin. And they'll never take that away from me again."[588] Heaney added that for him, the hardest part of returning home from Vietnam was the fact that we "…just came home alone."[589] Mike Rawson and Dave Dillard agreed that, "There was no fanfare, no crowds, no flag waving, nothing."[590] When Calvin came home he was forced to deal with his psychological and physical challenges alone.

Some of the men from Delta Company found temporary refuge by remaining in the military. First Lieutenant Jeffrey Wishik, First Sergeant Harjo and medic Ray Diaz, all retired from the service with proud records. Paul Bucha also stayed in the Army for nearly four years after the battle. Dave Dillard reenlisted and returned to Vietnam in 1970. Whether this continued association with the Army ultimately helped the men psychologically is unclear, but it certainly helped to establish at least some closure for them.

Many of the men sought the help of doctors, psychiatrists, and psychologists, but few found answers with these learned men and women as the effects of PTSD at that time were not completely understood. Other combat veterans buried themselves in projects, careers, religion, or personal missions that helped to deflect the issues of Vietnam, at least for a while. A few of the men, unable to cope with the unrelenting demons, simply gave up and took their own lives.

After returning home from the war, Dave Dillard was one of the men who attempted to move on with his life. He attended college at Monterey Peninsula College and San Francisco State University where he received a Bachelor of Arts Degree in Theater and Education. In 1980, working on his capstone project, Dave decided to write Delta Company's story hoping that it could at some point be turned into a screenplay. Dave felt Delta's story of March 16-19, 1968 needed to be told, for more than one reason, and it provided him a meaningful and relevant way to finish his scholastic work.

Dave began the project by locating as many of the men from Delta as possible. In 1981, Calvin's phone rang and the voice on the

[588] Dillard, Heaney, Rawson interview with author, October 9, 2013.
[589] Ibid.
[590] Ibid.

other end said, "[Calvin] this is Dave. Dave Dillard." Calvin, confused and not recognizing the voice at first, replied, "Don't know you..." Dillard persisted, "I was with the Company Commander, I was the RTO..."[591] Calvin thought for a moment and then it suddenly clicked. *Dave Dillard! Holy shit! It's Dave!* For the first time in 13 years, Calvin was finally talking to a battle mate. Before he understood the nature of the call, he immediately felt unimaginable relief as though a lifeline had been thrown to him. For the first time in a very long time, he realized that there were others who had survived the battle! A small portion of the unbearable loneliness and isolation he had been experiencing for years instantly faded. The call wasn't much, but to Calvin, it was something. It was hope! Calvin later said, "I was at a real low point [in my life then] and just hearing Dave's voice made things a whole lot better."[592]

Dillard informed Calvin of the purpose of his call and the two men talked for the better part of an hour. Over the next few years, they reconnected several times and Calvin eventually informed his old friend about the difficulties he had with the Army and VA since being medevac'd from the battle site. Dillard listened with genuine interest and for the first time since leaving Vietnam, Calvin finally had the sympathetic ear of someone who was not only willing to listen but was truly able to understand his pain. Dillard didn't have any answers for Calvin and suggested that he should start by contacting one of the officers who was present that day.

Calvin gave Dave's recommendation considerable thought and in 1982, he decided that the best place to start was to establish whether or not his old platoon leader, Jeff Wishik was still alive. Calvin's last recollection of Wishik was with a priest bent over him administering Last Rites and the doctors at Long Binh confirming it would be highly unlikely that Jeff would survive the night. Not knowing where to start, Calvin wrote a letter to the current Company Commander of Delta Company, 3/187th Infantry Regiment, at Fort Campbell, Kentucky and

---

[591] Adam Piore interview with Calvin Heath, 2009.
[592] Calvin Heath interview with author, May 2013.

several weeks later, on Thursday, August 19, 1982, he received the following letter:

Department of the Army
Headquarters, D Co. 3d Bd, 187th Inf.
Fort Campbell, KY

16 August 82

Mr. Calvin W. Heath
46 Smith St.
Putnam, CT 06260

Dear Mr. Heath,

Thank you for your recent letter. We always appreciate hearing from former soldiers of the Rakkasan battalion and D Company. The Regimental colors still unite us in spirit, whether on active duty or in civilian life.

Regretfully, the information you requested about 1LT Jeffrey Wishik is not available at this headquarters; if it were, we would not hesitate to provide it. I have researched a register of officers myself but was unable to locate him or his address. A possible source of information might be:

Commander
Adjutant General Center
Attn: Soldier Support Center
Fort Benjamin Harrison, IN 46249

I wish you providence in your attempt to contact 1LT Wishik.

The D Company Wolfpack has changed quite a bit since the Vietnam War. Under its current organization, it is an anti-armor force, equipped with 22 TOW missile launchers and 7 motorcycle scouts. The unit packs firepower and mobility, two features which are necessary on the modern battlefield. The company deploys to and trains in areas throughout North America, including Panama, Alaska, New York, and California.

Again, thank you for writing, and best wishes for locating your comrade. If you are ever in the Fort Campbell area, please pay us a visit.

RAKKASANS!!

Sincerely,

John E. Marlin
CPT INF
Commanding

The letter seemed to confirm his worse fears – that his platoon leader did die that night in Long Binh. Why else would he not be listed on the Register of Officers? Calvin, once again disappointed, put Captain Marlin's letter aside, packed his softball gear and left for a game. That evening, he and his team had an important game and he tried to put the disturbing news out of his mind. *Maybe,* he thought, *after the game, one of the guys would lend an ear.* But these were men who did not understand. After the game, Calvin and the guys went out for a few beers. They talked about the game. He never mentioned First Lieutenant Jeff Wishik.

When Calvin arrived home that evening, he read the letter one more time and again, set it aside and got ready for bed. His hip was really bothering him, but the beer made the familiar pain tolerable. As he lay in bed that night, his thoughts went to Dave Dillard and how happy he was to have reconnected with him, and to Wishik, a friend he would never again see. He wondered how many of the other men were still alive, and how many were fighting the same battles he was fighting. He thought about how he would love to see them all again just one more time, but he knew that was impossible. That night he tossed and turned, his mind flooded with troubling thoughts and unanswered questions. He finally fell asleep thinking, *if I could only see the guys...*

Several years later, in May, 1985, Dave Dillard, who was still working on his Delta project, once again contacted Calvin. The two men made arrangements for Dave to visit Calvin in Putnam, Connecticut so Dave could speak with Calvin about his recollections of his time with Delta. Calvin enthusiastically agreed. With plans made, Dave flew to Boston, Massachusetts and made the short drive to Putnam, Connecticut. He stayed in Connecticut for a few days where he and Calvin talked about their experiences and "…everything Delta." Even though the discussions reminded Calvin of the most difficult day of his life, the visit was one of the happiest events he had experienced in years and it proved to be extremely therapeutic. The visit helped Calvin to reconfirm his horrific memories of the battle with someone who was actually there.

Dave also met with members of Calvin's family and described Calvin's role in the battle that day. Hearing the details about the battle and Calvin's heroism from someone other than Calvin helped to eliminate many of the doubts developed over the years, and they all now looked at their son, brother, and uncle differently. For Calvin, Dave's recollections provided long-overdue validation to his service in Vietnam and much-welcomed proof about his heroism and actions during the battle. It would finally prove to all the doubters in his life that they were wrong. Calvin's only regret was that his father, Wayland, did not live long enough to extinguish any doubts he might have had.

During the last night of Dave's visit, Calvin and he spoke about the men they had lost and those who would never be the same. Calvin told Dave about his unsuccessful attempt at contacting Jeff Wishik and mentioned his sad realization that Jeff had died that day in the hospital at Long Binh back in 1968. Sadly Calvin added, "I'm the only one left alive."[593] Stunned, Dillard looked at Calvin with a puzzled face and said, "No, Wishik's alive!" Calvin caught off guard replied, "That can't be. They read him his Last Rites when I was there at the hospital. They said he wasn't going to make it." He informed Dave of Captain Marlin's letter, which could only mean one thing. Dave smiled and said, "No Calvin, he's very much alive and well. He's still in the service."[594] Calvin was absolutely floored. He sat back and thought about all the time that had passed since the night he and Wishik spent together in the hands of death. Calvin later recalled being, "Just happier than [hell]... I mean, I was just doing the Irish jig!"[595]

Dave was leaving for home the following morning and told Calvin that he might have Wishik's contact information at home. Dillard quickly found the information, but not knowing how Wishik would feel about reconnecting with Calvin, he decided to first call Wishik to inform him that Calvin was still alive. Wishik was as

[593] Adam Piore interview with Calvin Heath, 2009.
[594] Calvin Heath interview with author, June 2013. Note: Bobby Dietch was still alive at this time. Calvin stated that he died later in a car crash.
[595] Adam Piore interview with Calvin Heath, 2009.

surprised and as happy as Calvin that his old battle mate was still alive and by 10:00 p.m. that same evening, Calvin and Jeff were on the phone talking. Calvin was pleased to hear his old LT's voice and extremely happy that he was indeed alive and doing quite well. Wishik told him that he recovered from his wounds and went on with his military career. He was now a Lieutenant Colonel stationed at Fort Sill, Oklahoma.

That evening, the two men, who had shared a lifetime together in just one short night 13 years earlier, talked for hours. By the end of the conversation, and despite having just assumed command of a 1,200 person Pershing Missile Battalion at Fort Sill, and recently becoming a new dad, Wishik and his wife Fay extended an invitation for Calvin to visit them at Fort Sill, to which Calvin happily agreed. The two men settled on a date and in June of 1985, Calvin was once again heading west.

Fort Sill, Oklahoma

As Lieutenant Colonel Jeffrey Wishik drove to the airport, he did not know what to expect. He wasn't exactly certain when he last saw Calvin. It could have been near the trail, in Colonel Mowery's helicopter, or while he lay in the hospital's post-op recovery room. Wishik later admitted that there wasn't much from those few days that he remembered clearly. He did remember being told that Calvin might not survive the night.

As he waited for Calvin, Jeff undoubtedly thought about that fateful night, what little he remembered, and how each man had saved the other man's life. He remembered Calvin risking his life to pull him, Dietch, and Sherrill off the trail and out of harm's way. He also remembered killing the NVA soldier who rifled through Calvin's clothes and who attempted to kill him when he found him still alive. He might have also remembered Calvin stabbing to death an NVA soldier before he had a chance to kill them both. Finally, he clearly remembered Calvin crawling back to the company perimeter despite being severely wounded and in incredible pain in order to save him and Dietch. This created a powerful bond between the two men, one neither he nor Calvin fully understood.[596]

Calvin also did not know what to expect as he disembarked the plane. The last 13 years had been hell with regards to the military and the way in which they had treated him. And even though Wishik was still part of that establishment, Calvin understood he had nothing to do with his current problems. The anticipation of seeing Jeff again allowed the happy-go-lucky Calvin to once again shine through. He decided to dwell on all that was right with the world and focus on the friend and fellow soldier who awaited him at the end of the concourse. At that moment, Calvin was the happiest he had been in a very long time and there was nothing else in the world that mattered.

---

[596] Note: This is Calvin's version of the events. I contacted Jeff Wishik in October 2013 after Calvin's Memorial Ceremony in Hartford, CT. On October 16, 2013, he promptly replied, "After Calvin's memorial I think I'd like to take a break from Vietnam."

When Calvin finally came into view, Wishik had a moment of disbelief. Yes, he had spoken to his RTO over the phone, but as the old saying goes, "Seeing is believing." Wishik recalled, "I remembered meeting him at the airport, and looking down the concourse in utter disbelief that he had survived March eighteenth."[597] The two men had several awkward seconds that old friends typically have when meeting each other for the first time in many years, but it quickly passed and the two men embraced each other. Calvin later recalled, "I remember fighting back tears – I thought he was dead."[598] The reunion was emotional for both men for many different reasons, but the main reason was the names chiseled into panel 45E of the jet-black stone of the Vietnam Memorial.

For the next week, Lieutenant Colonel Jeffrey Wishik showed Calvin Fort Sill and introduced him to his new command. Nearly 30 years later, Wishik recounted the pride and honor he felt introducing Calvin to his 1,200-person command.[599] Calvin later confirmed to me in 2013, that the event was special for him as well. After years of mistreatment, to be introduced as a war hero in front of that many military personnel was one of the highlights of his life. It was an event he would never forget. Calvin noted that on that day, "I felt like I was the most important person on the base!"[600] The large, scrapbook that Calvin meticulously kept until the day he died, complete with mementoes and pictures of the visit, clearly shows how important that week with Jeff Wishik was for Calvin.

Calvin and Wishik talked late into the evenings during that visit, discussing everything under the sun, but mostly they talked about that horrible night. They discussed their thoughts and feelings about being left alone on the trail outside Delta Company lines and how the event affected and formed their lives. They talked about how the enemy had repeatedly walked through their area while they attacked Delta's perimeter and how the NVA searched them and their gear looking for valuables, tripping over them, and finally sitting on them to eat their

[597] Heath Memorial Ceremony, October 10, 2013, Hartford, Connecticut.
[598] Calvin Heath interview with author, May 2013.
[599] Heath Memorial Ceremony, October 10, 2013, Hartford, Connecticut.
[600] Calvin Heath interview with author, May 2013.

breakfast. They spoke about being shot by a passing NVA soldier who wanted to make certain they were dead. Calvin explained to Wishik that in spite of several operations, the bullet he received from that NVA soldier was still deeply lodged in his hip and how over the years it continued to cause him great pain. They talked about the two NVA they killed in the most brutal of ways, and the soldier Calvin later killed on the trail while setting up to snipe at the men of Delta Company. Because they were both severely wounded, much of that night was unclear to both men, but their long conversations helped them to fill in missing pieces known only to them. For the first time, Calvin was beginning to see the full picture. What became crystal clear to both men was that neither would have survived that night without the other.

Above: LTC Jeffrey Wishik's Pershing Missile Battalion as they marched away from a battalion formation at which Calvin was introduced. Calvin later exclaimed that "... I felt like I was the most important person on the base!" Calvin Heath photo.

There was another very important aspect of that trip. Toward the end of the week, Calvin spent a full day at the Fort Sill Indian Museum. Fort Sill was the last home of Geronimo, one of the most recognized and important Native American figures. Calvin spent hours at Geronimo's grave contemplating his own heritage and his time as a Native American warrior. As he said a prayer over Geronimo's grave, he wondered what this distinguished warrior would have thought about his short time as a soldier.

When Calvin returned to the Wishik's home after his visit, he and Jeff stayed up until the early morning hours discussing all that was important, to include their shared love for their country. Years later, at Calvin's memorial service, Jeff described the conversation with great clarity and emotion. It was clearly a conversation that neither man ever forgot.

Visiting the large base with his friend, a highly decorated soldier, must have been difficult on some level for Calvin. All around him were reminders of what he loved most about the Army, but he could not help but think how this very system, the one he once valued so deeply, had abandoned him. It was difficult for him not to consider the pain of his damaged honor and how many people still considered him a coward, a liar and a deserter and how the Army stripped him of the dignity and recognition for what was rightfully his. He thought about how different things could have been if he could have continued to serve under Wishik instead of the CO in Colorado. Maybe he could have stayed around long enough to become Wishik's Sergeant Major. The thoughts of what could have been began to consume Calvin's thoughts.

Calvin eventually told Wishik of his troubles with the Army and the VA over the past 13 years. Wishik was flabbergasted at how his old RTO, a decorated war hero, was so poorly treated by the very country who sent him in harm's way. He later stated, "Unknown to me, and those who had been close to Calvin [in Vietnam], after 1968, those were troubled times."[601] There was little Wishik could do for his old friend, but he promised to do all he could.

Before he left Fort Sill, Wishik gave Calvin a picture of himself in his Class A uniform, medals and qualification badges all perfectly pinned in place. It was signed, "Calvin, one has never lived until he has almost died. Life has a flavor the protected will never know.

---

[601] Heath Memorial Ceremony, October 10, 2013, Hartford Connecticut.

Thanks for saving mine."[602] Wishik later recalled that, "Those days with Calvin would always be incredibly special for me."[603] They were certainly incredibly special for Calvin.

Above: Calvin and Jeff Wishik during Calvin's 1985 visit to Fort Sill, OK. Calvin Heath photo.

During the long trip home, Calvin reflected on his visit with Jeff Wishik and the Indian Museum. He was saddened by the course his life had taken, but very happy that life and the Army had treated his former Lieutenant and friend so well. He was also pleased that now there were two people who could validate his role in the battle and the huge price he had paid. While Wishik's and Dillard's validation did little to get Calvin any closer to the benefits he deserved, it did somehow ease his pain.[604]

It is uncertain how much help Jeff Wishik was able to provide Calvin. There is little doubt that he did what he could, but even as a battalion commander, he had no influence over the VA, and certainly had no ability to modify official U.S. Army records.

---

[602] Calvin Heath 201 File.

[603] Heath Memorial Ceremony, October 10, 2013, Hartford, Connecticut.

[604] Calvin Heath interview with author, June 2013.

Dave Dillard kept in touch with Calvin over the next few years. He continued with his project by locating other members of Delta Company to get their perspective and individual recollections of the battle and their time in Vietnam. His dedication and work not only helped to preserve Delta's 1967-1968 history, it became the springboard from which many, to include Calvin, began to heal.

Above: A picture of LTC Jeffrey Wishik presented to Calvin by Wishik during his visit at Fort Sill, OK. Wishik wrote, "Calvin, one has never lived, til he has almost died. Life has a flavor the protected will never know. Thanks for saving mine." Calvin Heath photo.

LIFE IN THE 1980s

During the early 1980's Calvin once again applied for VA benefits hoping President Ford's Amnesty Law would allow him to secure his benefits. Ford's amnesty, in part, read:

> *By Executive Order, I have this date established a Presidential Clemency Board which will review the records of individuals within the following categories: (i) those who have been convicted of draft evasion offenses as described above, (ii) those who have received a punitive or undesirable discharge from service in the armed forces for having violated Article 85, 86, or 87 of the Uniform Code of Military Justice between August 4, 1964 and March 28, 1973, or are serving sentences of confinement for such violations. Where appropriate, the Board may recommend that clemency be conditioned upon completion of a period of alternate service. However, if any clemency discharge is recommended, such discharge shall not bestow entitlement to benefits administered by the Veterans Administration.*[605]

Calvin quickly discovered that the President's new law concentrated on clemency for draft evaders and did little to help combat veterans with no VA benefits. Calvin, naively thinking the new law would help him secure the medical and psychological help he desperately needed, once again applied for benefits from the VA, but was once again turned away.

Around 1981, Calvin was hired by The Furniture Place located in Putnam, Connecticut. The work of delivering furniture suited him well as he was usually by himself and did not have to deal with a

---

[605] Citation: Gerald R. Ford: "Proclamation 4313 - Announcing a Program for the Return of Vietnam Era Draft Evaders and Military Deserters," September 16, 1974. Online by Gerhard Peters and John T. Woolley, the American Presidency Project. Found at: www.presidency.ucsb.edu/ws/?pid=4714.

large number of people. The owners treated him well and for the next 13 years, Calvin found a nice niche for himself.[606]

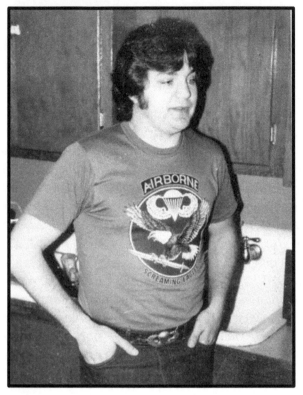

Above: Calvin circa 1985 with a Screaming Eagle shirt. After being mistreated by the Army for years, he was still proud of being airborne. Calvin Heath photo.

By 1985, Calvin's wife Maryanne was long gone, and he had little contact with his son. He had several relationships with other women, but none of them ever lasted long. One-on-one relationships were still very difficult for Calvin for a variety of reasons, but mostly because they would eventually become overwhelming and he would start to back away and become distant. His women friends were not the only ones who witnessed this behavior. Many of his friends and family noted how Calvin would stop by their homes a few times in

---

[606] Authier, Rob, interview with author, March 28, 2014.

one week and then they would not see him for several months. That intermittent contact, some called the "gypsy" in him, would stay with Calvin for the rest of his life.

Throughout the 1980s, athletics remained Calvin's most important sanctuary. At the age of 36, he continued to play basketball and softball better than most men ten years his junior. He could still hit the ball hard, throw a softball underhand at 85 MPH, and shoot three-pointers with the best of them. It was easy to imagine that Calvin, in a different life, could have become a high school athletic standout eventually playing college sports. The down side to playing ball, however, was the constant pain he had to endure and the danger of the bullet fragments moving, severely damaging the nerves to his right leg. Those of us who played with Calvin during those years, and knew of his condition, always held our collective breath when he pulled up lame running down the basketball court or up the first base line. His strength and good physical conditioning helped to keep the pain and discomfort in his hip at bay, but as he aged it became more and more difficult to play through the pain.

Throughout the rest of his life, Calvin found relief from the demons of war and his physical pain in marijuana. For thousands of years, humans have used cannabis as an effective relief for chronic pain, anxiety, depression, and insomnia, all conditions Calvin grappled with on a daily basis. Without help from the VA, and with no medical insurance, Calvin self-medicated with "weed." It made his life tolerable and he could play ball, sleep most nights, and usually felt a little better about himself, and life, in the process.

Over the past decade, more and more researchers have found that cannabis can have a significant positive effect on those who suffer from PTSD and other psychological ailments. While illegal, most of the people close to Calvin did not object to his use and could clearly see the positive effect it had on him. Others saw Calvin's use of marijuana as just another negative aspect in a pathetic life. Today, in many States, marijuana, or a similar medication, would have been simply prescribed with no one questioning its use. If there was ever a case to be made for medicinal marijuana, Calvin was it.

Another interesting side effect of Calvin's marijuana smoking, to which I personally witnessed, was the higher Calvin got, the better a softball pitcher he became. He could make a knuckle ball dance better than Fred Astaire and better than any pitcher I had ever caught or faced. As his catcher, I would always check with Calvin before the game. If I found him especially "happy," I would always make the trek back to the car to get my larger, oversized, 14-inch outfielder's glove in hopes of better catching his pitches. While it helped, it did not eliminate the multiple bruises I received each game when forced to block the dancing ball with my body. When Calvin was on as a pitcher during those years, he was among the best in New England.

Above: Pub on 44 basketball team. Top row (L-R): Bill Stiehl, Scott Tetreault, Mike Stiehl. Bottom row (L-R): Steve LaPointe, Calvin, Mike Castonguay. Paul Duquette photo.

THE FIGHT CONTINUES - 1990S

On September 17, 1988, Wayland Heath, Calvin's father passed away at the age of seventy-five. Five years later, almost to the day, on September 16, 1993, Calvin's mother Eva passed away, she was 70 years old. The two events were significant for Calvin in several ways. First, with the death of his mother, Calvin lost one of the few sources of strength he had. Eva, in Calvin's eyes, was a strong woman, whom Calvin greatly loved and respected. "I was always close to my Mom," he told me in April 2013.[607] Second, both parents died before Calvin was able to rectify the injustices he had endured with the Army. Both parents, especially his Dad, passed away having doubts about his son's time and performance in Vietnam. This bothered Calvin for the rest of his life.

1997 was a critical year for Calvin and his fight to restore his benefits and honor. Reconnections with Dave Dillard, Jeff Wishik, and other men of Delta, opened other lifelines Calvin did not dream possible years earlier. It took some time before he was completely honest with Dave about his troubles, and Dillard later stated, "He never said anything to me – for the longest time. Finally, it all came out."[608]

When the details of his lost benefits finally emerged, Dillard and several of the other men rallied to help their old battle mate. Calvin, who once felt that taking on the VA and the U.S. Army was an insurmountable task, now saw a glimmer of hope. "I spoke with Dave a bunch of times and he said with my Silver Star... What the Army did was illegal, and he said he would help me."[609] Calvin explained to Dave that the paperwork for his Silver Star was never processed in Vietnam and that all his records were lost. "I told [Dave] that they

---

[607] Calvin Heath interview with author, April 26, 2013.

[608] Dillard, Heaney, Rawson interview with author, October 9, 2013.

[609] Calvin Heath interview with author, April 26, 2013.

told me I got it (Silver Star) at the hospital [in Long Binh] but the paperwork was never done."[610]

Dillard, who had previously spoken with Paul Bucha, called his old company commander and told him the story of Calvin's mistreatment by the Army and the VA. Dillard stated, "I called Bucha and told him that [Calvin] had been dishonored."[611] Bucha, who was now an outspoken advocate for veterans' rights, was outraged and agreed to help in whatever way he could. Bucha was not hesitant to use his Medal of Honor as leverage to help those veterans who had difficulty helping themselves. Calvin's case was especially upsetting for Bucha as this was one of his own men and he was determined to set things right.

Within weeks, Dillard also contacted First Sergeant Harjo. Harjo was then heavily involved with the Military Order of the Purple Heart (MOPH) and Dillard reasoned that his former position as a highly-decorated retired senior NCO, the company's first sergeant, and his current position in MOPH, might provide the weight necessary to assist Calvin. This coupled with Bucha's help might make something happen.

Old first sergeants, like Austin Harjo, are a special breed of men. They dedicate their entire lives to the soldiers in their charge and gladly accept responsibility for every aspect of their needs to include their discipline, health, morale and training. They become the heart and soul of the company and few first sergeants ever walk away from that at retirement. They carry the responsibility for their men until the day they die, no matter their age or how many years have passed. This was how Austin Harjo felt about Calvin and the men of Delta Company.

Harjo made a number of phone calls and provided documentation to the VA, but after several months of trying, he was also hitting roadblocks. Due to Calvin's BCD, the lack of citations listed on his DD-214, his bad evaluations from his CO in Colorado, and his AWOL arrests, no one wanted to listen. After a few months of work,

---

[610] Calvin Heath interview with author, April 26, 2013.
[611] Dillard, Heaney, Rawson interview with author, October 9, 2013.

Harjo had a sense of the frustration that Calvin had felt for years. No one, outside of the men of Delta, understood that it was the *Army* that was primarily responsible for Calvin's problems – not Calvin. Prior to being wounded, Calvin was a model soldier, excelling in every aspect of soldiering. No one was willing to recognize that it was General Barsanti and a complete breakdown in his chain of command, Calvin's unsympathetic CO in Colorado, and the doctors who botched Calvin's medical discharge, not Calvin, who had failed first! Harjo became a man committed and determined, and he sought other avenues. A few weeks later, according to Calvin, he spoke with Paul Bucha and the two agreed on the next course of action.[612]

After Harjo's phone call, Bucha sat back and reflected on the battle at Bau Co Bong and Calvin's role in its successful outcome; successful because men survived. Bucha remembered telling Calvin to turn his radio off and play dead, understanding that this order might condemn the men to their deaths. Bucha remembered how Calvin, soaked in his own blood, and the blood of his friends and enemies, crawled back to the perimeter severely wounded, right leg useless, back laid out like someone took a shredder to it, to tell him that there were survivors and where they were located. He also remembered Calvin's heroic story about saving the wounded men, to include Wishik, by dragging them off the trail when others ran. He thought about the hand-to-hand combat that Calvin and Wishik endured while they were seriously wounded and how each man fought to save the other man's life and the life of Bobby Dietch. Bucha remembered when the medics loaded Calvin, Wishik and Dietch into Colonel Mowery's helicopter and medevac'd them out of the battle area, wondering if they would survive. He remembered visiting his torn-up troopers in the hospital, after that having no idea where they travelled.[613] Bucha, trusting the system, had assumed that Calvin had received proper medical care and his medals, to include his Silver Star, for which he was so deserving. He had no idea how badly Calvin had been treated, and when he finally heard the entire story, he like

---

[612] Calvin Heath interview with author, April 26, 2013.
[613] Calvin Heath memorial ceremony, October 9, 2013.

Harjo, was "pissed off" and vowed to do everything he could to fix this injustice.

After Harjo hung up with Bucha that day, he called Calvin and said, "Look, here's what you need to do... you've got to call Captain Bucha. He can help you out. I'm getting closed doors."[614] Calvin called Bucha and later said:

> *When I called Bucha he said, "About time you called me!" I told him everything that was going on with [my] discharge... He said, "They can't do that. That's illegal!" [I said], "Well they told me that there was nothing I can do about it." He said, "I'm going to send you a paper stating that you've given me Power of Attorney. We'll get this all straightened out."[615]*

Bucha found Calvin's case a complete travesty of justice that no honorable warrior should experience.[616] He was furious with the way in which one of his troopers was treated, and he, like Harjo, became determined to right this unimaginable wrong.[617] It was apparent to Bucha that the officers to whom Calvin later reported and the doctors at Fort Devens had completely botched Calvin's case. He also found that after months and months of being jerked around, and tired of being called a coward, Calvin had enough and simply went home. Bucha then found that several years later after being in and out of military jails that Calvin was ordered to Indianapolis where he signed a discharge without being properly advised as to its ramifications.

Bucha understood that the overall priority was to reestablish Calvin's VA benefits and get him the medical and psychological help he desperately needed. How to do that would be difficult. In January of 1997, Bucha developed a plan. The first step was to obtain a battle summary from Calvin's perspective. Shortly thereafter, Calvin sent the following hand-written letter to Bucha:

---

[614] Adam Piore interview with Calvin Heath, 2009.
[615] Ibid..
[616] Ibid.
[617] Calvin Heath memorial ceremony, October 9, 2013.

Letter Written to Paul Bucha by Calvin W. Heath – 1997

I was second platoon RTO.

When you called on the horn to get the wounded back to you in the perimeter, our M-60 man was hit by machine-gun fire nearly cutting him in half. I ran to him, picked him up, and headed back to the perimeter. He died in my arms. He was my best friend Paul Conner.

When we got back to you, you asked for volunteers to go back down the trail to set up a LZ to get the wounded out.

We had gone about 50 yds. back down the trail when the lead element was hit hard. Then to our left the NVA hit us with mines, machine guns, [and] with AK fire.

Lt. Wishik, who was right in front of me, was hit hard by the mines and gunfire.

At this time, I was also hit by the mines, the man behind me was killed.

There were five of us hit, with me being the only one who could still walk.

At this time, the lead element came running back, going by us, back to the company. I grabbed one of them, asking for his help to carry back out wounded. He was really scared, [because he kept] on going saying "you are dead men. You are all dead. We don't want to die."

I then pulled the wounded off the trail into the jungle. I could hear and see gunfire from the NVA on the men heading back to you. I still don't know if they made it.

After I pulled Lt. Wishik off the trail, he told me to go back to the company. I told him I could not and would not leave them.

I then called you on the horn and told you of the situation.

You told me that you would be right out to get us. I told you that we were surrounded; don't try to get us that you would not make it.

You then said to stay put, shut the radio off, and you [would] get us at first lite (light).

Right after that is when we were hit again, this is when I was hit with AK fire.

They ran right over us and kept going. We were playing dead when the NVA came in and [one took] the radio, one took my watch off of me, and was going into my pants when he hit where I was shot (R HIP) making me move, but before he could do me in Lt. Wishik reached up and grabbed him, killing him with his knife, saving me.

We were overrun 6 or 7 times through the [night]. We had hand to hand fighting 3-4 times.

At first [light], the NVA were still all around us, of the 5 of us only 3 were still alive. I then crawled [through] their lines (I WAS PARALYZED ON THE RIGHT SIDE [from the] WAIST DOWN) to let you know we were still alive. Just outside of your perimeter there was an NVA sniper, who I killed with my knife. Then I called to you.

When 2nd Platoon was pulling the dead and wounded back to the perimeter we were under intense fire, this is when Paul Conner, our M-60 man was hit, nearly cutting him in half. I picked him up and carried him back. He died in my arms. He was my best friend.

When we "2nd" was cut off, we were run over 6-7 times, it was during this time that Lt. Wishik saved my life by killing the NVA who knew I was still alive. I was shot in the right hip by AK-47 and been hit by mines. I was paralyzed on my right side from waist down.

We had hand to hand combat with the NVA 3-4 times through the [night].

God had to be with us that night. None of us should have made it [through] the [night] with the size of the force against us.

CALVIN HEATH

Determining that more information was needed, Bucha requested further details from Calvin and on February 12, 1997, Calvin faxed Bucha the following report:

FAX TO PAUL BUCHA
12 Feb 1997

The company had set up for resupply in a [hand-cut LZ] in the clearing, some of the men found an ox cart trail, on the trail, there were fresh ox cart tracks. The C.O. called 2nd Platoon First Lt. Wishik to come to his position to look at the ox-cart wheel marks. We could tell that they were very freshly made marks. The C.O. and the Lt. talked, and they decided not to go down the trail at this time, as it was getting dark and they didn't want to get ambushed. After re-supply, the C.O. sent a lead element with scout dogs to set up a night perimeter. The scouts had gone into the jungle about fifty yards when the lead dog alerted. The scouts saw two NVA and went after them.

They followed the [trail] another fifty yards when they got hit hard by the NVA, The C.O. sent the 2nd Platoon to reinforce them, by the time we got up to them, the NVA. had the scout lead element pinned down. 2nd Platoon was sent to the left to outflank them. We went about twenty-five yards and they were still to our left, we tried two more movements to the left, we could not outflank them. They were now pushing 2nd Platoon back towards a hastily set up perimeter of the company. The company was setting up a defensive perimeter, 2nd Platoon was pulling dead and wounded back to the perimeter at this time. The C.O. called Lt. Wishik on the horn to come back into the perimeter to go back down the trail to secure an L.Z. for the dead and wounded. As we went about fifty yards down the trail, the NVA blew mines to our left front and opened up with machinegun fire hitting Lt. Wishik, myself, and killing the man directly behind me.

During this time, four or five guys came running back down the trail in front of us, the NVA had missed them, I asked them to help pull the other men with me, back to the company, but they refused, they just kept running, saying 'You are dead men, you are all dead. We don't want to die." I do not know if those men made it back or not. The NVA did open fire on them. I pulled the Lt. off the trail into the jungle about five yards. There were five of us who set up a small little perimeter.

At this time Lt. Wishik told me to go back to the company, I told him, I could not and would not leave them. At this time, I called the C.O. and told him of the situation. I told him 'they are all around us Sir, don't try to get out here, you'll never make it.' The C.O. said, 'stay where you are, turn the radio off, and we'll do our best to get you at dawn,' I took the radio off, I was facing into the jungle, away from the trail. Lt. Wishik was to my right and another man was to his right also. To my left was a 2nd Lt. and facing the trail was the last man. At this time the NVA overran us, hitting all of us with AK 47 fire, they did not stop, they kept going, 'I believe, they did not know how small of a unit we were.'

The gun ships were now shooting all around us, hitting within five feet of us, hitting the NVA all around us. The NVA were yelling and screaming from being hit, the Lt. on left, started yelling at the NVA, 'What's the matter, you fuckers can't take it? Go ahead, fuck with us some more! Die you fuckers die.' At this time a NVA guy shot him in the head, killing him. Next the NVA came to me and started to search me, took my watch, I was face down, and when he went into my pants he touched me where I was hit, making me move, but before he could kill me, Lt. Wishik, who was face up, reached up and cut his throat, killing him, saving me. For the rest of the night, the NVA were running away on both sides of us, to get away from the gun ships, I believe that the size of the NVA forces had to be in the thousands because it would not take hundreds of men four or five hours to move away from us. We could hear the company still being attacked throughout the night.

Towards daylight, in front of me, someone started to talk to us, saying 'Hey man help me. I've been hit' his voice was a southern accent, as I started to move to go to him, Lt. Wishik grabbed me, asking me 'Where do you think you're going?' I answered, 'to go get him', the Lt. said, 'Listen to his voice, nobody in our outfit talks like that." So, we stayed still. In four or five minutes, he started to talk in Vietnamese, with other Vietnamese, and then they moved off. I believe that they thought that we were all dead. They didn't want to take the chance of coming in to find out for sure.

At dawn, we could hear the choppers coming in and out of the company A.O. (Area of Operation). We still had movement to my front and left, moving away from the company moving into the jungle.

We knew we had to move out from where we were, we knew the NVA would be sending snipers into our area, waiting to shoot anyone coming for us. The Lt. and Sergeant were hurt real bad and needed immediate help. My right leg was useless, but I could still crawl. I crawled on the side of the trail heading towards the company, at about twenty-five yards from the company, there was an NVA soldier looking up the trail into the company. I don't know if he heard me or not, with all the noise from the choppers coming and going, he could and probably did think that I was one of them. His mistake. I was able to get up to him and knifed him before he knew shit. The fight with him lasted about thirty seconds and he was dead. I moved to about fifteen yards from the company when I heard Top and Sergeant Quick talking, so I yelled to them not to shoot, that it was me. Top and Sergeant recognized my voice, they came right out to get me, we were still being sniped at, at this time. I told Top that Lt. Wishik and the Sergeant were still alive back down the trail, about a hundred yards back down the trail, and that they needed help bad, Top said 'don't worry, I will go after them right now and bring them back', and he did.[618]

Bucha refined the above summaries and used it to submit the proper applications and requests to the VA's, Army Discharge Review Board, and to the Board for the Correction of Military Records.

A week and a half later, Calvin sent a modified Statement of Support Claim to the VA. The letter appears to have been modified with advice of a long-overdue advocate, possibly Bucha and/or Harjo,

---

[618] Fax dated February 12, 1997 from Calvin, destination unknown. Calvin Heath file.

who understood the system. With the advocate's help, Calvin was better able to frame the psychological issues he had been dealing with since March 1968. It read:

Department of Veterans Affairs
Statement of Support of Claim
(Form 21-4138)

I wish to amend my service-connected disability to include post-traumatic stress disorder.

My problems are, since the combat experience in Vietnam in 1968, depression, anger, anxiety, isolation, irritability, painful intrusive memories of stressful events, nightmares, sleep disturbance, and sadness.

This limiting and disabling disorder is such severity and persistence and has caused me to experience a considerable inability to obtain or retain an employment; inability to establish and maintain effective or favorable relationships with people.

I request the DVA to schedule me for an examination as I am not financially able to obtain – furnish the medical evidence for the support of this claim as soon as possible. Thank you.
(This is my informal notice to the V.A.)

Calvin W. Heath
Feb. 27, 1997
Po Box 342
North Grosvenordale, CT 06255

The next few months were filled with phone calls, letter writing, and form submissions. Every "i" was dotted and every "t" was crossed. Soon, the VA responded and it became clear that some progress was finally being made.

Pressure was also brought to bear from sources outside Calvin's military circle. By 1997, the U.S. military, Congress, and society in general, viewed returning Gulf War combat veterans much differently than they viewed returning Vietnam War veterans. Returning Gulf War soldiers were treated as heroes and liberators and were welcomed home in a manner fitting their accomplishments. Unlike their Vietnam counterparts, they received the attention, accolades, and parades they well deserved. This improved perception and sensitivity of our returning veterans helped develop a greater awareness of their special needs, especially with PTSD and serious war-caused injuries. Now, more than ever, appropriate attention was given to the men and women who fought in Vietnam. Whether this collective change was the reason that Calvin finally obtained his long-overdue benefits is impossible to know, but it certainly helped. It is also certain that without the men from Delta, it would not have happened at all.

In June of 1997 First Sergeant Harjo was asked to provide a letter of support, specifically addressing his opinions about Calvin's need for PTSD therapy. On June 30, 1997, Harjo, a two-war senior NCO who had seen his share of the condition, faxed the following letter from the Muskogee Public Library to the VA. It read:

TO WHOM IT MAY CONCERN

This statement in in behalf of Calvin W. Heath, SSN XXX-XX-XXXX, for whom I am a strong advocate and have closely observed and counseled. Heath also served with me as one of the radio telephone operators (RTO) and all-do-it helper for Second Platoon Leader, while I was 1st Sergeant of "D" Company, 3rd BN, 187th ABN Infantry, 3rd Brigade, 101st Airborne Division. A unit that highly distinguished itself (citations and streamers) within the 101st Airborne Division in Vietnam.

After training together for nearly a year and being inseparable, we developed [into] a perfect fighting machine. We went right into the thick of it in Vietnam on November 17, 1967. I was thoroughly familiar with my men and their needs as I operated my administration and logistics from the field.

Heath demonstrated skills, zeal in his job, possessed dependability, diligence, promptness, always accurate in reports and constantly ready for action. We trained, worked, tired, sweated, bled hard, cried and nearly died together. I had my men realiz[ing] that we were dealing and fighting against a very hard, very experienced and battle-hardened soldiers dedicated to the communist cause.

After 29 years, I still feel responsible for their welfare. In many letters, telephone calls, and counseling with Heath, I have concluded that his complaints [about] depression, anxiety, anger, irritability, isolation, and painful intrusive memories causing flashbacks and nightmares from his combat experiences are directly related to the tour Heath served in the Infantry in the 101st Airborne Division (1968).

He has survived disasters and life-threatening traumatic events in combat in Vietnam along with lots of unpleasant after effects. Calvin W. Heath has been experiencing many stressor/combinations, since his separation from service. He told me recently that the smell of a butcher shop is revolting, reminding him of a battle we both fought in Vietnam in March 1968. Now he is beginning to isolate himself, not socializing, not relating even to family members.

Heath experienced intense firefights and frequent contact with the enemy. He was in an element that was cut off from the main body of the Company, earlier in evening of the 18th March 1968, while engaged with the fresh NVA Regulars, estimated to be two Bns. (Battalions). He remained out of the Company perimeter all through the night during the furious fighting (stand-off). He was severely wounded, bleeding, blinded, dragging his wounded buddies, playing dead, exposed to the enemy casualties, living, dead, crawling with his friends, continued killing the enemy with his knife, and stampeded by NVA soldiers to and fro, praying, crying, hurting, exhausted and dying until he heard my voice calling his name. I personally formed a search party to retrieve my men before they were discovered, killed or dragged off with their wounded (NVA). Heath in his dying cry, "Help-Help-Here-Here, 1st SGT!" And then he told me where the others were, and we were able to retrieve our wounded men.

Heath's condition is now at its most severe point. He is becoming a recluse. The attitudes of all contacts, even his family, are so adversely affected as to result in virtual isolation from the community. The symptoms are of such severity and persistence that there [is] severe impairment in Heath's ability to obtain or retain employment with other people.

The undersigned believes that the Veteran deserves all the assistance [that] our Government agency (VA) can give him as I have never encountered a combat soldier with greater caring to his soldiers or greater dedication to his country than Calvin W. Heath, in my lengthy tenure in service in the United States Army.

Austin A. Harjo
Retired 1SG E-8, US Army[619]

---

[619] Harjo letter "To Whom It May Concern," date unknown. Calvin Heath file.

Less than two weeks later, the VA agreed to hear Calvin's case and Calvin was instructed to meet Dr. Laurence R. Schweitzer, an expert in neuropsychiatry on August 27, 1997 at the Veterans Administration's Medical Center located in Newington, Connecticut. If the psychiatrist could first determine that psychological issues existed, and then determine that they were a result of the combat Calvin experienced in Vietnam, then maybe Calvin might finally obtain the help he sought, and so desperately needed.

Calvin made the one-hour drive to Newington, Connecticut not knowing what to expect. He arrived shortly after noon and completed the administrative preliminaries that would allow the VA to track his case. At 1:05 p.m. on Wednesday, August 27, 1997, he was escorted to Dr. Schweitzer's office. The psychiatrist introduced himself, asked Calvin to take a seat in the poorly decorated office and sat in a chair opposite him so he could observe his body language and movements. At exactly 1:34 p.m. Dr. Schweitzer looked at his watch and feeling he had what he needed, told Calvin they were done. Calvin was utterly confused as he did not expect such a short meeting. He remembered thinking, *how the hell can the doctor determine anything in just 29 fucking minutes?*[620] He left the meeting with Dr. Schweitzer feeling completely disheartened. He drove home angry and upset assuming the meeting was nothing more than the "same old bull shit." It was not. While Calvin drove home, Dr. Laurence Schweitzer dictated the following report:

MEDICAL RECORD   Progress Notes

Location: MHC SCHWEITZER INDIV (NEWT)

Patient is a 48 y.o. white divorced male who is a veteran of Vietnam Conflict. Veteran served in Vietnam 1967-1968 and saw significant battle experience. The Veterans MOS was 11-bp (airborne infantry) and was radio transmitter operator. While in Vietnam he was primarily [in] War Zone D but covered such areas such as Parrots Beak, Hue, Tran Rang, Hobo Woods, etc. These missions involved search and destroy activities in jungle terrain. While there he experienced several significant traumas. Among these are:

---

[620] Calvin Heath interview with author, June 2014.

1. Paul Connor, the veteran's best friend, died in his arms while on [a] mission. They encountered 2 battalions of NVA and two regiments of VC and Paul was killed by machine gun fire. "He was on his knees holding his guts right in his hands." He cried "Help me!" The veteran held him till he died and the[n] carried his friend back to the perimeter they were setting up. This event comes back to the veteran in nightmares, intrusive memories and depression. "He was right on the side of me and how he got it ... I don't know..."

2. "Later that night the company commander was on the horn with my Lt. and we were to go back to secure an LZ. The gooks were waiting for us and they opened up with machine guns and they blew mines that were set for an ambush. I was wounded in my left arm, both legs, back and left side of my head with little pieces of shrapnel. I saw the Lt. get blown over my head. Four men ran toward him from the front and said 'your all dead men and then they ran, the bastards. I radioed to the company commander not to come back and he told me to get off the radio and scramble it which made me very happy. Later that night they tried to hide and they were found and it was hand-to-hand combat all night. The dead were everywhere. I killed enemy in hand-to-hand combat. One thing that bothers me is that I tore one's throat out by biting him. I am not proud of that, but I didn't want to die. In the morning, we were taken out by chopper. The Lt was shot three times in the chest and once in [the] head. Others were seriously wounded. I was shot with an AK47 in my right hip. The bullet is still in me. I was put in for a Silver Star but never heard anything. I also knifed an NVA soldier who was unaware of me."

3. "When I was hospitalized, they [had] NVA right across from me."

Since that time the patient has been depressed, suffers from nightmares, [is] frightened by nighttime noises, has flashbacks almost daily, is always on guard, has trouble being close to people, fearful of getting angry, uncomfortable in crowds, has taken to living in the woods, and lives a highly restricted lifestyle. He is not comfortable dealing with people who have not been in Vietnam and has had difficulty holding a steady job.

On the basis of these data and a mental status exam which reveals no thought disorder, I believe that the veteran suffers from Post-Traumatic Stress Disorder (309.81) and I have recommended that he apply for compensation for what has been a chronic disability that is 100% disabling.

Signed by: /es/ LAURENCE R SCHWEITZER, SCHWEITZER 8/27/97 13:34

HEATH, CALVIN W   WEST HAVEN, CT   PRINTED: 08/27/97 13:35
DOB: 1/24/49 Pt Loc: OUTPATIENT   Vice SF 509[621]

Twenty-nine years after it had all begun, Dr. Laurence Schweitzer, a man who had never before met Calvin, in just 29 short minutes, finally properly diagnosed Calvin with chronic PTSD and recommended him for 100% disability. Calvin had won a major battle, but the war was far from over.

As the efforts to obtain Calvin's VA benefits continued, the battle to secure Calvin's long-overdue medals and to permanently change his BCD discharge intensified. Further support from family and friends was solicited to prove Calvin was mistreated and should have been medically discharged from Fort Devens in 1969. On December 3, 1997, Calvin's older brother Glen submitted the following:

Riverside Dr.
N. Grosvenordale, CT 06255

December 3, 1997

To whom it may concern:
THIS LETTER WRITTEN ON BEHALF OF CALVIN HEATH

After Calvin Heath was injured in Vietnam, he was a patient at Fort Devens Hospital. The Doctor spoke with the members of our family on our first visit to Fort Devens. At that time, he said there was a probability that Calvin would be receiving a Medical Discharge upon leaving Fort Devens.

Sincerely,
Glen W. Heath[622]

Harjo, using his position as the National Service Officer of the MOPH, was also still hard at work on Calvin's behalf. He contacted a number of people that could help Calvin secure his well-deserved

---

[621] Dr. Schweitzer report, August 27, 1997.
[622] Glen Heath letter dated December 3, 1997.

278

Silver Star. A memo dated January 13, 1998 to his staff at MOPH, shows Harjo still in the thick of the process. He had contacted Dickie Quick, Calvin's old platoon sergeant. The memo stated:

Military Order of the Purple Heart
Chartered by Congress

1-13-98

Dickie Quick was at work, and I left the message of this transaction. Be advised that Calvin will call, that if Dickie will recommend Heath for Silver Star, with my assistance – I will take care of the Purple Heart request today. Let Calvin know this evening. I will [be] out until 10 p.m. tonight for wake service out of town.[623]

The memo went on to state, "Note: I talked with Mrs. Quick about the whole deal, now, please call Dickie this evening after 5:30 CST."[624] Harjo was using every resource he could muster to include the wives of the men with whom Calvin served. A copy of the memo was faxed to Calvin later that day.

---

[623] Harjo memo dated January 13, 1998.
[624] Ibid.

PROGRESS - 1999

Approximately one and a half years after Calvin's visit with Dr. Schweitzer, Calvin still had no VA benefits. Despite Dr. Schweitzer's recommendation for full disability, the VA had yet to provide Calvin any assistance. Once again, frustrated with nowhere to turn, he sought Paul Bucha's help. According to Calvin, Bucha requested a summary of all events, this time focusing on Calvin's time *after* Vietnam and the events leading to his BCD. Calvin wrote:

March 15, 1999

Dear Paul,

I am writing to you in hopes that you can help me get my VA benefits.

My problems started after I was medevac'd from Vietnam back to the United States of America in March of 1968. I was sent to Fort Devens in Lee, Mass. I was operated on while I was a patient at Fort Devens. My right hip was operated on because a bullet was lodged in my hip. The joint was cleaned as much as possible and the bullet was stabilized at that time. I was told they couldn't remove it because they would only do more damage if they tried and possible[ly] paralyze me and I would never walk again. I have nerve damage to the area. [Grenade] and mine fragments were also removed from my back, legs, and side of head. At this time the attending doctor told me I would be getting a medical discharge. The doctor at this time also sent me to see a psychiatrist due to the nightmares and problems I was having. The psychiatrist told me that I needed treatment and I would be hearing from them. I never heard from the psychiatrist again. At this time a new doctor was taking over my case because the doctor that I had in the beginning was being discharged. At this time, I was told that if I wanted to stay at Fort Devens for a medical discharge, I had to sign a waiver to be released from airborne duty or be transferred to Fort Bragg waiting for the medical discharge. I chose to stay at Fort Devens because it was within driving distance for my family to visit me.

I was told that because of the injuries I was no longer able to make jumps, so I was put on a medical profile. It was C and D and another code that I don't recall. It stated no marching, no running, no prolonged standing, no lifting of anything heavy. The next thing I knew I received orders to report to Fort Carson, Colorado. When I asked my doctor, what was happening to my medical discharge he brushed me off stating it would be taken care of at Fort Carson. I went to Fort Carson in late fall of 1968. I was [transferred] into an Infantry Co. and was treated like a piece of garbage. My Co. Commander would not recognize my profile and said I was faking it. I was forced to go on marches and do maneuvers in the field although the doctors there said that I could not do this. The CO said if I did not [do] the assignment I would not get any passes or leave to go off post for the rest of my tour.

At this time, which was January of 1969, my doctor called the CO and again the CO told the doctor that I was faking it and he was covering for me. At this time the doctor decided to put me back into the hospital to [do] surgery on my right hip again due to no improvement in my condition due to all the activity I had been required to do. While in the hospital, I was harassed by the CO who continued to tell me that while I was in the hospital, I would not get paid. My doctor told me that what was happening was not right and he would take care of it. At that time, he had me reassigned to the hospital. After I had surgery, I was given a hospital leave so I could recover at home. While at home the CO called my home and told my mother that I didn't have to return to Fort Carson. Orders would be sent to me where to report. I was on crutches all this time in the summer of 1969 when I was waiting for orders to arrive when I was picked up by the FBI. I was returned to Fort Devens at that time. By this time, I was disillusioned by the military for their mistreatment of me both mentally and physically. At Fort Devens I was put in a holding company for AWOL's, deserters and the like. Because I didn't have any paperwork with me the profiles were not recognized. I received no help. I was treated like [a] lowlife. From this point on I was in and out of Fort Devens. I would be picked up for AWOL by the police and sent back to Fort Devens; once at Fort Devens they would just release me with a pass and I would leave to wait for them to come after me again. During this time, I was never offered any treatment by a psychiatrist.

In 1974 or 1975 I got a letter from the military telling me to go to Fort Benjamin Harris for discharge. Once there I was told I could either go back in the Army or be discharged. With all the ways I was being treated I chose the discharge. When I was going through the discharge procedure, I was told to just sign the papers and I would be out in a day or two. If I didn't sign the papers, I could be there for at least a month. I signed everything that was put in front of me. I did not realize that I was signing my rights away. I do not always understand very [technical] things as I only have a seventh-grade education. At this time, I was put in front of a Court Martial Hearing consisting of five officers. Two of these were Army officers and three were Marines. I was given the choice of a discharge or return to service. Because of the Purple Heart and combat in Vietnam I had my choice. I told them I wanted out. They told me because I couldn't prove that I had the Silver Star they would not give me an Honorable Discharge. (The 2 Army officers voted to give me an Honorable Discharge and the [3] Marine officers voted to give me a Bad Conduct Discharge.) Result BCD.

Any help that you are able to provide in my behalf would be gratefully accepted.

Sincerely,
Calvin Heath[625]

Fifteen days later, Calvin received a letter from the Department of Veterans Affairs, Hartford, Connecticut. He looked at the envelope and wondered how many of these he has seen over the years – always containing bad news. While hoping for the best, he fully expected the bureaucratic process of the VA to once again deny his benefits. He was not disappointed. The letter dated March 30, 1999, coldly stated, "Benefits are *not payable* where the former service member was discharged or released... by reason of a discharge under other than honorable conditions issued as a result of an absence without official leave (AWOL)."[626]

The letter suggested the obvious – if Calvin was ever going to receive benefits, he would have to first appeal to the Army to change his BCD to an Honorable Discharge. Calvin could not help but to think, *No shit! That's what I'm asking help with!* The letter further stated that the Army would have to further investigate the reasons behind the BCD and that they were requesting his records, further details, and evidence of the events leading to Calvin's BCD. Calvin's frustration climbed to a whole new level. He thought, *the goddam records are the source of my problems! What records? I've sent*

---

[625] Letter to Paul Bucha. Calvin Heath Collection.
[626] Code of Federal Regulation 38 CFR 3.12 – Character of Discharge.

letters, affidavits from the guys who were with me, psychological reports, and doctor's reports... What the hell else do you need? Even Calvin, with a limited education, saw the mind-blowing lunacy in the government's continual reviews of the same government errors and life-changing blunders. It seemed that unless General Barsanti himself walked into the U.S. Army Personnel Center with the misfiled order that he signed in Vietnam on March 19, 1968, awarding the Silver Star to Spec-4 Calvin Heath, nothing had changed!

It did not matter to the U.S. Government what sacrifices Calvin had made, how badly he was wounded, what care he needed, or how desperately broken he was as a result of his service. What seemed to matter most were the actions of the lazy commanding general and an incompetent CO and not the actions of one of the rank and file soldiers. He was destined to be discarded as a piece of rubbish not worthy of the help provided to "honorable soldiers," despite the fact that he saved lives and fought courageously.

As discouraged as Calvin was in 1999, he did not give up hope. Other battle plans were in place and this time he had reinforcements. Bucha and Harjo were still on the case. *Don't let the bastards wear you down,* he thought. So, he read the letter one more time, informed Bucha, and placed it in his rapidly growing folder. The letter from the Department of Veterans Affairs read:

Department of Veterans Affairs
Varo Hartford
450 Main, Street
Hartford, CT 06103

March 30, 1999

CALVIN W. HEATH
PO BOX 342
633 RIVERSIDE DR
NO GROSVENORDALE CT 06255

In Reply To: 308/21, CSS 044-XX-XXXX, HEATH, Calvin W

Dear Mr. Heath,

We have your claim for compensation based on your military service together with copies of letters written by Mr. Paul Bucha on your behalf.

Any time a veteran receives a discharge that is not "honorable," we have to decide if he is eligible for VA benefits.

The military has said your service was not "honorable." Therefore, we have to make a decision about your service. As long as we decide that your service was not "dishonorable," you will be eligible for VA benefits.

WHAT YOU SHOULD DO:

There are some things you should do if you want to help us make our decision. We'll carefully consider any evidence you send us. In particular, you should:

- Read the regulations we've enclosed.
- Tell us about the events that led to your dishonorable discharge. You can use the enclosed "Statement in Support of Claim."
- Send us evidence to support your story. This might include statements from people who know about the events that led to your discharge. It could also include other documents which show that your statements are true.
- Tell us why you think your service was honorable.
- Tell us if you want to have a personal hearing. Personal hearings are explained in the enclosed "Your Right to Representation and a Personal Hearing."

WHEN WE NEED THE EVIDENCE:

You should send us the information you want to submit right away. If we don't hear from you by May 30, 1999, we'll make our decision based on the evidence we have from the military service records.

WHAT WILL WE DO:

We will look at your military records and any other evidence you can give us. We'll also use the enclosed regulation, *38 Code of Federal Regulations, section 3.12,* to make our decision. Then we will decide whether your service entitles you to VA benefits.

We are also asking Newington VAMC to schedule you for examinations in connection with your claims for service connection for residuals of shrapnel wounds and post-traumatic stress disorder. They will notify you of the dates and times of the appointments. If you have any questions, please contact us at our toll-free telephone number 1-800-827-1000

Sincerely yours,

EDWARD O'BRIEN

Veterans Service Center Manager

Enclosure(s): VA Form 21-4138(2) Hearing Rep Info, 38 CFR 3.12 Excerpt
Cc: CTDVA

A day later, he received a form letter acknowledging receipt of his claim. It read:

Department of Veterans Affairs
450 Main Street
Hartford, CT 06103

March 31, 1999

CALVIN W HEATH   File Number: 044-XX-XXXX
PO BOX XXX   PAYEE NO OO
XXX RIVERSIDE DR   C W HEATH
NO GROSVENORDALE CT 06255

We have received your application for benefits. It is our sincere desire to decide your case promptly. However, as we have a great number of claims, action on yours may be delayed. We are now in the process of deciding whether additional evidence of information is needed. If we need anything else from you, we will contact you, so there is no need to contact us in the meantime. If you do write us, be sure to show YOUR file number and full name or have it at hand if you call.

If your mailing address is different than that shown above, please advise us of your new mailing address. You should notify us immediately of any changes in your mailing address...

MARK MAHALIK,
ACTING ADJUDICATION OFFICER[627]

The government was essentially telling Calvin, "We understand you have been waiting for benefits for 31 years, but you have to

---

[627] Mihalik letter, Department of Veterans Affairs, March 31, 1999. Calvin Heath file.

understand that we are very busy people, so this might take a while."
Sadly, Calvin was not the only Vietnam veteran going through this
miserable ordeal. This process was being repeated all across the
country to combat veterans who had earned their benefits and were
refused any help because of personnel file errors or command
incompetency.

During the early spring of 1999, Bucha, getting little results
from his efforts, changed direction and contacted Connecticut 2nd
District's U.S. House of Representative, Sam Gejdenson. Gejdenson
served in the U.S. House of Representatives 1981-2001 and had a
reputation for helping constituents with issues of this nature. Bucha
requested the Congressman's help in obtaining Calvin's long-overdue
Silver Star. He explained to the Congressman's office the nature of
his request and the problems Calvin had with the Army and the VA
since March of 1968. Gejdenson's office felt the cause was
worthwhile and agreed to assist in any way they could.

*Above: A small sample of the paperwork Calvin generated over the years. Much of
this was submitted to the government during the last phases of his benefit approval
process. There were more than a thousand pages. Calvin Heath file.*

During the initial phases of the process, Gejdenson's office found that a "timeliness requirement" had long-expired and they quickly moved to get that prerequisite waived. They also informed Calvin that a "...recommendation by someone who had personal knowledge of the event," needed to be secured, preferably from the commanding officer.[628] It is highly likely that Gejdenson knew Bucha in his capacity as the Chairman of the Board for Wheeling Pittsburg Steel Company as well as being the President of the Congressional Medal of Honor Society, and they "coordinated getting the recommendation from Paul Bucha and [forwarding] it to the Department of the Army."[629]

Gejdenson's work did not stop there. According to The Day newspaper located in New London, Connecticut, he went to work to write and sponsor a congressional resolution awarding Calvin his long-overdue medal.[630] Finally, in May, 1999, Frank Rowe, Congressman Gejdenson's Aide for Military Affairs, contacted Bucha with good news.[631]

---

[628] Gejdenson Email March 13, 2013. Letter found at the Dodd Center.
[629] Ibid.
[630] The Day, July 13, 1999. Vietnam Veteran gets his due – Three Decades Later.
[631] Ibid.

SILVER STAR

On May 28, 1999, Congressman Gejdenson's Washington, D.C. office was notified that the U.S. Army had approved Calvin's Silver Star for Valor while serving with the Delta Company, 3rd Battalion, 187th Infantry (ABN), 3rd Brigade, 101st Airborne Division, during operations in Vietnam on the March 16-19, 1968. Several days later, on June 2, 1999, the official orders were cut by the Army's Total Personnel Command. Calvin's Silver Star and the Purple Heart, awards he earned 31 years earlier, were sent to Congressman Gejdenson's office for presentation. The official order read:

DEPARTMENT OF THE ARMY
U.S. TOTAL ARMY PERSONNEL COMMAND
ALEXANDRIA, VA
22332-0471

PERMANENT ORDER 153-4
JUNE 1999

1.   HEATH CALVIN 044-XX-XXXX PFC Company D, 3rd Battalion, 187 Airborne Infantry, 3rd Brigade, 101st Airborne Division, in the Republic of Vietnam

  Announcement is made of the following award.

  AWARD: Silver Star Medal
  Date(s) or period of service: 16 March 1968 to 19 March 1968
  Authority: AR 600-8-22, Paragraph 3-9
  Reason: For gallantry in action against an armed enemy
  Format: 320

2.   This supersedes any previously issued order that may have been published announcing the Silver Star Medal.

  BY ORDER OF THE SECRETARY OF THE ARMY

  DANIEL B. GIBSON
  LTC, GS
  Chief, Military Awards Branch

The United States Army also issued the following official award (DA Form 4980-4) to Calvin. It was signed by Kathryn G. Frost, Brigadier General, Adjutant General, U.S. Army, and Louis Caldera, U.S. Secretary of the Army.

After receiving official notification from the U.S. Army, Gejdenson's office organized a formal ceremony to officially award Calvin his Silver Star. Working with VFW Post 270, Calvin's family, members of the Nipmuc tribe, Paul Bucha, local newspapers, and other local dignitaries, the long-overdue ceremony was finally planned for July 12, 1999 at Chelsea Parade, Norwich, Connecticut.

The ceremony began with the honor guard, comprised in part of Vietnam era veterans posting the colors. Calvin, by then 50 years old, stood at attention with the exact precision he was taught more than 30 years earlier. Standing next to him was U.S. Congressman Sam Gejdenson and Congressional Medal of Honor recipient Paul Bucha.

They assembled in front of large memorials honoring soldiers from wars long-ago fought. Large cast bronze plates listed the names of the men and women from Norwich, Connecticut, who, like Calvin, did their share when America needed them most. People in attendance could easily tell that this aging, grey-haired, barrel-chested man was once one of America's finest soldiers. More importantly to Calvin, those close to Calvin could finally see him as a proud and dignified, heroic soldier receiving the awards he so rightfully deserved. Calvin, well dressed, hair and mustache impeccably trimmed, stood at perfect parade rest, eyes looking down in the ultimate gesture of humility.

As the citation was read, Calvin fought back tears. Memories of that night long ago in the jungles of Vietnam came rushing back. Vivid pictures of Bobby Dietch and Jeff Wishik, both of whom were severely wounded, formed in his mind's eye and he felt terrible for what they endured. He felt sorry about Jimmy Sherrill and his family, and the other men he did not save. He remembered Paul Conner and wondered what could have been for Paul. He was such a great guy.

Calvin looked around and saw the newspaper photographers from The Day, the Norwich Bulletin and the Telegram and Gazette clicking off picture after picture. It brought a smile to his face and he wondered if his mother and father were now looking down on him with pride – pride they found difficult to express when they were alive. Calvin quickly determined they were, and that made him happy.

Gejdenson told the gathered crowd that, "We as a nation let him down… As a society we need to recognize the contributions and the valor of people who fought for this country when we faced a challenge. We should not do that one day a year when we're recognizing a particular veteran, but every day."[632] He went on to say that "Mr. Heath is an American hero and a credit to this great nation…"[633]

Calvin accepted the award with dignity and honor the way he would have 30 years earlier. He did not give into the anger and frustration many would have if faced with a similar situation. He

---

[632] The Day, July 13, 1999. *Vietnam Veteran Gets His Due – Three Decades Later.*
[633] Telegram and Gazette, July 9, 1999.

harbored no hate or ill feelings to those, in and out of the Army, who did not believe he was an honorable soldier who did his job with distinction when called upon. True to form, Calvin did not allow ugliness to rule the day. This was about the men who died in a terrible unnamed place in a terrible war in March 1968, and he would honor them in the best way possible.

Above: Paul Bucha pinning on Calvin's Silver Star at the July 12, 1999, Norwich, CT ceremony. Calvin Heath photo.

Immediately after Congressman Gejdenson finished reading Calvin's citation, Calvin asked for his family and members of his tribe to join him. He then turned to Paul Bucha and said, "Sir, would you please pin this on me?" Bucha later reported, "I cried, he cried, everybody cried. I think my daughter still cries as she remembers that event.[634]

In June 2013, Calvin stated that it was important to him to have Bucha pin the medal on him that day. For Calvin, it represented

---

[634] Calvin Heath memorial ceremony, Hartford, CT, October 9, 2013.

closure to an important piece of his life, probably the most important piece. All the doubts he and others had developed over the past 30 years about his role that day at Bau Co Bong were finally laid to rest. Having Bucha pin the Silver Star on him was affirmation that his actions were beyond reproach. It was as if Paul Conner, Bobby Dietch, Jimmy Sherrill, Juan Nazario, Steve Messerli, and all the others who fought that day, were there in Norwich, Connecticut telling Calvin in one collective voice, "You did great pal." Bucha later added, "It's the stuff of folklore…without Heath's cool actions, the entire unit might have been drawn into a disaster." He also added, "To go more than 30 years without help, and without recognition… this is a special human being."[635]

The ceremony ended an hour after it began and as people mingled, Calvin and Bucha caught up. Bucha told Calvin to, "Keep your Silver Star… that we are going to eventually [officially] present it right here in Hartford." At that time Calvin had no idea what that meant, but as before, he did as he was ordered. He thanked his old commander for the help he provided and watched as he walked away. When a reporter asked Calvin about his former CO, Calvin replied, "He's a great man. Even to this day, I'd follow him anywhere."[636]

Later that evening, outside in my driveway, I heard that all-too-familiar tooting of a horn that meant Calvin had stopped by to shoot the breeze, but this time the horn had a little more enthusiasm behind it than normal. At first, I thought that something was wrong. Outside I found Calvin yelling, "I got it Joe! I got it!" Going out to his car I asked, "Got what Cal?"

"My Silver Star!"

Calvin and I often talked about it and I was so happy to see he finally got what he deserved. I asked to see the Silver Star. I was in awe. The citation read:

---

[635] The Day, July 13, 1999. *Vietnam Veteran Gets His Due – Three Decades Later.*
[636] Norwich Bulletin, July 18, 1999, p. 6.

SILVER STAR
CALVIN W. HEATH
(THEN) PRIVATE FIRST CLASS, UNITED STATES ARMY

For gallantry in action against a hostile and superior force during the period 16 March 1968 to 19 March 1968 while combatting a hostile force in the Republic of Vietnam. During an intense battle at night when confronted by an overwhelming enemy force, Private First-Class Heath retained contact with the Company Commander and protected the lives and equipment of his unit. Due to a severe wound to his right leg, Private First-Class Heath crawled toward the company's position and continued to crawl toward the company location until he could hear the voices of the First Sergeant, 3rd Platoon Sergeant and Captain Bucha. A search and rescue team followed Private First-Class Heath's voice and rescued the wounded and dead from the 2nd platoon. Private First-Class Heath's conduct in spite of severe pain and intense fire from the enemy forces reflected great credit upon himself, his unit and the United State Army.

I had confused emotions about my old friend and what he had endured but was happy he finally received what he deserved. I had never seen Calvin more proud or happier than he was that day. I am certain for the first time in a very long time, he slept well that night, the nightmares and ghosts staying away.

VA BENEFITS

While Congressman Gejdenson pursued Calvin's Silver Star with the U.S. Army's Personnel Center, progress was also being made on other fronts. On April 2, 1999, Calvin received a letter from the VA scheduling several appointments with the Compensation and Ratings Board.[637] The C&R Board evaluates the nature of a soldier's claims and the disability he has incurred as a result of his injuries while serving in the armed forces of the United States. They then determine the soldier's monthly compensation rate, based on the "service-connected" impairment. This letter was extremely significant as it indicated the VA had approved Calvin's case, or at least saw enough merit in the claim to push it to the next level. The letter read:

04/02/1999
044-XX-XXXX

CALVIN W HEATH
P.O. BOX 342
NORTH GROSVENORDLE CONNECTICUT 06255

Dear Mr. Heath,
The VA Regional Office, Compensation and Pension Rating Board has requested the following C&P exam (s) be schedule on your behalf

SATURDAY APR 10, 1999, 12:00 PM COMP & PENSION MCLEAN (WHAV) Clinic
TUESDAY APR 13, 1999, 1:00 PM COMP & PEN DR. LIPSCHITZ (WHAV) Clinic

Office hours are Monday through Friday 8:00 a.m. to 4:00 p.m.

It is essential to make every effort to keep your appointment (s) and report to the West Haven Campus of the VA CT, Healthcare System, 950 Campbell Avenue, West Haven, Ct. Check-in with C&P Clerk located in Building Two, 2nd Floor, East Wing, room 2-213.

---

[637] VA CT Healthcare System letter (No. 044421350), April 2, 1999. Calvin Heath file.

Please complete any forms that may be enclosed and bring them with you when you report for your exam. If you have any additional medical documentation that would support your claim, please bring this documentation with you for the physician to review.

Failure to report for any portion of the above appointment (s) may result in this request being returned to the VA Regional Office without action. This will ultimately delay your compensation and pension benefits.

VA Connecticut Healthcare System
West Haven Campus
950 Campbell Avenue
West Haven, CT 06516

After receiving the above appointment notification, Calvin was informed by telephone that there were several more pieces of information the VA needed for the file. Several days after the initial phone call and four days before his first appointment, Calvin faxed the following Department of Veterans Affairs Statement in Support of Claim to the VA. Calvin wrote:

Department of Veterans Affairs
STATEMENT IN SUPPORT OF CLAIM
Form: 21-4138

Please see attached copy of the letter I wrote on March 15, 1999, for the events that led to my discharge. Please see a copy of the attached letter written by Paul W. Bucha dated February 23, 1999, which is evidence to support my statement. Also, please see a copy of the attached letter written by Glen W. Heath dated December 3, 1997. Also, please read my records on file at the Norwich Vets Center (June 4, 1997 to present) where I was diagnosed with Post Traumatic Stress Disorder on October 2, 1997 related to my military service. Further, I was seen and treated by two psychiatrists (Dr. Laurence Schweitzer, MD; and Dr. Teresa Bergherr, MD) at the Norwich Vets Center relating to medication for my psychological condition.

I believe my service was totally honorable because I was told by my company commander (Captain Paul W. Bucha) and commanding general of the 101st Airborne Division (Major General Barsanti) that I was being awarded the Silver Star for Valor and Heroism. I took direct gunshot wounds and shrapnel wounds while defending my fellow comrades in battle; the shrapnel is still in my body 31 years later. I also was afflicted with a condition now known as Post Traumatic Stress Disorder, which altered my behavior.

Yes, I want a personal hearing with my service officer representative.[638]

Calvin W. Heath 4/6/99
Riverside Drive
North Grosvenordale CT 06255

By the end of the summer of 1999, shortly after the Norwich ceremony, Calvin received word that his benefits had been approved and his "service-connected" disability rating was 70 percent.[639] He was also informed that he now had the right to use, without limitations, the full power of the VA medical system. Calvin recalled:

Within six months, everything was a go. [Captain Bucha] had straightened it out. The VA didn't want to give me benefits, but after he talked to them, they changed their minds. And they rated me 100% because of Post-Traumatic Stress, not counting the shrapnel [wounds] and [stuff]. When Bucha talked to them they listened to him. They had to pass a bill in Congress and now a lot of the guys are getting their medals all the way back to World War II now that couldn't get them before.[640]

At Calvin's final compensation hearing, the VA offered Calvin a one-time substantial amount of money for back benefits and

---

[638] Note: Statement in Support of Claim (VA-Form 21-4138), Department of Veterans Affairs, submitted on April 6, 1999. Calvin Heath records.
[639] Note: While Calvin states he was 100% disabled, VA reports dated February 1, 2009 shows a 70% disability rating, but also notes that he was "entitled to a higher level of disability payment due to being unemployable," possibly due to 100% PTSD rating.
[640] Adam Piore interview with Calvin Heath, 2009. Note: The bill to which Calvin refers is most likely H.R. 1090 "To amend Title 38, United States Code, to allow revision of veterans' benefits decisions based on clear and unmistakable error." First introduced April 18, 1997, by Illinois Congressman Lane Evans and approved as law on November 21, 1997. It also could have been the resolution that Gejdenson introduced earlier. Further investigation is needed on this point.

compensation lost over the past 31 years. The amount, somewhere in the neighborhood of $125,000 was significant for someone like Calvin who had not earned a great deal of money throughout his life, but the larger amount, if accepted, would substantially reduce his future VA benefits, especially his medical treatment. Calvin sought Bucha's advice and agreed with his old commander that he should accept a smaller upfront settlement and keep the long-term medical coverage.

Shortly thereafter, at the age of 53, Calvin finally received monthly VA payments of $2,300 per month.[641] It was the first time since leaving the Army in 1968 that he had a stable source of income *and* proper medical care.

As soon as he secured his VA medical benefits, Calvin made an appointment with an orthopedist seeking relief from the constant pain in his right hip. As he aged, the bullet lodged in his hip was causing increasing pain and discomfort. After a number of tests, examinations, and X-Rays, the doctors determined that the bullet, lodged deep inside the iliac crest, was just millimeters from the femoral nerve, a large nerve bundle which controls the leg muscles. Removing the bullet could cause permanent nerve damage and the possible loss of the use of his right leg. Calvin opted not to have surgery and lived with the pain for the balance of his life.[642]

---

[641] Based on his 2009 VA statement dated February 1, 2009.
[642] Calvin Heath interview with author, June 2013.

WEST POINT SOCIETY DINNER - 2002

For the next three years, things improved for Calvin. He was receiving medical care, and with the help of the VA, his nightmares began to subside. The greatest change, however, seemed to be in the people around Calvin. Many who once viewed Calvin with fear and disappointment, now saw him as a hero. Calvin reported, "I had friends that wouldn't give me the time of the day back in the '70s and '80s, now all of a sudden they wanted to introduce their kids to me because I was a war hero!" [643] This bothered Calvin greatly and was something he never quite understood.

In February of 2002, Calvin received a phone call from Paul Bucha. Three years after the Norwich, Connecticut Silver Star presentation, and almost 34 years after the battle near Phuoc Vinh, Bucha found the perfect venue in which to properly award Calvin his Silver Star. Bucha was asked to speak at the annual West Point Society Dinner, this one celebrating the 200th birthday of the U.S. Military Academy.

Bucha informed Calvin that he could invite several guests, and Calvin invited his brother Bert and nephew Paul Duquette to join him. Bucha also informed Calvin that the affair was formal, requiring him to wear a tuxedo. This threw Calvin off a bit, as this would be the first time in his life that he would attend a formal military affair. He later admitted being "...scared shitless."[644] Photos of Calvin during the event indicate this was an understatement.

When Calvin arrived at the dinner he could not have been in a more unfamiliar environment. If it weren't for the support of his brother and nephew, it would have been impossible for him to get through the event. Upon entering the large dining room, he found it quickly filling with highly-decorated, retired, and active duty military officers, most of them West Point graduates. There was also a U.S. Coast Guard Admiral and several USCG cadets in attendance. The

---

[643] Calvin Heath interview with author, June 2013.
[644] Ibid.

spouses of the officers looked like something you would see at a presidential ball. Many of the men were former warriors like Calvin, and in this, he gained some comfort. Calvin later noted, "I wasn't completely certain what Paul had in mind for dinner. I knew I was getting the medal pinned on in front of the West Pointers." When asked how he felt about that, Calvin replied, "I was proud as hell, but I was scared. I've never done anything like that before in my life." After a few seconds he added, "I just wished my father could have seen it."[645] Seeing his son in front of such a distinguished group formally receiving the Silver Star would have extinguished any doubts Wayland had about his son's actions in Vietnam.

Above: Calvin at the West Point Society Dinner. L-R: Paul Duquette, Calvin, Medal of Honor Recipient, Paul Bucha, and Bert Heath. Paul Duquette photo.

When dinner finished, a former U.S. Army officer, acting as the emcee, who had not lost his authoritative voice, took the microphone, and very loudly announced, "Attention to orders!" All the former and current military officers in attendance jumped to their feet and stood at attention, the West Pointers looking like "they had when they were

---

[645] Calvin Heath interview with author, April 26, 2013.

cadets."[646] Their spouses and guests looked around confused trying to determine what was happening. The emcee then announced, "Specialist Fourth Class Calvin Heath, front and center!"[647] While Calvin was fully expecting to be called to the podium, he did not expect the "Attention to orders" command and he nearly fainted. Determined not to embarrass himself, his family, or Bucha, Calvin rose and unsteadily walked to the front of the room, uncomfortably dressed in his rented black tuxedo that suddenly seemed to be three sizes too small and cutting off circulation in every part of his body. Former Company Commander Paul Bucha, Delta Company, 3/187th Infantry (ABN), 3rd Brigade, 101st Airborne Division, then took the mic and waited for Calvin to post himself at the dais. When he arrived, the two men shook hands and exchanged a few words off mic. Calvin, not knowing what to do next, assumed a modified parade rest position next to his former commander.

On the dais was a well-prepared speech, but Bucha did not need it – he knew this story all too well. Trying to control his emotions, he began to talk about March 16 through March 19, 1968, and Calvin's role in the battle that Dave Dillard would later call, "...our defining moment." As Bucha explained the sequence of events and the men who fell during the battle, tears began to flow from the eyes of the two old warriors as they remembered their fallen comrades, with Calvin remembering Paul Conner most of all. Calvin hoped his old friend was looking down on him now and wished he was here. The crowd "listened stoically, and let the tears flow without embarrassment, as Bucha read what [Calvin] did on the night of March [18], 1968, in the jungles near Phuoc Vinh."[648] Bucha explained the horrors Calvin endured that terrifying evening 34 years ago and how he was cut off from the main group, hit by mines, shot several times, and severely wounded and how he refused to leave the side of the other injured men with whom he shared a small piece of blood-soaked ground.

[646] Bert Heath interview with author October 24, 2013.
[647] Heath Memorial Ceremony, October 10, 2013, Hartford, Connecticut.
[648] McCaughey and Dean, May 28, 2002.

The memories of the friends lost touched a nerve that was still extremely painful for both men. Bucha struggled to close his remarks without completely breaking down. When he completed his speech, he called upon Admiral J. William Kime to step forward.[649] Admiral Kime took the Silver Star from its blue case, handled it with great respect and carefully – *and finally* – officially pinned it on Calvin, who was now standing at attention. The crowd of old, and not-so-old soldiers, and their guests erupted in a loud and enthusiastic standing ovation that overwhelmed Calvin. Never in his life had he experienced such gratitude.[650] 12,406 days after Specialist Fourth Class Calvin "Willy" Heath earned the Silver Star, "For gallantry in action against a hostile and superior force …" and 12,404 days after it should have been pinned on this remarkably brave soldier by General Barsanti at Long Binh Hospital, Vietnam, Calvin finally received justice.

Above L-R: The Silver Star and the Purple Heart. The Silver Star is the nation's third highest award and is awarded for gallantry in action. It is often referred to as the Warrior's Medal. The Purple Heart is the oldest American military award and is given to soldiers wounded in action. It is awarded in the name of the President of the United States. These are the two medals worn by Calvin during the West Point Dinner on March 14, 2002.

---

[649] Note: During his October 2013, Hartford, CT speech, Paul Bucha referred to the admiral who officially pinned on Calvin's Silver Star as the commandant of the USCG Academy. Records show this was Rear Admiral J. William Kime. Found at:
www.uscg.mil/history/people/JWKimeBio.asp.
[650] Dumont, Stephen, CT West Point Association, conversation with the author May 17, 2017.

Overcome with emotion, Calvin scanned the room as the men and women in attendance showed their gratitude for his service. For the second time in his life, he was recognized for the hero he was, but this time was especially meaningful as it was among men and women who truly understood the sacrifices he made during and after the war. For Calvin the world once again made sense. When asked if he wanted to say a few words, he choked down his tears and simply said, "Thank you." It was two of the most heartfelt words spoken that evening.

Calvin was then presented two round trip all-expenses-paid tickets to London, England from the West Point Society of Connecticut. The following day, Morton Dean, long-time anchor and news correspondent for ABC and CBS News, co-authored the article *A Call to Remember Those Who Fought or Fell for U.S.* It powerfully recalled the sacrifices Calvin made in March 1968.[651]

---

[651] McCaughey and Dean, May 28, 2002.

REUNIONS

"We can only heal through each other."
Bill Heaney, Mike Rawson, Dave Dillard, October 2013

Since the early 1960s, American psychiatrists were witnessing a rapid growth in a previously unidentified mental disorder among returning American combat soldiers. While post-combat diagnoses were available and thoroughly studied, the men and women who returned from Vietnam did not fit the typical disorders and conditions previously identified. For more than a decade, psychiatrists struggled to understand, and then develop treatments for this new disorder.

No man from Delta Company, and in fact, few who fought in Vietnam, came home emotionally, physically, and psychologically unscathed. Unfortunately for the returning warriors, the VA was ill-prepared for the magnitude of the problems they faced. Worse, few in the psychological community, especially the VA's, fully understood the true nature of the battles that raged within these particular veterans' psyche. Diagnosis and treatment, at first, was incredibly ineffective, especially for those with latent symptoms. Dr. Richard Kulka, a distinguished social psychologist noted that, "Well before 1982, it had become clear to both scientific and policymaking communities concerned about Vietnam veterans that a definitive study was needed."[652] The National Vietnam Veterans Readjustment Study (NVVRS), commissioned by Congress in 1983, helped to fill this void, but much work was still needed, especially in educating the veterans on how and where to seek appropriate help.

In 1980, the disorder – Posttraumatic Stress Disorder (PTSD) – was finally officially identified and added to the American Psychiatric Association's *Diagnostic and Statistical Manual of Mental Disorders* (*DSM–III*; American Psychiatric Association, 1980).[653] Posttraumatic stress, however, has been around since prehistoric man first walked

---

[652] Kulka, et al., p. xix.
[653] Baldwin, Williams, and Houts, p. 1.

303

the earth. Soldiers were always especially vulnerable due to their high level of contact with extreme and traumatic events. In military circles, similar disorders have had several labels to include "shell shock," "battle fatigue," "the thousand-yard stare," "nervous disease," and even "irritable heart." In his article, *PTSD from the Vietnam War*, Dr. Matthew Tull, Associate Professor and Director of Anxiety Disorders at the University of the Mississippi Medical Center, outlines the findings from the congressionally mandated NVVRS. According to Tull:

The findings from this study were alarming. At the time of the study (middle to late 1980s), among Vietnam veterans, approximately 15% of men and 9% of women were found to currently have PTSD. Approximately 30% of men and 27% of women had PTSD at some point in their life following Vietnam.[654]

What remains unclear in Tull's summary is the actual combat role and combat frequency of the subjects tested. Assuming the study includes subjects assigned to combat support units, and those who had limited combat roles, might suggest the numbers represented above are much higher for soldiers like Calvin who saw intense combat for long periods of time.

The VA and the psychology world quickly adjusted their treatment plans, but found the more proficient they became in helping soldiers deal with the problems of PTSD, the more and more veterans sought their help. The scale of the problem was enormous. While this additional service remained inadequate for years, it was at least a step in the right direction. Unfortunately, outliers like Calvin, who had no VA benefits, no insurance or personal means to help themselves, were forced to deal with these very complicated issues alone.

The NVVRS report, according to Tull, also suggested that in a small number of cases, symptoms diminished as time went on, but he was quick to note that based on studies by Harvard, Columbia, and

---

[654] Tull, *PTSD From the Vietnam War*, January 29, 2012 found at: http://ptsd.about.com/od/ptsdandthemilitary/a/Vietnamlongterm.htm.

SUNY, "Veterans who continued to have PTSD 14 years after their first interview, were found to have considerably more psychological and social problems." He also suggested that "...persistent PTSD can have a tremendous negative effect on a person's life and physical health."[655] Calvin was clearly among this group of veterans.

Over the past 30 years, much work has been accomplished in developing treatment methodologies to assist those with PTSD. The recent wars in Iraq and Afghanistan have facilitated better PTSD awareness, education and treatment, but in the 1970s and 1980s, when Calvin and his battle mates fought the disorder, little assistance was available and much work, with regards to understanding its long-term ramifications, remained.

Many Vietnam veterans who understood they had a serious problem, sought treatment and found that counselling sessions with psychologists, counsellors, and support groups achieved little, and in many cases, aggravated the condition. Calvin himself later shared his opinion about group sessions that he eventually attended:

Well, you talk to other guys. You talk to them about it but depending on [their experience] – you got like clerks who got PTSD, because they got hit by a mortar round. Well I'm sorry, I can't relate to you. You're rear echelon. You weren't out in the shit. I can't relate to somebody like that.[656]

Many researchers and psychologists have suggested that the most effective way to heal long-term PTSD is for the veteran to work through the traumatic event(s) with those who shared the incident or had similar experiences. Calvin unknowingly agreed with this assessment and was living proof that this worked as he always felt better during and after his long talks with Dillard, Harjo, Heaney, Wishik and the other men with whom he served.

In 2013, Bill Heaney noted, "It's like pulling the scab off a [wound] and cleaning out the pus. We can only do it through each

---

[655] Tull, *PTSD From the Vietnam War,* January 29, 2012 found at:
http://ptsd.about.com/od/ptsdandthemilitary/a/Vietnamlongterm.htm.
[656] Adam Piore interview with Calvin Heath, 2009.

other."[657] No matter who tried to help them throughout their lives, the men of Delta Company agreed with Calvin and felt "[Nobody except us] has been where we've been. They can't help us because they don't know how it feels. They don't know what it's like to be in that kind of inner turmoil. [It's] a wound that will not heal."[658] No matter the level of education or skill a counselor might possess, no matter the psychological merit of the medicine du jour, the only thing that helped many of the men of Delta Company was the man who fought on their right or left.

The Rakkasan Association, a group for all past and serving Rakkasans, was formed in 1981.They held their first reunion in 1982 in Atlanta, Georgia and a few of the men from 3/187th attended. Building on what the association was doing, the men of Delta Company felt a more specifically focused reunion would be better, and around 1998, they held their own reunion in Washington State at the hotel of Harold Mayer, a former member of the 3/187th.[659] That year, six men from Delta Company attended. They were, Dave Dillard, Tom Hartman, Austin Harjo, Peter Colantuoni, Jerry Jarrett, and Tim Hurley. They decided to hold more reunions and over the next several years, 90 of their former battle mates were eventually found and contacted, Calvin included.

The men found great value in reconnecting with one another and all agreed that the healing process had only began when they reunited. The hugs, the tears, the stories, and the discussions allowed each of them the opportunity to piece together the missing parts of their time in the field and address the demons they each faced. In 2013, Mike Rawson stated:

> *I've been to the reunions, and me and him* (pointing to Dave Dillard) *and the other guys are tearing this stuff apart... "And I don't remember this, and I don't remember that...."*

---

[657] Dillard, Heaney, Rawson interview with author, October 9, 2013.
[658] Ibid.
[659] Heaney interview with author, September 10, 2014.

It just helps us to complete all the incompletes that's been in us because we stuffed it [all away] for so long...[660]

Bill Heaney added:

If you were just a combat veteran and you weren't there that night – you had to be there that night for the healing to begin. You had to be there for the days leading up to it, and the days after it. Otherwise it just didn't mean anything talking to [other] people about it. They weren't there.[661]

For Calvin, the final stretch of healing began in 2003 when he attended his first reunion. Dave Dillard convinced him that it would be good for him and the guys if they were all to see each other again. Calvin agreed, but was uneasy and worried about attending. When he arrived at Ardmore, Oklahoma, he checked in, looked around and suddenly felt extremely uncomfortable. His stomach turned and a piece of him just wanted to turn around and go home. For 35 years, people at home thought of him as a coward and he reasoned that the men here, at least some of them, might feel the same way. How would he handle that? He also thought about answering the inevitable questions about his time in the Army after the battle and his arrests for desertion. In spite of finally receiving his Silver Star, the bad conduct discharge would be difficult to explain.

Questions and concerns filled his head. Sudden bouts of anxiety and survivor's guilt overwhelmed him. *Would they blame me for Sherrill, and the others?? How many died that day that I should have saved? Why am I here and not them?* He looked around and saw the guys with whom he served, but he didn't recognize anyone except Dillard. The rest of the men just seemed to ignore him. Calvin recalled that "...at first I thought they were mad at me [because] they weren't really talking to me."[662] The decision to go to the reunion carried great emotional and psychological risk for Calvin and was one

---

[660] Dillard, Heaney, Rawson interview with author, October 9, 2013.

[661] Ibid.

[662] Adam Piore interview with Calvin Heath, 2009.

he began to seriously question. At one point early in the process, he thought, *My God this is all wrong…*

In 2009, Adam Piore asked, "So who made the first move?" Calvin replied, "Actually the combat photographer. I was talking to Earl Vanalstine, I was talking to him and then one of the other guys introduced who he was and we started to talk a little bit."[663] Another member of Delta Company, besides Vanalstine, who made Calvin feel welcomed and therefore made all the difference in the world that day, was Ray Palmer.[664] Ray eased Calvin's sudden panic with a simple extended hand and "Hi, I'm Ray Palmer." The two men shook hands and Ray introduced Calvin to a number of the other men. The men now recognized Calvin and welcomes, and hugs were soon exchanged. Calvin was soon at ease; more lifelines had been thrown.

Left: SGT Ray Palmer March 1968, Phuoc Vinh, Vietnam. Photo taken by Dennis Moore. Dennis was killed in action March 18, 1968. 2008. Right: Ray Palmer 2008. Ray was instrumental in Calvin's healing and one of the first to welcome him at the 2003 reunion. Palmer photo.

When Calvin was later asked how he felt about reuniting with the men that day, Calvin responded, "I wanted to cry. It was the best day

---

[663] Adam Piore interview with Calvin Heath, 2009.

[664] Ray Palmer was with Delta during 1967/1968 assigned to HQ Platoon and was a battalion S-5 (Civil Affairs) NCO. He helped Harjo organize a reaction force on March 18/19, 1968, the night Calvin, Dietch, Sherrill, and Wishik were isolated.

of my life in a very long time."[665] "[It was like] the first Christmas that you can remember – *that's* what the reunion is. You're giddy as hell. You're nervous…"[666]

Above: Calvin with First Sergeant Austin Harjo at a Delta reunion. Calvin's deep respect for "Top" lasted until the day he died. Calvin stated that Harjo, "Was one of the greatest men I ever met." Calvin Heath photo. Above right: Harjo after his retirement in his Class Bs complete with decorations and awards. Heath photo.

Calvin's concerns and worries quickly disappeared and so did the question as to whether he should have attended the reunion. Calvin continues, "Everybody was starting to talk and that's when they said they thought I was mad at them for not coming out [to rescue us] and they were being apologetic for it. I said, you don't need to be."[667] Never in his wildest dreams did Calvin expect that turn of events. *How could they have possibly thought that I would be mad at them?*

For several days, the men talked. They passed no judgment on Calvin because of his problems with the post-battle Army. What

---

[665] Calvin Heath interview with author, April 26, 2013.
[666] Adam Piore interview with Calvin Heath, 2009.
[667] Ibid.

mattered most to them, was their shared experiences during the war and the long journey each had taken since. Calvin noted:

It was good to be able to talk to somebody that was there... because you can talk it out. What everybody did [that night] was the right thing. We should have been overrun, absolutely we should have gotten overrun, but the way we did things, they just thought we were a bigger unit than what we were...[668]

The exchange of details about those days, the ability to put the pieces together, and finding each other once again meant the world to Calvin and the other men. It opened doors for healing that many of them felt did not exist. Mike Rawson added, for years "the worst place I had was in my own head and I spent too much time in my own head."[669] The reunions helped Rawson and Calvin escape from their "own heads."

Calvin discussed the battle and the horrors he experienced during Vietnam, as well as the demons he still fought. Remarkably, for the first time he spoke with a group of men who completely understood. For the first time he felt something positive occurring, something therapeutic – restorative. That happy-go-lucky boy at Ciconne's farm *was* still alive, and for the first time in years, Calvin felt *that* little boy had a chance to live again, "Because you are talking to somebody who's been through hell, just like you have, and he knows what you know and that makes it a lot easier."[670]

When asked about something specific with regards to healing, Calvin told of a reoccurring nightmare that he had for years. Each night he found himself back in the jungle trying to change the battle's outcome. Night after night he attempted a different scenario, but each scenario kept leading him back to the same inevitable outcome. Paul was dead; the others were dead, and he was completely powerless to save more men. Every night the nightmare ended with the same

---

[668] Adam Piore interview with Calvin Heath, 2009.
[669] Dillard, Heaney, Rawson interview with author, October 9, 2013.
[670] Adam Piore interview with Calvin Heath, 2009.

frustrating outcome – he, Dietch, and Wishik were cut off and he was unable to get them to safety.[671]

The dreams might suggest that Calvin fought suppressed notions of self-doubt and self-loathing due to the ever-present feeling of failure. This was supported and reinforced by many close to him who thought him a "screw-up" and doubted his actions, and the ungrateful Army for whom he fought. Speaking with the men of Delta Company in 2003 helped Calvin to understand that he did all he could that day and they all praised his extraordinary effort. Those conversations with the men that day were far more therapeutic and meaningful than anything he could have possibly received elsewhere. Calvin later said. "That was so good to talk to the guys. I don't remember having that dream after that."[672]

Another story Calvin shared from the first reunion was an incident he had with the men of Bravo Company. Calvin stated:

[During] the first-year reunion, B Company was sitting over on the knoll and as we walked by them one of the guys yelled out, "Dead men walking!" and he was referring to us and I thought he was being a wise-ass. I was ready to fight. I was pissed – and Dillard grabs me and says, "No, no, no... they're actually giving us a compliment." When they're talking about D Company everybody should have been dead – they were saying that we made it through [that night].[673]

Other men from Delta Company also found the reunions to be incredibly healing. Bill Heaney later stated that, "The healing could not even begin until we, the guys who were there, started talking to each other." Dave Dillard, who for years began to doubt many of the details of that night added, "When he (pointing at Heaney) sat down at the reunion, I realized what I remembered was true."[674]

Mike Rawson battled debilitating guilt about not being with the men on March 16-19, 1968. Rawson had nothing to feel guilty about.

---

[671] Calvin Heath interview with author, June 2013.
[672] Ibid.
[673] Adam Piore interview with Calvin Heath, 2009.
[674] Dillard, Heaney, Rawson interview with author, October 9, 2013.

He had done far more than his share during his time in Vietnam, but he was unavailable during Operation Rakkasan Chaparral because he was recovering from a serious wound obtained in a previous mission. He, like Calvin, always felt he should have done more to help his unit. He later stated:

> *I was wounded and healing up, and the best I could do was to jump on the chopper with Harjo and try to help these guys out. And I never got over that, feeling guilty about that night. I didn't have a choice, but it didn't dismiss the guilt.*[675]

Bill Heaney added, "Whether you liked the guy that was in your squad or you hated him, when you're on that battlefield you're brothers."[676] And all the men were quick to add that strong bond remains unbroken forever. Dillard added:

> *Even though we were slammed together – these bunch of misfits, it made a cohesive unit. If you ask me, there are no other men on this planet that I would rather spend my time with. Why? Because we were brothers, and we were put together and sealed for time and eternity. No question...*[677]

Dillard stopped, took a moment, and then proudly added as he looked at the other men, "The strength of the family."[678]

Left: Dave Dillard during Jump School. Right: Paul Bucha, Dave Dillard and Sam Spencer during a reunion. "The strength of the family." Still exists today.

---

[675] Dillard, Heaney, Rawson interview with author, October 9, 2013.
[676] Ibid.
[677] Dillard, Heaney, Rawson interview with author, October 9, 2013.
[678] Ibid.

Above: Calvin holding two Delta Company, 3/187th commemorative flags to include the D, 3/187th guidon. Ray Palmer photo.

As Calvin attended more reunions, he found a developing inner peace with the men of Delta that he could not find anywhere else in the world. Outsiders looking at these aging Rakkasans saw pot-bellied old men with crops of gray and white hair. Their wrinkled and weathered looks made it easy to see that their best years were far behind them. Calvin saw them differently. While their frames had changed greatly, to him they were still warriors. These were men who crawled through the snake-infested jungles of Vietnam stalking their quarry like savage animals. They brought death and destruction down upon anyone who crossed their paths in the most horrible of ways with little consideration for the crying mothers, fathers, wives or children they left behind. They were the best the United States Army had ever produced and were once among the most feared men in the world, and Calvin loved them more than anything. It was a love "forged in the fires of hell" and cultivated by the horrors of war.

These aging men understood Calvin, and Calvin understood them. They experienced the same thoughts, nightmares, had the same problems and wandered the same paths on which Calvin often found himself wandering while seeking help and understanding. These old men were the answer Calvin so desperately sought. Here, *with them*, he could find peace, that peace increasing with every reunion and every phone call. Every part of the reconnection process brought Calvin to a better place. Visits with Bill Heaney and his wife, phone calls with These aging men understood Calvin, and Calvin understood them. They experienced the same thoughts, nightmares, had the same problems and wandered the same paths on which Calvin often found himself wandering while seeking help and understanding. These old men were the answer Calvin so desperately sought. Here, *with them*, he could find peace, that peace increasing with every reunion and every phone call. Every part of the reconnection process brought Calvin to a better place. Visits with Bill Heaney and his wife, phone calls with Dave Dillard, Top, Ray Palmer, Paul Bucha, Billy Ford, Earl Vanalstine and the other men allowed Calvin to find a place in which he Dave Dillard, Top, Ray Palmer, Paul Bucha, Billy Ford, Earl Vanalstine and the other men allowed Calvin to find a place in which he felt understood – a place in which he felt safe. For the first time in a very long time Calvin was feeling good about himself – almost.

While happy to reconnect with the men of Delta, the reunions were also a constant reminder of the shameful manner in which he was treated. With the help of Dave Dillard, Austin Harjo, Paul Bucha and the other men, much had been gained over the past five years, but Calvin still had a long way to go. His permanent record still showed that he was a deserter... but that would soon change.

Above: Calvin while he attended the 2006 reunion. According to Ray Palmer, he is holding three candles to honor those lost during their time in Vietnam. Calvin's candles include one each for Paul Conner and Jimmy Sherrill. It is uncertain who the third is for. Holding the microphone is Bob Friedrichs, former commander of Bravo Company. Bob earned the Distinguished Service Cross for action in Trang Bang Corridor. Ray Palmer photo.

Above: The men of Delta Company during a reunion at Fort Campbell, Kentucky. Calvin is 2nd from the left, Dave Dillard 8th from the left (including the young man standing in the front), and Paul Bucha 11th. Calvin Heath photo.

VINDICATION

During 2002 and most of 2003, Calvin used the momentum created by the receipt of his Silver Star and the change of his VA benefits status to address the final injustice – the correction of his permanent military records. Changing permanent U.S. military records is a lengthy and often futile process. Many requests get dismissed out of hand and many applicants, finding the process hopeless, simply give up. Calvin, most likely with Paul Bucha's continued help, felt that he had one more battle in him.

The last round of vindication began with Calvin submitting an Application for Correction of Military Records to the Army Board of Correction of Military Record (ABCMR). The ABCMR is a civilian department that reports directly to the Office of the Secretary of the Army in Washington D.C. According to the Department of the Army, The ABCMR is the highest level of administrative review within the Department of the Army with the mission to correct errors in, or remove injustices from Army military records.[679] Among the several requests an applicant can make are the two major items Calvin was requesting; an upgrade to his BCD to an Honorable Discharge, and to have his permanent records reflect the medals and awards he had earned while in combat.

The ABCMR process is challenging and can take more than 12 months to complete. The applicant is responsible to obtain and submit all pertinent records and information, any omission typically results in an automatic non-approval. Calvin also had an additional obstacle as the ABCMR will not disturb military court dispositions.[680] Because he was found guilty by a military court of law for AWOL and

---

[679] U.S. Pentagon website, Army regulation 15-185, Army Board for Correction of Military Records, found January 23, 2014 at: http://arba.army.pentagon.mil/abcmr-overview.cfm

[680] Applicant's Guide to Applying to the Army Board for Correction of Military Records, p.5 Found March 1, 2014 at:
http://arba.army.pentagon.mil/documents/ABCMR%20Applications%20Guide%202005.pdf

desertion, changing his permanent records to reflect an Honorable Discharge was clearly a long shot.

After all the forms and information are submitted, the ABCMR reviews the evidence to determine if the application merits further attention. If the application is found worthy, it is then assigned to a special board consisting of three civilian members from the executive level of the Department of the Army for review and determination.[681]

The paperwork was checked and double checked before Calvin submitted it to the ABCMR. For months, he heard nothing. Then on Monday August 18, 2003, Calvin received the following report from the Department of the Army. It read:

Department of the Army
BOARD FOR THE CORRECTION OF MILITARY RECORDS
1941 JEFFERSON DAVIS HIGHWAY, 2ND FLOOR
ARLINGTON, VA 22202-4508

PROCEEDINGS

IN THE CASE OF: HEATH, CALVIN
044-XX-XXXX

BOARD DATE: 14 August 2003
DOCKET NUMBER: AR2003086947

I Certify that hereinafter is recorded the true and complete record of the proceedings of the Army Board for Corrections of Military Records in the case of the above-named individual.

Mr. Carl W. S. Chun   Director
Mrs. Nancy L. Amos   Analyst

The following members, a quorum, were present

Mr. Raymond V. O' Conner   Chairperson
Mr. James E. Anderholm   Member
Ms. Linda M. Barker   Member

The applicant and counsel if any, did not appear before the board.

The Board considered the following evidence:

Exhibit A - Applications for correction of military records

---

[681] U.S. Army, Regulation 15-185, p. 2.

Exhibit B - Military Personnel Records (including advisory opinion, if any)

FINDINGS:

1. The applicant has exhausted or the Board has waived the requirement for exhaustion of all administrative remedies afforded by the existing law or regulations.
2. The applicant request, in effect, that his upgraded discharge be affirmed.
3. The applicant states his problems started when he was medically evacuated from Vietnam to Fort Devens, MA. His hip was operated on, but the bullet lodged there could not be removed. The attending doctor (who soon thereafter was reassigned) told him he would be getting a medical discharge. He signed a waiver to be taken off airborne duty and chose to stay at Fort Devens to await his medical discharge. The next thing he knew he received orders to report to Fort Carson, CO. When he asked his new doctor about his medical discharge, the doctor brushed him off saying it would be taken care of at Fort Carson.
4. The applicant states that his company commander at Fort Carson would not recognize his physical profile and said he was faking it. He was forced to go on marches and field maneuvers although the doctors there said that he could not do that. Around January 1969, he was placed back in the hospital for further hip surgery, but his company commander still harassed him. After the surgery, he was placed on convalescent leave. His company commander called his home and told his mother he did not have to return to Fort Carson. That summer, while he was still on crutches, he was picked up by the Federal Bureau of Investigation. He was returned to Fort Devens and put in a holding company for absentees. He did not have his medical paperwork with him, so his physical profiles were not recognized. He was treated like a lowlife. He would be placed on pass, only to be picked up for being absent without leave (AWOL).
5. The applicant further states that in 1974 or 1975, he got a letter telling him to go to Fort Benjamin Harrison, IN for discharge. He was told he could return to the Army or be discharged. With all the ways he was being treated, he chose the discharge. He just signed the papers he was told to sign. He only had a 7th grade education and did not understand he was signing away his rights. At that time, he was put in front of a board consisting of two Army officers and three Marine Corp officers. Because he could not prove he had the Silver Star, he was told he would not get an honorable discharge.

6. As supporting evidence, the applicant provides a summary statement from his former first sergeant; a supporting statement from his former company commander; the narrative to the recommendation for the Silver Star prepared by his former company commander, dated 16 December 1998; and his Representative in Congress's endorsement of the recommendation for the Silver Star.

7. The applicant's military records show that he enlisted in the Regular Army on 17 May 1967. He completed basic combat training and advanced individual training and was awarded military occupational specialty 11B (Light Weapons Infantryman).

8. The applicant arrived in Vietnam on or about 16 December 1967. He was assigned to Company D, 3d Battalion (Airborne), 187th Infantry as an airborne qualified rifleman. He was wounded on 18 March 1968 and medically evacuated to the U.S. Army Hospital, Camp Zama, Japan after receiving participation credit for two campaigns.

9. The applicant was assigned to Medical Holding Detachment, U.S. Army Hospital, Fort Devens, MA on 3 April 1968.

10. The applicant's service medical records are not available.

11. The applicant's DA Form 20 (Enlisted Qualification Record) shows he was AWOL from 20-30 June 1968.

12. The applicant was reassigned to Company C, 1st Battalion, 10th Infantry, Fort Carson, CO on or about 5 October 1968.

13. The applicant's DA Form 20 shows he had 10 periods of AWOL/dropped from the rolls/confinement between 22 January 1969 and 8 September 1971. He was departed AWOL again on 24 September 1971.

14. By letter dated 21 November 1974, the applicant was notified of the provisions of Presidential Proclamation Number 4313 (PP 4313). On 2 December 1974, he turned himself in under the provisions of PP 4313.

15. On 3 December 1974, the applicant was discharged, with a discharge under other than honorable conditions, under the provisions of PP 4313. He had completed 2 years, 4 months, and 25 days of creditable active service and had a total of 1872 days of lost time. His DD Form 214 shows he was awarded the National Defense Service Medal, the Expert Qualification Badge with Rifle bar, the Parachute Badge, the Purple Heart, the Republic of Vietnam Gallantry Cross with Palm Unit Citation, the Expert qualification Badge with Machine Gun bar, and the Vietnam Service Medal.

16. On 11 February 1977, the Army Discharge Review Board (ADRB) upgraded the applicant's discharge to general under honorable conditions under the provisions of the 19 January 1977 extension of PP 4313.

320

17. On 23 May 1978, the ADRB voted, in a 3 to 2 decision, not to affirm the applicant's upgrade characterization of service under uniform standards. The ADRB considered the applicant's initial excellent service; however, it did not consider that to be of sufficient magnitude to outweigh his acts of [in]discipline which led to his discharge.

18. The applicant was awarded the Silver Star on U.S. Total Army Personnel Command Permanent Order 153-4, dated 2 June 1999, for the period 16 to 19 March 1968.

19. Presidential Proclamation 4313 (PP 4313), dated 16 September 1974, was issued by President Ford and affected three groups of individuals. One group was members of the Armed Forces who were in an unauthorized absence status. These individuals were afforded an opportunity to return to military control and elect either a discharge under other than honorable conditions under PP 4313 or to stand trial for their offenses and take whatever punishment resulted. For those who elected discharge, a Joint Alternative Service Board composed of military personnel would establish a period of alternative service of not more than 24 months that the individual would perform. If they completed the alternative service satisfactorily, they would be entitled to receive Clemency Discharge. The Clemency Discharge did not affect the underlying discharge and did not entitle the individual to any benefits administered by the VA.

20. A Presidential Memorandum was issued by President Ford on 19 January 1977 (sometimes referred to as PP 4313 Extension). This memorandum mandated the issuance of a general discharge to individuals who had: (1) applied for consideration under PP 4313; (2) been wounded in action or decorated for valor; and (3) records free of any compelling reason to deny relief. This was a mandate to the ADRB from the President and was to be applied by the ADRB without any applications from the affected individuals. Whether the individuals had performed alternative service or not is an issue to be consider.

21. The Department of the Army Special Discharge Review Program (SDRP) was based on a memorandum from the Secretary of Defense Brow and is often referred to as the "Carter Program." It mandated the upgrade of individual cases in which the applicant met one of the several specified criteria and when the separation was not based on a specified compelling reason to the contrary. The ADRB had no discretion in such cases other than to decide whether recharacterization to fully honorable as opposed to a general discharge was warranted in a particular case. An individual who had received a punitive discharge was not eligible for consideration under the SDRP. Absentees who returned

to military control under the program were eligible for consideration after they were processed for separation. Individuals could have their discharges upgraded if they met any one of the following criteria: wounded in action; received a military decoration other than service medal; successfully completed an assignment in Southeast Asia; completed alternate service; received an honorable discharge from a previous tour of military service; or completed alternative service or excused therefore in accordance with PP 4313 of 16 September 1974. Compelling reasons to the contrary to deny discharge upgrade were desertion/AWOL in or from the combat area; discharge based on a violent act of misconduct; discharge based on cowardice or misbehavior before the enemy; or discharge based on an act or misconduct that would be subject to criminal prosecution under civil law.

22. Public Law 95-126 provided in pertinent part for a "Relook Program." All cases upgraded from under other than honorable conditions under the SDRP or extension to PP 4313 had to be relooked and affirmed or not affirmed under uniform standards. Two of the principal features of the Public Law 95-126 were: (1) the addition of 180 days of continuous unauthorized absence to other reasons (e.g., conscientious objector, deserters) for discharge which act as specific bar to eligibility for Veterans Administration (VA) benefits. Such absence must have been the basis for discharge under other than honorable conditions and is computed without regard to expiration term of service; and (2) prospective disqualification for receipt of VA benefits for those originally qualifying as a result of upgrade by Presidential Memorandum of 19 January 1977 or the SDRP. Unless an eligibility determination is made under the published uniform standards and procedures.

23. Army Regulation 600-8-22 (Military Awards) provides for the award of the Combat Infantry Badge to a soldier who is an infantryman satisfactorily performing infantry duties, who is assigned to an infantry unit during such time as the unit is engaged in active ground combat and must actively participate in such ground combat. Campaign or battle credit is not sufficient for award of the CIB.

24. Army Regulations 600-8-22 provides for award of the Republic of Vietnam Campaign Medal with Device 1960 to personnel who have served in the Republic of Vietnam for 6 months during the period 1 March 1961 to 28 March 1973, inclusive, have served for less than 6 months and have been wounded by hostile forces.

25. Army Regulation 600-8-22 provides for the wear of one bronze service star on the appropriate service medal for each credited campaign.

26. Department of the Army Pamphlet 672-3 (Unit Citation and Campaign Participation Credit Register) lists the unit awards received by units serving in Vietnam. This document shows that, at the time of the applicant's assignment to 3d Battalion, 187th Infantry, it was cited for award of the Valorous Unit Award for the period 16 through 22 March 1968 by Department of the Army general Orders Number 22, dated 1976.

27. Department of the Army Pamphlet 672-3 also shows that, at the time of the applicant's assignment to 3d Battalion, 187th Infantry, it was credited for award of the Meritorious Unit Commendation for the period 14 March through 3 October 1968 by the Department of the Army General Orders Number 22, dated 1976.

CONCLUSIONS:

1. On May 23, 1978, the ADRB voted, in a 3 to 2 decision, not to affirm the applicant's upgrade characterization of service under uniform standards. The ADRB considered the applicant's initial excellent service, however, it did not consider that to be of sufficient magnitude to outweigh his acts of indiscipline which led to his discharge.

2. In 1999, the applicant was awarded the Silver Star for gallantry in action during the period 16 to 19 March 1968. The Board considers that this award is of "significant magnitude" to outweigh the applicant's acts of indiscipline enough to warrant affirming his upgraded general under honorable conditions discharge.

3. The applicant should be mindful that he had had over 180 days of continuous absence. Under Public Law 95-126, 180 days of continuous unauthorized absence acts as a specific bar to eligibility for VA benefits. Although this Board has concluded that the applicant's discharge, as upgraded by the ADRB, should be affirmed, the Army has no jurisdiction over the VA, which operates under its own policies and procedures.

4. The Board also concludes that the applicant met the eligibility criteria for award of the Combat Infantryman Badge. His DD Form 214 should be amended to add this award.

5. The Board notes that the applicant met the eligibility criteria for award of the Republic of Vietnam Campaign Medal with Device 1960 by virtue of his being wounded while in Vietnam. He also met the eligibility criteria for wear of two bronze service stars on the Vietnam Service Medal. His DD Form 214 should be amended to add these awards.

6. The applicant was assigned to a unit during a period of time that unit was awarded the Valorous Unit Award and the Meritorious Unit Commendation. These unit awards should be added to his DD Form 214.

7. In view of the forgoing, the applicant's records should be corrected as recommended below.

RECOMMENDATION:

1. That all of the Department of the Army records related to this case be corrected by showing that the applicant's discharge, upgraded to general under honorable conditions under the provisions of the 19 January 1977 extension of Presidential Proclamation 4313 by the ADRB, is affirmed.

2. That the applicant's DD Form 214 be amended to add the Combat Infantryman Badge, the Republic of Vietnam Campaign Medal with Device 1960, the Valorous Unit Award, and the Meritorious Unit Commendation and to show he is authorized to wear two bronze service stars on the Vietnam Service Medal.

Note: the form shows the Board all voting "Grant as stated in the recommendation."

Calvin was uncertain at first what the document meant, and he reread it in its entirety. He put the document down, thought about what he read, picked it up and reread the recommendation section several more times. It took him awhile before he could accept what it said. It clearly stated, "That all of the Department of the Army records related to this case be corrected to show that the applicant's discharge, upgraded to general under *honorable conditions... is affirmed.*" Calvin sat and looked at the document in disbelief. Thirty-five years and five months after the battle at Bau Co Bong, he finally regained the honor taken from him so many years ago.

On June 21, 2004, one year and ten months after the ABCMR's final decision, the final piece of Calvin's long journey was completed. His DD Form 214 was reissued by the United States Government, the old DD-214 issued in 1974, unfairly showing a man dishonorably discharged because he had dishonored the proud uniform of the United States Army was finally destroyed. The reissued June 21, 2004 document showed a soldier who had served his country honorably and with great distinction. It now clearly noted the character of his service as "Honorable," and that he had earned through great sacrifice and courage, the right to wear:

- The Silver Star
- Purple Heart
- Combat Infantryman's Badge
- National Defense Service Medal
- Vietnam Service Medal with two Bronze Service Stars
- Republic of Vietnam Campaign Medal with Device 1960,
- The Valorous Unit Award
- Republic of Vietnam Gallantry Cross with Palm Unit Citation
- Expert Qualification Badge with Rifle and Machine Gun Bars
- Parachutist Badge
- Meritorious Unit Commendation Medal.

Other medals added to that list were the American Indian Nations of the United States of American Warrior's Medal of Valor, one of their most honorable awards, and the Connecticut Wartime Service Medal.

2004 - 2013

After 2003, Calvin attended a number of reunions and looked forward to each with great anticipation. The reunions, and the men with whom he served, helped him see through the darkness and by 2004, he recognized a very unfamiliar light at the end of the long dark tunnel, something he once thought impossible.

On Memorial Day weekend 2004, Rakkasans young and old once again gathered at Ardmore, Oklahoma for their annual reunion. There, Calvin was able to meet some of the younger soldiers who fought in Iraq. It was a special event for Calvin, one he and the older Rakkasans greatly enjoyed. Although the two groups of soldiers were separated by decades, they shared much. Calvin was pleased that this new generation deeply respected and enjoyed the company and advice of these old soldiers.

Also, on hand for the event was long-time news correspondent Ed Lavandera of CNN's *American Morning,* a daily show that first aired the day after 9/11 and ran for ten years. Lavandera was there to produce a Memorial Day piece using the Rakkasans' reunion as a backdrop. One of the old soldiers he interviewed that day was Calvin "Willy" Heath of Putnam, Connecticut. Lavandera's piece centered on the differences and similarities between the Vietnam veterans and their Iraq War counterparts. Calvin added his thoughts to the differences between the two eras. He stated, "People back here [in the United States], I think they got it right this time. Instead of taking it out on the soldiers, they're taking it out on the politicians, the people that are making the decisions. And that's the way it should be."[682] Calvin was pleased that this new generation of returning combat veterans would not have to face the unpleasantness of an ungrateful country the way the Vietnam veterans did. The country had learned much since Vietnam – so had Calvin.

---

[682] CNN piece aired May 31, 2004.

By 2008, much of Calvin's life was moving in the right direction. He was collecting VA benefits and he continued rebuilding his friendships with the men of Delta Company. During a trip to Maryland to visit Earl Vanalstine, the incredibly talented combat photographer who captured much of Delta's time in Vietnam, Calvin met Terri Jackson, Earl's secretary. Terri, 20 years younger than Calvin, was a single 40-year-old woman to whom Calvin took a liking. The two hit it off well and approximately a year later they were married.[683]

Also, in 2008, Calvin visited Dave Dillard in Livingston, Texas, and fell in love with the area. Calvin discussed moving to Texas with Dave, and Dave agreed that if Calvin was serious about moving to the area, he would put him up for a short period of time while he and Terri got their feet on the ground. Calvin returned to Connecticut, packed his things, and made the long drive to Livingston.

Above: 2008 reunion held at Fort Campbell Kentucky. Calvin is seventh from the left. Calvin Heath photo.

---

[683] Note: Calvin and Terri were married in Polk, Texas, on April 6, 2009, while Calvin was living there.

For the first few weeks, Calvin stayed with Dave Dillard living in Dave's guest house, fondly called "The Eagles Nest." Dave was a gentleman rancher with a large piece of land that appealed to Calvin. Maybe it was the various animals that roamed the property, the well-stocked fishing pond, or the peacefulness of the area that attracted Calvin; whatever it was, Calvin liked it and was at great peace there – at least for a while.

Before Calvin left Connecticut he approached his tribe and asked if he could make his Delta friends honorary members of the tribe. The Nipmuc council agreed and issued Honorary Awards of Valor to the men who fought alongside Calvin in 1968. Calvin did not expect how important this gesture would be for the men. Mike Rawson later stated:

When Calvin moved down here to Texas, before he left [Connecticut], he went to his tribe and he had them adopt a number of us from our company and he brought us these medallions he got from them, that are Native American recognition of Vietnam and I brought this specially to show you guys. See that's one of the things, the last things that Calvin did for me. Is that a brother or what? It's called the Warriors Medal of Valor, Native American Nations of the United States of America...[684]

Left: The Native American Nations of the United States Warriors Medal of Valor presented to the men of Delta by Calvin on behalf of a grateful Native American Nation. When Mike showed me the medal, he handled it as if it was his most prized possession. Joe Lindley photo.

---

[684] Dillard, Heaney, Rawson interview with author, October 9, 2013.

Calvin soon found a small house to rent on Jack Nettles Road, located about 15 minutes from Dillard's ranch. It was an inexpensive one-floor house in a good neighborhood, and for the first time in his life, Calvin felt that he finally found a place where he could live a well-deserved "normal life." During this time Calvin also had a great deal of discussion with Dave Dillard about religion. While Calvin chose to keep this part of his life private during my 2013 interviews, it was clear that Calvin gave the matter a great deal of thought, and it was easy to see it had a profound and positive effect on his life. [685]

For a while, things were going well for Calvin and Terri in Texas, but the elusive normalcy he so desperately sought throughout his life was still out of reach, and within a year of their April 6, 2009 wedding, Terri and he began to argue. Soon the wheels of their marriage began to wobble. The oppressive summer Texan heat exacerbated the problem and they soon decided to return east, she wanting to return to Baltimore and Calvin looking to return home to Connecticut. Calvin's good friend, Rob Authier later reported, "He hated the heat, and a couple years after he went out there, they came home. Terri, she wanted to go to Baltimore, but Calvin didn't want to live there so they came back, and he found a place by the lake." When I asked about Calvin's and Terri's state of affairs, Rob simply replied, "Things weren't going very well."[686]

By 2012, the stress of the unhappy marriage soon became intolerable for Calvin and he began experiencing severe headaches. Calvin reported that at times "the pain was absolutely unbearable."[687] At first, he thought they were the result of the stress of the unpleasant marriage, but they continued to increase both in frequency and in intensity. By January 2013, he realized there was something seriously wrong.

---

[685] Calvin Heath interview with author, May 2013.

[686] Authier, Rob, interview with author, March 28, 2014. Note: The lake Authier refers to is Quaddick Lake located in Thompson, CT.

[687] Calvin Heath interview with author, June 2013.

2013 - SICKNESS

In January 2013, Calvin's headaches were getting more intense, and they were now accompanied by random memory loss, confusion, constant pain, and persistent dizziness. He made an appointment at the Providence VA Hospital where doctors quickly determined the symptoms presented indications of something very serious and they immediately ordered a series of tests to include blood work and a CT scan. When the tests returned, they confirmed the doctor's worse suspicions. Calvin was suffering from Glioblastoma Multiforme (GBM), an aggressive malignant brain tumor. GBM is difficult to treat and even more difficult to surgically remove. It is often fatal within a few years when caught early and properly treated, and fatal within months when not. Calvin's case was, unfortunately, not caught early.

There has been a great deal of research suggesting a strong connection between GBM among Vietnam veterans due to the use of Agent Orange, but any lengthy discussion as to why he had GBM would have to wait for now. The CT scan showed a large, highly developed tumor in his right temporal lobe. If the doctors did not operate right away, Calvin's life expectancy was measured in days, if not hours.

Not expecting such bad news, Calvin was staggered. The doctors were honest with Calvin and explained that the prognosis for this type of cancer at that stage of development was never good. They explained that even with surgery, and then aggressive radiation and chemotherapy, he might only have a year to live. This old soldier was about to engage in another life or death struggle, and like other battles he fought during his life, this enemy also held overwhelming odds.

On Thursday January 31, 2013, the surgeon briefed Calvin and a few family members on the lengthy surgical procedure and the most likely outcomes. They explained that brain surgery, in and of itself, is an extremely dangerous affair that always carries serious risks both during and after surgery. Even if all went according to plan, strokes and cardiac failure were real possibilities while on the table, and while the doctors expressed "very guarded" hope for success, they were convinced Calvin had no options. While he wasn't prepared for such news, Calvin, when weighing the options, agreed to the immediate surgery and it was scheduled for the following day, Friday, February 1, 2013.

In the early morning hours of Friday, February 1, Calvin was prepped, and his head shaved. The nurses reviewed the procedures with him and attempted to make him as comfortable as possible. He took the activity in stride, joking with the nurses as they went about their duties. As he was wheeled into the operating room, thoughts of death certainly entered his mind. He understood the surgery was dangerous and he understood there was a good chance he would not survive. But it was not death he feared most, he had stared that particular devil down more than once in his life. It was living – living physically or mentally impaired that troubled him.

The humming monitoring equipment was set up along one side of the brightly lit room where nurses and physicians of the surgical team would monitor Calvin's vital signs. IV lines were set, and the masked anesthesiologist was busy prepping the solution that would send Calvin to another world, at least for a while. Nurses prepped Calvin with blue surgical cloth and there was little showing of the man who lay beneath except the right side of his head. Had he been flipped on his belly he would have looked like the March 19, 1968, Vanalstine picture of him on the stretcher during the battle near Phuoc Vinh. The surgical instruments were wheeled into place, the head surgeon was ready and gave the anesthesiologist the nod. "OK Mr. Heath, we're about to begin. I'm going to give you something to go to sleep. I want you to count back from ten." Calvin complied, "Ten, nine…" He was out.

After the long and complicated surgery, Calvin was wheeled back to the recovery room where he was closely monitored. He slept most of the night and the doctors and nurses were anxious to see how successful they were. GBM can imbed itself deep within the complicated interstices of the brain and any nick of brain tissue, or a portion of the tumor left behind, could have serious ramifications. The medical team knew they removed most of the tumor, but they did not know at what price. The loss of speech, memory, motor skills, etc., are all among the more probable postsurgical issues with which Calvin would have to deal.

During the following morning, Calvin's brother Bert made the drive to Providence to visit his younger brother, hoping for the best, but prepared for the worse. Bert stated:

> *I went Saturday a.m. to see him and I was shocked because I thought I'd find a guy on death row with tubes hanging out... and I walked in and he said, "Hey brother!" with a patch on the side of his head and the nurse and doctors are shaking their heads. "This is not what we expected. We expected he would have a stroke or a massive heart attack because the operation was that invasive."*[688]

On Saturday morning, Bert found his brother sitting up in bed in a good mood, smiling. "After all that [he went through], he's sitting there in bed and says to me 'it was only a little thing...'"[689] The doctor's postsurgical check went well, and the medical team was amazed at how well Calvin was doing. Having come through the surgery better than expected, Calvin asked the surgeon, "How long do you think I have now?" The surgeon replied the best way he knew how. "I'm not God. I can't tell you that."[690] The surgeon knew that while the surgery was a success, it did little to change the ultimate prognosis. Success in Calvin's case only meant he had a few more months to live.

On February 5, 2013, Calvin was released from the hospital and was admitted to the Orchard View Rehabilitation Center located in Providence, Rhode Island. Due to the nature of the surgery, and the high risk of a debilitating stroke and/or heart attack, Calvin required constant monitoring.

---

[688] Bert Heath interview with author October 24, 2013.
[689] Ibid.
[690] Ibid.

With the stress of the surgery and their already-shaky relationship, Calvin felt it best for Terri to return home to Maryland. Terri agreed and later, Rob Authier brought Terri to Worcester, Massachusetts, where she boarded a train heading for Baltimore. Calvin never saw her again.

For the next 11 days, Calvin responded reasonably well and experienced no major incidents or events. He was released from Orchard View on February 16, 2013, and stayed at the home of his good friends, Russell and Kelly Tiffany. There he awaited the next phase of his treatment, which included radiation and chemotherapy. His nephew Jesse and Jesse's wife Tammy, lived nearby and assisted with Calvin's appointments and medication. Younger brother Frank also lived nearby and helped Calvin during this phase of his illness. Everyone in the family pitched in and did what they could.

Between February 16 and March 21, 2013, a visiting nurse ensured that Calvin was taking his medication properly and was following the doctor's instructions. She reported that he still had mild headaches, some memory issues, and required some oversight with his medicinal routine.

On March 22, 2013, the doctors and Calvin decided to move ahead with radiation treatments. Over the next four weeks Calvin had 23 radiation treatments at the VA Hospital. They were intended to kill any remaining cancer cells.[691] With the radiation and follow up chemotherapy, the doctors hoped to add a few more months to Calvin's life.

Four days later, in the early afternoon of March 26, 2013, I heard that all-too-familiar horn tooting in my driveway.[692] I had not seen Calvin for some time, and I was very happy to see my old friend again. I immediately dropped what I was doing and ran out to the driveway and sure enough there he was in his familiar blue, Chevy S-10, pick-up truck with stickers of his Vietnam medals and the 101st Airborne Division eagle proudly displayed in the rear window.

---

[691] Calendar of events provide by Chasidy and Paul Duquette.
[692] Estimated date based on calendar provided by Chasidy Duquette.

As stated in the prologue, I went out and said, "Hey Cal! How the hell are you?" As soon as the words came out of my mouth, I knew something was seriously wrong. He told me about the cancer and that he had less than a year to live. I invited him in and over a cup of coffee, we spoke for more than an hour.

Calvin told me about the cancer, the operation, the treatments and the doctor's prognosis. I asked him how long he had, and he replied, "Less than a year, maybe a few months." Once the initial discussion subsided, I could tell he was beating around the bush on something else, and I could not imagine anything more important than the problem at hand. I asked, "Cal, do you need anything?" He teared up, something I'd never seen him do until that day. "Joe, I need your help, I want to see the guys one more time. Could you and our old softball buddies run a benefit to help me get to my unit reunion one more time?" Without hesitation, I replied, "Of course Cal, we'll do what we have to."[693]

I was amazed at the fact that of all the things that could be bothering him, to include being sick and dying, the most important thing to him at that moment was attending one more reunion with the men of Delta Company. I had little understanding of how important these men were to Calvin or how important these men were to each other. Over the next few months Calvin gave me a life lesson on friendship and brotherhood that I'll never forget and will always deeply appreciate.

That afternoon I was on the phone with my American Legion Post (Post 67, Grosvenordale, Connecticut). Within a week I attended an executive meeting, and the Post agreed to hold a benefit breakfast. Over the same period of time, I ran into a few of the guys with whom Cal and I played ball and without hesitation they all agreed to do what they could. My wife and I agreed whatever we did not raise, she and I would cover. No matter what happened, Calvin would get to one more reunion.

When Calvin next visited me during the week of April 15, I was in the middle of finishing my last book *A Thousand Days to Live* and

---

[693] Calvin Heath interview with author, April 26, 2013.

the material was laying all over the kitchen. It prompted me to ask Calvin about his time during and after the war. He looked at me, asked for another coffee, and we settled in for a long discussion. After a few minutes, for the first time since we met decades before, Calvin finally opened his heart to me and told me all the gruesome details. After listening to his story and all the subsequent injustices, I knew what needed to be done. "Calvin, I am almost done with this project and I would be honored to write your story." Calvin, stunned for a moment, lit up and said, "You would do that for me?" "Cal, I would be honored. Your story is one that needs to be told."[694]

Through May and June, Calvin, ecstatic over the prospect of having a book written about him, came to the house and spent hours reviewing boxes of information that included his medals, scrapbooks, and military records. We began the long interview process and the more information he provided, the more amazed I became. This was a friend who stared adversity in the eye almost every day of his life, and he somehow was able to hide the demons he fought and, with us, his friends, maintain that all-too-familiar positive attitude we always saw.

On April 25, 2013, two days after the radiation treatments finished, the oncology team reviewed Calvin's progress and determined, that like the surgery, he had pulled through better than expected and they suggested to Calvin that he might have more time than they originally thought.

Shortly after the April 25 visit, Bert spent some time with his brother and observed, that despite Calvin's recent "good news," he had physically and noticeably deteriorated. Bert stated:

Calvin said he was going to fight it and he came home... came up to the house and we would talk, but I could see a physical deterioration. I could see it in his walk. When he used to come to the house he would be whistling and singing. Normally when he came to see me because he wanted some of my oldie CD's "Hey what do you have?" In the end Calvin came to my house a lot and it would never fail, my brother Chet would come up – he was the one from Korea –

[694] Calvin Heath interview with author, April 26, 2013.

*and we took him to the [car] races. We went to the Spring
Open at Thompson [Speedway], but we had to help him up
the steps and then we had to help him down the steps. Then
he wanted to go to Stafford [Speedway] – so we called him,
and he said he really doesn't feel right...*[695]

Throughout the balance of April and into May and June of 2013,
Calvin stopped by the house numerous times and we worked on the
details of his experiences during and after Vietnam. The research
began to pile up and the full picture began to emerge. By the end of
May, I felt we were well on our way.

*Above: The Heath family June 22, 2013, shortly before Calvin passed away. From
R-L: Melzer, Calvin, Frank, Chet, Bert, Corrine, Evelyn, Lorraine. Picture
compliments of Karen Weir and her daughter Vanessa Ouimet.*

On June 26, 2013, Calvin returned to the VA Hospital in
Providence for a follow up visit. He saw Dr. Nancy J. Freeman, Chief
of Hematology and Oncology. Doctor Freeman concluded that Calvin
was responding better than expected. She wrote, "64 [year old male]
with GBM [right] temporal lobe status post-surgery (not fully
resected) and returns to clinic for F/U [follow up]."[696] The report goes
on to indicate that the entire tumor was not removed and she

---

[695] Bert Heath interview with author October 24, 2013.
[696] Freeman report, June 26, 2013.

recommended another cycle of chemotherapy. Calvin, according to the report, "...at first did not wish more Rx (treatments), but then changed his mind to try another cycle."[697]

Above: The day he received good news that he had pulled through his treatments better than expected. Calvin Heath photo.

That afternoon on his way home, Calvin stopped by my house very excited and informed me that after the new round of treatments, the doctors now felt he might have another year or two, and that "we had plenty of time to work on the book." As he was explaining the doctor's visit, he caught himself, and like an excited child about to unwrap Christmas gifts, he looked at me and said, "By the way, how the hell long does it take to write a book?" I replied, "We got plenty of time pal."

That afternoon we called several of Calvin's battle mates and he introduced me over the phone to the guys. He left messages for those not home, and those who were home agreed to speak with me in depth at a later date.

---

[697] Freeman report, June 26, 2013.

That day, Calvin and I spoke about the battle near the trail and the men he killed. We talked about Paul Conner and Jimmy Sherrill, Juan Nazario, Steve Messerli, and the others who died that day. He told me about the jungle, what it looked like and how it felt, the barracks where they stayed, Phuoc Vinh, the "crazy-ass airplanes," the helicopters, Wishik, Spooky, the full effect of a Claymore mine, NVA tactics, the medevac, … He was all over the place and I sat back and recorded detail after detail, name after name, and memory after memory. He was in a good place both mentally and emotionally. In spite of his illness, he was very much alive that day.

By June 30, 2013, Bert noticed further changes in his brother. "I got the feeling that at the end he knew he was close. I went for a ride with him and he never got over 25 miles per hours. That scared the bejesus out of me. I told him he shouldn't be driving anymore, and he stopped driving after that."[698] Bert continued:

> *So, he was over to the house and I asked him, "How you feeling?" And he said, "I'm doing OK," but he was bullshitting me, I could see it. I could see it in his eyes. I have seen death before, and I looked at my wife and she said, "What's the matter?" And I said Calvin's going, and then the next thing I hear is he's back at the hospital. They couldn't regulate his blood pressure because he was on so much Coumadin and if they gave him anymore, he would bleed out. So they said, "The only thing we can do is send him home and have somebody monitor him."[699]*

On July 4, 2013, just a week after our last meeting, Calvin experienced chest discomfort and was admitted back into the hospital. The doctors found he had experienced two small heart attacks. The medical staff at the VA concluded that Calvin now needed constant care. Going back to the Tiffany's made Calvin uncomfortable. They had two young children that he deeply cared about, and he did not want to expose them to any medical emergencies, which were now

---

[698] Bert Heath interview with author October 24, 2013.
[699] Ibid.

more likely to happen. Calvin also struggled with remembering to take his medications on time and it was most likely this that led to the last cardiac episode. The nurses and doctors at the VA could not emphasize enough how important taking his meds on time was, and he knew he needed some assistance with this. The doctors also wanted Calvin to restrict his physical exertion by avoiding stairs, walking any distance, etc.

Several family members, to include his brother Glen and sister-in-law Betty, and nephew, Paul Duquette, who considered Calvin "…like a father," and his wife Chasidy, offered to take Calvin into their homes. Betty was a nurse and Chasidy was a medical assistant and were both qualified to care for Calvin. Paul and Chasidy had three daughters Tanya, Samantha, and Corey. Corey was autistic and already required 24-hour attention, so there was always someone at their house. The Duquette's also had a first-floor bedroom and bath that Calvin could use, so it was at the Duquette's that Calvin decided to live his remaining days.

On July 7, 2013, the day before he was discharged from the hospital, Paul moved his uncle's belongings to his home. The Duquettes relocated Paul and Chasidy's bedroom downstairs to the basement and set Calvin up in their master bedroom. Seventeen-year-old daughter Samantha did all her great-uncle's laundry that day, and "…set up Calvin's new room so he would be comfortable."[700] The Duquettes had previously purchased the sports package on their cable TV for Calvin, allowing him to watch all the sports programs he wanted. There were few places on earth that Calvin was happier than in Paul's recliner, in charge of the clicker, while watching sports on his big screen TV.

The care and support the Duquettes and other family members displayed revitalized Calvin's commitment to live as long as possible, and he promised to be more diligent with his medications. He looked around the Duquette's home – his new home – and said to Chasidy, Paul and the girls, "We're gonna make this happen!"[701]

---

[700] Chasidy and Samantha Duquette interview with author, April 8, 2014.
[701] Ibid.

That evening the three girls, Paul and Chasidy said their goodnights and Calvin stayed up to watch the sports channels. After four days of being in a hospital bed, he just wanted to be by himself and watch TV. By all accounts, he was at great peace.

On the following morning, July 9, 2013, Chasidy and Paul rose and prepared for work. Chasidy had set up Calvin's medications, prepared food, which was now in the refrigerator, and had already given their daughters a few instructions the evening before. Calvin looked well enough and he, Paul and Chasidy expected no issues.

Around 9:30 a.m. Calvin was up and around and needed to go to the bathroom. On his way there, he felt dizzy and collapsed in the hallway. Samantha heard Calvin fall to the floor and immediately ran to his side. When she found him, she knew something was seriously wrong and immediately called 911. Knowing that he had nitroglycerin available, Samantha asked her great-uncle if he had chest pains to which he replied, "No, no, no, I'm OK... I don't have any chest pain."

As the ambulance was dispatched, Samantha made her uncle as comfortable as she could and called her Mom at Day Kimball Hospital, Putnam, Connecticut. Chasidy left work immediately. Calvin attempted to collect himself, most likely trying his best not to alarm his great-niece. Samantha later said that through the whole ordeal, "He was smiling and seemed happy."[702]

Shortly before Chasidy and the ambulance arrived, the Duquette's dog, possibly sensing he was needed, went to Calvin and nudged and licked his face. Calvin looked at the dog and, perhaps seeing his favorite dog Boo, said, "Hey pretty girl!"[703] At that very moment, the spirits of his ancestors came through the haze of Calvin's mind. He was pleased they had appeared and this time he was eager to follow them down that long river to the place where the spirits of honorable warriors dwell. I am certain he thought of all those he would leave behind, including his family, close friends, and the remaining men of Delta Company. He knew they would all be fine

---

[702] Chasidy and Samantha Duquette interview with author, April 8, 2014.
[703] Paul, Chasidy and Samantha Duquette interviews with author February 3, 2014 and April 8, 2014.

without him. He then turned, looked at his niece, smiled, and at 10:00 a.m. he closed his eyes and quietly passed away.

When Chasidy arrived home, the ambulance had Calvin out of the house, and she had seen enough emergency care to know he was gone. At first, she was angry and said to herself, "You bastard! You didn't let me say goodbye!"[704] But Calvin would not have left in such a manner. The night before, he told Chasidy that he would be around after he passed away to keep an eye on things. Over the next few weeks, the Duquettes put together a picture montage that celebrated Calvin's life. Soon thereafter one picture kept falling for no apparent reason. During my interview with her, Chasidy, now crying stated, "I know it was Calvin..." She stopped, thought, and then laughing through her tears, added, "...and I told him, 'One more time and you're going downstairs!"[705]

The Duquettes also told of a dream Calvin had while in the hospital a day or two before coming to their home. This dream, however, was not like the nightmares that so often shattered his sleep. This dream was set far away from the jungles of Vietnam and the ugliness of war. This one involved his mother coming to him and informing her son, "You have something you need to do."[706] Calvin was confused as to what that could have been, and maybe I can offer an answer.

Throughout his life, Calvin "Willy" Heath faced hardships that few are forced to experience. But through it all, he took every step in stride and never gave into the hatred or despair to which so many do. Paul Bucha, at the Silver Star ceremony held in Norwich, Connecticut in July, 1999, stated that Calvin was a very "special human being." One that should "serve as an example of the potential that resides in each and every one of us."[707] For many of us, he did just that. That *one more thing* his mother told him he needed to do was already done. He gave us an example by which to live our lives. Chasidy told me

[704] Paul, Chasidy and Samantha Duquette interviews with author February 3, 2014 and April 8, 2014.
[705] Ibid.
[706] Ibid.
[707] The Day, July 13, 1999, p. a5.

that one of Calvin's favorite expressions was, "If we're going to argue, you're the only one leaving here pissed off." Calvin did not leave this life pissed off – he left this life happy.

On July 13, 2013, Calvin's family organized a small ceremony at the Shaw-Majercik Funeral Home, located in Webster, Massachusetts to say a final goodbye to Calvin. It was only for two hours and the family did not expect a large crowd. Before the event was through, there were several hundred people who lined up outside to give their last respects to a fallen hero and friend. Brother Bert later said:

To be honest with you I think the most respect given to my brother, aside from his military friends, were the people who showed up at his wake because they were there for only one reason – because they respected my brother for who he was. You saw that different part of him too...[708]

At his wake Bert Heath, also known as Rain Maker, read the following Native American prayer for his brother Calvin – Lone Wolf:

Manittoo-oo Manittoo-oo wame masugkenuk Manittoo-oo
Ken nootah nunnepoh anaquabean Manittoo-oo
Tabottne kutabottamish newutche yeu kesukok wunnegin
Kutabottamish newutche wunanumoo-onk
Nupeantam asekesukokish newutche wame ninnimmissinnuonk
Nupeantam newutche paomoo-onk nesausuk tashe pomettuonk
Nupeantam newutche nishnoh ohhaas pomotak
Nupeantam newutche enkesuquad nishnoh mohtompan
Neenawun tabuttantamoo-onk newutche kepennemoo-onk wunnegin
Neenawun tabuttantamoo-onk newutche towohkomuk wunnegin
Neenawun tabuttantamoo-onk newutche wame mettugquash kah uppeshauawawarnash wunnegin quinnupohki
Neenawaun tabuttantamoo-onk newutche nippisspog kah pawtuck wunnegin
Neenewaun tabuttantamoo-onk newutche nishnoh teage wunne Nukketetookum Sokaanum Nattayam Aho

---

[708] Bert Heath interview with author, October 24, 2013.

FORGOTTEN HERO

Great Spirit, Great Spirit, Almighty Great Spirit

Hear me, I stand before you Great Spirit

I thank you for this beautiful day,

I thank you for my health and well-being,

I pray daily for all my people,

I pray for the future to come of seven generations,

I pray for all living things,

I pray with the sun each morning,

We give thanks for a bountiful harvest,

We give thanks for the beautiful forests,

We give thanks for all of the trees and beautiful flowers surrounding us,

We give thanks for the Beautiful lakes and waterfalls,

We give thanks for all good things.

I have spoken, Rain Maker, amen.

FINAL TRIBUTE

Behind the neatly arranged folding chairs that faced the dais was the Connecticut Army National Guard State Armory, a huge, impressive, turn-of-the-century stone facility. Uniformed soldiers were coming and going, and it seemed a fitting place for the ceremony that was about to take place. It was October 10, 2013. The day was cloudy, but the temperature hung comfortably around 65 degrees. Off to the side were a half dozen chairs for the speakers and special guests. A homeless man sat in the back on one of the many stone walls and, in spite of his obvious struggles, carried himself with great dignity and respect – undoubtedly a veteran who recognized the importance of the ceremony about to take place.

Approximately 50 people, including soldiers, guests, Calvin's family and friends, and men of Delta Company, including Paul Bucha, Dave Dillard, Bill Heaney, Ray Palmer, Mike Rawson, and Jeff Wishik, were in attendance. Representatives of the 1st Cavalry Color Guard, the Vietnam Veterans Association, Veterans of Foreign Wars, the American Legion, Connecticut Commission of Veterans affairs, U.S. Congressman John Larson's office, and high-ranking officials of the Connecticut Army National Guard were also present. Several newspapers and radio stations were also in attendance to capture the story about to unfold.

Dave Dillard approached the microphone and asked everyone to take their seats. The 1st Cavalry Color Guard marched to a designated area behind the dais with great precision and pride and posted the colors. Everyone stood as the National Anthem was played. As the Nation's song played, it was easy to see that all those who once wore the uniform of this great country, especially the men of Delta Company, 3/187th Infantry (ABN), 3rd Brigade, 101st Airborne Division, stood a little straighter and a little taller... for one of their own was being honored here today.

Once the colors were posted and the Anthem played, Dave Dillard then introduced Father Michael Galasso from the Connecticut VA for the invocation. Father Galasso prayed:

Let us pray. We gather here this afternoon in memory of the valor of Calvin Heath. We ask Your blessing upon his family here gathered, [to honor his] tremendous example of service to the state and our country. We ask this in Thy name. Amen.

Dillard then asked everyone to be seated and welcomed those in attendance. He then introduced Linda Schwartz, Commissioner for the Connecticut VA. Schwartz was a flight nurse during the Vietnam War, and witnessed firsthand the horrors of war and the remarkable bonds that war creates. She stated:

There is a belief that those of us who go to war together are bonded together by a unique and intrinsic understanding of what it means to leave your home and challenge the unknown, and to put your life on the line for the freedoms that we all enjoy. There's a brotherhood, a brotherhood that I could not be a part of that I see very visible here today. That after all these years you come today to remember your comrade with whom you were young... and had your whole life ahead of you. So, please know that we are very, very honored by your presence here today.

Dillard thanked Commissioner Schwartz and introduced the next speaker, John Rossi, Chief of Staff for U.S. Congressman John Larson. Rossi passed on the congressman's well wishes and read a letter written by Larson for the event. It read:

U.S. Congressman John Larson

To the family of Calvin Heath:

Today our community honors the life of Specialist Calvin Heath, a decorated Unites States Army veteran, father, grandfather, son, brother, uncle, and friend. During his time of service, Specialist Heath's exceptional bravery and love of country would earn him the Combat

345

Infantry Badge, the Silver Star, the Bronze Star, and the Purple Heart. A true patriot, his sacrifice deserves our nation's highest praise.

At home Calvin demonstrated a joyous demeanor and distinct humility, well known in his community. In the years ahead, each of us should mirror the quiet courageousness that made him a true hero to his family, friends, and loved ones.

Thank you for your gracious invitation to today's service and know that my thoughts and prayers continue to be with you during this difficult time.

Sincerely,
U.S. Congressman,
John Larson

Dillard returned to the microphone and thanked Rossi. Dave, a large formidable man, even in his 60s, clearly struggled to maintain his composure. He removed a prepared speech from his jacket's breast pocket, took a deep breath, hesitated and then began:

At this point, it is my privilege to share some thoughts with you and some comments because this is a very special day.

Today we will honor a comrade who passed on to the splendor and serenity of the hereafter.

Many called him Calvin. His family called him Willy. To those of us who served with him, we called him Brother. As I pondered the text from my remarks today, I was transported back in time nearly 45 years, a very turbulent time when our country was embroiled in an extremely controversial issue called Vietnam. To me and my comrades, there was no time to worry about which side of the issue we stood. We were standing in the issue. We were standing in Vietnam.

It is very important, I think, to set the stage so you can better understand the levity of this memorial today for those of us who served with Calvin in Vietnam in 1968. Understand the following speakers will be his company commander and his platoon leader from Delta Company, 3rd Battalion of the 187th Airborne Infantry, 101st Airborne Division. And the defining moment that has truly bonded us [together] all these years really boils down to one mission...

346

and that mission took place March 16th to March 19th in 1968.

The Tet Offensive of 1968 had just finished with an amazing victory for the allied troops, yet there were still 65,000 infiltrators from North Vietnam still in the jungles trying to escape back to their safe havens in Cambodia and Laos. Having only scouted intelligence, as to their whereabouts, our battalion was deployed into the jungles of War Zone D with a mission to locate the insurgents, converge on their location, and destroy them, but there were many battalions involved with this particular mission.

Spec 4 Heath – Calvin – Willy – was an RTO, a radio-telephone operator for his platoon leader on this mission. I'm very familiar with the job, because I was an RTO for my company commander. The job of RTO is very difficult… one that is extremely dangerous. The job means that you're going to have a radio on your back, and that antennae may oftentimes be extended, and that means you put yourself in a very ominous situation – a very dangerous situation. Because it was well known that the radio meant that either the man in front of you or the man in back of you was an officer, and so you were an easy target. Few RTOs went home without being wounded in 1968, I assure you. In fact, one of our company RTOs was wounded three times. After returning to the field after his third wound, Harry's smiling face was greeted by many of us finding cover as he walked over to our position. Sporting a brand-new PRC-77 and with that antennae extended, the closer he came, the more dispersed we became. We realized that somehow, he was drawing bullets and we better find a place to hide. Having a sense of humor is good for a laugh but having a good sense of humor was another quality of a fine RTO.

One of the most important aspects of the RTO's life in combat is the relationship [he has] with his commander or his platoon leader. Besides carrying and communicating with the radio, as the operator of the radio, he was the voice, and the secretary, and special assistant, the bearer of the classified codes, which we called an SOI. He was sometimes cook, and many times the sounding board for his boss. He must be alert, patient, and fluent in the phonetic alphabet. He must be able to understand the language, which I call, Stress-eese, that is, recognizing an extreme pressure on the commander and not repeating "exactly" what the commander had to say when reporting to the higher [ups]. Most importantly, the RTO must be the commander's confidant. He must be able to hear all and say nothing. And all of these duties must be accomplished while under fire. And in all these areas, and many more, Calvin Heath was amazing.

During this mission in 1968 the company was in contact with the enemy every day. But in the evening of the 18th just before dark while moving off an LZ, where the company had been resupplied, contact was made with what was believed to be a North Vietnamese Army regiment. The company of 85 men found themselves in a 13-hour, all-night firefight with an enemy whose strength has since been estimated from anywhere from 1,000 to 2,500 North Vietnamese regulars.

During the course of the night battle, Calvin and his lieutenant, another platoon leader, and three others were separated from the main element. Soon, their position was overrun, leaving only Calvin, his lieutenant, and one NCO still alive, but ALL very seriously wounded. They were stripped of their weapons and radio by the enemy; they began an all-night horror, praying that morning would come quickly. When first light came, Calvin the only one of the three capable of moving, crawled with his wounds, past the bodies of dead enemy soldiers to find the main element... or what was left of it. He did this with a deep wound in his back, that exposed his spine, and the first words out of his mouth were, "My lieutenant is still alive, go to him, get him, please hurry."

You see sometimes an RTO has a higher calling. He must be an angel. And for his lieutenant that morning, Calvin was an angel. Both the lieutenant and the NCO were found and survived. Calvin was everything one could ever expect from an RTO and more. I know this is true, because I was there. I was with him in the main element that night.

He and I connected some years later and remained close friends until the end of his life. And though the actions of that night took an emotional toll on Calvin for the rest of his life, I will forever remember him as a kind and loving free spirit.

Rest my Brother is my prayer... until we meet again in that place where spirits dwell.

Dillard took a deep breath then said:

It is my profound privilege now to introduce to you the commander... for which I was his RTO. He is also known to many as the recipient of the Medal of Honor for his actions that particular night – may I introduce Paul Bucha.

Paul Bucha, former company commander of Delta Company, 3rd Battalion, 187th Infantry (ABN), 101st Airborne Division approached the dais. He gave his former RTO a long and heartfelt hug. Forty-five years earlier, the two men had been through hell together. Around Bucha's neck hung the nation's highest military award – The Congressional Medal of Honor. Bucha earned the CMH during the same action in which Calvin earned his Silver Star. His action and quick decisions, and the extraordinary bravery of his men, saved the remnants of Delta Company. Bucha began his speech:

I am not in the habit of correcting Dave, but I have to. This medal belongs to each and every member of Delta Company, Calvin included – because this medal recognizes what we did that night and the day before, and the day before that. So I'd like all the members of Delta Company to stand up please, so you can see who they are.[709]

The men of Delta stood and the crowd gave the old warriors a resounding round of applause. When they sat down, Bucha continued.

I thought I would tell you a little about what Calvin meant to me and what Calvin was. A lot of people talk about the military side of things, but I last saw Calvin when he was being medevac'd that day in March of 1968. I heard him last when he yelled out about his lieutenant. Then he disappeared into the wondrous thing called military medicine. I had no idea where he went and how he travelled. But he eventually made it to Fort Carson Colorado. At Fort Carson, Colorado, his lieutenant looked at his form – his DD-214 and saw nothing in it. No medals, no recognition, nothing. And the lieutenant concluded that since his wounds were primarily in his back that he was a coward – he must have been shot and wounded running away. The psychologist and psychiatrist to whom Calvin was talking understood because they were willing to listen, and they were willing to hear. No one, with a wound like that and circumstances like that – no matter what you thought – could have been called a coward.

Calvin was tired of being called a coward. He was tired of the typical military things – he just wanted to find a psychologist that would listen, and a commanding officer that would take [the] care to let him speak his mind and to try and heal. Having had enough of that, Calvin left. He said, "I'm going home." And he did. He went home. They eventually found Calvin here in Connecticut and they said you have to go to Indianapolis. You have to sign some papers and we'll let you go back. Calvin went back, signed the papers, went on home. Not knowing what those papers included... which was a renunciation of all his benefits with

---

[709] Note: Members of the Co. D, 187th present included: Mike Rawson, Dave Dillard, Ray Palmer, Jeffrey Wishik, Paul Bucha, and Bill Heaney.

the Department of Veterans Affairs. No one read them to him. No one cautioned him. They just said sign here and you can go home – and Calvin wanted to go home.

Some 30 plus years after that, I got a phone call. "Captain this is Calvin, you probably don't remember me." I said, "I remember you! Where the hell are you?" He said, "I'm in Connecticut and I need help. I'd like to get someone to help me handle these dreams I have at night, and the concerns I'm living with." I said, "Why don't you go to the V.A.?" He said, "I don't have any benefits. They took those away." I said, "They can't take them away with your Silver Star, your Bronze Star, and your Purple Heart." He said, "Sir, I don't have a Purple Heart, I don't have a Bronze Star, and I don't have a Silver Star." It then became my realization that General Barsanti, after whom a house in Fort Campbell is named, and [one] in which I refuse to stay, was too busy to go to the hospital to award those who have been medevac'd the medals to which they were entitled. He was also too busy to have his staff enter into the permanent records what Calvin Heath had achieved. As a result, emptiness followed Calvin wherever he went... because one man was too busy.

So...we said it's about time to get everything that he earned and get it all restored – and we did. We got his disability, we got his back disability pay, we got his Silver Star, his Bronze Star, and we got his Purple Heart.

And after he received his Silver Star in [Norwich] Connecticut, he took off the medal and I thought he was going to throw the medal down and stomp on it. He didn't. He turned to the members of his tribe and family, and said, "Come on up here." And then he turned to me and said "Sir, will you pin this on [me]?" I cried, he cried, everybody cried. I think my daughter still cries as she remembers that event. Not out of sadness, but out of happiness. It may be small... but a life in this world cosmos had a major error corrected on his behalf [that day].

351

Calvin went through this and he called me about three weeks later and he said "Sir, I'm doing fine." And I said, "What's changed?" He said, "I don't buy coffee anymore in [Putnam], Connecticut. Everybody knows I have the Silver Star. I said, "Well, what did you learn from all this Calvin?" He said, "The important people in my life didn't need a medal to tell me they loved me." I told him, "Keep your Silver Star... that we are going to eventually [officially] present it right here in Hartford." The West Point Society was having a dinner at which the Coast Guard Superintendent was going to speak. That's a two star. This is the Warriors medal – the Silver Star is called the Warrior's Medal, and for that it requires the highest-ranking warrior which is two-stars – a division commander. The Coast Guard Academy Superintendent had never even had a Silver Star in his hand – and he said, "It would be my honor." So, we gathered there that night, and no one knew what was going to happen except Calvin and his brother – and they announced, "Attention to orders!" and all the West Point Graduates jumped out of their chairs as they had when they were cadets. The wives were screaming, "Oh my God! What is going on?" "Specialist Calvin Heath front and center!" And the two-star admiral pinned on the Silver Star, the Purple Heart, and the Bronze Star.

Now if you think of that – and you think about those 30 years, I would be angry. I would have been furious. There would be no ceremony to which I would be willing to attend if I had been mistreated, misunderstood, called a liar, and called a coward, and in fact – been guilty of the fact that my father who had the right to ask for my records to see what I had done found that there was no record. And therefore, even someone like that (Calvin's Father) would question what I had done. If I were Calvin, I would have been furious, and I would have reached no quarter with any person. Instead – at the West Point dinner [that night], Calvin received two first-class tickets to London and a week's stay in a hotel, and he turned around and gave them to his brother. I called him later on and said, "That was wonderful! What are you doing with your disability pay?" "I gave it to them too, because they took care of me when no one else cared. Sir, they didn't need a medal." But if you look back on that, you say to yourself, "How can this kid, who went to war, be so soft – so caring – so loving." I can tell you that each member of Delta Company that's here, and everyone that I spoke to, faces life and approaches their problems the same way. There is no anger. There is no coveting. There is no "I wish someone would give me a handout." There's none of that. It's just, "I wonder how my brothers are doing."

Above: Paul Bucha during the Calvin Heath memorial ceremony held in Hartford, CT, October 9, 2013. Joe Lindley photo.

The commissioner talked about the special relationship. Among us, it is love. More intense than any other love that has been defined or found on this earth. It is between people who go to the gates of hell because someone asked them to, and then returned home, to come back to a grateful country, or an indifferent country, depending on the time, the politics, or the moment. So today, as you think of Calvin, think of the gentle person. Think of a person who had every right to be angry, but instead was happy. Think of a person who was so happy to receive the medal, but when he looked at it realized that the people who loved him most were the people who did not need a medal to say he was lovable. That was Calvin. I thank you for being here to honor Calvin. God bless you all.

By the time Bucha finished, most in attendance were wiping away tears. Dillard, also clearly moved by the words of his old commander, moved to the microphone to introduce the concluding speaker. He started with, "I sent an Email to Jeff and said, 'I would like a copy of your bio so I can introduce you.' He wrote me back and he said, 'Just tell them I was Calvin's friend.'"

Jeffrey Wishik stayed in the Army after being severely wounded on March 18, 1968. In that action, Wishik earned the country's second highest award – The Distinguished Service Cross. The term "friend" seemed fitting when describing Wishik, as Calvin noted during several of our interviews, "When we were away from the men, I would call him Jeff, and he would call me Calvin. I mean how many times does that happen?"[710]

As Wishik approached the dais, he stopped at Calvin's family and spoke with them for a few moments. He had never met them before. He was also visibly moved by the presence of the Delta men present as this was the first time since Vietnam that he had seen the men. Wishik said off mic:

I realized that this is the first time that I had the opportunity, except I guess for once – this is my first time seeing any of

---

[710] Calvin Heath interview with author, June 2013.

these guys, and certainly my first time getting the honor and privilege of meeting Calvin's family. I have prepared remarks. I wish I was as eloquent as David, and especially Bud, but I am not. But what I will try to do is share with you a piece of Calvin that he shared with me. But Willy! Boy, after all these years I never knew, and he and I had some really close conversations, so if you give me just a moment, I'm going to write that part in my speech...

Jeff Wishik moved to the microphone and began:

Thank you kindly for that – and also like to thank you for honoring me and allowing me to spend today and say goodbye with you to a very special soldier. I'm proud – incredibly proud – to say that I was Calvin's lieutenant and he was my RTO. You could say that we were always extremely close – about four or five feet apart. That's about the length of the cord between the radio and the lieutenant or the company commander who's usually using it (Laughs).

As you could imagine, the world of an RTO is incredibly special, and one of implied and complete trust. It is also a job with major responsibility and unquestionable confidence by the leader. In truth – and David said it well – the RTO is the life line of communication, instruction, and very importantly – feedback, to the leader – in each and every element of the unit. Calvin knowingly and enthusiastically accepted that role, and he performed it magnificently. Throughout my military career I had countless numbers of RTOs, but none ever better, more capable, more loyal, [and] more dedicated, than Calvin Heath. I am also honored, extremely honored, to know him as a friend and a confidant.

Actually, when I look back, I thought I knew Calvin very well, especially after all that we had been through together in 1968. But it wasn't until 1985 that I really got to know, and intensely respect him for the man he was and his Native American heritage. Calvin called in early 1985, actually revealing to me that he was still alive, and asked to visit my wife and me at Fort Sill, Oklahoma. I had taken command of a Pershing Missile Battalion there in early May. Our only daughter was born in the early part of June and Calvin came to visit a couple weeks after her birth. There are not many people that you would welcome in your home shortly after that, but Calvin understood, and we wanted Calvin to be with us. One might say that those times were a bit active to say the least.

I remembered meeting him at the airport and looking down the concourse in utter disbelief that he had survived March 18th. He most likely thought the same way about me. For the next week, once again, we were virtually inseparable. And I can't tell you the pride I felt, and the honor it was for me to introduce Calvin publicly to my 1,200-person Pershing Missile Battalion – I think it was special for him also.

There was also another special day during that visit, when my wife Fay suggested that Calvin spend the day at the Fort Sill Indian Museum. As many of you know, Fort Sill was the place of incarceration, and the ultimate burial location of Geronimo, clearly a Native American legend in U.S. history. Calvin spent the entire day visiting all the facilities, walking the land occupied by Geronimo's followers and spending a long time at the grave site of Geronimo. That evening, and through most of the night, we talked. He shared his intense pride for his Indian heritage, his family, and the love of his country.

Unknown to me, and those who had been close to Calvin, after 1968... those were troubled times. But those days with Calvin would always be incredibly special for me. Come to think of it, our relationship was built on nights to remember, or those to forget.

On the night of 18 March, Calvin, Lieutenant Jimmy Sherrill, Bob Dietch, and I, found ourselves lying next to each other... (Long pause)... badly wounded, and separated from our battle brothers. With increasing hostilities and a very long and eventful night – most of you know the story. We finally saw light and felt the warmth of the morning sun. I remember slowly reaching to my right and touching Calvin's leg, thinking that I had felt it move earlier, I done the same thing to Dietch on my left, but there was no response, and there had not been for hours. Then, in a very soft voice, Calvin asked, "LT you alive?" At first, I hesitated to answer because we'd been called a number of times through the night [by the Vietnamese]. As best I remember, I replied, "Maybe." To this day I still don't think I was sure. We then set to a plan that would allow us to return to the company perimeter, since we were convinced that our comrades believed that we had all perished. One thing for sure, we would not be making that journey together.

So, Calvin, severely wounded, struggled to crawl for help. I am not sure of much after that, but I thank God he was successful, because the next thing I remember was waking up in an evacuation hospital in the middle of what appeared to be a five-alarm fire drill. There will always be a lot that I am not sure of, when it comes to Vietnam. But there is one thing of which I am absolutely certain. My Native American RTO, and battle friend, saved the lives of Dietch and his LT [that day]. To his family... (Long pause) *... You should be so incredibly proud of Calvin for his love of you, his heritage, his country, his interpersonal strength and character, and his willingness to save and sacrifice for others. To his tribal family, Calvin Heath was an incredible warrior, an American soldier intensely proud of his heritage. To his battle brothers here today, and those no longer with us, Calvin Heath was a very special soldier, warrior, and patriot, intensely committed to each of you and the dangers [we faced], and the difficult and dirty task you were all challenged with. To me, Calvin Heath was – and will always be – my exceptional RTO, my trusted battle buddy, my friend – and my hero.*

Rest easy my warrior friend. The mission is complete, and we are going home.

Those who were not already crying, were by the time Wishik finished his last sentence. The VFW then removed the American flag, folded it perfectly, and presented it to Calvin's family. Benediction was offered by Father Galasso and then Taps was played by a lone bugler who stood off to the side. Dillard thanked everyone for attending and the veteran groups that attended. After the ceremony concluded, there was a little of the normal mingling that takes place after an event of this nature, hands were shook, and people left one by one. The men of Delta spoke a while longer, and it was easy to see the bond they shared. They had truly been to the gates of hell together, and that will forever be, the burden – and honor – they carry together.

Above: U.S. Army LTC Jeff Wishik (Ret.) during the Calvin Heath memorial held in Hartford, CT, October 9, 2013. Joe Lindley photo.

Above: Dave Dillard during the Calvin Heath memorial held in Hartford, CT, October 9, 2013. Dave Dillard photo.

Above: Men of Delta, 3/187th, 101st Airborne holding Calvin's ashes during the Calvin Heath memorial held in Hartford, CT, October 9, 2013. L-R: Ray Palmer, Jeff Wishik, Bill Heaney, Paul Bucha, Dave Dillard, and Michael Rawson. Joe Lindley photo.

HEALING

Now arises from hallowed ground a delicate cloud of bugle notes that softly say, go to sleep... Comrades true, born anew, peace to you. Your souls shall be where the heroes are and your memories shine like the morning star... Slumber well, where the shells screamed and fell... the danger has passed, and now at last, go to sleep.

SGT Joyce Kilmer

When I began this project in March of 2013, I had no idea where it would lead me. I thought I knew Calvin William Heath well. Over the years, our many conversations failed to reveal the gravity of the deep pain, both physically and psychologically Calvin endured most of his life. But therein lies Calvin's true story. He faced his problems throughout his life the way he faced the enemy in Vietnam, with bravery and with great strength.

During the first six months of this project, I was transfixed on the pain he suffered, the challenges he endured, and the injustices he faced after giving everything to what was, for the most part, an ungrateful country. But as the project evolved, I saw past this to find the real story – Calvin's remarkable character.

During our many conversations about his time in the Army, Calvin did not dwell on his own pain or the problems he faced during and after the battle. He was more interested in telling me about Paul Conner, his best friend who died while laying down covering fire to support a rapidly developing potential disaster; he was more interested in talking about Dave Dillard, Bobby Dietch, Earl Vanalstine, Mike Rawson, Juan Nazario, Jimmy Sherrill, Billy Ford, Ray Palmer and the great leaders under whom he served, men like Captain Paul Bucha, First Sergeant Austin Harjo, Platoon Sergeant Dickie Quick, and First Lieutenant Jeffrey Wishik and all the other men. He spoke of all these men as if they were gods among men. King Leonidas, the great Spartan leader at Thermopylae, could not

360

have spoken about better warriors or braver men than did Calvin when he spoke about the men with whom he served. They helped to mold *the* defining moment in his life, one in which he was immensely proud and one that haunted him every day of his life.

Calvin was also a proud member of the 101st Airborne Division. He became a piece of the greatest airborne fighting force ever assembled by man. He helped to establish the record held by the 187th Airborne Infantry as the most decorated airborne unit in Vietnam by adding to their overall total with ten of his own medals.

There were many other bright spots in Calvin's life along the way, to include his life-long commitment to his Native American heritage. He was especially proud to have been a Nipmuc Indian and even prouder to be the recipient of the Warriors Medal. Being an honorable warrior meant everything to Calvin.

Calvin also found great solace in his family, especially those who stuck with him through thick and thin. Having them understand who he was, and what he did, was important to him. He was especially proud of his granddaughter Rebecca. She rose above great challenges and became every grandfather's dream. Calvin knew that he did not excel in the art of being a father, a husband, or a grandfather, and there was much along those lines he wished he could have changed. During one of our last talks in June of 2013, he stopped at the door before leaving for the day, turned and said, "Joe could you do me a favor?"

"Sure Cal, what?"

"Could you tell Becca everything?" He hoped that someday, with all the details provided, she would understand. On March 2, 2014, ten months after that request, I sat with Rebecca and her fiancé Karl for several hours explaining, to the best of my very limited abilities, the horrors her grandfather faced during the Vietnam War and the hardships he faced after the war. And more importantly, what made him a hero. I only hope I was successful.

Looking back on Calvin's life, it is easy to see that there were many dark places in which he was forced to dwell. He navigated a life-long storm of the mind that once entered, few emerge unscathed. He always sought a way to heal, a way to make things right, and a way to restore his honor. This was a battle he fought alone for many years, until a lifeline was thrown by a man who, in 1968, ate the same dirt as he in Vietnam.

Above: Connecticut Senator Mae Flexer presenting the Connecticut War Time Service Medal to Calvin's granddaughter Rebecca and great-granddaughter Avery during a May 18, 2016 award ceremony. More than one hundred people attended. Work continues to obtain further awards earned by Calvin. Lindley photo.

Unfortunately for Calvin, he did not find complete peace, and on the day he died there remained unresolved issues. But, without doubt, his greatest opportunity for healing did not come from the long-overdue medals he was finally awarded, or his military and VA records that were eventually corrected. It came from reuniting with the men with whom he fought.

Combat veterans share a remarkable bond that does not exist anywhere else in life. It is often shaped in the furnaces of hell that makes each fighter forever interwoven as the molecules of a well forged sword. They cannot be separated, they cannot be one without the other. As Paul Bucha stated, "We have truly been to the gates of hell together."[711] It was there – at the gates of hell – that their lives

---

[711] Paul Bucha, October 9, 2013, Hartford, CT.

were forged. All the men of Delta, including Calvin, who fought those few days in March 1968 agree.

EPILOGUE

On February 27, 2014, after eight months of searching for Paul Conner's family, I unexpectedly found an article about U.S. Air Force Lieutenant Colonel Paul Allan Conner. Finding it odd that he had the exact same name as Calvin's friend, I searched for his phone number and found that all the numbers listed were no longer valid, very common for servicemen who moved from one assignment to the next. Discouraged, I set the article down and then suddenly noticed a line near the end of the page that referred to his father Nathan, who lived in Plantation, Florida. Understanding how important Paul was to Calvin, and with nothing to lose, I tracked down Nathan's phone number and gave it a try. A gentleman at the other end quickly picked up the phone and said, "Hello."

"Hello, Mr. Conner, my name is Joe Lindley. I'm from Thompson, Connecticut, I am looking for the family of Paul Allan Conner who died in Vietnam on March 18, 1968."

"You found them! I'm his older brother Nathan."

Ecstatic that I found Paul's family, I informed Nathan about the project and what I learned about his brother from Calvin. For an hour we spoke about Calvin and Paul. He told me more about Paul as a child, where they lived, what he did, and why he chose the Airborne. He told me that his son was named after Paul and that he became a career United States Air Force officer, something in which Nathan was extremely proud. I told him more about the battle in which Paul died and the men with whom he served. At the end of the conversation I tentatively offered, "Mr. Conner, for what it's worth, Paul wasn't forgotten. Calvin thought about him every day of his life up until the day he died." There were a few seconds of silence at the end of the line, and he finally asked, "Can you do me a favor Joe, and call my son?" That evening, USAF Lieutenant Colonel Paul Allan

Conner and I spoke for another hour. Lieutenant Colonel Conner's pride in his uncle was unmistakably clear.[712]

Seven months later, I had a similar conversation with Jan Sherrill Hampton, Jimmy Sherrill's younger sister. Jan met Calvin at the 2008 reunion and stated that meeting Calvin was the most healing experience she had ever had in her life.[713] Jan was only in 7th grade when her family received the Western Union telegram informing them of his death. For 31 years she had so many questions. "The strength of the family" were not just words for Calvin. Jimmy Sherrill and his little sister Jan were part of the family and in 2008 Calvin did what he could to help Jan Hampton heal. In her Rakkasan book he wrote, "Jan, I was with Jim at the end. He was a soldier to the end. He was one of the bravest men I have ever known [and] he fought, never worrying about himself." It was signed "Lone Eagle," Calvin Heath.

On September 22, 2014, after my discussion with Jan, I tried to imagine how Calvin would have felt about the conversations I had with the Conners and Jan. I went to bed that night with thoughts of Calvin, Paul and Jimmy discussing my conversations with their families. The thought made me feel good and I felt that at least through this work these *Forgotten Heroes* – and the men with whom they fought – would be remembered.

For weeks I struggled with how to finish this piece appropriately, and for days I searched through my research for inspiration. I went back to my notes of October 9, 2013, the day Adam Piore and I interviewed Bill Heaney, Dave Dillard and Mike Rawson at Bill's house in Connecticut. Among my notes was a message Bill's wife Alecia wrote on a small piece of paper. She handed it to Bill, who read it, looked at his wife, smiled and nodded. She wrote:

One of the most important messages you told me, was that you knew that when you went over to Vietnam, you were fully aware that you might give your life for your country... But

---

[712] Nathan and Paul Conner phone conversations with author, February 27, 2013.
[713] Hampton phone conversation, September 22, 2014.

you did not realize that it would be <u>every</u> day for the rest of your life.[714]

At the Connecticut State Veteran's Memorial there is a bench on which people can sit and ponder the many sacrifices our men and women in the armed forces have made and continue to make. It reads:

To the Rakkasans and All Who Served,
Delta Company, 3/187th ABN INF, 101st ABN DIV,
Vietnam 1967-1968

If those who walk these grounds look down, they will see the names of those willing to pay the ultimate sacrifice. One of those grey marble pavers bears the name "Calvin Heath, Delta 3-187th Infantry, 101st Airborne Division, Vietnam 1967-1968, Silver Star."

Above: Calvin's memorial paver located at the Connecticut State Veterans' Memorial, Hartford, CT. Joe Lindley Photo.

---

[714] Bill Heaney, October 9, 2013.

I opened this book with Quarles' poem and find it fitting to end it the same way.

God and the soldier, all men adore
In time of danger, and not before.
When the danger has passed, and all things righted,
God is forgotten, and the soldier slighted.

APPENDICES

Appendix 1: Abbreviations Used in this Book

1LT – First Lieutenant, O2

2LT – Second Lieutenant, O1

ABN – Airborne

AIT – Advanced Individual Training

AK-47 – A gas-operated 7.62×39mm assault rifle, first developed in the Soviet Union by Mikhail Kalashnikov and used by the enemies of the United States.

ARVN – Army of Vietnam (South Vietnam Army)

AWOL – Away Without Leave

BCD – Bad Conduct Discharge

BCT – Basic Training

C&C – Command and Control

CPT – U.S. Army Captain, 03

CO – Commanding Officer

COL – Colonel, O6

CS – Tear Gas

DI – Drill Instructor

DSC – Distinguished Service Cross. The Nation's second highest award behind the Medal of Honor.

DSJ – Daily Staff Journal

Dust Off – Medevac choppers

DVA – Department of Veterans Affairs

GBM – Glioblastoma Multiforme – Brain Cancer

GIR – Glider Infantry Regiment

IG – Inspector General's Office

JAG – Judge Advocate General

KHA – Killed in Hostile Action

KIA – Killed in Action

LRRP – Long Range Reconnaissance Patrol

LTC – Lieutenant Colonel, O5

LZ – Landing Zone

M-16 – Lightweight, 5.56 mm, air-cooled, gas-operated, magazine-fed assault rifle used by the United States and its allies.

M-60 – A 7.62 X 51mm general-purpose machine gun used by the United States and its allies.

M-79 – Portable single-shot, shoulder-fired, break-action grenade launcher that fires a 40x46mm grenade.

MACV – Military Assistance Command, Vietnam

MBA – Master of Business Administration

MOPH – Military Order of the Purple Heart

MOS – Military Occupational Specialty

NCO – Non-Commissioned Officer

NDP – Night Defensive Perimeter

NVA – North Vietnam Army

NVVRS – National Vietnam Veterans Readjustment Study

OPORD – Operations Order

PAVN – Peoples' Army of Vietnam (North Vietnam)

PFC – Private First Class, E3

PIO – Public Information Office

PLF – Parachute Landing Fall

PP4313 – Presidential Pardon, September 16, 1974

PRC-77 – Portable Radio, Communications, "Prick-77"

PTSD – Posttraumatic Stress Disorder

REMF – Rear Echelon Mother Fuckers

RTO – Radio Telephone Operator

S-2 – Intelligence Section

SDRP – Special Discharge Review Board

SFC – Sergeant First Class (Platoon Sergeant) E-7

SGT – Sergeant E-5

SOI – Signal Operating Instructions

SPEC4 – Specialist Forth Class, E4

SSG – Staff Sergeant E-6

TAC – Tactical Air Control

TO&E – Table of Organization and Equipment

TOP – Top Sergeant, First Sergeant E-8

UCMJ – Uniform Code of Military Justice

UH-1 – Huey Helicopter

USARECSTA – U.S. Army Reception Station

USARPAC – U.S. Army – Pacific Command

VA – Veterans Administration

VC – Viet Cong

VFW – Veterans of Foreign Wars

VNAF – Vietnam Air Force

WHA – Wounded in Hostile Action

WIA – Wounded in Action

Appendix 2: Paul Bucha – Medal of Honor Citation

Paul Bucha – Medal of Honor

Issued May 14, 1970, for his gallant actions March 3, 1968,

The President of the United States in the name of The Congress takes pleasure in presenting the Medal of Honor to:

Rank and Organization: Captain, U.S. Army, Company D, 3d Battalion. 187th Infantry, 3d Brigade, 101st Airborne Division.

Place and Date: Near Phuoc Vinh, Binh Duong Province, Republic of Vietnam, 16-19 March 1968.

Entered service at: U.S. Military Academy, West Point, N.Y.

Born: 1 August 1943, Washington, D.C.

Citation: For conspicuous gallantry and intrepidity in action at the risk of his life above and beyond the call of duty. Capt. Bucha distinguished himself while serving as commanding officer, Company D, on a reconnaissance-in-force mission against enemy forces near Phuoc Vinh, The Company was inserted by helicopter into the suspected enemy stronghold to locate and destroy the enemy. During this period Capt. Bucha aggressively and courageously led his men in the destruction of enemy fortifications and base areas and eliminated scattered resistance impeding the advance of the company. On 18 March while advancing to contact, the lead elements of the company became engaged by the heavy automatic weapon, heavy machinegun, rocket-propelled grenade, Claymore mines and small-arms fire of an estimated battalion-size force. Capt. Bucha, with complete disregard for his safety, moved to the threatened area to direct the defense and ordered reinforcements to the aid of the lead element. Seeing that his men were pinned down by heavy machinegun fire from a concealed bunker located some 40 meters to the front of the positions, Capt. Bucha crawled through the hail of fire to single-handedly destroy the bunker with grenades. During this heroic action Capt. Bucha received a painful shrapnel wound. Returning to the perimeter, he observed that his unit could not hold its positions and repel the human wave assaults launched by the determined enemy. Capt. Bucha ordered the withdrawal of the unit elements and covered the withdrawal to positions of a company perimeter from which he could direct fire upon the charging enemy. When 1 friendly element retrieving casualties was ambushed and cut off from the perimeter, Capt. Bucha ordered them to feign death and he directed artillery fire around them. During the night Capt. Bucha moved throughout the position, distributing ammunition, providing encouragement and insuring the integrity of the defense. He directed artillery, helicopter gunship and Air Force gunship fire on the enemy strong points and attacking forces, marking the positions with smoke grenades. Using flashlights in complete view of enemy snipers, he directed the medical evacuation of 3 air-ambulance loads of seriously wounded personnel and the helicopter supply of his company. At daybreak Capt. Bucha led a rescue party to recover the dead and wounded members of the ambushed element. During the period of intensive combat, Capt. Bucha, by his extraordinary heroism, inspirational example, outstanding leadership and professional competence, led his company in the decimation of a superior enemy force which left 156 dead on the battlefield. His bravery and gallantry at the risk of his life are in the highest traditions of the military service, Capt. Bucha has reflected great credit on himself, his unit, and the U.S. Army.

Source: http://homeofheroes.com/moh/citations_living/vn_a_bucha.html

Appendix 3: Austin Harjo – Silver Star Citation

Austin Harjo
(The First Sergeant, United States Army)

For gallantry in action on 18-19 March 1968. First Sergeant Austin A. Harjo, Company D, 3d Battalion (Airmobile), 187th Infantry, distinguished himself in the vicinity of Phuoc Vinh, Republic of Vietnam. The Third Brigade Long Range Reconnaissance Patrol, while walking point for Company D, made initial contact with an estimated reinforced Viet Cong Battalion. As the intense firefight increased in volume, Company D became engaged in a ravaging battle resulted continuing into the night. First Sergeant Harjo had remained in Phuoc Vinh preparing for annual Inspector General's inspection. During this time, he had been monitoring radio and heard that the needed resupply helicopter had not yet arrived. He left for the helicopter pad, assisted in loading the ship, and remained with the aircraft. As the aircraft approached the area, First Sergeant Harjo guided the pilot into the small landing zone despite a heavy volume of intense automatic and small arms fire which the enemy directed at the incoming ship. After breaking down the supplies, he immediately moved about the perimeter distributing badly needed ammunition and encouraging his struggling men. First Sergeant Harjo's personal bravery and devotion to duty were in keeping with the highest traditions pf the military service and reflect great credit upon himself, his unit, and the United States Army.[715]

Note: First Sergeant Harjo was recommended for the Distinguish Service Cross and the Medal of Honor by his men. All attempts were rejected, but the ongoing effort is still alive.

---

[715] Source: Harjo family files.

Appendix 4: Dennis Moore – DSC Cross Citation

Dennis Moore – Distinguished Service Cross

Rank and Organization: Specialist Five, Company D, 3d Battalion (Airborne), 187th Infantry, 3d Brigade, 101st Airborne Division

Date and Place: March 18, 1968, Republic of Vietnam

Reason: Specialist Five Dennis F. Moore distinguished himself by extraordinary heroism while serving as the Senior Aidman with Company D, 3d Battalion (Airborne), 187th Infantry, 3d Brigade, 101st Airborne Division which was actively engaged in ground combat against enemy forces in the vicinity of Tan Uyen, Republic of Vietnam, on 18 March 1968. As the lead element of the company came under intense hostile small arms, rocket, grenade and machinegun fire, Specialist Moore left the security of the company headquarters element voluntarily to go to the aid of the wounded in the front element. As he approached the first of eight wounded comrades, he was seriously wounded in the leg and stomach. Completely ignoring his own wounds and safety he pushed ahead into the enemy fire. He discarded his personal weapon so as to better aid the wounded. In the course of moving from the first to the sixth man who lay only ten feet from an enemy machinegun bunker, Specialist Five Moore was wounded repeatedly. Not once did he stop to tend his own wounds but continued to crawl to the front, treating the wounded as he moved. He courageously moved to the lead man and began treating him, when he was mortally wounded by machinegun fire. Specialist Five Moore's extraordinary heroism and willing self-sacrifice are in the highest traditions of the United States Army and reflect great credit upon him and the Armed Forces of the country.

Appendix 5: Jeffrey Wishik – DSC Citation

Jeffrey Wishik – Distinguished Service Cross

Rank and Organization: First Lieutenant, U.S. Army, Company D, 3d Battalion. 187th Infantry, 3d Brigade, 101st Airborne Division.

Place and Date: Near Phuoc Vinh, Binh Duong Province, Republic of Vietnam, 18- 19 March 1968.

Reason: The President of the United States of America, authorized by Act of Congress, July 9, 1918 (amended by act of July 25, 1963), takes pleasure in presenting the Distinguished Service Cross to First Lieutenant (Infantry) Jeffrey Wishik (ASN: 0-5334937), United States Army, for extraordinary heroism in connection with military operations involving conflict with an armed hostile force in the Republic of Vietnam, while serving with Company D, 3d Battalion (Airborne), 187th Infantry, 3d Brigade, 101st Airborne Division. First Lieutenant Wishik distinguished himself by exceptionally valorous actions on 18 and 19 March 1968, as a platoon leader during a reconnaissance-in-force mission conducted by his company and an attached reconnaissance platoon near Phuoc Vinh. The combined American forces engaged an estimated reinforced battalion of Viet Cong and North Vietnamese Army regulars. The fierce enemy onslaught of small arm, automatic weapon, claymore mine, and grenade fire inflicted heavy casualties on the point platoon, including the platoon leader. Charging through the storm of bullets, Lieutenant Wishik took command of the stricken lead element. While exposed to the hostile fire, he positioned the men and carried the wounded back to the defensive perimeter. Receiving the order to pull back, he directed an orderly withdrawal, and then began to lead a scouting party to secure a trail to a landing zone where the casualties could be evacuated. As they made their way to the site, the communists exploded a command detonated mine, injuring three members of the party and killing the others. As he staggered to his feet, bleeding profusely from multiple fragmentation wounds, Lieutenant Wishik was assaulted by six screaming enemy soldiers. Dropping to one knee, he switched his rifle to full automatic and shot the assailants with one long burst. Through the remainder of the long night the three survivors feigned death to avoid capture by hostile troops who passed within inches of their position. Just before dawn and shortly before they were rescued, a lone North Vietnamese Army regular came upon them. After rifling Lieutenant Wishik's body to obtain "C" rations, the soldier turned him over, sat on him and began to eat his food. With his last bit of strength, Lieutenant Wishik drew his survival knife and slit the throat of the intruder. First Lieutenant Wishik's extraordinary heroism and devotion to duty were in keeping with the highest traditions of the military service and reflect great credit upon himself, his unit, and the United States Army.

General Orders: Headquarters, U.S. Army, Vietnam, General Orders No. 501 (February 13, 1969)[716]

---

[716] Source: http://projects.militarytimes.com/citations-medals-awards/recipient.php?recipientid=4901

Appendix 6: Calvin Heath – Awards and Medals

Calvin Heath Awards and Medals

- Silver Star

- Purple Heart

- Combat Infantryman Badge

- Parachutist Badge

- National Defense Service Medal

- Republic of Vietnam Gallantry Cross with Palm (Unit Citation)

- Vietnam Service Medal with 2 Bronze Service Stars

- Republic of Vietnam Campaign Medal with Device (1960)

- Valorous Unit Award

- Meritorious Unit Commendation

- Expert Qualification Badge Rifle

- Expert Qualification Badge Machine Gun

- American Indian Nations' Warrior's Medal

- Connecticut Veterans Wartime Service Medal

Appendix 7: 3/187th Casualty List 16-19 March 1968

(Source: Daily Staff Journal, S-1 Section, 3/187, 17-19 March 1968)

16 March 1968
1. Scholer, Co. C, wounded in action.
2. Hein, Jeffrey, SGT, Co. D., wounded in action.

17 March 1968
1. Cox, Michael, E-4, HHC, fragmentation wound to right arm.
2. *Dick, Jonnie E., E-4 Co. D, gunshot wound left foot.
3. *Harbert, Charles W., E-4, Co. D, gunshot wound to right arm and right leg.
4. *Itzoe, Robert A., E-7, Co. E, KHA fragmentation wound to head.*
5. Jones, Donald E., E-3, Co. C, fragmentation wounds to left leg.
6. Middleton, James, W., E-4, Co. E, fragmentation wounds to head and body – performed Tracheotomy.
7. Owens, Jimmie, E-4, Co. B, fragmentation wounds left shoulder.
8. Patrick, Eldridge, SP4, Co. B, fragmentation wounds to back.
9. Royalty, Richard D., E-6, Co. B, gunshot wounds right hand and left arm.
10. *Spencer, Samuel C., E-5, Co. D, shrapnel wound to the knee.
11. Stewart, Michael J., E-4, Co. E, fragmentation wound to the wrist.

18 March 1968
1. House, Herbert, SP4, Co. B, gunshot wound to right shoulder.
2. Johnson, Ronald D. PFC, Co. A, fragmentation wound left leg.
3. Mullinax, Ronald D., Co. B, SP4, gunshot wound left leg.
4. Nugent, Joseph, E-5, Co. A, fragmentation wound to corner right eye.
5. Patridge, Steve, E-5, Co. B, gunshot wounds to left side of face and back.
6. *Williams, Walter A, Co. A, KHA gunshot through chest and abdomen.*

19 March 1968 (Note: Many of those listed below were killed or wounded on 18 March)
1. *Bricker, Raymond P., SGT, Co. D, fragmentation wounds right wrist, forearm and chest.
2. *Bucha, Paul W., Captain, Co. D, fragmentation wounds left hand.
3. *Carroll, Michael, PFC, Co. D, KHA, received chest wounds.*
4. *Chambers, James F., PFC, Co. D, fragmentation wounds to chest, burns on right hand.
5. *Clark, Beauford A., PVT, Co. D, fragmentation wounds back and left hand.

6. *Conner, Paul A., PFC, Co. D, KHA, fatal wounds to the head.*
7. *Cook, Albert W., SP4, Co. D, fragmentation wounds left side of back.
8. *Davis, Cecil, SGT, Co. D, KHA, gunshot to chest.*
9. *Day, Kenneth F., SP4, Co. D, fragmentation wounds on right hand and leg.
10. Descoteaux, Gene R., SP4, HHC, gunshot wound to right knee and back.
11. *Diaz, Raymond, SP4, Co. D, numerous frag wounds on neck and chest.
12. *Dietch, Robert M., SP4, Co. D, multiple gunshot wounds to both legs and arms.
13. Doyle, Michael B., SP4, HHC, shrapnel wound to stomach.
14. *Ellard, Sherman E., SGT, Co. D, fragmentation wounds right arm.
15. *Estrada, Roy L., SGT, Co. D, KHA, wounds to chest.*[717]
16. *Evans, Linus C., SGT, Co. D, fragmentation wound to right calf.
17. *Folkews, James, SP4, Co. D, fragmentation wounds on back.
18. *Fuller, John R., PFC, Co. D, fragmentation wounds on right thigh.
19. *Green, Larry V., PFC, Co. D, KHA received wounds to abdomen and spleen.*
20. *Green, Walter, Sp-4, Co. D, gunshot wound left arm.
21. *Halloran, William, SGT, Co. D, multiple gunshot wounds to right thigh and right arm.
22. *Haygood, Russell, Co. D, gunshot wound right arm and head.[718]
23. *Heath, Calvin W., PFC, Co. D, fragmentation wound to buttocks.[719]
24. *Hickman, Franklin D., SP4, Co. D, gunshot wounds in left arm and fragmentation wound in left arm.
25. *Hilburn, Kenneth H., SGT, Co. D, fragmentation wound right shoulder.
26. *Holland, Michael B., SP4, Co. D, fragmentation wounds to right thumb and forearm.
27. *Jimenez, Ross K., SP4, Co. D, gunshot wound to right leg.
28. *Kuykendall, Stephen R., Co. D, fragmentation wound to right elbow.
29. *Macklin, Robert M., PVT, Co. D, gunshot wound to left leg and left shoulder.
30. *Matthew, James M., Sp4, Co. D, fragmentation wound right shoulder.
31. *McGee, Stevain [Steven] R., SP4, Co. D, fragmentation wounds both legs and left arm.

---

[717] Note: In an Email dated February 3, 2016, Lin Evans reports that he carried the seriously wounded Haygood back to the company's defensive perimeter.
[718] Note: In an Email dated February 3, 2016, Lin Evans reports that he carried Estrada's body back to the company's defensive perimeter. Estrada had sustained fatal wounds to the kidney area.
[719] Note: Calvin's wounds were much more extensive than those listed above.

32. *Messerli, Steven L., Co. D, KHA, received decapitation.*
33. Moesle, James W., Jr., PVT, Co. B., fragmentation wounds left leg.
34. Moore, Dennis F., SP5, HHC, wounds to head, neck and left arm.[720]
35. *Morgan, Joseph A., SGT, Co. D, fragmentation wound to left wrist and left elbow.
36. *Nazario, Juan J., SP4, Co. D, KHA penetrating wound to skull.*
37. *Perkins, Audrey L., SP4, Co. D, fragmentation wound and burns left side of face and ear.
38. *Pierce, Richard L., PVT, Co. D, fragmentation wound to neck and right arm.
39. Quinchocho, Juan B., SGT, Co. B., fragmentation wound right thigh.
40. *Recio, Arguello, PSG, Co. D, fragmentation wound on left elbow.
41. *Sain, Larry D., PFC, Co. B, KHA, wounds to head.*
42. *Savage, James F, SP4, Co. D, fragmentation wound to right elbow.
43. *Sherrill, Jimmy L, 2LT, Co. D, KHA gunshot to skull.*
44. *Smith, Thomas L., SGT, Co. B, KHA, severe face and head wounds.*
45. *Wishik, Jeffrey, 1LT, Co. D, gunshot wound to right arm and back, fragmentation wound right leg.
46. *Zwicke, Edward M., PFC, Co. D, fragmentation wound left thigh.

Note: The Daily Staff Journal did not report the men of Phantom Force who were wounded and killed. They include:

47. Davis, Jeffrey, wounded in action.
48. Messer, Forrest, wounded in action.
49. Shoup, Rick, wounded in action.
50. Karrell, Clark, wounded in action.
51. *Cunningham, Dennis*, killed in action.
52. *Cooley, Monte*, killed in action.

"*" – Delta Company
Italics – Killed in Hostile Action (KHA)

---

[720] Note: Moore was killed in hostile action.

Appendix 8: Congressman Gejdenson's Assistance

The following was received by the author on March 13, 2013 in response to an inquiry about Congressman Gejdenson's help in securing Calvin's Silver Star.

March 13, 2013

Dear Mr. Lindley,

I thought I had found more information recently, since Paul Bucha was keynote at the Middlesex Chamber of Commerce Veterans Luncheon in November 2011. I spoke to him about Calvin. Below is his side given to at West Point.

Background:
Calvin Heath asked for your assistance in getting his Silver Star in 1999. Though you could request waiver of the "timeliness" requirement, he needed a recommendation by someone who had personal knowledge of the event. He stated that his commanding officer was Paul Bucha, Congressional Medal of Honor awardee who was the President of the CMOH org and Chairman of the Board of Wheeling-Pittsburgh Steel Company at that time. You and Calvin coordinated getting the recommendation from Paul Bucha and forwarding it to the Department of the Army.

Based on his recommendation and your request, the Army approved the award of the Silver Star. The Medals were forwarded to you for presentation. You coordinated with Paul Bucha in order for him to be present. You presented his medal(s) at an event at the Veterans Memorial section of Chelsea Parade in Norwich.
Note from VVA:

Calvin W. Heath of Putnam, Connecticut, was recently awarded the Silver Star for his gallantry in action in March 1968. The decoration was presented by Rep. Sam Gejdenson (D-Conn.) during ceremonies at the Chelsea parade. Heath's former company commander, Paul Bucha, president of the Congressional Medal of Honor Society, attended the ceremony.

Reference by Paul Bucha

Appendix 9: Paul Allan Conner from the Virtual Wall

PAUL ALLAN CONNER

On the Wall: Panel 45E Line 19
Home of record: Fort Lauderdale, FL
Date of Birth: 06/04/1947
Military Data:
    Service: Army of the United States
    Grade at loss: E3
    Rank: Private First Class
    ID No: 53579680
    MOS: 11B10P: Infantryman (Airborne Qualified)
    Length of Service: 00
    Unit: D CO, 3rd BN, 187th Infantry, 101st ABN DIV, USARV
Casualty Data:
    Start Tour: 12/03/1967
    Incident Date: 03/18/1968
    Casualty Date: 03/18/1968
      Age at Loss: 20
      Location: Binh Duong Province, South Vietnam
      Remains: Body recovered
      Casualty Type: Hostile, died outright
      Casualty Reason: Ground casualty
      Casualty Detail: Multiple fragmentation wounds[721]

Paul Conner Silver Star Citation
3 August 1968
Action Date: 18 March 1968
Theater: Republic of Vietnam

For gallantry in action in the Republic of Vietnam on 18 March 1968. Private First-Class Conner distinguished himself while on a company size combat operation in the vicinity of Tan Uyen, Republic of Vietnam. A large enemy force attacked the company, hitting hardest at the lead element. Private First-Class Conner, along with the rest of his squad was engaged by a numerically superior enemy force while attempting to lay

---

[721] Source: www.VirtualWall.org/dc/ConnerPA01a.htm

down a protection base of fire for the lead element. Upon spotting the enemy fire coming from a fortified bunker, Private First-Class Conner unhesitatingly and with complete disregard for his own safety single-handedly assaulted the enemy position with automatic rifle fire until he was only a short distance away. He then silenced the position with a hand grenade. As he was returning to his squad, he noticed one of his companions lying in an open position, seriously wounded, and calling for a medic. Private First-Class Conner immediately moved to the site of the wounded man, administered first aid and courageously carried him back to a more secure area. While doing so, he was mortally wounded, but still managed to carry the wounded man back to safety. Private First-Class Conner's personal bravery and devotion to duty were in keeping with the highest traditions of the military service and reflected great credit upon himself, his unit, and the United States Army.

Appendix 10: Colleen Price Letter

Note: Chuck Whitten was a member of Delta Company, 3/187th Infantry (ABN), 101st Airborne Division and served with Calvin during his time in Vietnam. His story is tragic and provides a great deal of information about the battles the men (and their families) fought after Vietnam.

THE VIRTUAL WALL (www.VirtualWall.org)

On Behalf of Reference Desk, The American War Library
Sent: Saturday, December 10, 2005 5:00 PM
To: paratrooper@yahoogroups.com

My name is Colleen Whitten Price and I am the widow of a 101st Airborne soldier who served proudly with honor in Vietnam. My husband's name was Charles "Chuck" Whitten.

He was awarded 2 Bronze Stars, one with a 'V' and the Purple Heart. He was wounded in Chu Chi and spent the next 8 months at Fort Riley in the Irwin Army Hospital. We have discovered before he was released from the hospital and the Army on the same day, he had a fatal disease.... PTSD.

Tragically for his family and friends Charles committed suicide on October 12, 1971, 2 1/2 years after his release. For 32 years I believed he had become a madman in Vietnam, not knowing how much he was together during his time spent in country.

In June of 2003 Charles' and my daughter, Lori, was able to get in touch with four men he served with while in the 3/187 Infantry Airborne Division stationed in Phuoc Vinh. We were told of his heroic actions, bravery, devotion, kindness, and dedication to the 101st Airborne Mission.

On July 3rd of 2003 the Elkhart Truth in Elkhart, Indiana, did a 71-inch article named "He Wasn't the Same" written by Steph Price who is no relation to me. She was about 25 years old when she wrote the article. I dropped off a book, 3 days prior to the article being written about PTSD that a Veteran friend of mine had given me so she might understand what Charles suffered with. What a fantastic job she did for someone so young.

The story started off telling of how we met, married, spent Charles' R&R in Hawaii, the sad decline of a once proud man, who we now know suffered with a disease unknown at the time of his suicide, and of his death by carbon dioxide poisoning.

I was told the night he died he honked the horn of our car while it was in the detached garage for over 3 hours. The neighbors told me they thought "Crazy Charlie" was just drunk and no one investigated his actions. Sadly, his brother found him dead just inside the service entrance of the garage the next night.

I filed for a service-rated death for about 10 years, but this was denied time after time until I gave up in 1980. I had letters from Congressman John Brademas and Senator Birch Bayh, Charles' mother, my mother, supporting my request to no avail.

No one knew of the deadly disease PTSD and I read about suicide after suicide until I contacted the Phil Donahue Show in the late 70's to do a show on the suicides that unfortunately still are occurring to this day. I was told the widows of these proud misunderstood band of brothers probably had remarried and would not want to bring their dead spouse into their new lives. No show would be done.

Soon after contacting Jerry Jerett, Nick Goudoras, Dave Dillard and Kenny Gaddy in June of 2003 another member of the 3/187 December 13, 1967 to December 13, 1968 Rakkasans killed his wife and then himself so the madness continues to this day.

As I was warned in the late 70's about widows not wanting to bring their dead hero into their new lives, I sadly lost my husband of 15 years this last month because of bringing my dead HERO into our lives. My husband Bob, who I married after being single for 19 years, felt he was in competition with a man who died 34 years ago.

When the reporter was at my home, in 2003, our oldest daughter Lori told how she thought for 32 years it was my fault her father died. So did her sister think the same thing, unknown to me. I had not revealed the abuse I suffered, to our children, not wanting to burden our kids with that knowledge.

All I told the kids, over the years, was how much their father loved them. Now I was telling the reporter how I fled our home in the middle of the night, after being beaten, with our 2 daughters, Lori and Stacy, after being rescued by the police. They had been called to our home many times before, but Charles had already left, and nothing was done about domestic violence back then.

This time he was there, as I called the operator, while he was down stairs locking doors and windows and turning the stereo up loud. He resumed to beat me. I listened for someone beating on the door and when this happened, I made a dash down the stairs. I heard him yell "No one is going to help you" as I fled into the protective arms of the police who took us to my mother's home.

Charles killed himself about two weeks later. He called my mother's and told me to come home the night before he died. I told him I would come the next day but that did not pacify Charles. He became verbally abusive and I gave the phone to my mom who loved Charles like a son. He told her he would not be there the next day. She replied, "You aren't going to go anywhere" and told him I would come home the next day. He then became verbally abusive with her.

After his calling 3 times we took the phone off of the hook. I did go to the house the next day and looked throughout our home but did not find him. I did find the end table pulled in front of the sofa and a small pad of paper, punched full of tiny holes, and a beer can on the table. Not knowing what had happened I left and was summoned home by Charles' brother, that same evening, telling me he had found Charles dead.

How I drove over to our home, a few miles away from my mom's home that evening, I still do not know to this day. When I pulled up to our home, I saw the police and neighbors gathered, outside of the garage, at the back of our lot. I could not make myself go in to the garage, so I stood outside and stared at Charles' covered body on the dirty floor, dead by his own hand. He had survived Vietnam but could not survive coming home.

His suicide note was written from the pad of paper and contained those tiny holes. He wrote "Colleen I love you." I knew he was thinking of me and the 101st Airborne. I found his uniform in our coat closet with all the braids and medals in place. I had not seen the uniform since his release from the service.

Sadly, this find was after his burial when my sister, Carolynn, was helping me gather his things together. We found a box with his momentous of his time in Vietnam including one of the bullets taken from his body when he was shot in Chu Chi. Also, in the box was a picture of Charles with four men and wrote "These are all the squad leaders I have" and listed their names, Nick Goudoras, Kenny Gaddy, Dave Dillard, and Jerry Jerrett, and myself".

I called information in New York City, as Charles had written to me about Nick in his letters home and got Nick's phone number. The only part of the conversation I remember, after telling Nick Charles had killed himself, is Nick saying, "I wish you had not told me this."

After talking to Jerry Jerrett, I asked how the other 3 men were doing. I was told Jerry had 10 tough years after tour, Dave Dillard was doing ok, Kenny Gaddy was shot with a portable rocket in the face and had endured endless surgeries, but Nick was having a hard time.

The other 3 men were dealing with their PTSD but Nick was just admitting he too suffered with PTSD. I did not know Charles and Nick had been best friends in Vietnam and my call partnered with his time in Vietnam sentenced him to a life filled of sorrow, guilt, and endless mental pain.

Jerry explained Nick did not like his phone number given out, so we waited until he called Lori's home the next day. Nick exclaimed "I cannot believe I am talking to you. This has to be fate. I just wrote to the VA explaining my health problems with PTSD and I wrote a paragraph telling how Charles helped me in Vietnam and of the call you made to me in 1971."

In 2004 Lori and I attended the 3/187, 12/13/67-12/13/68 reunion, in Oklahoma, and met Dave Dillard and Jerry Jerrett. Nick was supposed to go but was in poor health at the time and could not attend that year.

Kenny also did not attend the reunion in 2004. I hope they all can make it next year as I will try and go to it again in hopes of meeting Nick and Kenny. After going in 2004 I was to attend in 2005. This time I had health problems & husband problems, due to our discovery, and could not go. Now I have no reason not to go in 2006.

The gist of my story is PTSD. I hired Dr. Harold Bursztajn, co-director of Harvard Medical School, to do a psychological autopsy, on Charles and his suicide. Dr. Bursztajn's specialties are PTSD and suicide.

The Doctor's initial report claims Charles died of untreated or undiagnosed PTSD.

Captain (retired) Paul Bucha, Medal of Honor recipient, was the Captain of Charles' Company 'D' and is now trying to help me right the wrong done to Charles and his family by denying Charles suicide as service-rated.

I furnished records to back up my claim to Charles' band of brothers and they too are behind our claim. Charles had PTSD, I then had PTSD, and my children will suffer forever with the illness that seems to keep on giving.

I write this story so the new HEROS, who are now fighting for their lives in Iraq, may identify with our story and have some knowledge of what untreated PTSD can do and will do if they do not seek the help they need.

Please publish this sad story so others might benefit from my words written from my heart. The reason I started this journey back down memory lane is 3 men from Fort Bragg, where Charles and I were our happiest, came home from Iraq and killed themselves and their families. I could not believe the Army and the VA were not aware of the harm PTSD would cause, if untreated, in 2003.

Now I am again alone, losing another husband because of PTSD, second hand, and can write with no reason not to.

Respectfully yours,
Colleen Whitten Price

Appendix 11: Contact Information

Delta Company 3/187th, 101st Airborne Division

- Rakkasan Delta site: http://www.rakkasan-delta6768.com/
- Rakkasan Association: http://www.rakkasan.net/contact.html
- Delta Company 3/187th, 101st ABN Facebook page found at: https://www.facebook.com/groups/433389746755997/

Appendix 12: Phantom Force Members

- 1LT Jeff Davis – *Wounded in Action*
- PLT SGT Forest Messer - *Wounded in Action*
- SGTT Rick Shoup - *Wounded in Action*
- Gene Hobson
- Dennis Cunningham – *Killed in Action*
- Don Lescault
- Monte Cooley – *Killed in Action*
- Sammy Washburn
- Clark Karrell - *Wounded in Action*
- Peter Gliha
- John Hunt
- Roger Elling
- James Martinez
- Ed Crowley
- Don Lescault
- Doug Pinder
- Bill Graham
- Jerry Brown

INTERVIEWS

- Authier, Rob, Calvin's friend, interview, March 28, 2014.
- Authier, Jason, Calvin's friend, interview, March 28, 2014.
- Blackmar, Romeo, Email, August 28, 2013.
- Blalock, Michael 1LT, Combat Engineer assigned to the 3/187th on March 18, 1968, various communications.
- Bopp, Kenneth, 24th Evacuation Hospital, Long Bien, Vietnam, April 2014.
- Callahan, Don, member of Delta Co., 3/187th INF (ABN), 101st Airborne Division, meeting at the University of South Carolina, April 13, 2016.
- Conner, Paul, COL, U.S. Air Force, interview February 27, 2014 and various emails and communications.
- Conner, Nathan, Paul Conner's older brother, phone conversation, February 27, 2014, visit December 9, 2016 and various emails.
- Cripe, John, 3/506th, LRRP reunion, Ft. Benning GA, March 16-18, 2017.
- Cutler, John, Calvin's childhood friend, interview, October 20, 2013.
- Davis, Floyd "Jeff," COL RET, U.S. Army, LRRP, 3/187th INF (ABN), 101st Airborne Division, phone conversation January 19, 2016, correspondence September 12, 2016, phone conversation October 2, 2016, various Emails. LRRP reunion, Ft. Benning GA, March 16-18, 2017.
- Decker, John, LRRP, 3/187th INF (ABN), 101st Airborne Division, LRRP reunion, Ft. Benning GA, March 16-18, 2017.
- Diaz, Raymond, former medic 3/187th INF (ABN), 101st Airborne Division, phone interview, February 5, 2014.
- Dillard, David, former member Co. D, 3/187th INF (ABN), 101st Airborne Division , interview, October 9 and 10, 2013, February 5 and 6, 2014, February 19, 2014, November 25, 2014. Numerous Email contacts.
- Dufrene, Ed, LRRP, 3/187th INF (ABN), 101st Airborne Division, LRRP reunion, Ft. Benning GA, March 16-18, 2017.
- Dumont, Stephen, former president of the CT West Point Society, several communications May 2017.
- Duquette, Chasidy, Samantha and Paul, Calvin's nephew, wife and niece in-law, February 3, 2014. March 8, 2014.
- Eader, Doug, LRRP, 3/187th INF (ABN), 101st Airborne Division, LRRP reunion, Ft. Benning GA, March 16-18, 2017.
- Esposito, Richard, LRRP, 3/187th INF (ABN), 101st Airborne Division, LRRP reunion, Ft. Benning GA, March 16-18, 2017.

- Evans, Linus, SGT, member Delta Co., 3/187th INF (ABN), 101st Airborne Division, multiple discussions to include phone conversation on January 21, 2016.
- Ford, Billy, former member Co. D, 3/187th INF (ABN), 101st Airborne Division, interview, February 5 and 6, 2014.
- Goudoras, Nicholas, former member Co. D, 3/187th INF (ABN), 101st Airborne Division, email dated September 21, 2014.
- Hampton, Jan, Jimmy Sherrill's sister, phone call conversation, September 22, 2014, various Emails.
- Harjo, Billy, 1SGT Austin Harjo's son, June 15, 2018, phone interview.
- Harjo, Teresa, Burger, 1SGT Austin Harjo's daughter, June 15, 2018, phone interview.
- Heaney, William, former member Co. D, 3/187th INF (ABN), 101st Airborne Division, October 9-10, 2013 and September 10, 2014, various mails.
- Heath, Bert, Calvin's brother and former member, 173rd INF (ABN), 101st Airborne Division, October 18, 24, 2013, March 30, 2014.
- Heath, Betty, Calvin's sister-in-law, interview, August 25, 2014, October 3, 2014.
- Heath, Calvin, subject of book, numerous interviews between March 23, and June 26, 2013.
- Heath, Curt, Calvin's cousin, interview, January 31, 2014.
- Heath, Frank and Karen, Calvin's brother and sister-in-law, interview, May, June, July 2013.
- Heath, Melvin, Calvin's brother, interview, January 31, 2014.
- Hisert, Linda Broan, Paul Conner's fiancée, phone interview December 20, 2016.
- Jakeway, Jon, C. Co. 3/187th, 101st Airborne DIV, telecom interview with author, March 8, 2019.
- Jackson, James, Major (Retired), 101st Airborne Division, LRRP reunion, Ft. Benning GA, March 16-18, 2017. Major Jackson was a OCS classmate of Jimmy Sherrill.
- Jackson, Thomas, member of Delta Co., 3/187th INF (ABN), 101st Airborne Division, phone interview, November 3, 2016.
- Jarrett, Jerry, member of Delta Co., 3/187th, 101st Airborne Division, phone interview, November 11, 2016. Delta's 50th reunion at Fort Campbell, KY, September 2017.
- Keiper, Paul, Paul Conner's childhood friend, visit, December 9, 2016.
- Lechner, William, 1st Platoon Leader, telecom interview with author March 7, 2019.
- Lefevre, Joyce, Calvin's half-sister, interview, interview, March 30, 2014.

- Lefebvre, Rebecca, Calvin's granddaughter, interview, March 2, 2014.
- Lester, Joan, Nipmuc Indians, interview, November 2013.
- Messer, Forest, LRRP, PLT SGT, , 3/187th INF (ABN), 101st Airborne Division, LRRP reunion, Ft. Benning GA, March 16-18, 2017.
- Mooney, Claire, Paul Conner's aunt, various communications and visit, November 11, 2016.
- Mulholland, William, Paul Conner's childhood friend, Veteran's Administrator, Becket, MA, and former USAF member stationed at Tan Son Nhut Air Base during TET, various emails and phone communication, November 4, 2016.
- Mullis, Nancy (Vanalstine), Earl Van Al Stine's sister, email December 10, 2014.
- Nelson, Ron, Delta Co., 3/187th INF (AND), 101st Airborne Division, Delta's 50th reunion at Fort Campbell, KY, September 2017.
- Palmer, Raymond, former member Co. D, 3/187th INF (ABN), 101st Airborne Division, October 10, 2013. Email contacts throughout October – November 2013, February 2014. Delta's 50th reunion at Fort Campbell, KY, September 2017.
- Perrier, Kevin, E. Co. 2/7th Cavalry, telecom interview with author, March 11, 2019.
- Podolski, Brenda, Paul Conner's cousin, various communications and visit November 17, 2016.
- Pray, Sandra, Bill Pray's (Member of Delta Company, 3/187th) wife. Phone call conversation, September 29, 2014. Delta's 50th reunion at Fort Campbell, KY, September 2017.
- Pray, Bill, former member of Co. D, 3/187th INF (ABN), 101st Airborne Division, numerous phone interviews, various Emails, visit University of South Carolina, April 13, 2016. Delta's 50th reunion at Fort Campbell, KY, September 2017.
- Orlomoski, Alton, 187th INF ABN, 11th Airborne Division, Japan 1946-1948. Interviewed March 30, 2017.
- Orlomoski, Stephen, Lt. Col. (Ret) USAF. Interviewed March 30, 2017.
- Quick, Dickie, PLT SGT, Delta Co., 3/187th INF (ABN), 101st Airborne Division, phone conversation November 11, 2016. Delta's 50th reunion at Fort Campbell, KY, September 2017.
- Robbins, Andrew, Co. B., 3/187th INF (ABN), 101st Airborne Division, phone discussions, February 2017, April 12, 2017.
- Rawson, Michael, former member Co. D, 3/187th INF (ABN), 101st Airborne Division, interviews, October 9-10, 2013, February 5 and 6, 2014.
- Satterfield, Eugene, Delta Co., 3/187th INF (AND), 101st Airborne Division, Delta's 50th reunion at Fort Campbell, KY, September 2017.
- Scheets, Teresa, Colonel Scheet's daughter, telecom interview with author March 6, 2019

- Shaw, Tamara, life-long friend of Calvin's, interview, November 17, 2013.
- Shoup, David, son of Richard Shoup LRRP, various communications and visits.
- Shoup, Richard, LRRP, 3/187th INF (ABN), 101st Airborne Division, numerous communications and visits. LRRP, reunion, FT Benning, GA, March 16-19, 2017.
- Smith, Eugene, Delta Co., 3/187th INF (AND), 101st Airborne Division, Delta's 50th reunion at Fort Campbell, KY, September 2017.
- Smith, Karen (Eugene's wife), Delta Co., 3/187th INF (AND), 101st Airborne Division, Delta's 50th reunion at Fort Campbell, KY, September 2017.
- Smith, Michael, LRRP, 3/187th INF (ABN), 101st Airborne Division, LRRP reunion, Ft. Benning GA, March 16-18, 2017.
- Smith, Tim, conversations at the Vietnam Memorial Wall. Telecom with author arch 11, 2019.
- Spencer, Samuel, WO5, U.S. Army Retired, former member of Delta Co., 3/187th INF (ABN), 101st Airborne Division, interview, University of South Carolina, April 13, 2016.
- Stowers, Clint and Kathy, Paul Conner's cousin, visit, November 11, 2016.
- Stinnett, Terry, member of Delta Co., 3/187th INF (ABN), 101st Airborne Division, phone interview May 8, 2016.
- Thoksakis, Nikos, Echo Co., 3/187th INF (AND), 101st Airborne Division, Delta's 50th reunion at Fort Campbell, KY, September 2017.
- Wishik, Jeffery, member of Delta Co., 3/187th INF (AND), 101st Airborne Division, Delta's 50th reunion at Fort Campbell, KY, September 2017.

OTHER SOURCES

- Department of Veterans Affairs, Washington, D.C.
- Dodd (Thomas J.) Center, University of Connecticut, Storrs, CT.
- Don Pratt Museum, Fort Campbell, KY.
- Heath, Calvin, U.S. Army Personnel Records to include, 201 File, DD-214, Medical Records, qualification orders, etc.
- Heath, Calvin, personal records collection.
- National Archives, St. Louis, MO.
- National Personnel Records Center. St. Louis, MO.
- National Rakkasan Association (187th Airborne Infantry Regiment), found at: www.rakkasan.net/index.html
- Pritzker Military Museum, 104 S. Michigan Ave. 2nd Floor Chicago, IL 60603. Also found at: http://www.pritzkermilitary.org/
- Rakkasan Delta Site, found at:www.rakkasan-delta6768.com/
- Texas Tech University, The Vietnam Center and Archive, found at: www.vietnam.ttu.edu/virtualarchive/.
- U.S. Army, After-Action Reports, 3rd Battalion, 187th Infantry (ABN), 101st Airborne Division, March, April 1968.
- U.S. Army, After-Action Report for the period ending April 30, 1968, Department of the Army. Headquarters, 3rd Brigade, 101st Airborne, Colonel Mowery, dated 30 April 1968.
- U.S. Army, Board of for the Correction of Military Records. In the Case of Calvin Heath, August 14, 2003.
- U.S. Army, Corp of Engineers maps: Phuoc Vinh, Vietnam, (1:50,000) Sheet No. 6331 I, Series L7014, 1969, and Tan Uyen, Vietnam, (1:50,000) Sheet No. 6331 II, Series L7014, 1969.
- U.S. Army, Daily Staff Journals, 3rd Battalion, 187th Infantry (ABN), 101st Airborne Division, March 15 through March 22, 1968. These included S1, S2, and S3 reports with map overlays.
- U.S. Army, Operational Reports of 3rd Brigade, 101st Airborne Division, 16 May 1968. Colonel Mowery commanding.
- Vietnam Conflict Aviation Resource Center found at: www.vietnam.warbirdsresourcegroup.org
- West Point Society of Connecticut. Founders Day event brochure, March 14, 2002.
- Wahcona Regional High School – Paul Allan Conner Memorial.

BIBLIOGRAPHY

3rd Brigade Troopers Blast 215 Enemy Fortification. (1968, March 1). *The Screaming Eagle Newspaper*, p. 1.

Ants Prompt Boonie Strip. (1968, March 8). *The Screaming Eagle Newspaper,* p. 3.

Arnold, J., (1990). *Tet Offensive 1968*. United Kingdom. Osprey Publishing.

Baldwin, S., Houts, A., Williams, D. (2004). The Creation, Expansion, and Embodiment of Posttraumatic Stress Disorder; A Case Study in Historical Critical Psychopathology. *The Scientific Review of Mental Health Practice*. Retrieved January 2014 at: http://www.srmhp.org/0301/hcp.html.

Bond, J. (2006). *Rakkasans; A History and Collection of Personal Narratives from Members of the 3rd Battalion (airborne), 187th Infantry, 101st Airborne Division, Republic of Vietnam.* Self-published.

Cronkite, W. (1968, February 27). Who, What, When, Where, Why: Report from Vietnam by Walter Cronkite. *CBS Evening News*. Retrieved December 12, 2013 from: https://facultystaff.richmond.edu/~ebolt/history398/Cronkite_1968.html.

Firefight Nets 36 VC Near Song Be City. (1968, March 29). *The Screaming Eagle Newspaper,* p.1.

Flanagan, E., M. (1997). *The Rakkasans; the Combat History of the 187th Airborne Infantry*. Novato, GA. Presidio Press.

Hamilton, R. (1999, July 13). 30 Years Later, A Soldiers Valor is Rewarded. *The Day*, pgs. A1, A5.

Harrell, D. (1968, March 8). Two Rescued from Swirling River. *The Screaming Eagle Newspaper*, p. 1.

Inaugural Address of John F. Kennedy (1961, January 20). The Avalon Project, Yale Law School. Retrieved January 2014, at: http://avalon.law.yale.edu/20th_century/kennedy.asp.

Jeffries, W. (2006). *Trap Door to the Dark Side*. Author House, Bloomington, IN.

Jones, R. (2005). *History of the 101st Airborne Division; Screaming Eagles, The first 50 Years.* Nashville, TN. Turner Publishing Co.

Kulka, R., A. et.al. 1990. *Trauma and the Vietnam War Generation*. New York. Brunner, Mazel Inc.

Leo, V. (1999, July 18). Vietnam Vet Finally Gets Medals. *Norwich Bulletin,* p. B6.

Lewy, Guenter (1978). *America in Vietnam*. New York: Oxford University Press. Appendix 1, pp.450-453.

Lindley, J. (2013, October) Local Soldier Honored in Hartford; Speaker includes Medal of Honor Recipient. *Thompson Villager*, p. A5.

Jeffries, W. (2006). *Trap Door to the Dark Side*. Author House, Bloomington, IN.

Mann, Robert. (2002). *A Grand Delusion*, Basic Books.

Meacham, W. (1999). *Lest We Forget; The Kingsmen, 101st Aviation Battalion, 1968*. Ivy Books, New York, New York.

McCaughey, B., Dean, M. (2002, May 28). A Call to Remember Those Who Fought or Fell for U.S., *Investor's Business Daily*. Retrieved November 18, 2013 at: http://news.investors.com/052802-487921-a-call-to-remember-those-who-fought-or-fell-for-us.htm#ixzz2NWMkzRL2.

Moise, E. (1996). *Tonkin Gulf and the Escalation of the Vietnam War*. North Carolina University Press.

Moore, H. (1992), *We Were Soldiers Once... and Young: Ia Drang--The Battle That Changed the War in Vietnam*. Random House, New York, New York.

Murphy, E. (2007), Dak To; America's Sky Soldiers in South Vietnam's Central Highlands. Random House, New York.

Olsen and Roberts, *Where the Dominoes Fell*, Blackwell Publishing, Malden, MA.

Shoup, David (2017), *Phantom Force Revisited*. Found at: https://www.youtube.com/watch?v=tDS-p036meg

Smith, L. (2003). *Beyond Glory; Medal of Honor Heroes in Their Own Words*. W.W. Norton Co., Inc. NY, NY.

Sullivan, R. (Ed.) (2008). Remembering Martin Luther King Jr. 40 Years Later. *Life Magazine*.

The President's News Conference of April 7, 1954, *Public Papers of the Presidents of the United States: Dwight D. Eisenhower, 1954*. Government Printing Office, Washington, D. C.

Tolson. J. (1999). *Vietnam Studies; Air Mobility 1961-1971*, Department of the Army. Washington, D.C. Retrieved December 2013 at: http://www.history.army.mil/html/books/090/90-4/CMH_Pub_90-4-B.pdf.

Tonsetic, R. (2007). *Days of Valor*, Casemate, Haverton, PA and Newbury, Berkshire.

Tull M., PhD. (2012). PTSD From the Vietnam War. *About.com.* Retrieved January 29, 2012 found at:
http://ptsd.about.com/od/ptsdandthemilitary/a/Vietnamlongterm.htm.

Vietnam Heroism Recognized 3 Decades after Fateful Night. (1999, July 9). *Worcester Telegram and Gazette*, pgs. B1-B3.

Willbanks, J., H. (2007). *The Tet Offensive; a Concise History.* Columbia University Press, New York, New York.

INDEX

D

Z